Little Lulu®

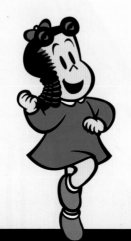

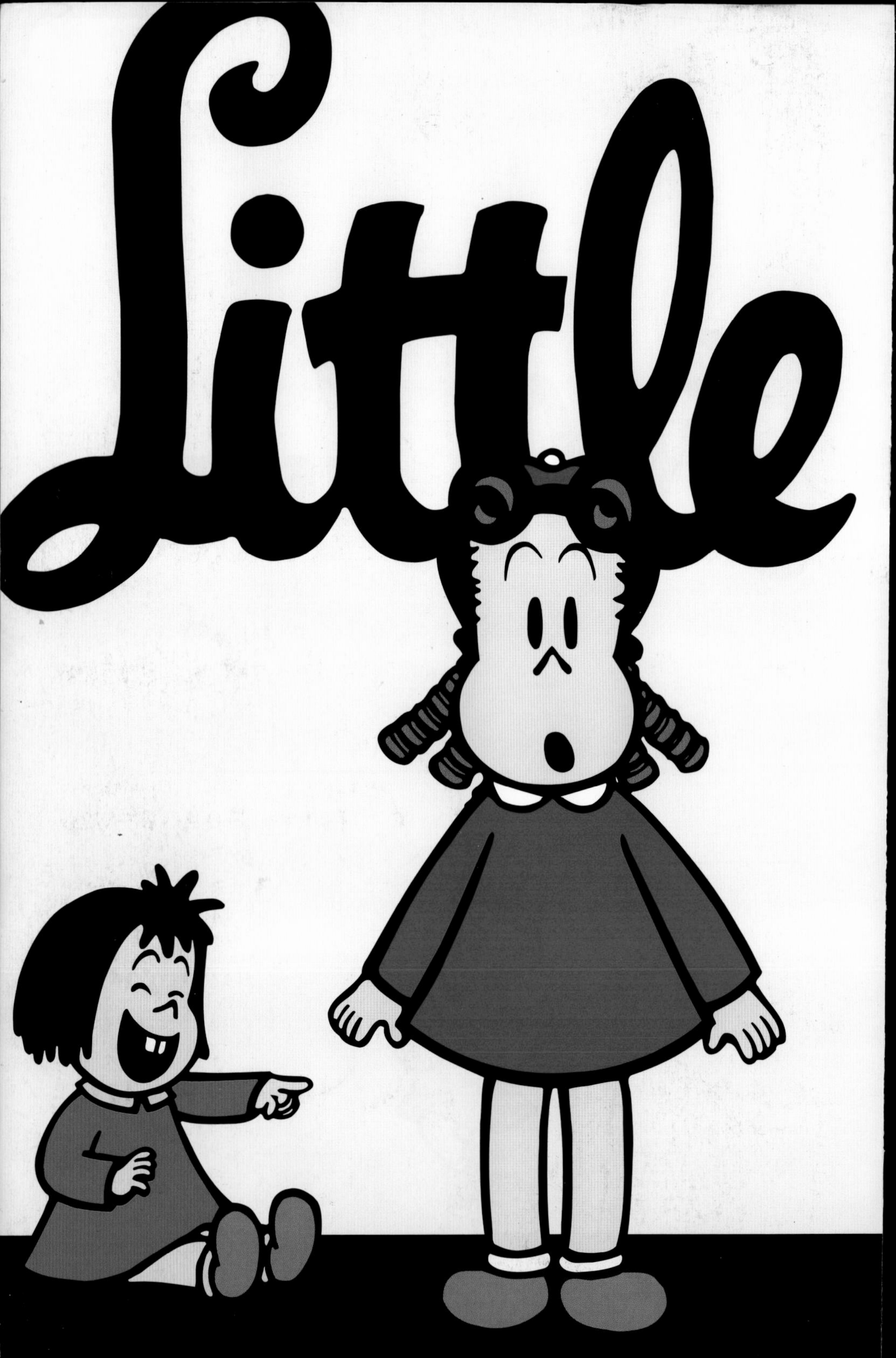
Little

Lulu®

The Big Dipper Club and Other Stories

Story and Art
John Stanley & Irving Tripp

Based on the character created by
Marge Buell

Dark Horse Books®

Publisher **Mike Richardson**

Editor **Dave Marshall**

Assistant Editor **Brendan Wright**

Collection Designer **Krystal Hennes**

Published by Dark Horse Books

A division of Dark Horse Comics, Inc.

10956 SE Main Street

Milwaukie, Oregon 97222

First edition: February 2010

ISBN 978-1-59582-420-2

Little Lulu® Volume 22: The Big Dipper Club and Other Stories

This volume contains every comic from issues #106 through #111 of
Marge's Little Lulu, originally published by Dell Comics.

Mike Richardson, President and Publisher • Neil Hankerson, Executive Vice President • Tom Weddle, Chief Financial Officer • Ran
Stradley, Vice President of Publishing • Michael Martens, Vice President of Business Development • Anita Nelson, Vice President
Marketing, Sales, and Licensing • David Scroggy, Vice President of Product Development • Dale LaFountain, Vice President of Informati
Technology • Darlene Vogel, Director of Purchasing • Ken Lizzi, General Counsel • Davey Estrada, Editorial Director • Scott Allie, Seni
Managing Editor • Chris Warner, Senior Books Editor • Diana Schutz, Executive Editor • Cary Grazzini, Director of Design and Producti
Lia Ribacchi, Art Director • Cara Niece, Director of Scheduling

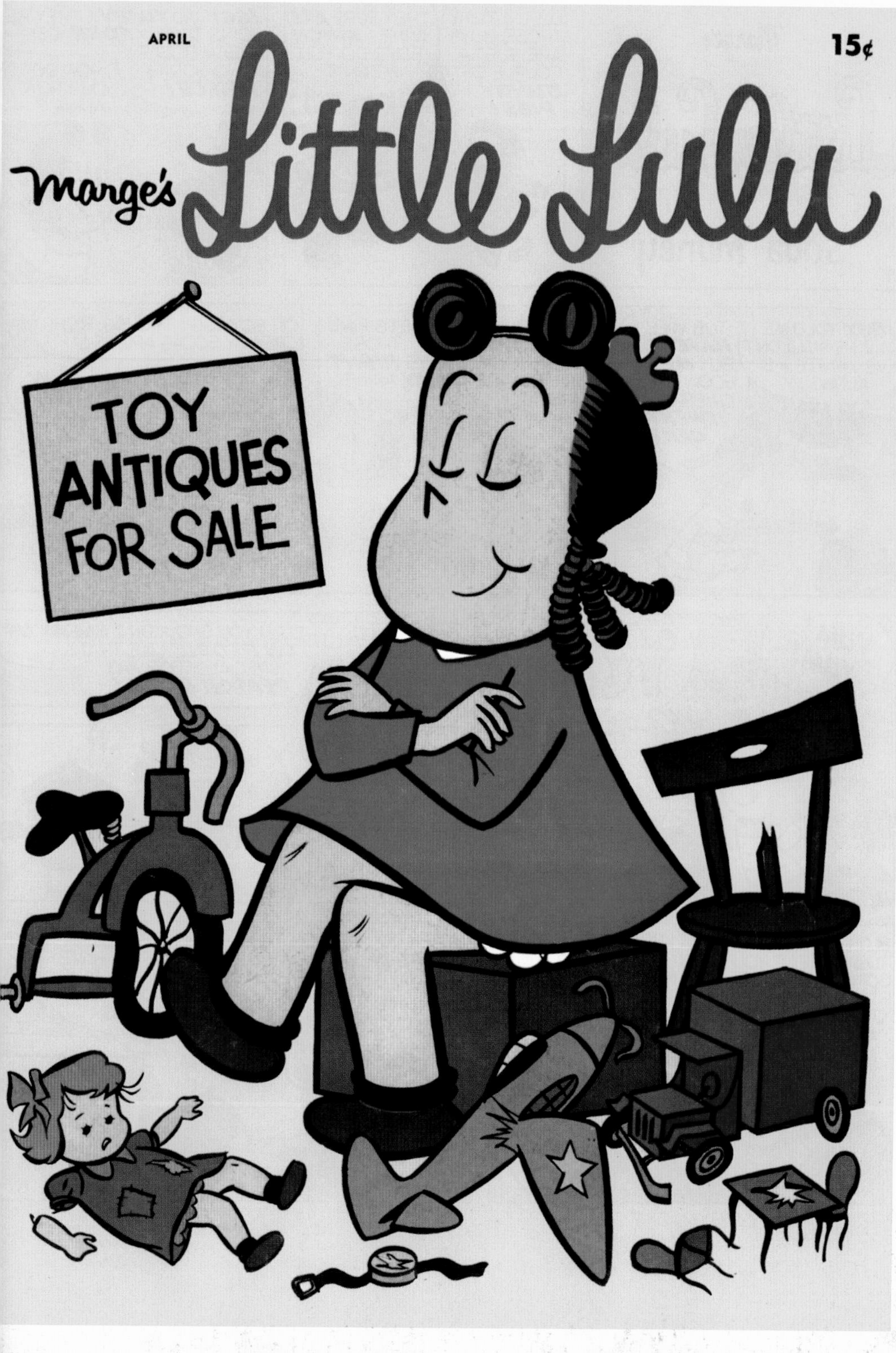
APRIL
15¢
Marge's Little Lulu
TOY
ANTIQUES
FOR SALE

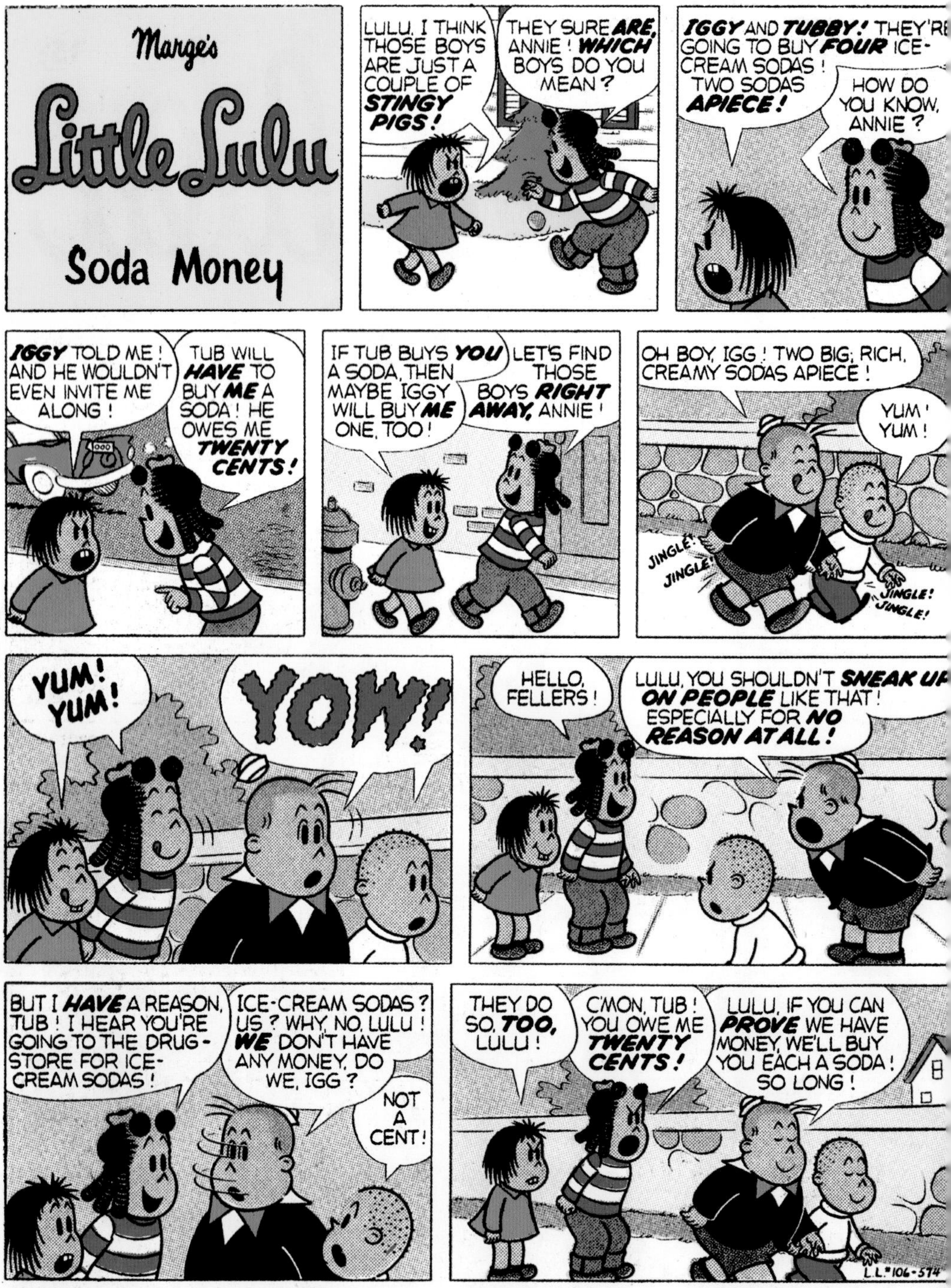
Marge's
Little Lulu
Soda Money
LULU, I THINK THOSE BOYS ARE JUST A COUPLE OF STINGY PIGS!
THEY SURE ARE, ANNIE! WHICH BOYS DO YOU MEAN?
IGGY AND TUBBY! THEY'RE GOING TO BUY FOUR ICE-CREAM SODAS! TWO SODAS APIECE!
HOW DO YOU KNOW, ANNIE?
IGGY TOLD ME! AND HE WOULDN'T EVEN INVITE ME ALONG!
TUB WILL HAVE TO BUY ME A SODA! HE OWES ME TWENTY CENTS!
IF TUB BUYS YOU A SODA, THEN MAYBE IGGY WILL BUY ME ONE, TOO!
LET'S FIND THOSE BOYS RIGHT AWAY, ANNIE!
OH BOY, IGG! TWO BIG, RICH, CREAMY SODAS APIECE!
YUM! YUM!
JINGLE! JINGLE!
JINGLE! JINGLE!
YUM! YUM!
YOW!
HELLO, FELLERS!
LULU, YOU SHOULDN'T SNEAK UP ON PEOPLE LIKE THAT! ESPECIALLY FOR NO REASON AT ALL!
BUT I HAVE A REASON, TUB! I HEAR YOU'RE GOING TO THE DRUG-STORE FOR ICE-CREAM SODAS!
ICE-CREAM SODAS? US? WHY, NO, LULU! WE DON'T HAVE ANY MONEY, DO WE, IGG?
NOT A CENT!
THEY DO SO, TOO, LULU!
C'MON, TUB! YOU OWE ME TWENTY CENTS!
LULU, IF YOU CAN PROVE WE HAVE MONEY, WE'LL BUY YOU EACH A SODA! SO LONG!
L.L.#106-574

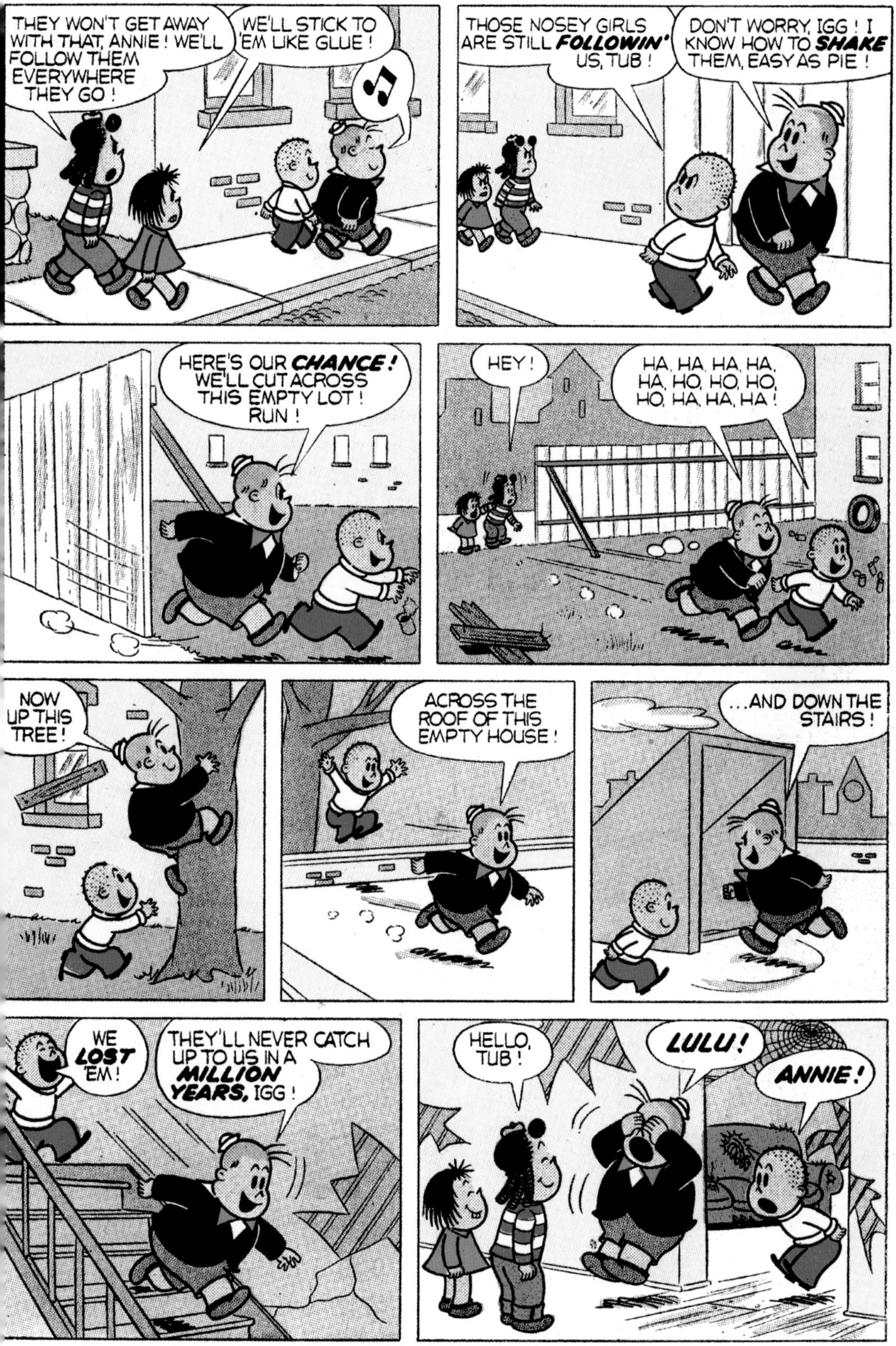
THEY WON'T GET AWAY WITH THAT, ANNIE! WE'LL FOLLOW THEM EVERYWHERE THEY GO!
WE'LL STICK TO 'EM LIKE GLUE!
♫
THOSE NOSEY GIRLS ARE STILL FOLLOWIN' US, TUB!
DON'T WORRY, IGG! I KNOW HOW TO SHAKE THEM, EASY AS PIE!
HERE'S OUR CHANCE! WE'LL CUT ACROSS THIS EMPTY LOT! RUN!
HEY!
HA, HA, HA, HA, HA, HO, HO, HO, HO, HA, HA, HA!
NOW UP THIS TREE!
ACROSS THE ROOF OF THIS EMPTY HOUSE!
...AND DOWN THE STAIRS!
WE LOST 'EM!
THEY'LL NEVER CATCH UP TO US IN A MILLION YEARS, IGG!
HELLO, TUB!
LULU!
ANNIE!

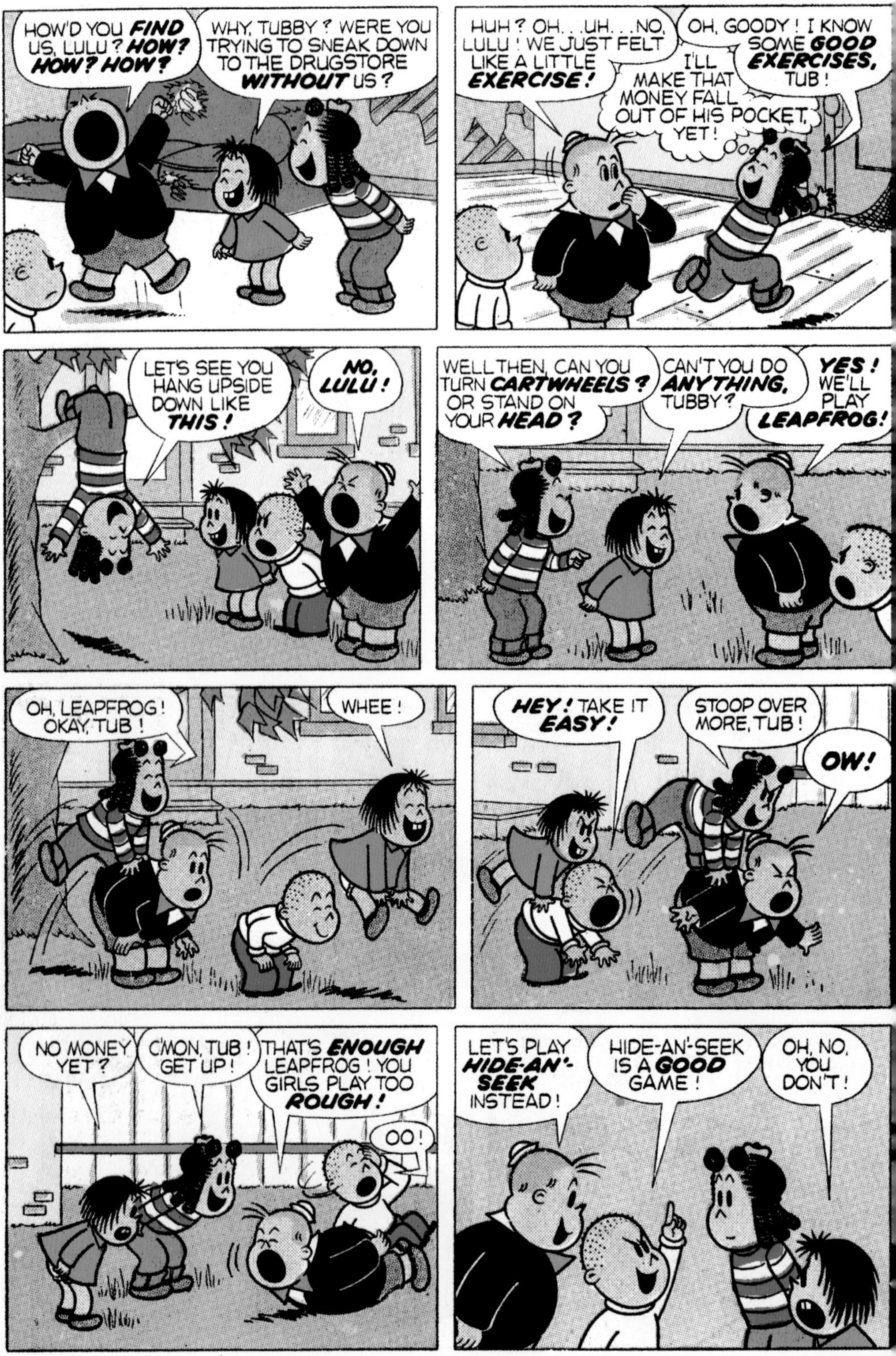

HOW'D YOU FIND US, LULU? HOW? HOW? HOW?
WHY, TUBBY? WERE YOU TRYING TO SNEAK DOWN TO THE DRUGSTORE WITHOUT US?
HUH? OH. . .UH. . .NO, LULU! WE JUST FELT LIKE A LITTLE EXERCISE!
I'LL MAKE THAT MONEY FALL OUT OF HIS POCKET, YET!
OH, GOODY! I KNOW SOME GOOD EXERCISES, TUB!
LET'S SEE YOU HANG UPSIDE DOWN LIKE THIS!
NO, LULU!
WELL THEN, CAN YOU TURN CARTWHEELS? OR STAND ON YOUR HEAD?
CAN'T YOU DO ANYTHING, TUBBY?
YES! WE'LL PLAY LEAPFROG!
OH, LEAPFROG! OKAY, TUB!
WHEE!
HEY! TAKE IT EASY!
STOOP OVER MORE, TUB!
OW!
NO MONEY YET?
C'MON, TUB! GET UP!
THAT'S ENOUGH LEAPFROG! YOU GIRLS PLAY TOO ROUGH!
OO!
LET'S PLAY HIDE-AN'-SEEK INSTEAD!
HIDE-AN'-SEEK IS A GOOD GAME!
OH, NO, YOU DON'T!

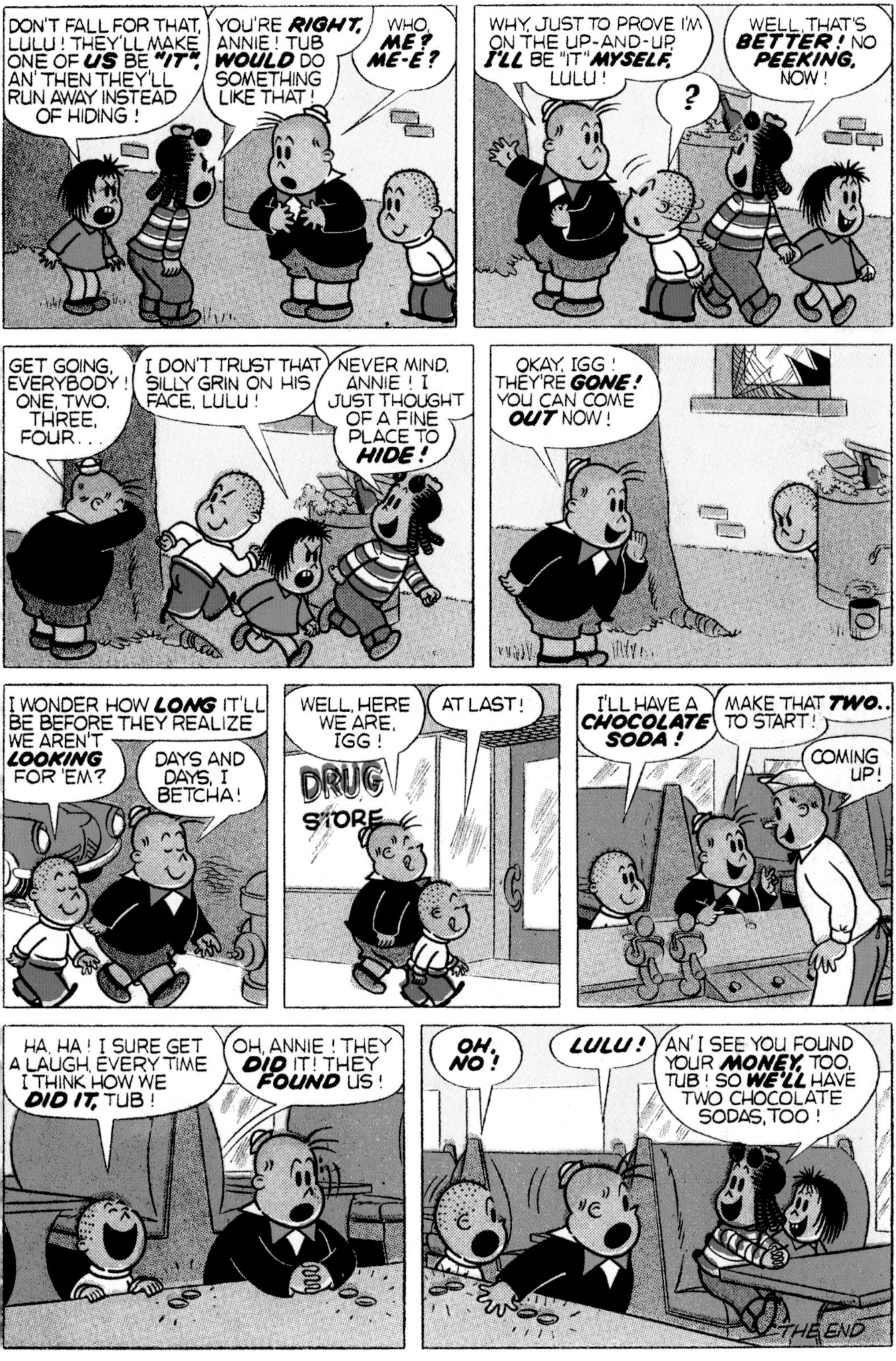
DON'T FALL FOR THAT, LULU! THEY'LL MAKE ONE OF US BE "IT", AN' THEN THEY'LL RUN AWAY INSTEAD OF HIDING!
YOU'RE RIGHT, ANNIE! TUB WOULD DO SOMETHING LIKE THAT!
WHO, ME? ME-E?
WHY, JUST TO PROVE I'M ON THE UP-AND-UP, I'LL BE "IT" MYSELF, LULU!
?
WELL, THAT'S BETTER! NO PEEKING, NOW!
GET GOING, EVERYBODY! ONE, TWO, THREE, FOUR...
I DON'T TRUST THAT SILLY GRIN ON HIS FACE, LULU!
NEVER MIND, ANNIE! I JUST THOUGHT OF A FINE PLACE TO HIDE!
OKAY, IGG! THEY'RE GONE! YOU CAN COME OUT NOW!
I WONDER HOW LONG IT'LL BE BEFORE THEY REALIZE WE AREN'T LOOKING FOR 'EM?
DAYS AND DAYS, I BETCHA!
WELL, HERE WE ARE, IGG!
AT LAST!
DRUG STORE
I'LL HAVE A CHOCOLATE SODA!
MAKE THAT TWO.. TO START!
COMING UP!
HA, HA! I SURE GET A LAUGH EVERY TIME I THINK HOW WE DID IT, TUB!
OH, ANNIE! THEY DID IT! THEY FOUND US!
OH, NO!
LULU!
AN' I SEE YOU FOUND YOUR MONEY, TOO, TUB! SO WE'LL HAVE TWO CHOCOLATE SODAS, TOO!
THE END

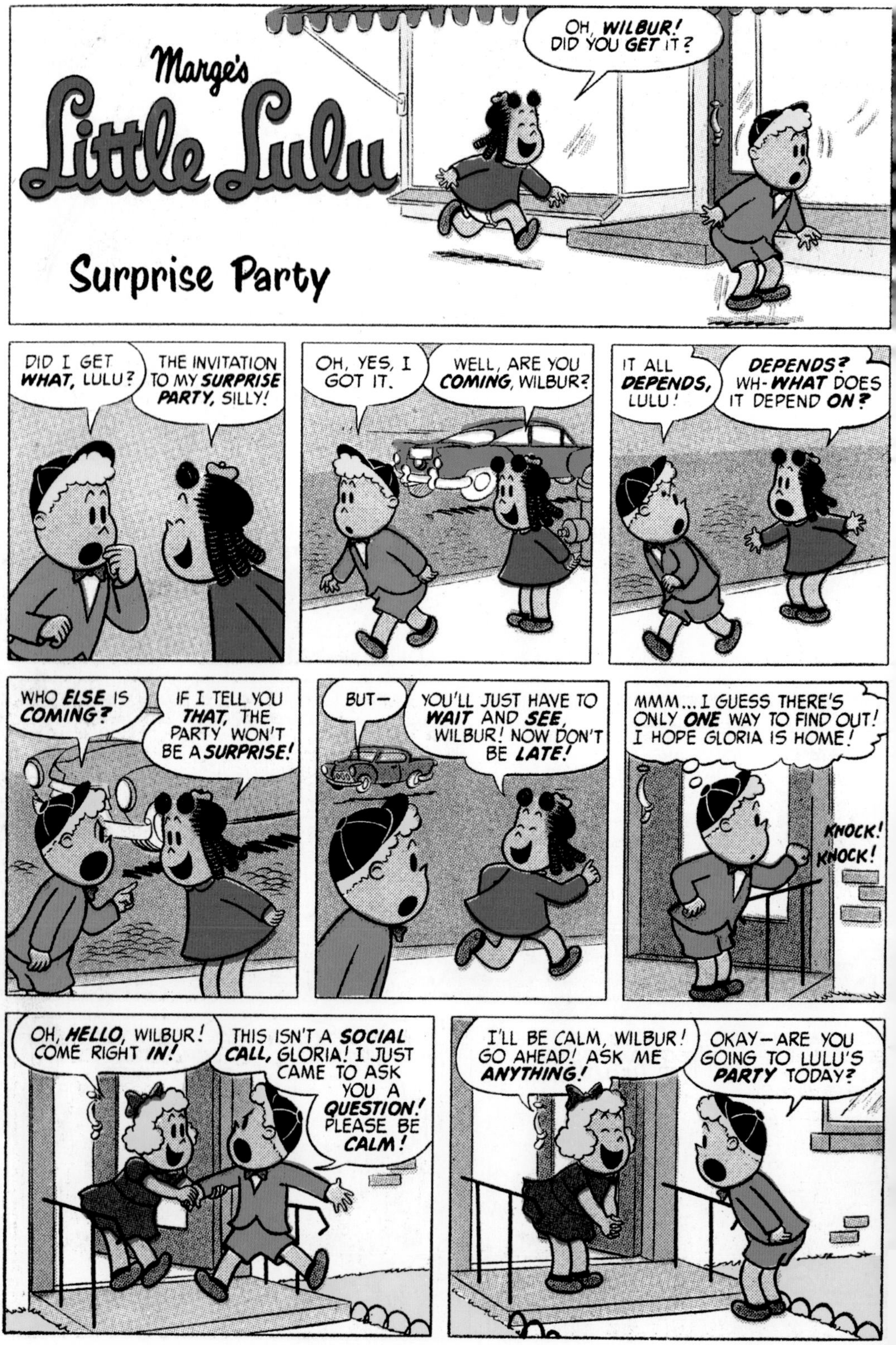
Marge's Little Lulu
Surprise Party
OH, WILBUR! DID YOU GET IT?
DID I GET WHAT, LULU?
THE INVITATION TO MY SURPRISE PARTY, SILLY!
OH, YES, I GOT IT.
WELL, ARE YOU COMING, WILBUR?
IT ALL DEPENDS, LULU!
DEPENDS? WH-WHAT DOES IT DEPEND ON?
WHO ELSE IS COMING?
IF I TELL YOU THAT, THE PARTY WON'T BE A SURPRISE!
BUT—
YOU'LL JUST HAVE TO WAIT AND SEE, WILBUR! NOW DON'T BE LATE!
MMM... I GUESS THERE'S ONLY ONE WAY TO FIND OUT! I HOPE GLORIA IS HOME!
KNOCK! KNOCK!
OH, HELLO, WILBUR! COME RIGHT IN!
THIS ISN'T A SOCIAL CALL, GLORIA! I JUST CAME TO ASK YOU A QUESTION! PLEASE BE CALM!
I'LL BE CALM, WILBUR! GO AHEAD! ASK ME ANYTHING!
OKAY—ARE YOU GOING TO LULU'S PARTY TODAY?

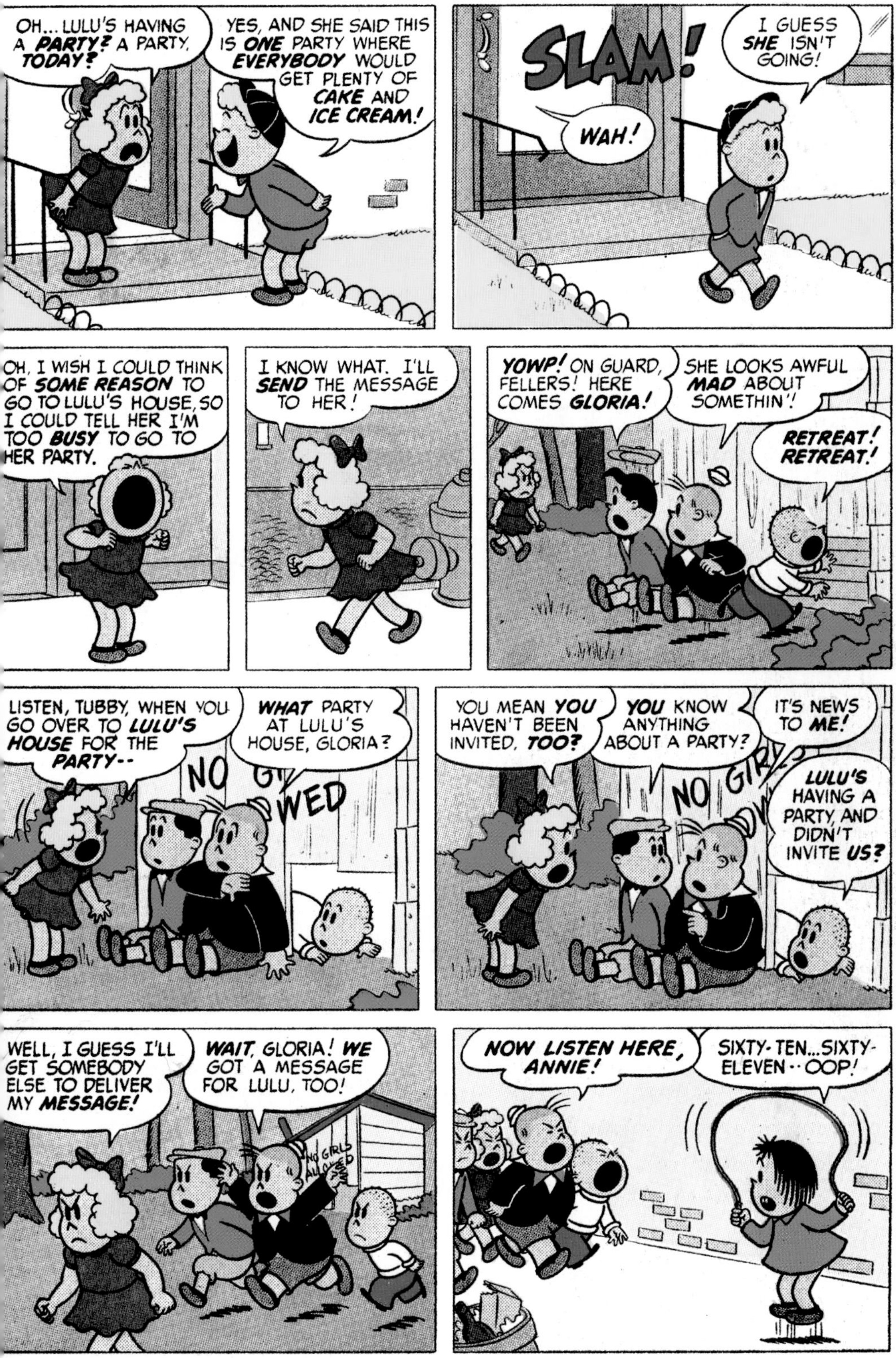
OH... LULU'S HAVING A PARTY? A PARTY, TODAY?
YES, AND SHE SAID THIS IS ONE PARTY WHERE EVERYBODY WOULD GET PLENTY OF CAKE AND ICE CREAM!
SLAM!
I GUESS SHE ISN'T GOING!
WAH!
OH, I WISH I COULD THINK OF SOME REASON TO GO TO LULU'S HOUSE, SO I COULD TELL HER I'M TOO BUSY TO GO TO HER PARTY.
I KNOW WHAT. I'LL SEND THE MESSAGE TO HER!
YOWP! ON GUARD, FELLERS! HERE COMES GLORIA!
SHE LOOKS AWFUL MAD ABOUT SOMETHIN'!
RETREAT! RETREAT!
LISTEN, TUBBY, WHEN YOU GO OVER TO LULU'S HOUSE FOR THE PARTY--
WHAT PARTY AT LULU'S HOUSE, GLORIA?
YOU MEAN YOU HAVEN'T BEEN INVITED, TOO?
YOU KNOW ANYTHING ABOUT A PARTY?
IT'S NEWS TO ME!
LULU'S HAVING A PARTY, AND DIDN'T INVITE US?
WELL, I GUESS I'LL GET SOMEBODY ELSE TO DELIVER MY MESSAGE!
WAIT, GLORIA! WE GOT A MESSAGE FOR LULU, TOO!
NOW LISTEN HERE, ANNIE!
SIXTY-TEN...SIXTY-ELEVEN--OOP!

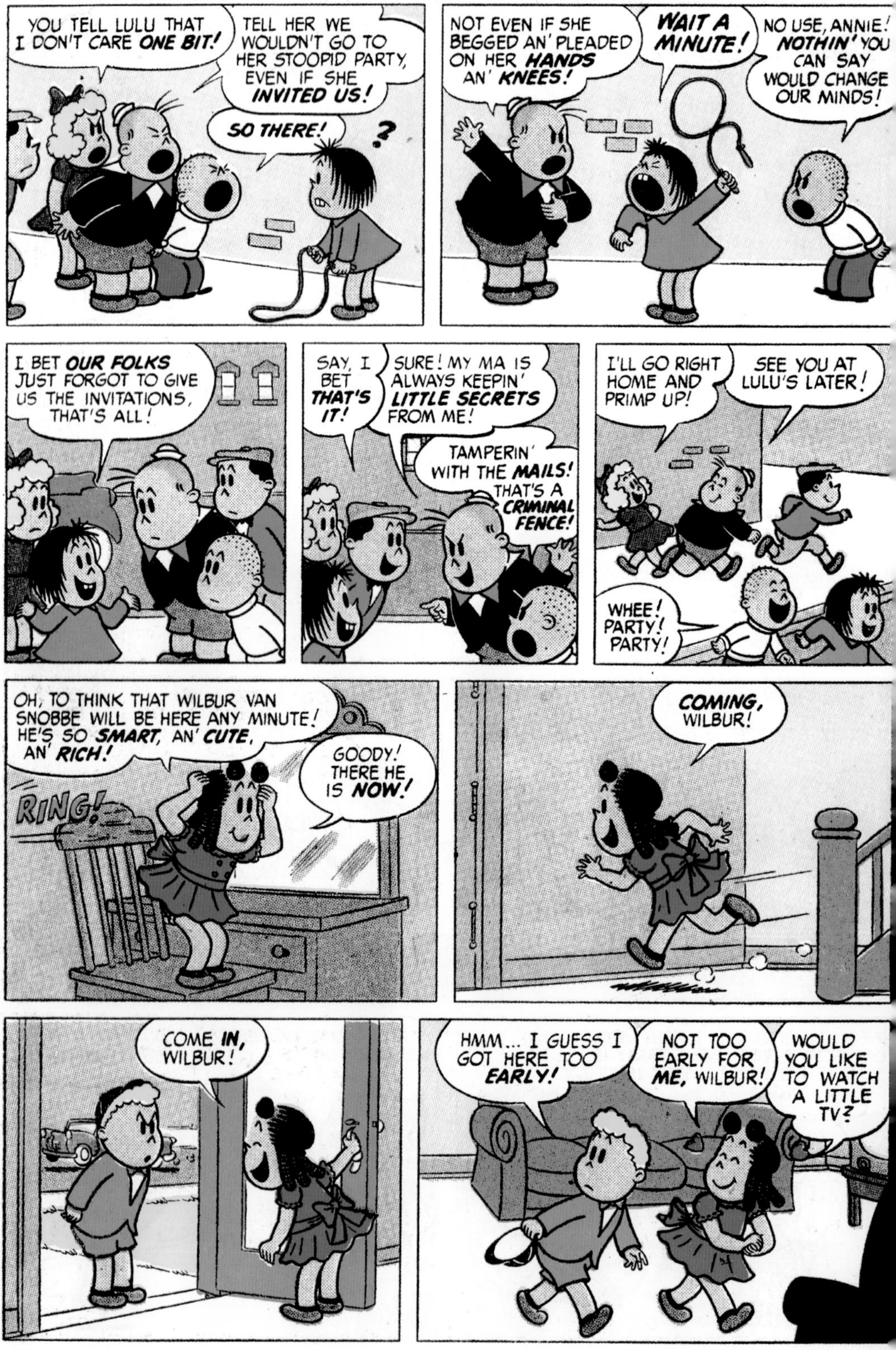
YOU TELL LULU THAT I DON'T CARE ONE BIT!
TELL HER WE WOULDN'T GO TO HER STOOPID PARTY, EVEN IF SHE INVITED US!
SO THERE!
?
NOT EVEN IF SHE BEGGED AN' PLEADED ON HER HANDS AN' KNEES!
WAIT A MINUTE!
NO USE, ANNIE! NOTHIN' YOU CAN SAY WOULD CHANGE OUR MINDS!
I BET OUR FOLKS JUST FORGOT TO GIVE US THE INVITATIONS, THAT'S ALL!
SAY, I BET THAT'S IT!
SURE! MY MA IS ALWAYS KEEPIN' LITTLE SECRETS FROM ME!
TAMPERIN' WITH THE MAILS! THAT'S A CRIMINAL FENCE!
I'LL GO RIGHT HOME AND PRIMP UP!
SEE YOU AT LULU'S LATER!
WHEE! PARTY! PARTY!
OH, TO THINK THAT WILBUR VAN SNOBBE WILL BE HERE ANY MINUTE! HE'S SO SMART, AN' CUTE, AN' RICH!
RING!
GOODY! THERE HE IS NOW!
COMING, WILBUR!
COME IN, WILBUR!
HMM... I GUESS I GOT HERE TOO EARLY!
NOT TOO EARLY FOR ME, WILBUR!
WOULD YOU LIKE TO WATCH A LITTLE TV?

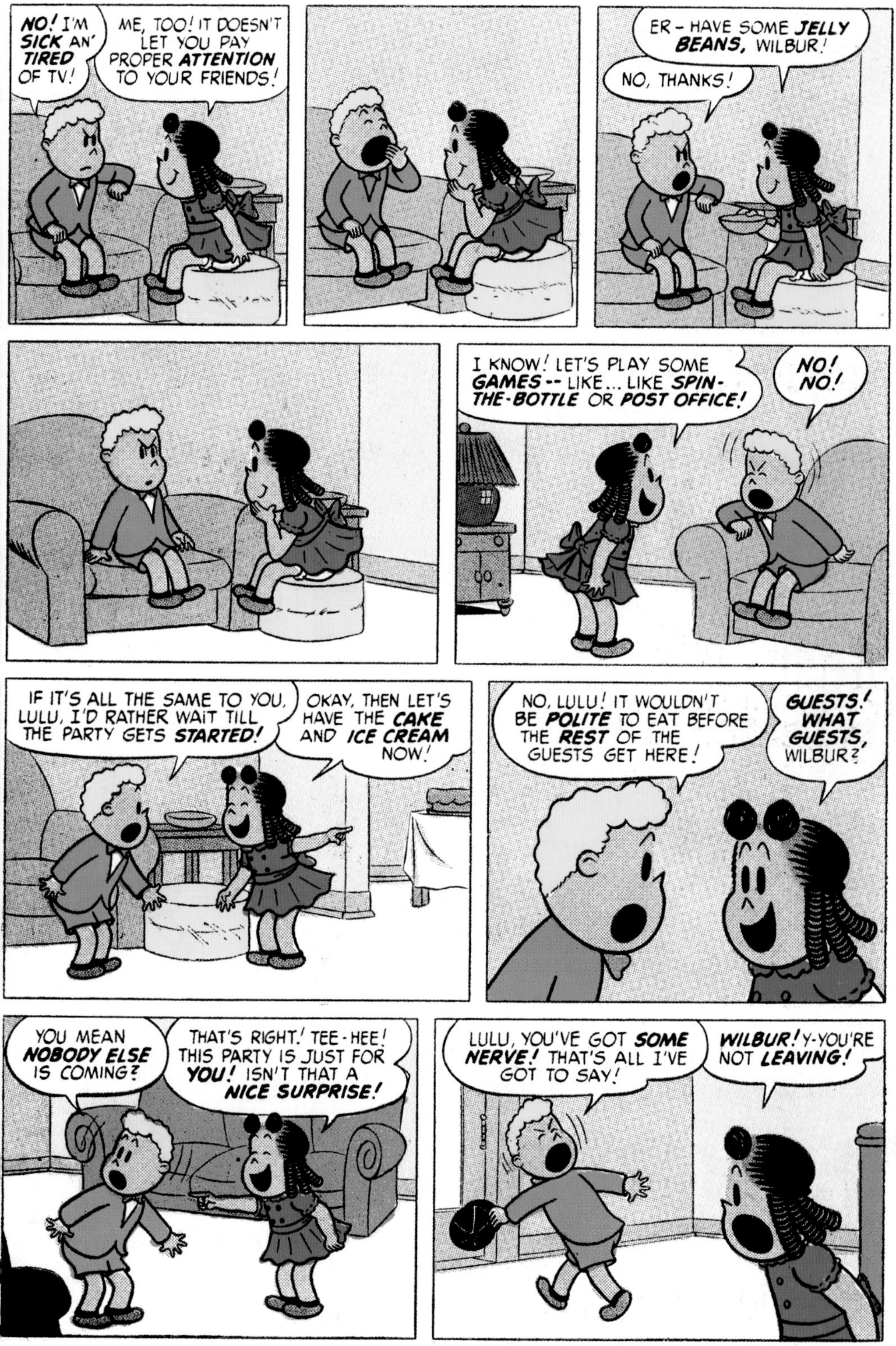
NO! I'M SICK AN' TIRED OF TV!
ME, TOO! IT DOESN'T LET YOU PAY PROPER ATTENTION TO YOUR FRIENDS!
ER - HAVE SOME JELLY BEANS, WILBUR!
NO, THANKS!
I KNOW! LET'S PLAY SOME GAMES -- LIKE... LIKE SPIN-THE-BOTTLE OR POST OFFICE!
NO! NO!
IF IT'S ALL THE SAME TO YOU, LULU, I'D RATHER WAIT TILL THE PARTY GETS STARTED!
OKAY, THEN LET'S HAVE THE CAKE AND ICE CREAM NOW!
NO, LULU! IT WOULDN'T BE POLITE TO EAT BEFORE THE REST OF THE GUESTS GET HERE!
GUESTS! WHAT GUESTS, WILBUR?
YOU MEAN NOBODY ELSE IS COMING?
THAT'S RIGHT! TEE-HEE! THIS PARTY IS JUST FOR YOU! ISN'T THAT A NICE SURPRISE!
LULU, YOU'VE GOT SOME NERVE! THAT'S ALL I'VE GOT TO SAY!
WILBUR! Y-YOU'RE NOT LEAVING!

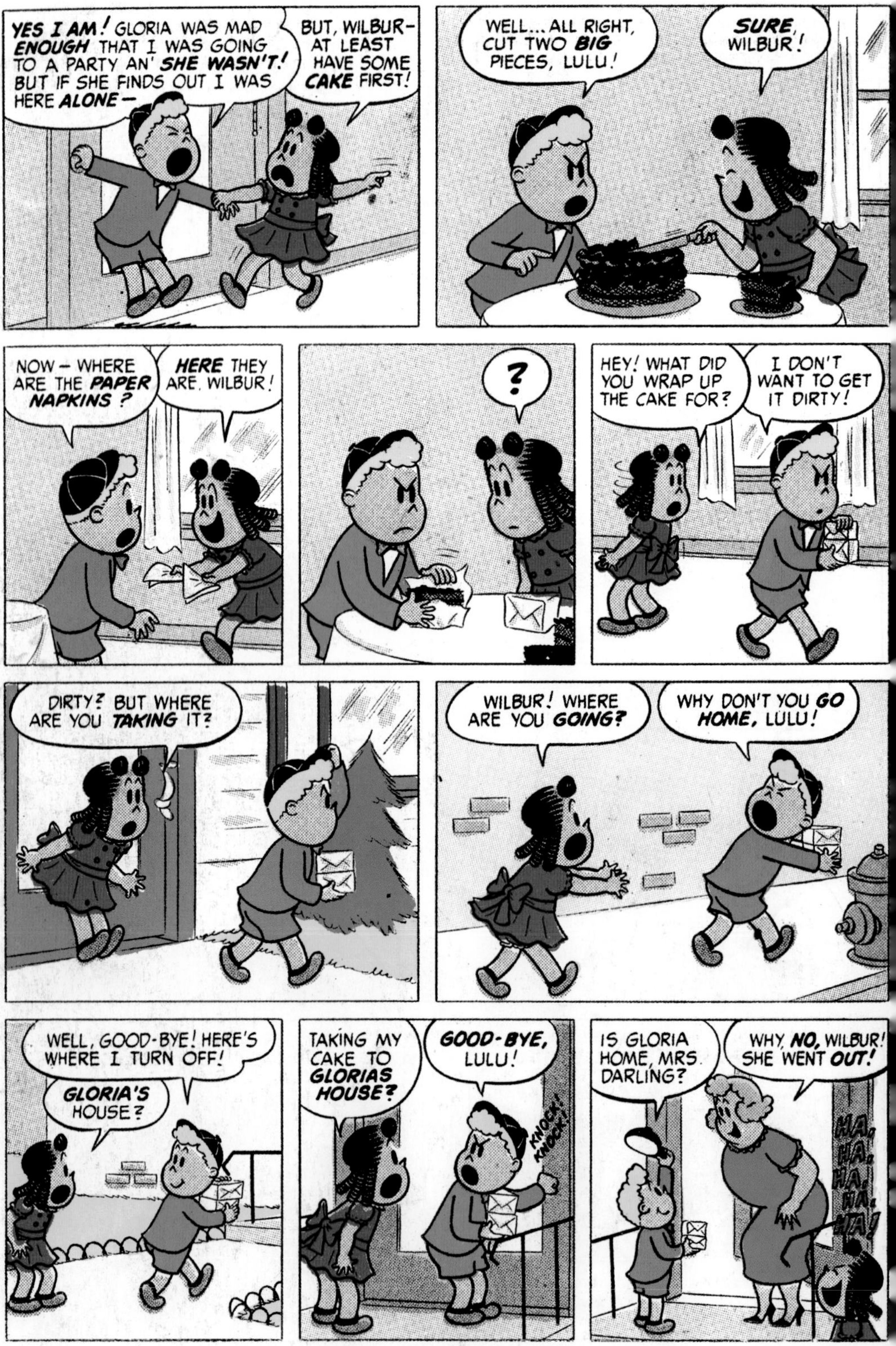
YES I AM! GLORIA WAS MAD ENOUGH THAT I WAS GOING TO A PARTY AN' SHE WASN'T! BUT IF SHE FINDS OUT I WAS HERE ALONE—
BUT, WILBUR—AT LEAST HAVE SOME CAKE FIRST!
WELL... ALL RIGHT, CUT TWO BIG PIECES, LULU!
SURE, WILBUR!
NOW—WHERE ARE THE PAPER NAPKINS?
HERE THEY ARE, WILBUR!
?
HEY! WHAT DID YOU WRAP UP THE CAKE FOR?
I DON'T WANT TO GET IT DIRTY!
DIRTY? BUT WHERE ARE YOU TAKING IT?
WILBUR! WHERE ARE YOU GOING?
WHY DON'T YOU GO HOME, LULU!
WELL, GOOD-BYE! HERE'S WHERE I TURN OFF!
GLORIA'S HOUSE?
TAKING MY CAKE TO GLORIAS HOUSE?
GOOD-BYE, LULU!
KNOCK! KNOCK!
IS GLORIA HOME, MRS. DARLING?
WHY, NO, WILBUR! SHE WENT OUT!
HA, HA, HA, HA, HA!

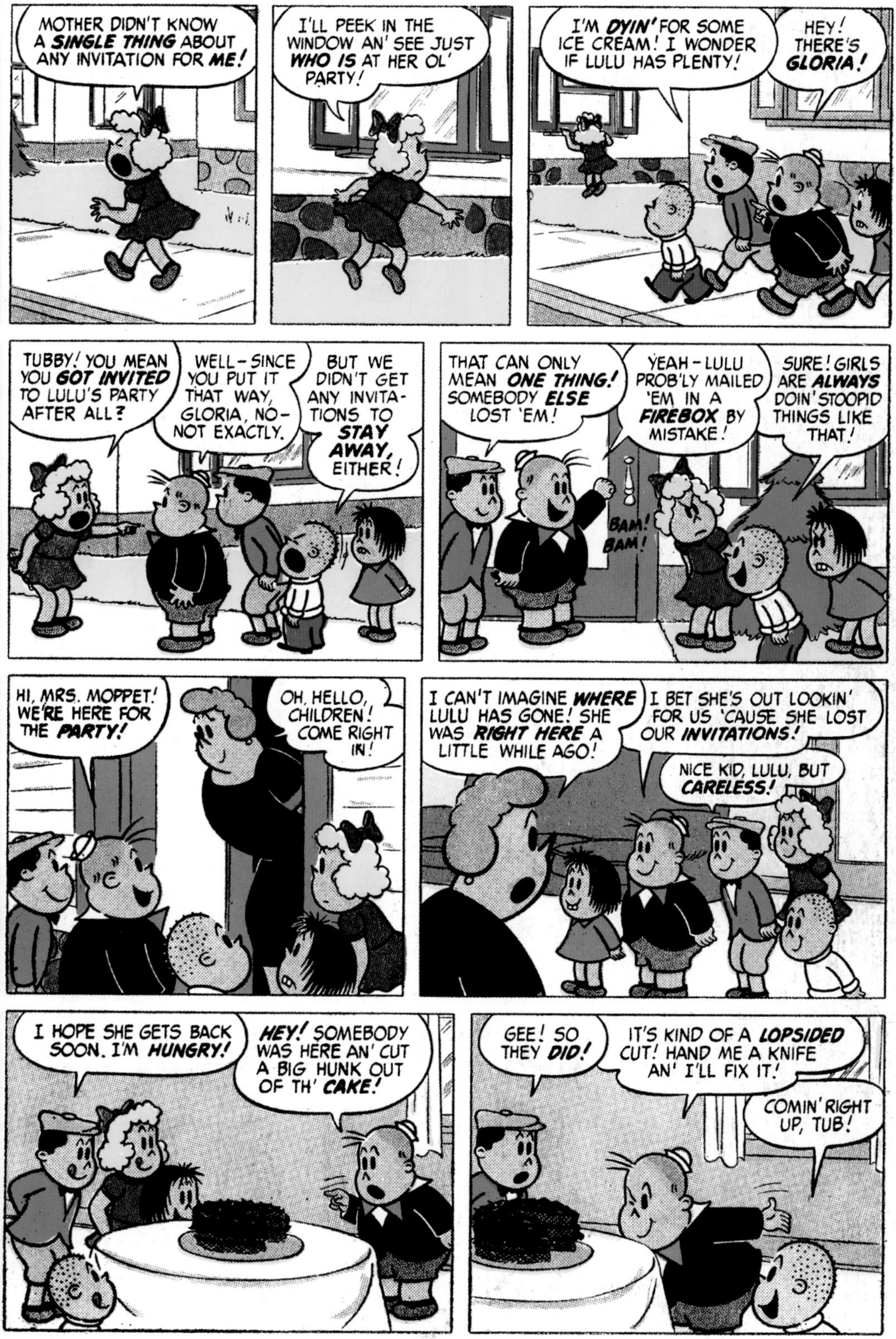
MOTHER DIDN'T KNOW A SINGLE THING ABOUT ANY INVITATION FOR ME!
I'LL PEEK IN THE WINDOW AN' SEE JUST WHO IS AT HER OL' PARTY!
I'M DYIN' FOR SOME ICE CREAM! I WONDER IF LULU HAS PLENTY!
HEY! THERE'S GLORIA!
TUBBY! YOU MEAN YOU GOT INVITED TO LULU'S PARTY AFTER ALL?
WELL-SINCE YOU PUT IT THAT WAY, GLORIA, NO-NOT EXACTLY.
BUT WE DIDN'T GET ANY INVITATIONS TO STAY AWAY, EITHER!
THAT CAN ONLY MEAN ONE THING! SOMEBODY ELSE LOST 'EM!
YEAH-LULU PROB'LY MAILED 'EM IN A FIREBOX BY MISTAKE!
BAM! BAM!
SURE! GIRLS ARE ALWAYS DOIN' STOOPID THINGS LIKE THAT!
HI, MRS. MOPPET! WE'RE HERE FOR THE PARTY!
OH, HELLO, CHILDREN! COME RIGHT IN!
I CAN'T IMAGINE WHERE LULU HAS GONE! SHE WAS RIGHT HERE A LITTLE WHILE AGO!
I BET SHE'S OUT LOOKIN' FOR US 'CAUSE SHE LOST OUR INVITATIONS!
NICE KID, LULU, BUT CARELESS!
I HOPE SHE GETS BACK SOON. I'M HUNGRY!
HEY! SOMEBODY WAS HERE AN' CUT A BIG HUNK OUT OF TH' CAKE!
GEE! SO THEY DID!
IT'S KIND OF A LOPSIDED CUT! HAND ME A KNIFE AN' I'LL FIX IT!
COMIN' RIGHT UP, TUB!

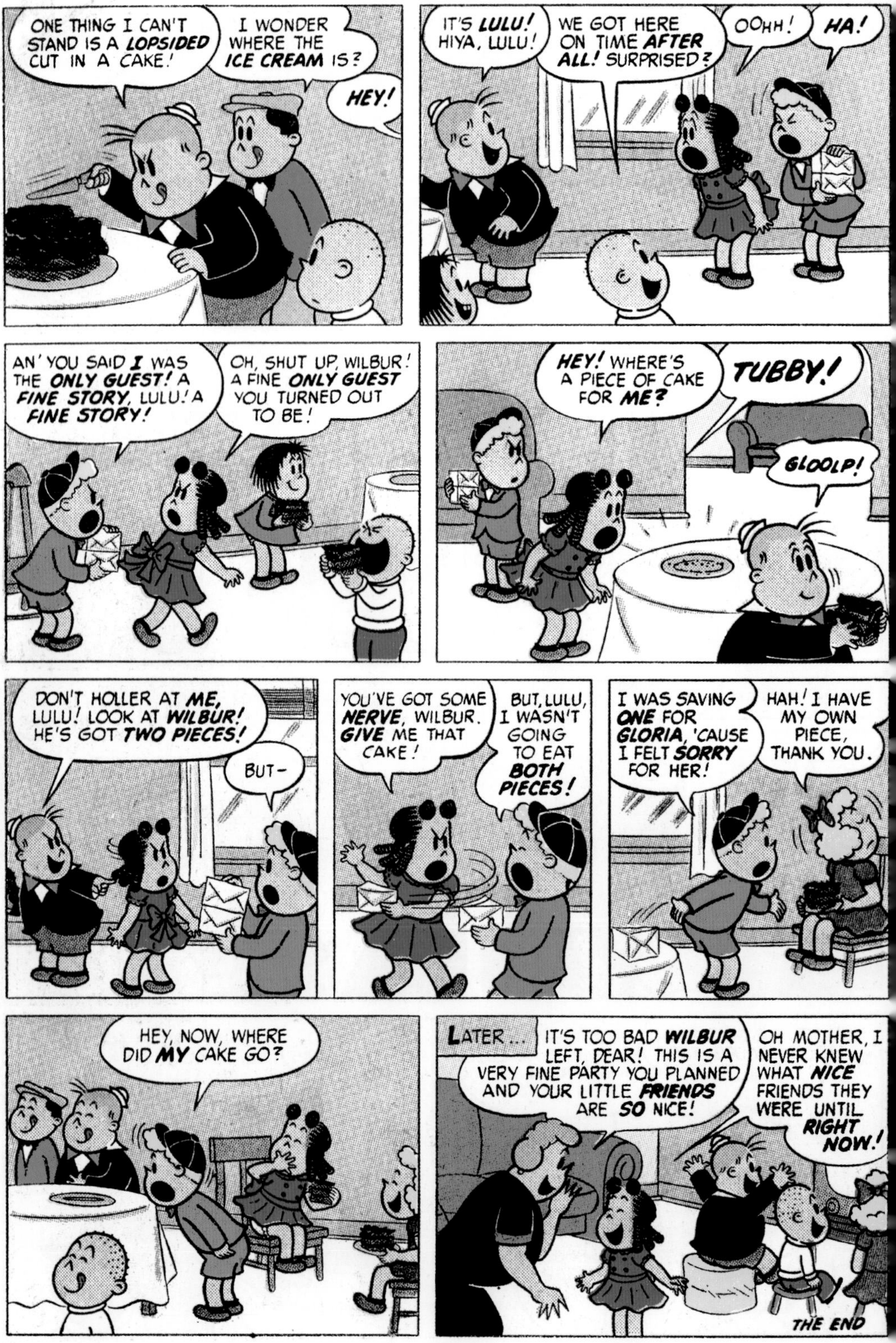
ONE THING I CAN'T STAND IS A LOPSIDED CUT IN A CAKE!
I WONDER WHERE THE ICE CREAM IS?
HEY!
IT'S LULU! HIYA, LULU!
WE GOT HERE ON TIME AFTER ALL! SURPRISED?
OOHH!
HA!
AN' YOU SAID I WAS THE ONLY GUEST! A FINE STORY, LULU! A FINE STORY!
OH, SHUT UP, WILBUR! A FINE ONLY GUEST YOU TURNED OUT TO BE!
HEY! WHERE'S A PIECE OF CAKE FOR ME?
TUBBY!
GLOOLP!
DON'T HOLLER AT ME, LULU! LOOK AT WILBUR! HE'S GOT TWO PIECES!
BUT—
YOU'VE GOT SOME NERVE, WILBUR. GIVE ME THAT CAKE!
BUT, LULU, I WASN'T GOING TO EAT BOTH PIECES!
I WAS SAVING ONE FOR GLORIA, 'CAUSE I FELT SORRY FOR HER!
HAH! I HAVE MY OWN PIECE, THANK YOU.
HEY, NOW, WHERE DID MY CAKE GO?
LATER...
IT'S TOO BAD WILBUR LEFT, DEAR! THIS IS A VERY FINE PARTY YOU PLANNED AND YOUR LITTLE FRIENDS ARE SO NICE!
OH MOTHER, I NEVER KNEW WHAT NICE FRIENDS THEY WERE UNTIL RIGHT NOW!
THE END

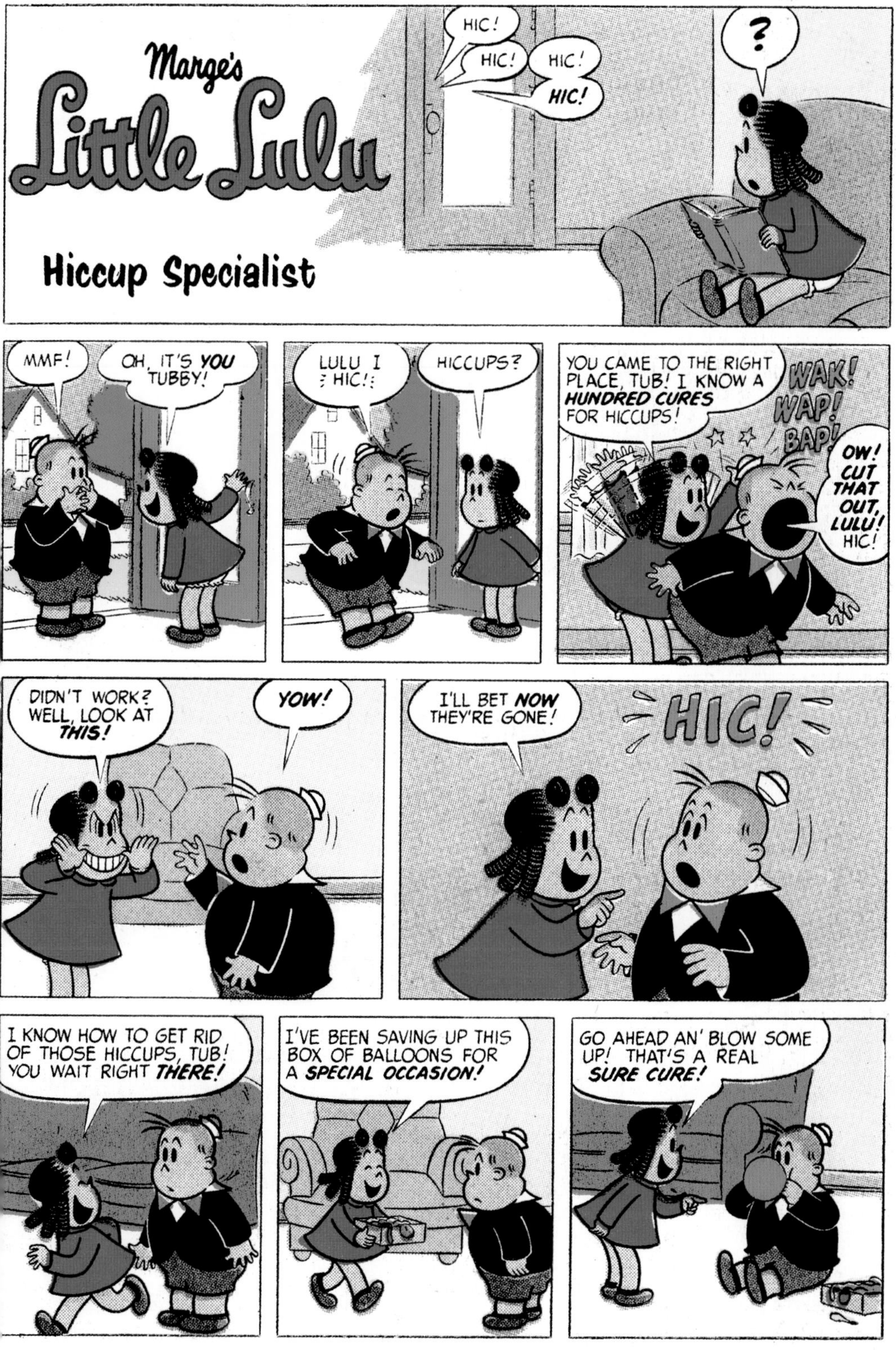
Marge's
Little Lulu
Hiccup Specialist
HIC!
HIC!
HIC!
HIC!
?
MMF!
OH, IT'S YOU TUBBY!
LULU I HIC!
HICCUPS?
YOU CAME TO THE RIGHT PLACE, TUB! I KNOW A HUNDRED CURES FOR HICCUPS!
WAK! WAP! BAP!
OW! CUT THAT OUT, LULU! HIC!
DIDN'T WORK? WELL, LOOK AT THIS!
YOW!
I'LL BET NOW THEY'RE GONE!
HIC!
I KNOW HOW TO GET RID OF THOSE HICCUPS, TUB! YOU WAIT RIGHT THERE!
I'VE BEEN SAVING UP THIS BOX OF BALLOONS FOR A SPECIAL OCCASION!
GO AHEAD AN' BLOW SOME UP! THAT'S A REAL SURE CURE!

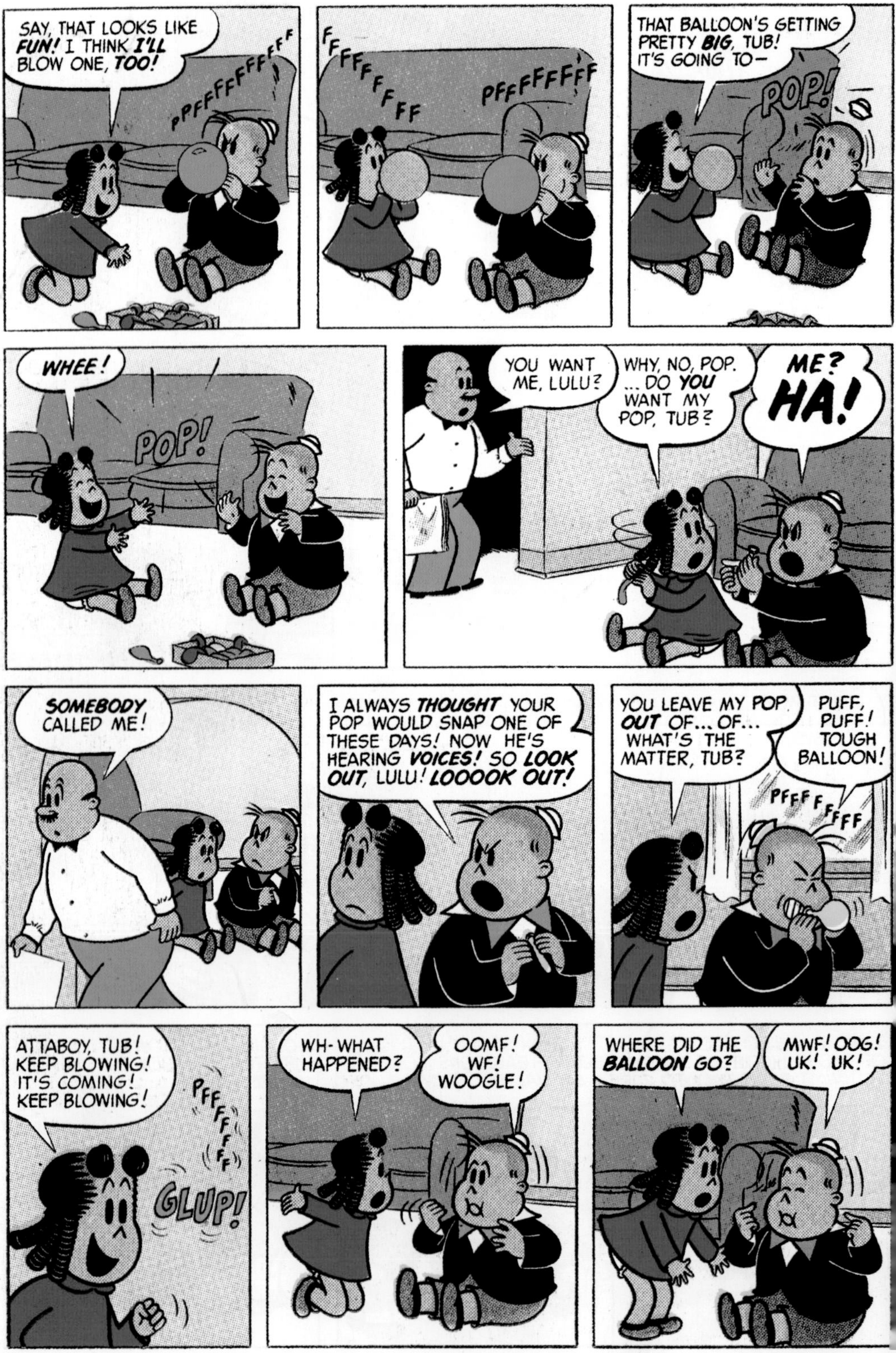
SAY, THAT LOOKS LIKE FUN! I THINK I'LL BLOW ONE, TOO!
PPFFFFFFFFFF
FFFFFFFFFF
PFFFFFFFF
THAT BALLOON'S GETTING PRETTY BIG, TUB! IT'S GOING TO—
POP!
WHEE!
POP!
YOU WANT ME, LULU?
WHY, NO, POP. ... DO YOU WANT MY POP, TUB?
ME? HA!
SOMEBODY CALLED ME!
I ALWAYS THOUGHT YOUR POP WOULD SNAP ONE OF THESE DAYS! NOW HE'S HEARING VOICES! SO LOOK OUT, LULU! LOOOOK OUT!
YOU LEAVE MY POP OUT OF... OF... WHAT'S THE MATTER, TUB?
PUFF, PUFF! TOUGH BALLOON!
PFFFFFFF
ATTABOY, TUB! KEEP BLOWING! IT'S COMING! KEEP BLOWING!
PFFFFFF
GLUP!
WH-WHAT HAPPENED?
OOMF! WF! WOOGLE!
WHERE DID THE BALLOON GO?
MWF! OOG! UK! UK!

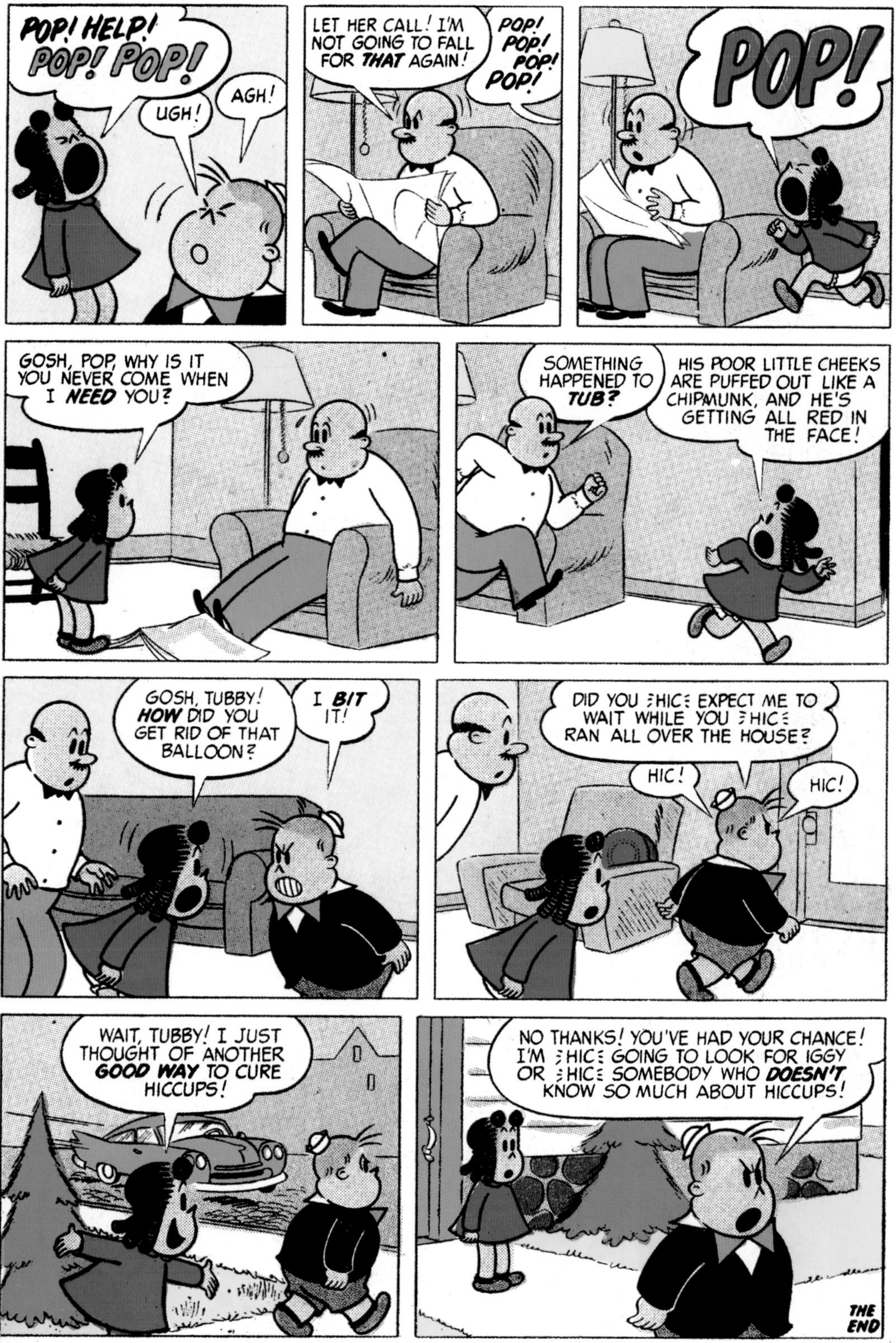
POP! HELP! POP! POP!
UGH!
AGH!
LET HER CALL! I'M NOT GOING TO FALL FOR THAT AGAIN!
POP! POP! POP! POP!
POP!
GOSH, POP, WHY IS IT YOU NEVER COME WHEN I NEED YOU?
SOMETHING HAPPENED TO TUB?
HIS POOR LITTLE CHEEKS ARE PUFFED OUT LIKE A CHIPMUNK, AND HE'S GETTING ALL RED IN THE FACE!
GOSH, TUBBY! HOW DID YOU GET RID OF THAT BALLOON?
I BIT IT!
DID YOU HIC EXPECT ME TO WAIT WHILE YOU HIC RAN ALL OVER THE HOUSE?
HIC!
HIC!
WAIT, TUBBY! I JUST THOUGHT OF ANOTHER GOOD WAY TO CURE HICCUPS!
NO THANKS! YOU'VE HAD YOUR CHANCE! I'M HIC GOING TO LOOK FOR IGGY OR HIC SOMEBODY WHO DOESN'T KNOW SO MUCH ABOUT HICCUPS!
THE END

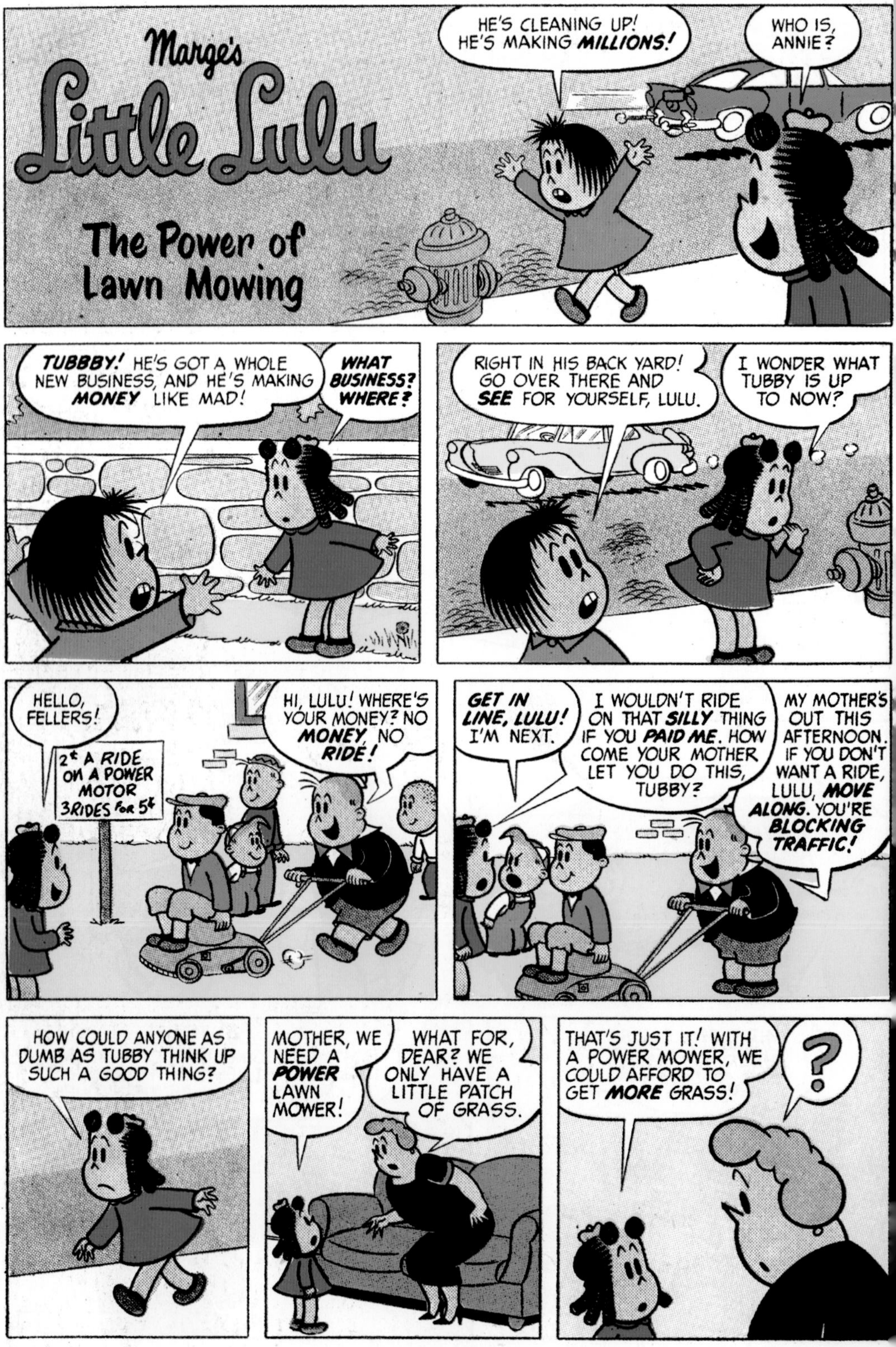
Marge's Little Lulu
The Power of Lawn Mowing
HE'S CLEANING UP! HE'S MAKING MILLIONS!
WHO IS, ANNIE?
TUBBBY! HE'S GOT A WHOLE NEW BUSINESS, AND HE'S MAKING MONEY LIKE MAD!
WHAT BUSINESS? WHERE?
RIGHT IN HIS BACK YARD! GO OVER THERE AND SEE FOR YOURSELF, LULU.
I WONDER WHAT TUBBY IS UP TO NOW?
HELLO, FELLERS!
2¢ A RIDE ON A POWER MOTOR 3 RIDES FOR 5¢
HI, LULU! WHERE'S YOUR MONEY? NO MONEY, NO RIDE!
GET IN LINE, LULU! I'M NEXT.
I WOULDN'T RIDE ON THAT SILLY THING IF YOU PAID ME. HOW COME YOUR MOTHER LET YOU DO THIS, TUBBY?
MY MOTHER'S OUT THIS AFTERNOON. IF YOU DON'T WANT A RIDE, LULU, MOVE ALONG. YOU'RE BLOCKING TRAFFIC!
HOW COULD ANYONE AS DUMB AS TUBBY THINK UP SUCH A GOOD THING?
MOTHER, WE NEED A POWER LAWN MOWER!
WHAT FOR, DEAR? WE ONLY HAVE A LITTLE PATCH OF GRASS.
THAT'S JUST IT! WITH A POWER MOWER, WE COULD AFFORD TO GET MORE GRASS!
?

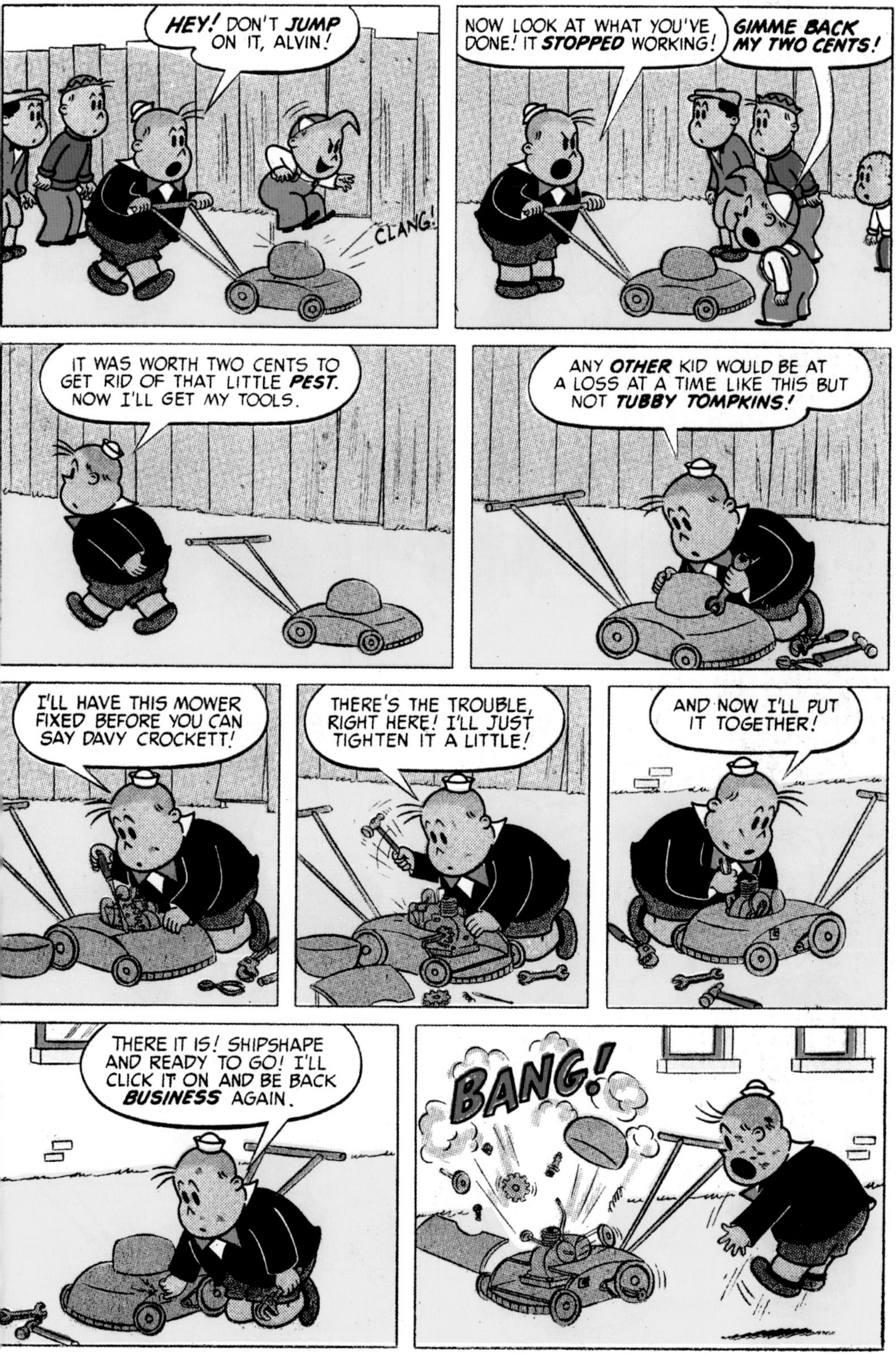
HEY! DON'T JUMP ON IT, ALVIN!
CLANG!
NOW LOOK AT WHAT YOU'VE DONE! IT STOPPED WORKING!
GIMME BACK MY TWO CENTS!
IT WAS WORTH TWO CENTS TO GET RID OF THAT LITTLE PEST. NOW I'LL GET MY TOOLS.
ANY OTHER KID WOULD BE AT A LOSS AT A TIME LIKE THIS BUT NOT TUBBY TOMPKINS!
I'LL HAVE THIS MOWER FIXED BEFORE YOU CAN SAY DAVY CROCKETT!
THERE'S THE TROUBLE, RIGHT HERE! I'LL JUST TIGHTEN IT A LITTLE!
AND NOW I'LL PUT IT TOGETHER!
THERE IT IS! SHIPSHAPE AND READY TO GO! I'LL CLICK IT ON AND BE BACK BUSINESS AGAIN.
BANG!

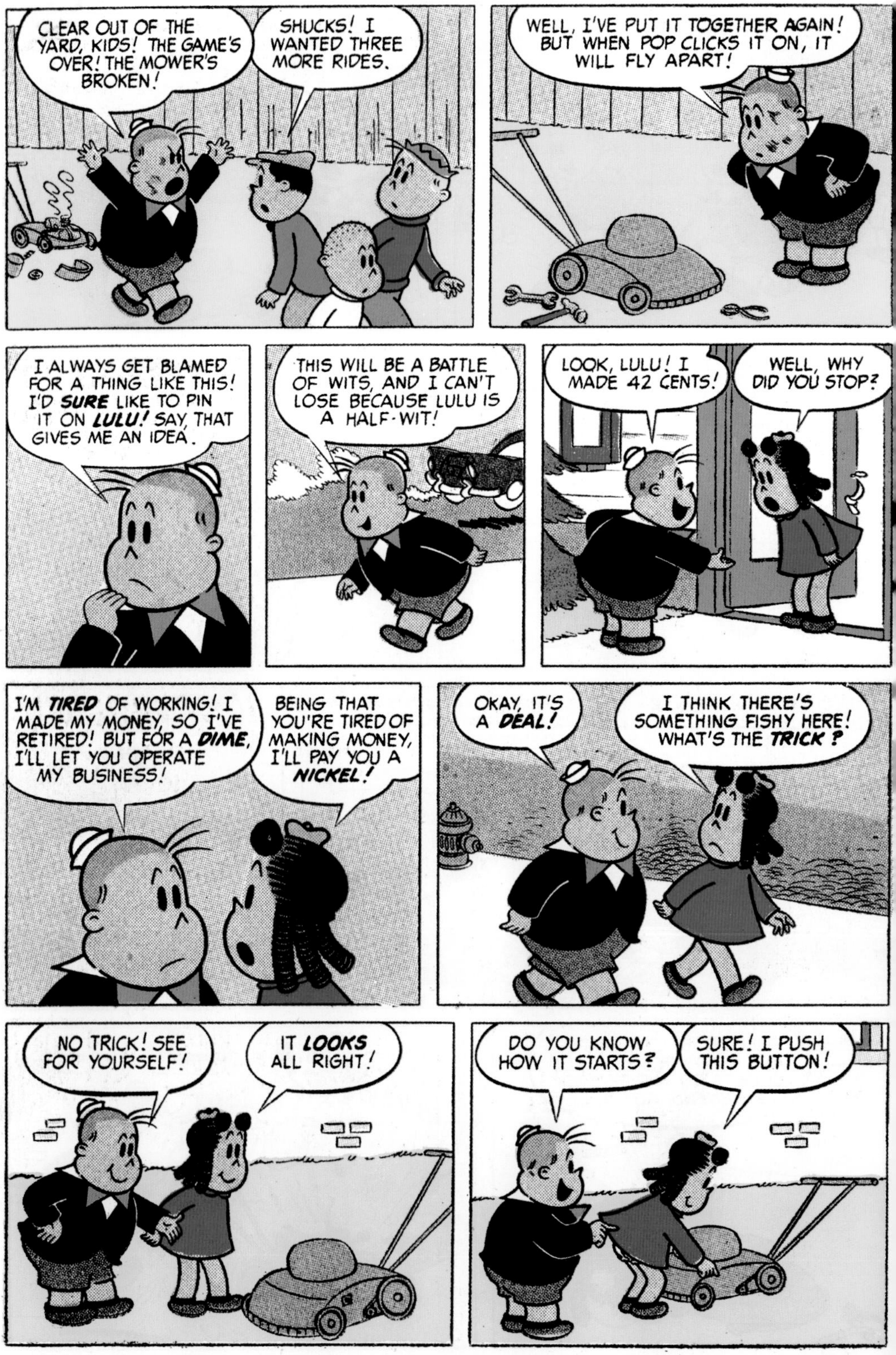
CLEAR OUT OF THE YARD, KIDS! THE GAME'S OVER! THE MOWER'S BROKEN!
SHUCKS! I WANTED THREE MORE RIDES.
WELL, I'VE PUT IT TOGETHER AGAIN! BUT WHEN POP CLICKS IT ON, IT WILL FLY APART!
I ALWAYS GET BLAMED FOR A THING LIKE THIS! I'D SURE LIKE TO PIN IT ON LULU! SAY, THAT GIVES ME AN IDEA.
THIS WILL BE A BATTLE OF WITS, AND I CAN'T LOSE BECAUSE LULU IS A HALF-WIT!
LOOK, LULU! I MADE 42 CENTS!
WELL, WHY DID YOU STOP?
I'M TIRED OF WORKING! I MADE MY MONEY, SO I'VE RETIRED! BUT FOR A DIME, I'LL LET YOU OPERATE MY BUSINESS!
BEING THAT YOU'RE TIRED OF MAKING MONEY, I'LL PAY YOU A NICKEL!
OKAY, IT'S A DEAL!
I THINK THERE'S SOMETHING FISHY HERE! WHAT'S THE TRICK?
NO TRICK! SEE FOR YOURSELF!
IT LOOKS ALL RIGHT!
DO YOU KNOW HOW IT STARTS?
SURE! I PUSH THIS BUTTON!

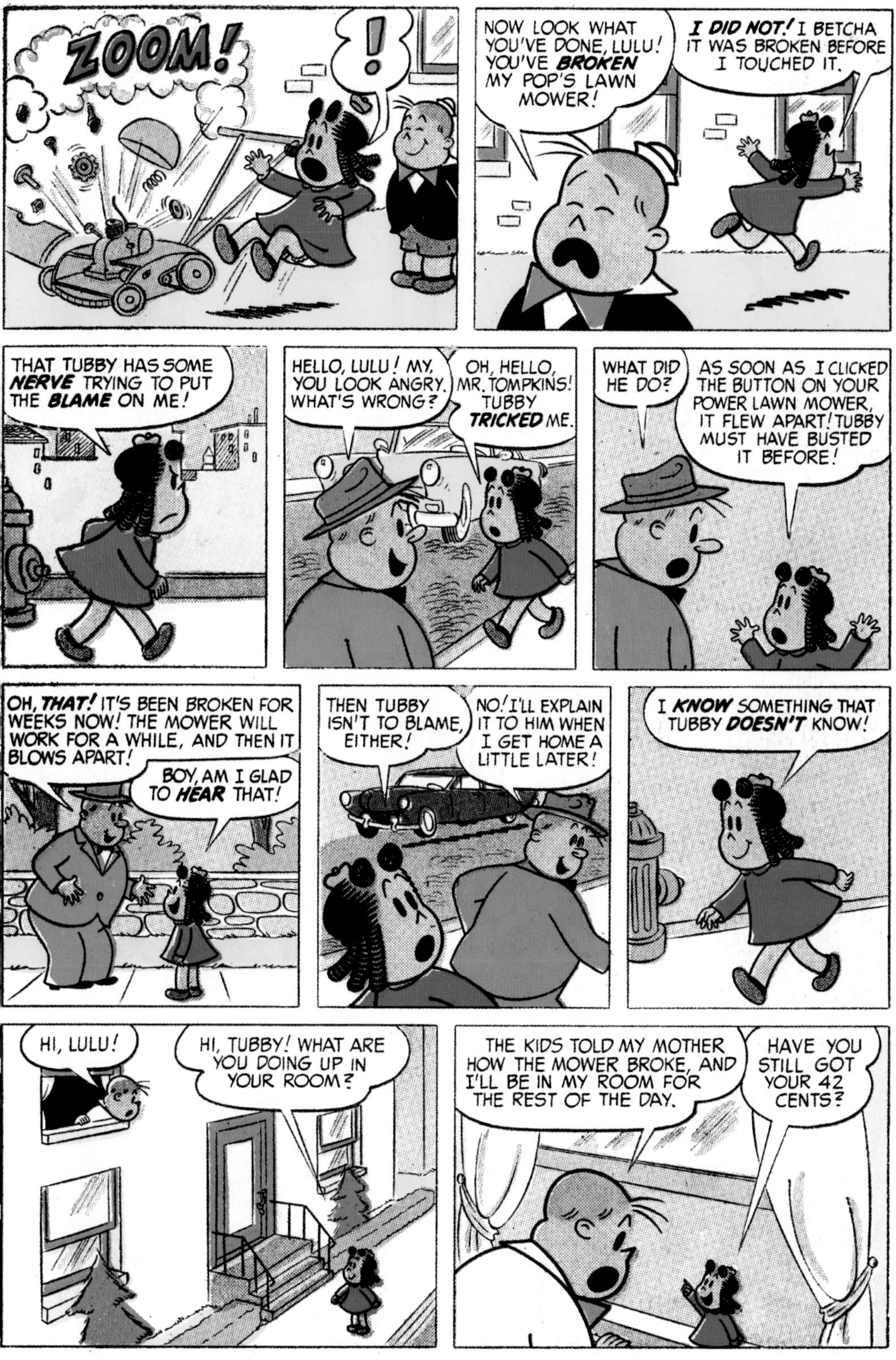
ZOOM!
!
NOW LOOK WHAT YOU'VE DONE, LULU! YOU'VE BROKEN MY POP'S LAWN MOWER!
I DID NOT! I BETCHA IT WAS BROKEN BEFORE I TOUCHED IT.
THAT TUBBY HAS SOME NERVE TRYING TO PUT THE BLAME ON ME!
HELLO, LULU! MY, YOU LOOK ANGRY. WHAT'S WRONG?
OH, HELLO, MR. TOMPKINS! TUBBY TRICKED ME.
WHAT DID HE DO?
AS SOON AS I CLICKED THE BUTTON ON YOUR POWER LAWN MOWER, IT FLEW APART! TUBBY MUST HAVE BUSTED IT BEFORE!
OH, THAT! IT'S BEEN BROKEN FOR WEEKS NOW! THE MOWER WILL WORK FOR A WHILE, AND THEN IT BLOWS APART!
BOY, AM I GLAD TO HEAR THAT!
THEN TUBBY ISN'T TO BLAME, EITHER!
NO! I'LL EXPLAIN IT TO HIM WHEN I GET HOME A LITTLE LATER!
I KNOW SOMETHING THAT TUBBY DOESN'T KNOW!
HI, LULU!
HI, TUBBY! WHAT ARE YOU DOING UP IN YOUR ROOM?
THE KIDS TOLD MY MOTHER HOW THE MOWER BROKE, AND I'LL BE IN MY ROOM FOR THE REST OF THE DAY.
HAVE YOU STILL GOT YOUR 42 CENTS?

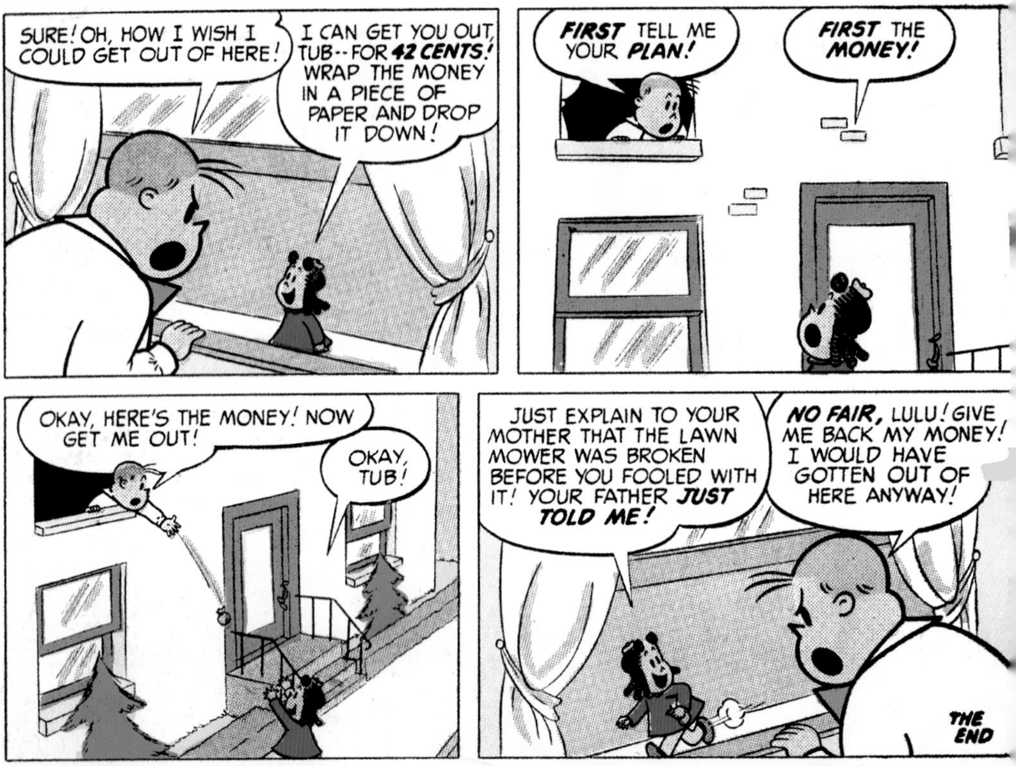
SURE! OH, HOW I WISH I COULD GET OUT OF HERE!
I CAN GET YOU OUT, TUB--FOR 42 CENTS! WRAP THE MONEY IN A PIECE OF PAPER AND DROP IT DOWN!
FIRST TELL ME YOUR PLAN!
FIRST THE MONEY!
OKAY, HERE'S THE MONEY! NOW GET ME OUT!
OKAY, TUB!
JUST EXPLAIN TO YOUR MOTHER THAT THE LAWN MOWER WAS BROKEN BEFORE YOU FOOLED WITH IT! YOUR FATHER JUST TOLD ME!
NO FAIR, LULU! GIVE ME BACK MY MONEY! I WOULD HAVE GOTTEN OUT OF HERE ANYWAY!
THE END

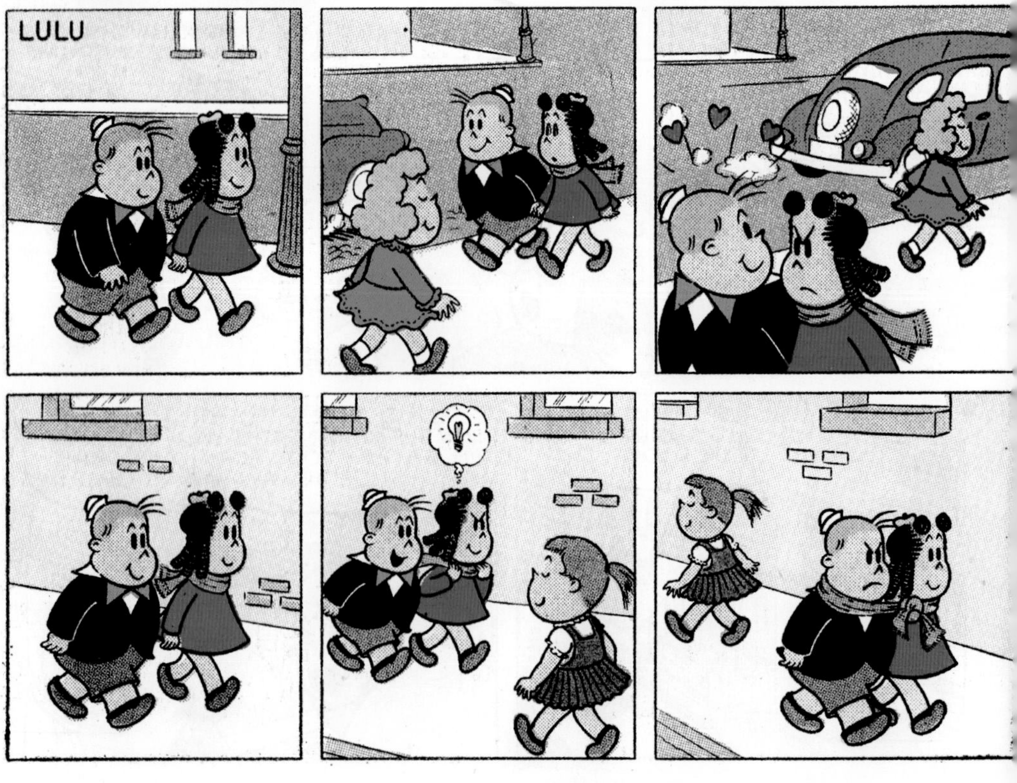
LULU

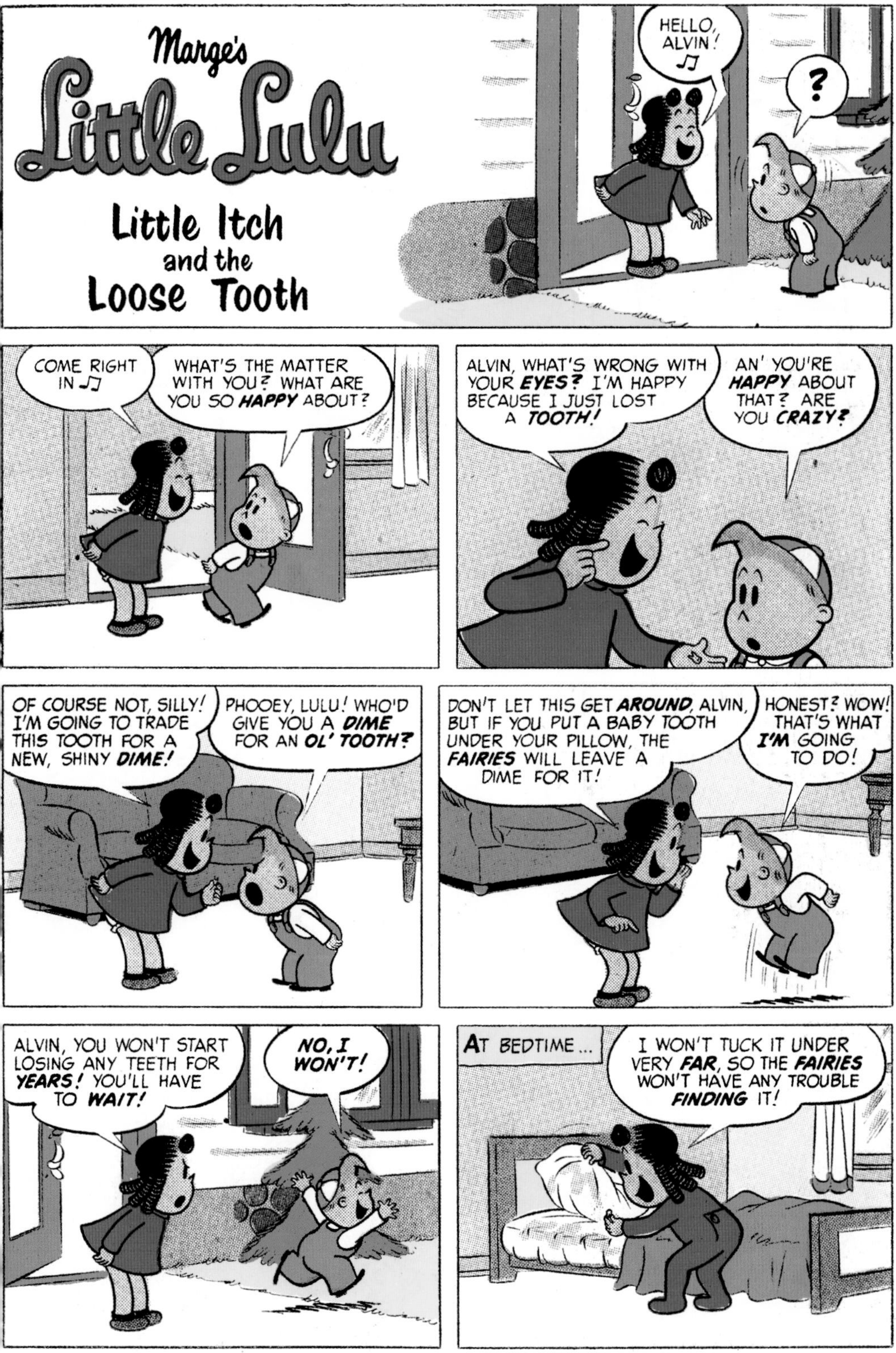
Marge's Little Lulu
Little Itch and the Loose Tooth
HELLO, ALVIN! ♫
?
COME RIGHT IN ♫
WHAT'S THE MATTER WITH YOU? WHAT ARE YOU SO HAPPY ABOUT?
ALVIN, WHAT'S WRONG WITH YOUR EYES? I'M HAPPY BECAUSE I JUST LOST A TOOTH!
AN' YOU'RE HAPPY ABOUT THAT? ARE YOU CRAZY?
OF COURSE NOT, SILLY! I'M GOING TO TRADE THIS TOOTH FOR A NEW, SHINY DIME!
PHOOEY, LULU! WHO'D GIVE YOU A DIME FOR AN OL' TOOTH?
DON'T LET THIS GET AROUND, ALVIN, BUT IF YOU PUT A BABY TOOTH UNDER YOUR PILLOW, THE FAIRIES WILL LEAVE A DIME FOR IT!
HONEST? WOW! THAT'S WHAT I'M GOING TO DO!
ALVIN, YOU WON'T START LOSING ANY TEETH FOR YEARS! YOU'LL HAVE TO WAIT!
NO, I WON'T!
AT BEDTIME...
I WON'T TUCK IT UNDER VERY FAR, SO THE FAIRIES WON'T HAVE ANY TROUBLE FINDING IT!

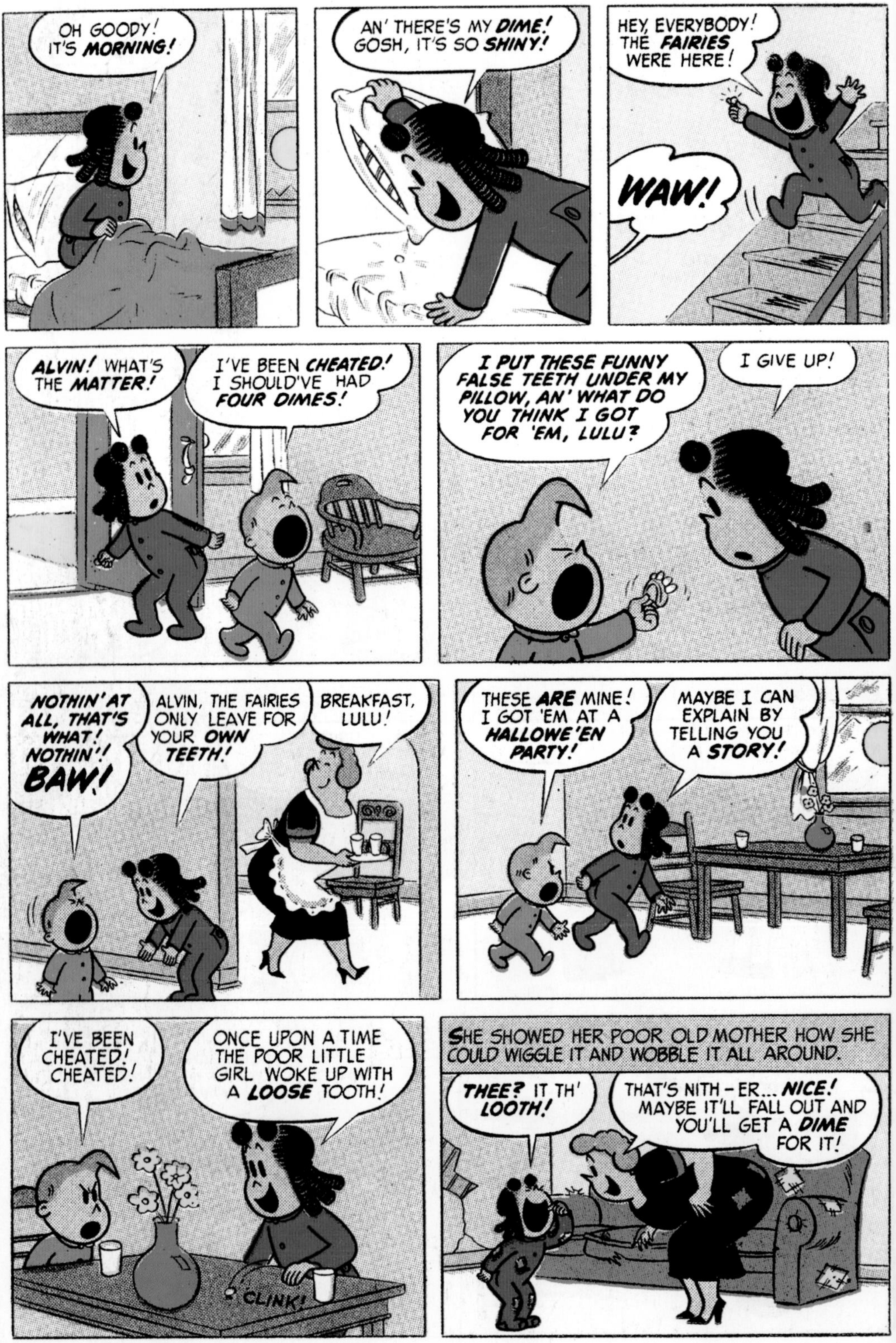

OH GOODY! IT'S MORNING!
AN' THERE'S MY DIME! GOSH, IT'S SO SHINY!
HEY, EVERYBODY! THE FAIRIES WERE HERE!
WAW!
ALVIN! WHAT'S THE MATTER!
I'VE BEEN CHEATED! I SHOULD'VE HAD FOUR DIMES!
I PUT THESE FUNNY FALSE TEETH UNDER MY PILLOW, AN' WHAT DO YOU THINK I GOT FOR 'EM, LULU?
I GIVE UP!
NOTHIN' AT ALL, THAT'S WHAT! NOTHIN'! BAW!
ALVIN, THE FAIRIES ONLY LEAVE FOR YOUR OWN TEETH!
BREAKFAST, LULU!
THESE ARE MINE! I GOT 'EM AT A HALLOWE'EN PARTY!
MAYBE I CAN EXPLAIN BY TELLING YOU A STORY!
I'VE BEEN CHEATED! CHEATED!
ONCE UPON A TIME THE POOR LITTLE GIRL WOKE UP WITH A LOOSE TOOTH!
CLINK!
SHE SHOWED HER POOR OLD MOTHER HOW SHE COULD WIGGLE IT AND WOBBLE IT ALL AROUND.
THEE? IT TH' LOOTH!
THAT'S NITH – ER... NICE! MAYBE IT'LL FALL OUT AND YOU'LL GET A DIME FOR IT!

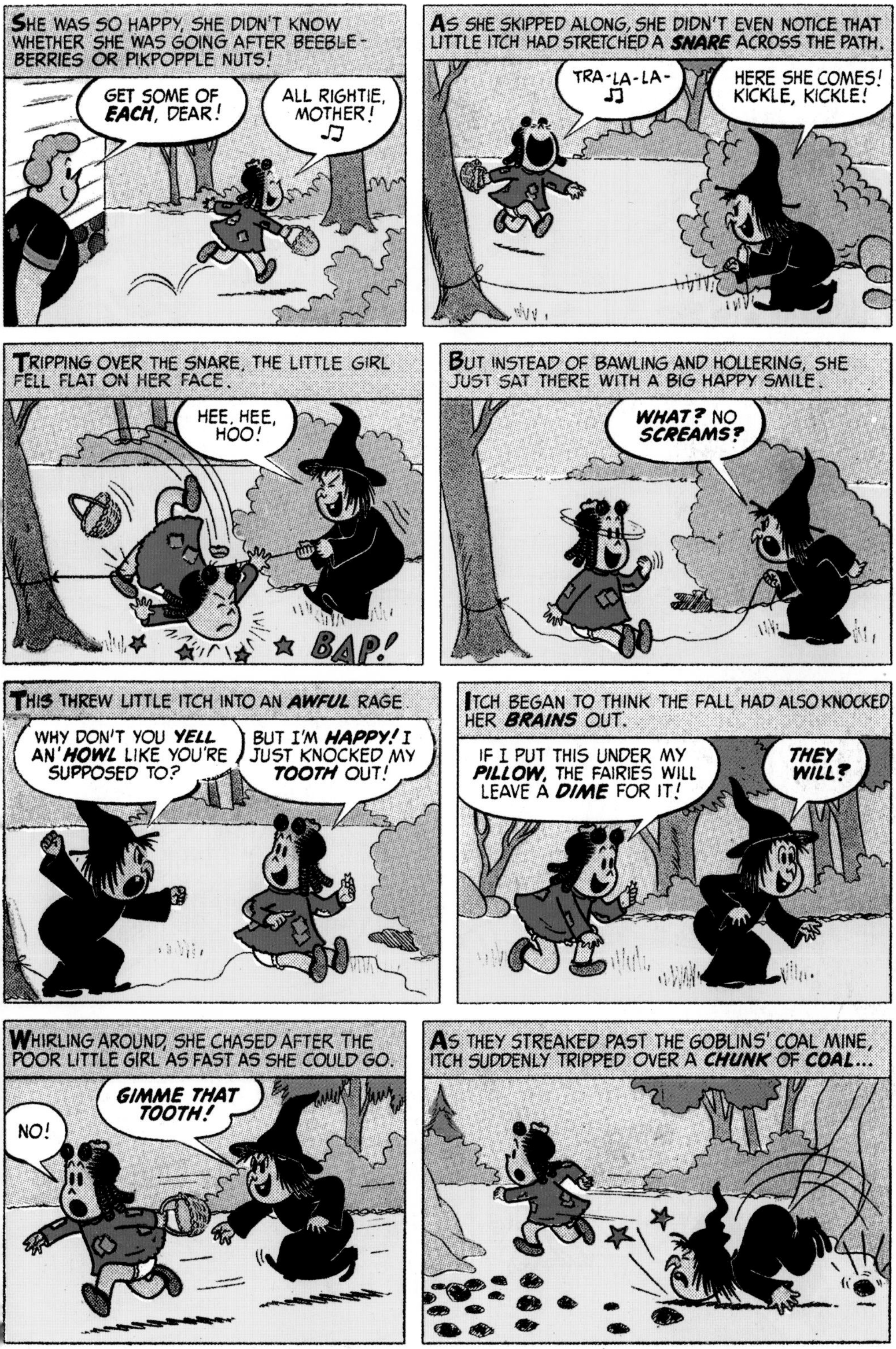
SHE WAS SO HAPPY, SHE DIDN'T KNOW WHETHER SHE WAS GOING AFTER BEEBLE-BERRIES OR PIKPOPPLE NUTS!
GET SOME OF EACH, DEAR!
ALL RIGHTIE, MOTHER! ♫
AS SHE SKIPPED ALONG, SHE DIDN'T EVEN NOTICE THAT LITTLE ITCH HAD STRETCHED A SNARE ACROSS THE PATH.
TRA-LA-LA- ♫
HERE SHE COMES! KICKLE, KICKLE!
TRIPPING OVER THE SNARE, THE LITTLE GIRL FELL FLAT ON HER FACE.
HEE, HEE, HOO!
BAP!
BUT INSTEAD OF BAWLING AND HOLLERING, SHE JUST SAT THERE WITH A BIG HAPPY SMILE.
WHAT? NO SCREAMS?
THIS THREW LITTLE ITCH INTO AN AWFUL RAGE.
WHY DON'T YOU YELL AN' HOWL LIKE YOU'RE SUPPOSED TO?
BUT I'M HAPPY! I JUST KNOCKED MY TOOTH OUT!
ITCH BEGAN TO THINK THE FALL HAD ALSO KNOCKED HER BRAINS OUT.
IF I PUT THIS UNDER MY PILLOW, THE FAIRIES WILL LEAVE A DIME FOR IT!
THEY WILL?
WHIRLING AROUND, SHE CHASED AFTER THE POOR LITTLE GIRL AS FAST AS SHE COULD GO.
NO!
GIMME THAT TOOTH!
AS THEY STREAKED PAST THE GOBLINS' COAL MINE, ITCH SUDDENLY TRIPPED OVER A CHUNK OF COAL...

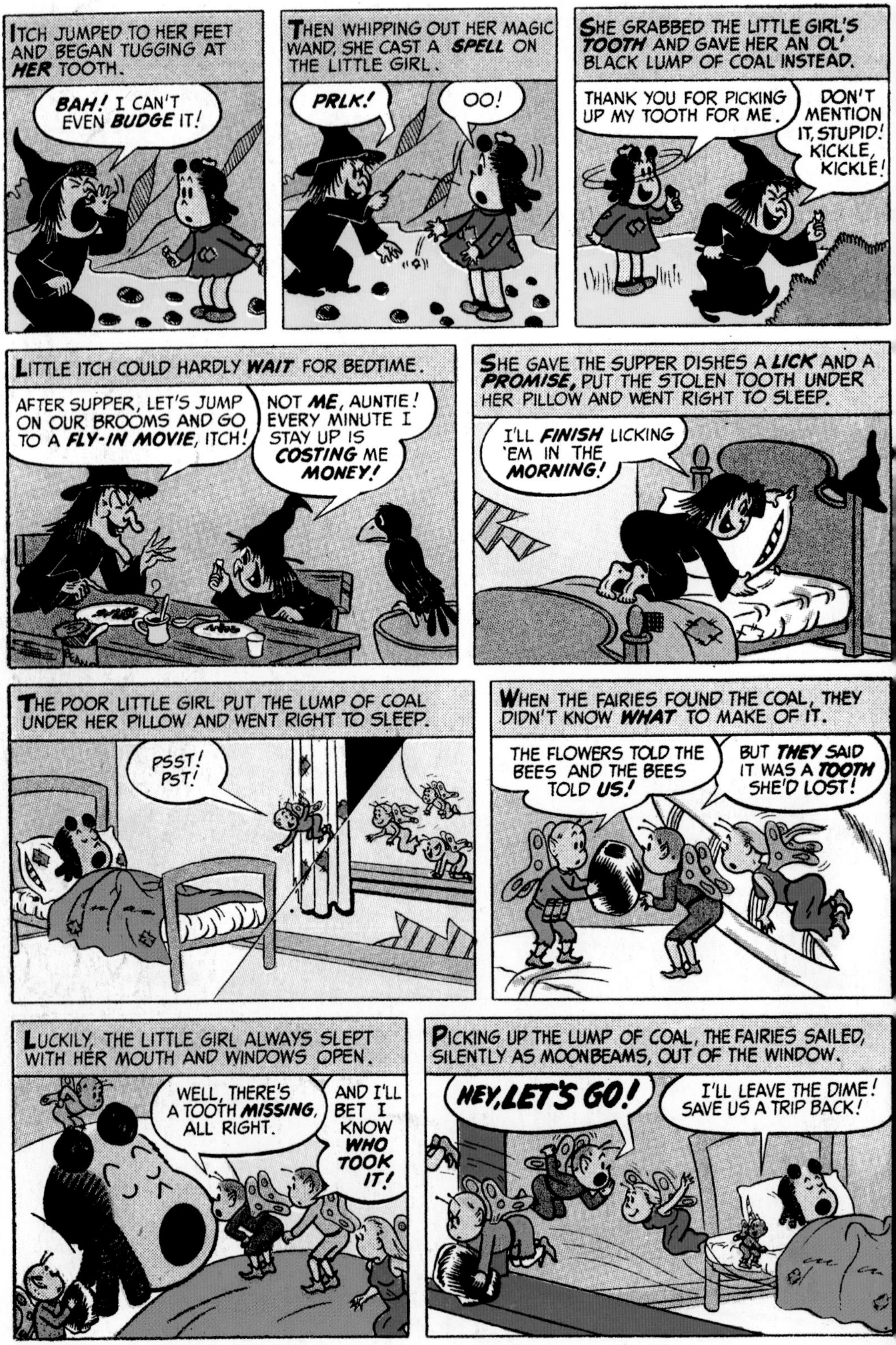
ITCH JUMPED TO HER FEET AND BEGAN TUGGING AT HER TOOTH.
BAH! I CAN'T EVEN BUDGE IT!
THEN WHIPPING OUT HER MAGIC WAND, SHE CAST A SPELL ON THE LITTLE GIRL.
PRLK!
OO!
SHE GRABBED THE LITTLE GIRL'S TOOTH AND GAVE HER AN OL' BLACK LUMP OF COAL INSTEAD.
THANK YOU FOR PICKING UP MY TOOTH FOR ME.
DON'T MENTION IT, STUPID! KICKLE, KICKLE!
LITTLE ITCH COULD HARDLY WAIT FOR BEDTIME.
AFTER SUPPER, LET'S JUMP ON OUR BROOMS AND GO TO A FLY-IN MOVIE, ITCH!
NOT ME, AUNTIE! EVERY MINUTE I STAY UP IS COSTING ME MONEY!
SHE GAVE THE SUPPER DISHES A LICK AND A PROMISE, PUT THE STOLEN TOOTH UNDER HER PILLOW AND WENT RIGHT TO SLEEP.
I'LL FINISH LICKING 'EM IN THE MORNING!
THE POOR LITTLE GIRL PUT THE LUMP OF COAL UNDER HER PILLOW AND WENT RIGHT TO SLEEP.
PSST! PST!
WHEN THE FAIRIES FOUND THE COAL, THEY DIDN'T KNOW WHAT TO MAKE OF IT.
THE FLOWERS TOLD THE BEES AND THE BEES TOLD US!
BUT THEY SAID IT WAS A TOOTH SHE'D LOST!
LUCKILY, THE LITTLE GIRL ALWAYS SLEPT WITH HER MOUTH AND WINDOWS OPEN.
WELL, THERE'S A TOOTH MISSING, ALL RIGHT.
AND I'LL BET I KNOW WHO TOOK IT!
PICKING UP THE LUMP OF COAL, THE FAIRIES SAILED, SILENTLY AS MOONBEAMS, OUT OF THE WINDOW.
HEY, LET'S GO!
I'LL LEAVE THE DIME! SAVE US A TRIP BACK!

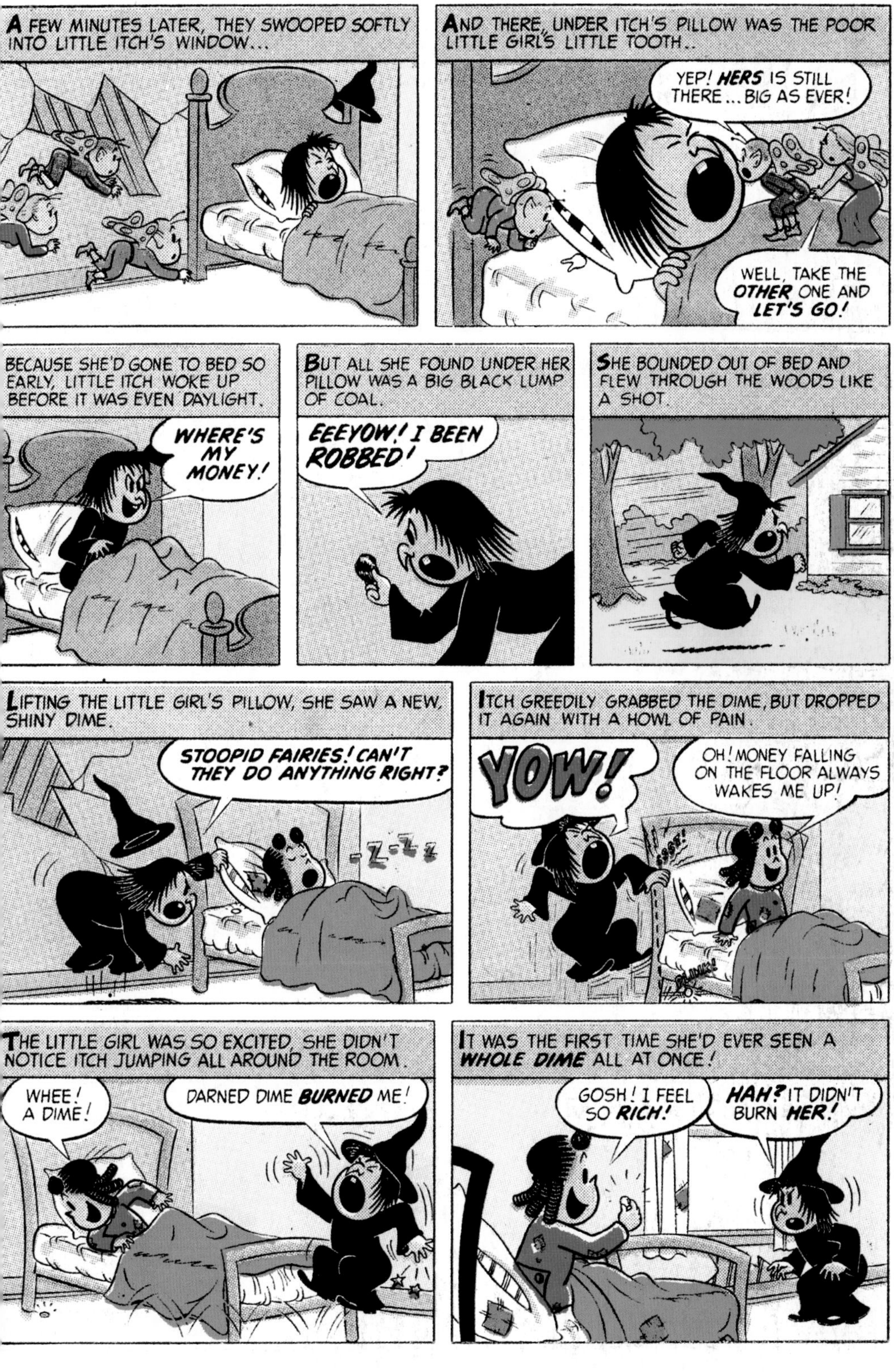
A FEW MINUTES LATER, THEY SWOOPED SOFTLY INTO LITTLE ITCH'S WINDOW...
AND THERE, UNDER ITCH'S PILLOW WAS THE POOR LITTLE GIRL'S LITTLE TOOTH..
YEP! HERS IS STILL THERE... BIG AS EVER!
WELL, TAKE THE OTHER ONE AND LET'S GO!
BECAUSE SHE'D GONE TO BED SO EARLY, LITTLE ITCH WOKE UP BEFORE IT WAS EVEN DAYLIGHT.
WHERE'S MY MONEY!
BUT ALL SHE FOUND UNDER HER PILLOW WAS A BIG BLACK LUMP OF COAL.
EEEYOW! I BEEN ROBBED!
SHE BOUNDED OUT OF BED AND FLEW THROUGH THE WOODS LIKE A SHOT.
LIFTING THE LITTLE GIRL'S PILLOW, SHE SAW A NEW, SHINY DIME.
STOOPID FAIRIES! CAN'T THEY DO ANYTHING RIGHT?
Z-Z-Z
ITCH GREEDILY GRABBED THE DIME, BUT DROPPED IT AGAIN WITH A HOWL OF PAIN.
YOW!
OH! MONEY FALLING ON THE FLOOR ALWAYS WAKES ME UP!
THE LITTLE GIRL WAS SO EXCITED, SHE DIDN'T NOTICE ITCH JUMPING ALL AROUND THE ROOM.
WHEE! A DIME!
DARNED DIME BURNED ME!
IT WAS THE FIRST TIME SHE'D EVER SEEN A WHOLE DIME ALL AT ONCE!
GOSH! I FEEL SO RICH!
HAH? IT DIDN'T BURN HER!

LIKE A BLACK TOAD, LITTLE ITCH SPRANG AT THE LITTLE GIRL.

IT MUST'VE **COOLED OFF!** I'LL GRAB IT AN' **RUN!**

?

THEN SHE WENT BACK TO **JUMPING** AGAIN.

OO!
AGH!
OW!
YOW!
WOW!
FWSST

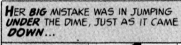

HER **BIG** MISTAKE WAS IN JUMPING **UNDER** THE DIME, JUST AS IT CAME **DOWN...**

S-P-S-S-T.
?

...SO THAT IT LANDED RIGHT INSIDE THE BACK OF HER ALL-PURPOSE NIGHTIE.

YOW! YOW! YOW! YOW!
YOW! YOW! YOW! YOW!

YOU SHOULDN'T JUMP AROUND SO HARD. YOU MIGHT **HURT** YOURSELF!

IT FINALLY JIGGLED ITS WAY DOWN FAR ENOUGH AND FELL ON THE FLOOR.

BAW!

IF YOU LIKE TO JUMP, YOU SHOULD DO SOMETHING **USEFUL**-- LIKE JUMPING **ROPE!**

...AND THE LITTLE GIRL PUT HER DIME IN THE **BANK,** SO SHE WOULD HAVE SOMETHING FOR HER **OLD AGE!**

PHOOEY! I DON'T BELIEVE IT! I DON'T BELIEVE THAT NONSENSE ABOUT THE DIME BURNING LITTLE ITCH--

'CAUSE IT DIDN'T BELONG TO HER!

HEY! DON'T **TOUCH** THAT DIME, ALVIN. IT'S **MINE!**

YOW!

THE END

30

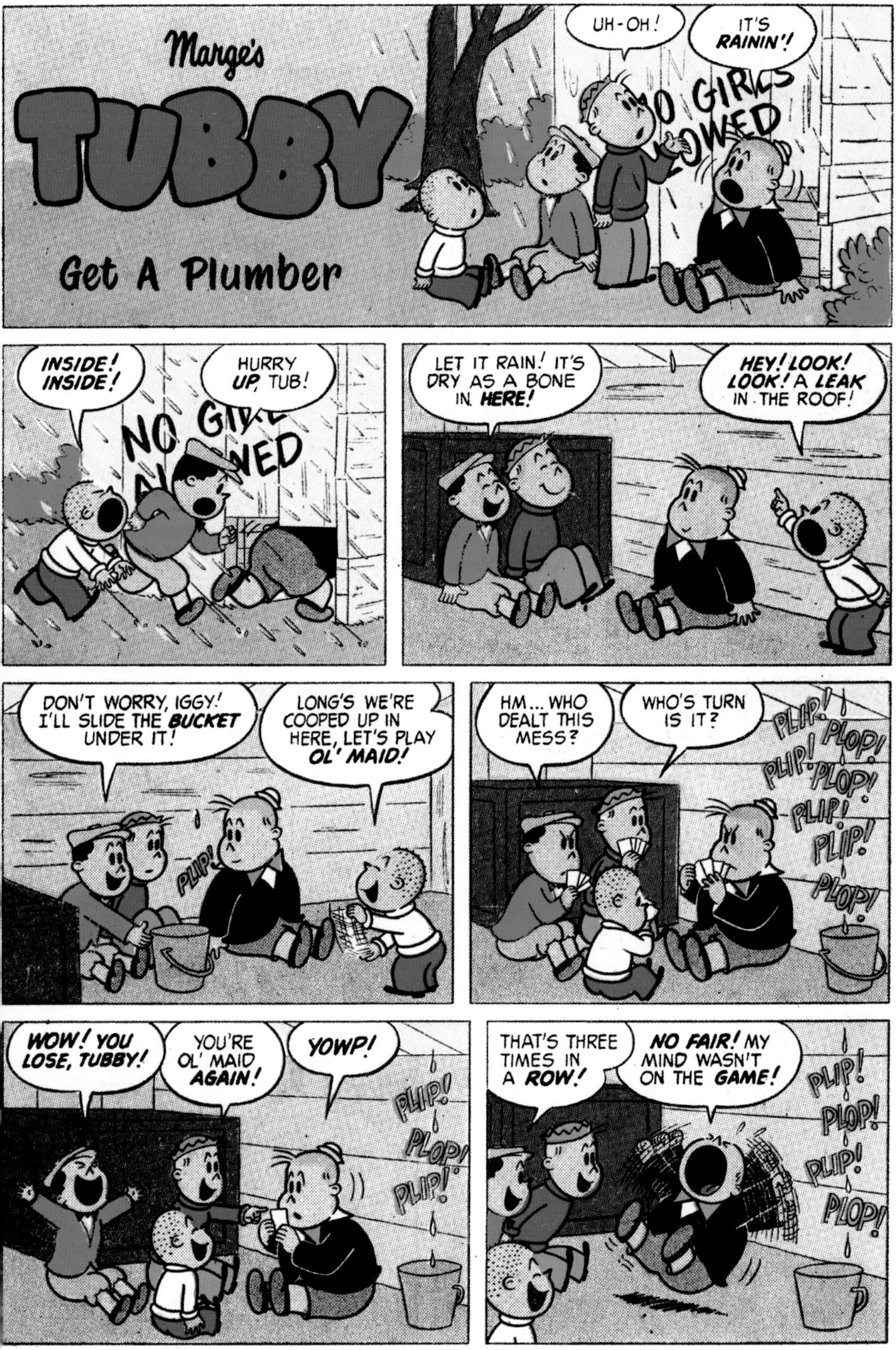

Marge's
TUBBY
Get A Plumber
UH-OH!
IT'S RAININ'!
NO GIRLS ALLOWED
INSIDE! INSIDE!
HURRY UP, TUB!
LET IT RAIN! IT'S DRY AS A BONE IN HERE!
HEY! LOOK! LOOK! A LEAK IN THE ROOF!
DON'T WORRY, IGGY! I'LL SLIDE THE BUCKET UNDER IT!
LONG'S WE'RE COOPED UP IN HERE, LET'S PLAY OL' MAID!
PLIP!
HM... WHO DEALT THIS MESS?
WHO'S TURN IS IT?
PLIP! PLOP! PLIP! PLOP! PLIP! PLIP! PLOP!
WOW! YOU LOSE, TUBBY!
YOU'RE OL' MAID AGAIN!
YOWP!
PLIP! PLOP! PLIP!
THAT'S THREE TIMES IN A ROW!
NO FAIR! MY MIND WASN'T ON THE GAME!
PLIP! PLOP! PLIP! PLOP!

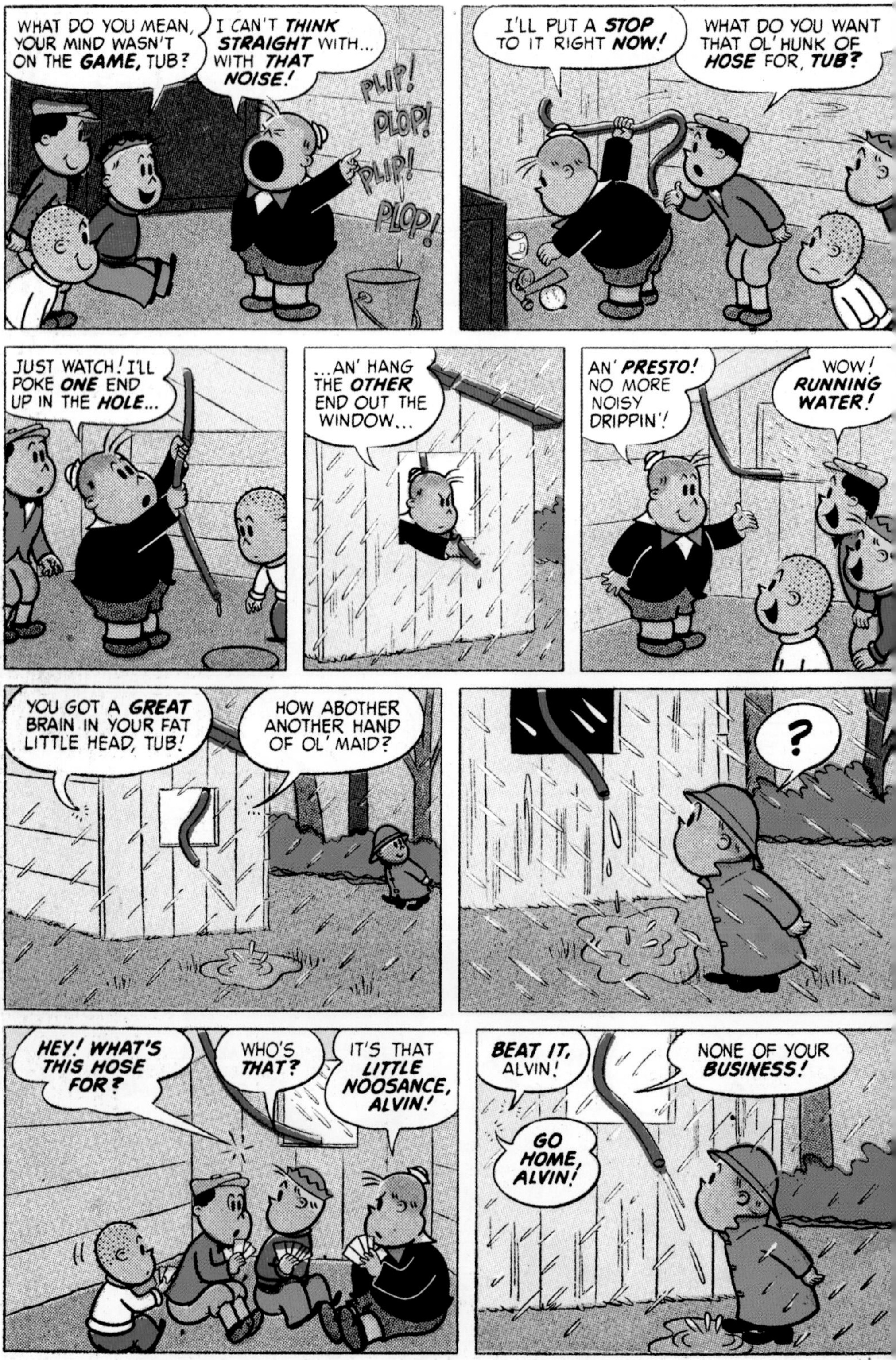
WHAT DO YOU MEAN, YOUR MIND WASN'T ON THE GAME, TUB?
I CAN'T THINK STRAIGHT WITH... WITH THAT NOISE!
PLIP! PLOP! PLIP! PLOP!
I'LL PUT A STOP TO IT RIGHT NOW!
WHAT DO YOU WANT THAT OL' HUNK OF HOSE FOR, TUB?
JUST WATCH! I'LL POKE ONE END UP IN THE HOLE...
...AN' HANG THE OTHER END OUT THE WINDOW...
AN' PRESTO! NO MORE NOISY DRIPPIN'!
WOW! RUNNING WATER!
YOU GOT A GREAT BRAIN IN YOUR FAT LITTLE HEAD, TUB!
HOW ABOTHER ANOTHER HAND OF OL' MAID?
?
HEY! WHAT'S THIS HOSE FOR?
WHO'S THAT?
IT'S THAT LITTLE NOOSANCE, ALVIN!
BEAT IT, ALVIN!
NONE OF YOUR BUSINESS!
GO HOME, ALVIN!

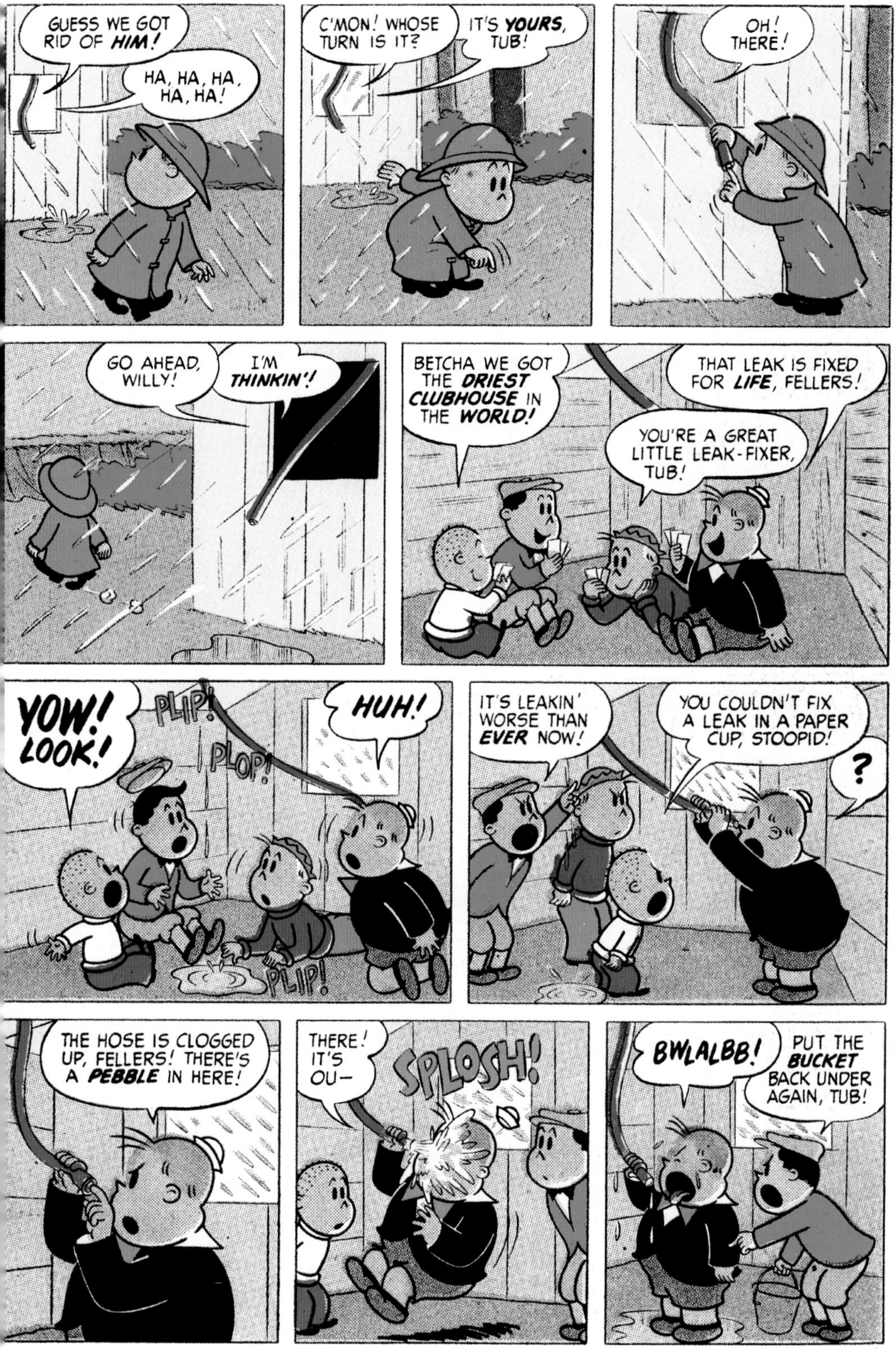
GUESS WE GOT RID OF HIM!
HA, HA, HA, HA, HA!
C'MON! WHOSE TURN IS IT?
IT'S YOURS, TUB!
OH! THERE!
GO AHEAD, WILLY!
I'M THINKIN'!
BETCHA WE GOT THE DRIEST CLUBHOUSE IN THE WORLD!
THAT LEAK IS FIXED FOR LIFE, FELLERS!
YOU'RE A GREAT LITTLE LEAK-FIXER, TUB!
YOW! LOOK!
PLIP!
PLOP!
HUH!
PLIP!
IT'S LEAKIN' WORSE THAN EVER NOW!
YOU COULDN'T FIX A LEAK IN A PAPER CUP, STOOPID!
?
THE HOSE IS CLOGGED UP, FELLERS! THERE'S A PEBBLE IN HERE!
THERE! IT'S OU—
SPLOSH!
BWLALBB!
PUT THE BUCKET BACK UNDER AGAIN, TUB!

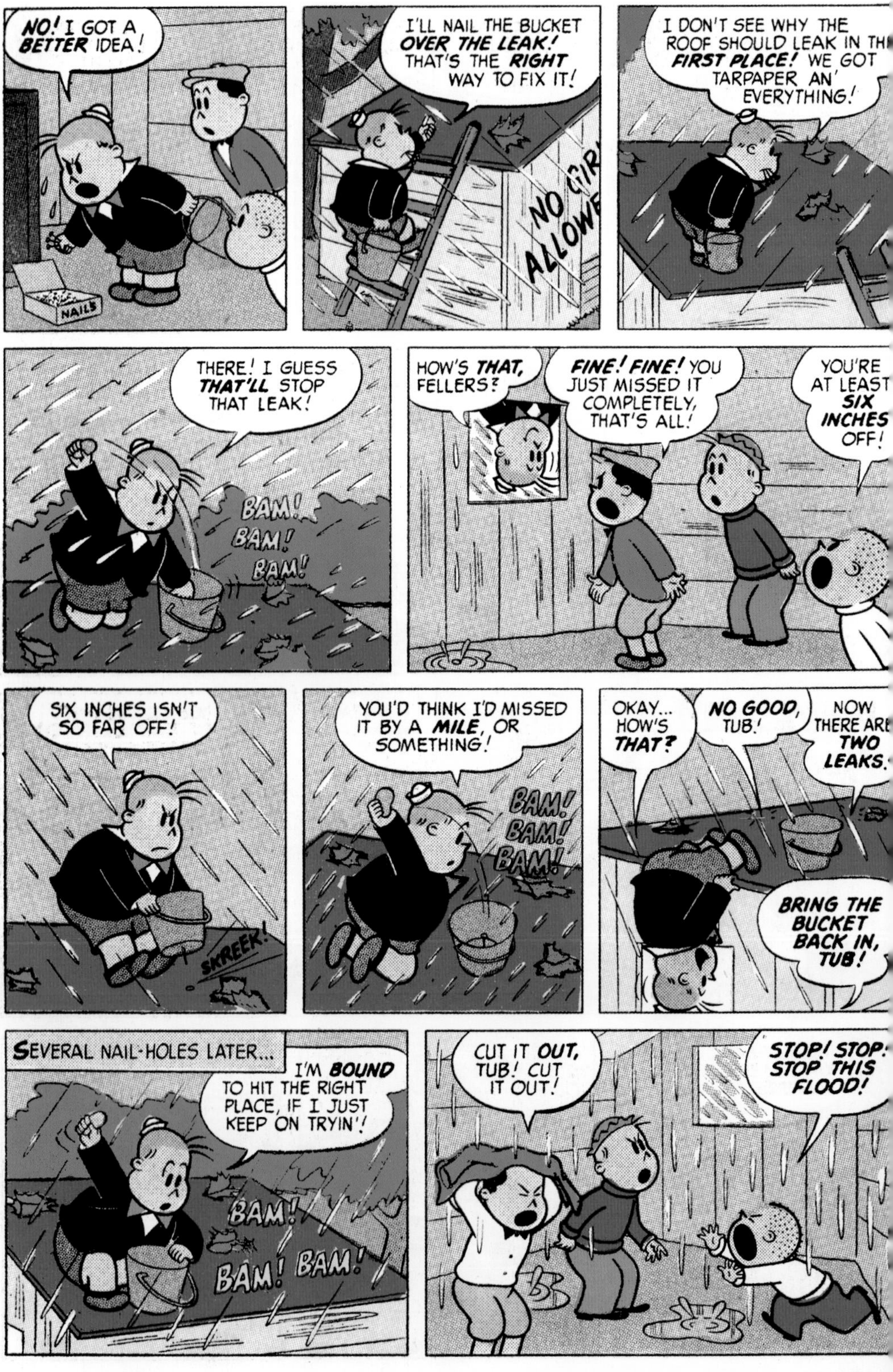
NO! I GOT A BETTER IDEA!
I'LL NAIL THE BUCKET OVER THE LEAK! THAT'S THE RIGHT WAY TO FIX IT!
NAILS
NO GIR ALLOWE
I DON'T SEE WHY THE ROOF SHOULD LEAK IN TH FIRST PLACE! WE GOT TARPAPER AN' EVERYTHING!
THERE! I GUESS THAT'LL STOP THAT LEAK!
BAM! BAM! BAM!
HOW'S THAT, FELLERS?
FINE! FINE! YOU JUST MISSED IT COMPLETELY, THAT'S ALL!
YOU'RE AT LEAST SIX INCHES OFF!
SIX INCHES ISN'T SO FAR OFF!
SKREEK!
YOU'D THINK I'D MISSED IT BY A MILE, OR SOMETHING!
BAM! BAM! BAM!
OKAY... HOW'S THAT?
NO GOOD, TUB!
NOW THERE ARE TWO LEAKS.
BRING THE BUCKET BACK IN, TUB!
SEVERAL NAIL-HOLES LATER...
I'M BOUND TO HIT THE RIGHT PLACE, IF I JUST KEEP ON TRYIN'!
BAM! BAM! BAM!
CUT IT OUT, TUB! CUT IT OUT!
STOP! STOP! STOP THIS FLOOD!

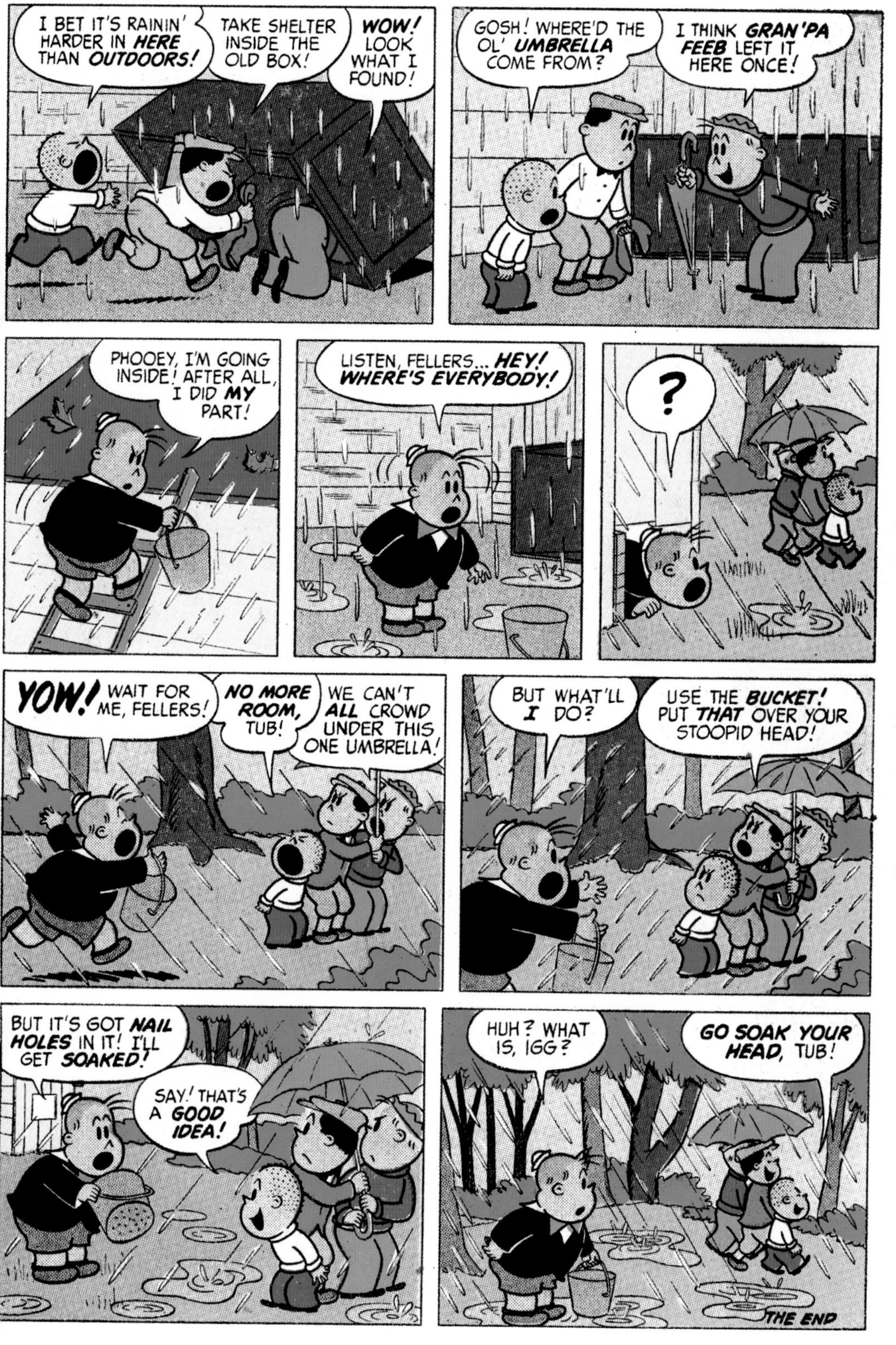
I BET IT'S RAININ' HARDER IN **HERE** THAN **OUTDOORS!**
TAKE SHELTER INSIDE THE OLD BOX!
WOW! LOOK WHAT I FOUND!
GOSH! WHERE'D THE OL' **UMBRELLA** COME FROM?
I THINK **GRAN'PA FEEB** LEFT IT HERE ONCE!
PHOOEY, I'M GOING INSIDE! AFTER ALL, I DID **MY** PART!
LISTEN, FELLERS... **HEY! WHERE'S EVERYBODY!**
?
YOW! WAIT FOR ME, FELLERS!
NO MORE ROOM, TUB!
WE CAN'T **ALL** CROWD UNDER THIS ONE UMBRELLA!
BUT WHAT'LL **I** DO?
USE THE **BUCKET!** PUT **THAT** OVER YOUR STOOPID HEAD!
BUT IT'S GOT **NAIL HOLES** IN IT! I'LL GET **SOAKED!**
SAY! THAT'S A **GOOD IDEA!**
HUH? WHAT IS, IGG?
GO SOAK YOUR HEAD, TUB!
THE END

LULU

WHAT CAN I DO FOR YOU, LULU?
I'D LIKE A PIECE OF RED CLOTH, MR. WOOLLEY!
...TO MAKE A NEW DRESS FOR MY DOLLY!
UMHM! LET ME SEE...
HOW'S THIS, LULU IS IT BIG ENOUGH
GOSH, THAT'S FINE!
I'LL WRAP IT UP FOR YOU...
HOW MUCH IS THAT, MR. WOOLLEY?
JUST ONE KISS, SWEETHEART!
ONE KISS?
ALL RIGHT...POP SAID HE'D COME AFTER WORK AN PAY FOR IT!

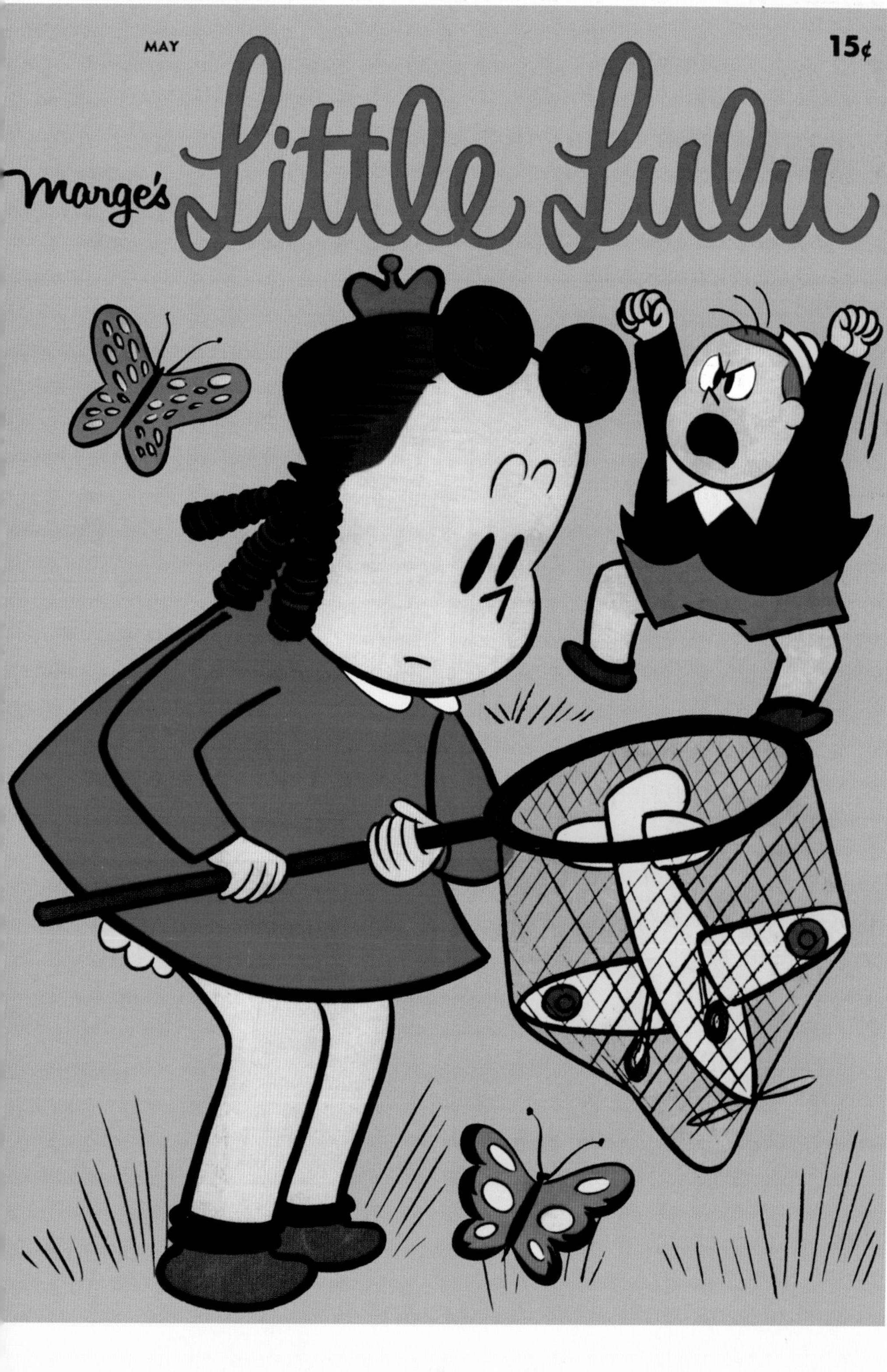
MAY
15¢
Marge's Little Lulu

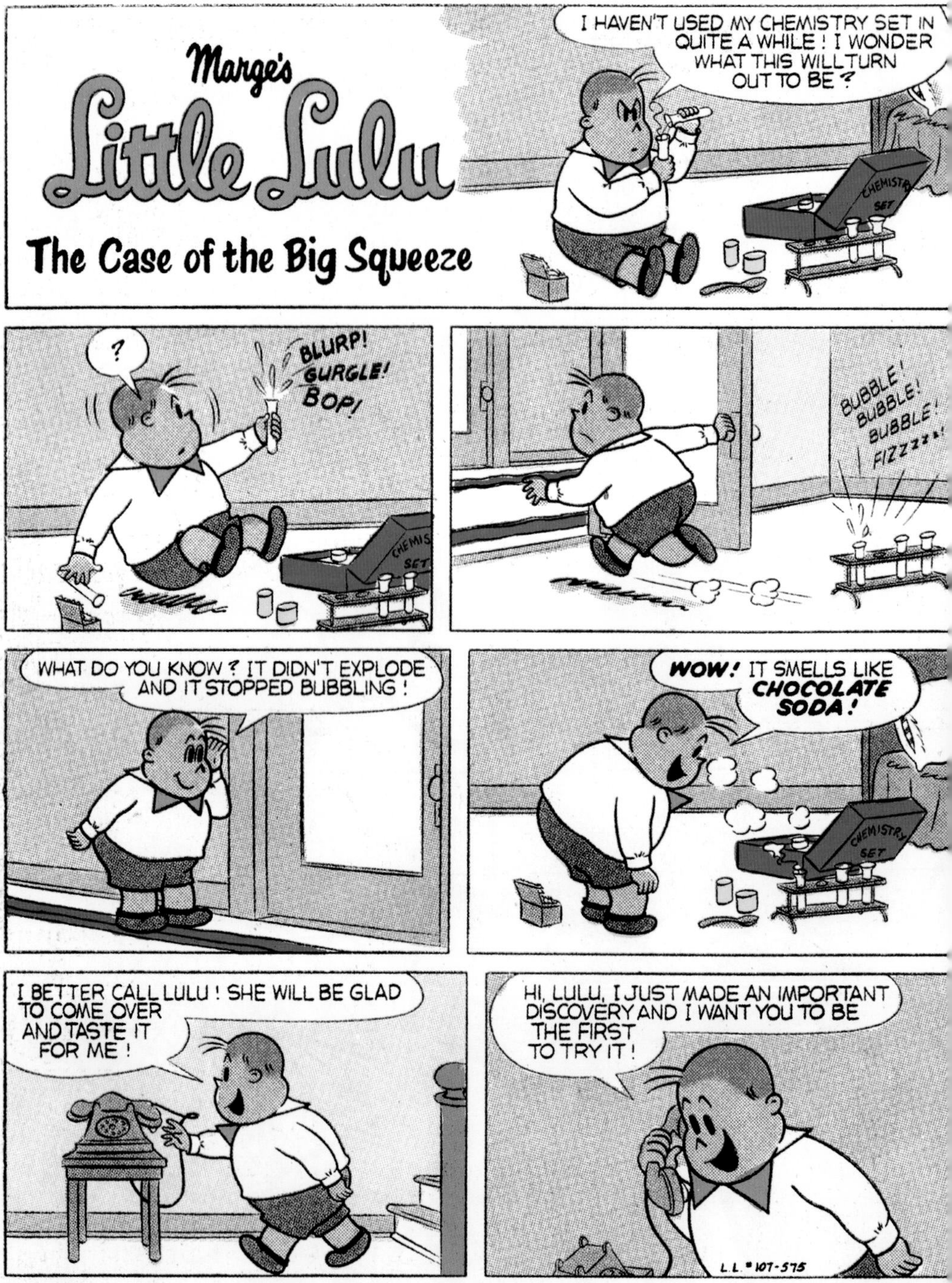
Marge's
Little Lulu
The Case of the Big Squeeze
I HAVEN'T USED MY CHEMISTRY SET IN QUITE A WHILE ! I WONDER WHAT THIS WILL TURN OUT TO BE ?
CHEMISTRY SET
?
BLURP! GURGLE! BOP!
BUBBLE! BUBBLE! BUBBLE! FIZZZZ!
WHAT DO YOU KNOW ? IT DIDN'T EXPLODE AND IT STOPPED BUBBLING !
WOW! IT SMELLS LIKE CHOCOLATE SODA !
I BETTER CALL LULU ! SHE WILL BE GLAD TO COME OVER AND TASTE IT FOR ME !
HI, LULU, I JUST MADE AN IMPORTANT DISCOVERY AND I WANT YOU TO BE THE FIRST TO TRY IT !
L.L. #107-575

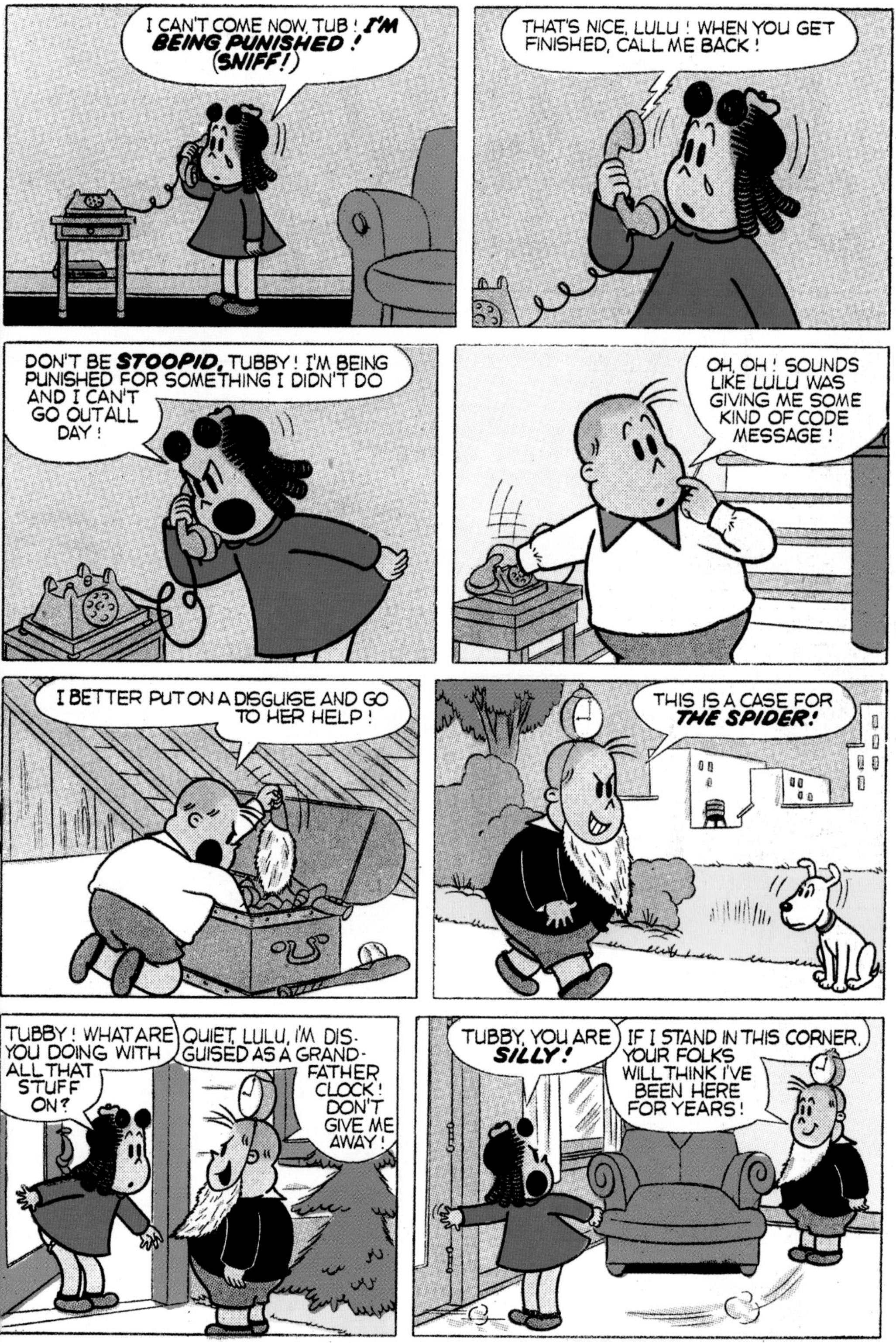
I CAN'T COME NOW, TUB! I'M BEING PUNISHED! (SNIFF!)
THAT'S NICE, LULU! WHEN YOU GET FINISHED, CALL ME BACK!
DON'T BE STOOPID, TUBBY! I'M BEING PUNISHED FOR SOMETHING I DIDN'T DO AND I CAN'T GO OUT ALL DAY!
OH, OH! SOUNDS LIKE LULU WAS GIVING ME SOME KIND OF CODE MESSAGE!
I BETTER PUT ON A DISGUISE AND GO TO HER HELP!
THIS IS A CASE FOR THE SPIDER!
TUBBY! WHAT ARE YOU DOING WITH ALL THAT STUFF ON?
QUIET, LULU, I'M DISGUISED AS A GRANDFATHER CLOCK! DON'T GIVE ME AWAY!
TUBBY, YOU ARE SILLY!
IF I STAND IN THIS CORNER, YOUR FOLKS WILL THINK I'VE BEEN HERE FOR YEARS!

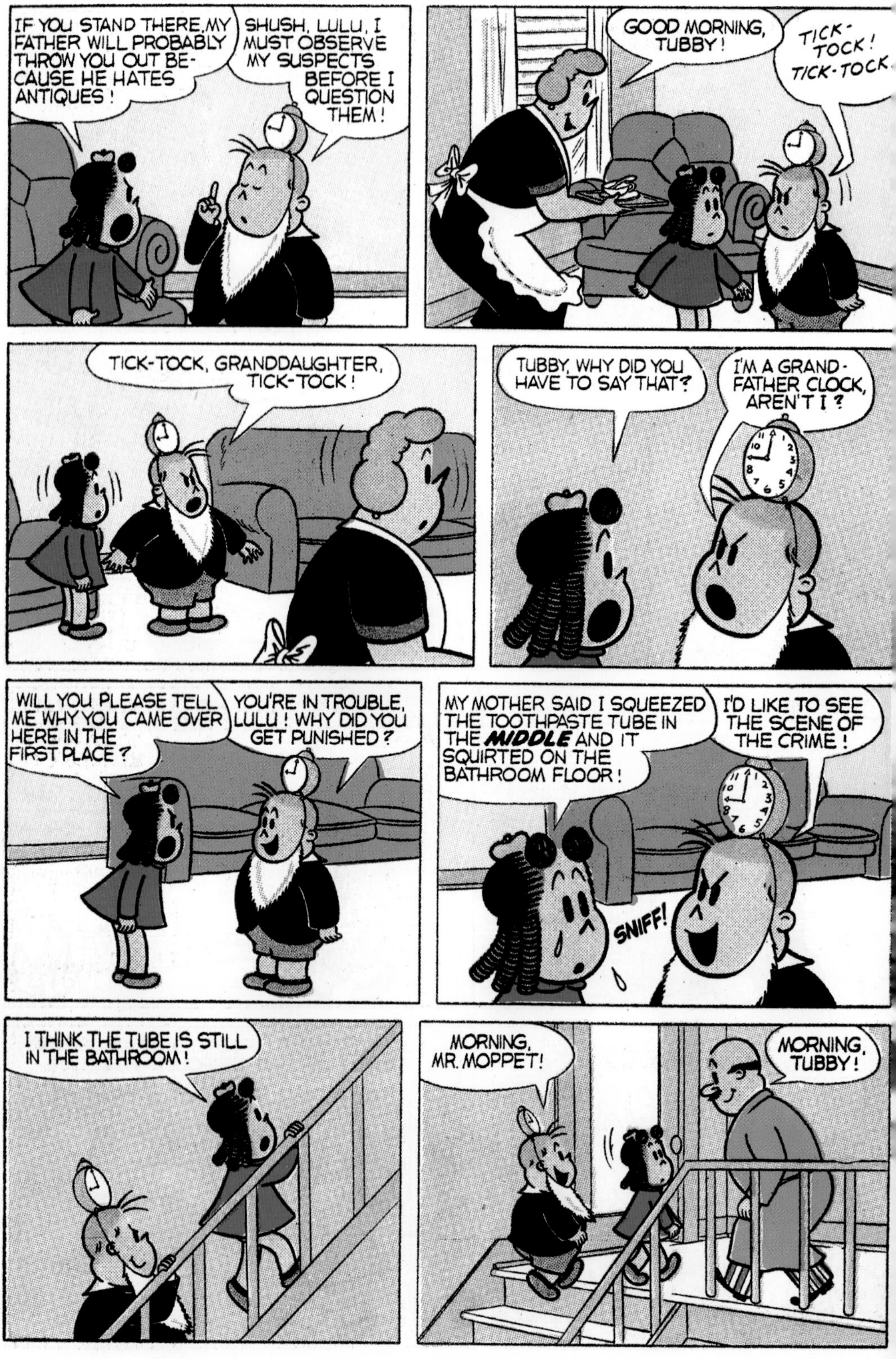
IF YOU STAND THERE, MY FATHER WILL PROBABLY THROW YOU OUT BE-CAUSE HE HATES ANTIQUES!
SHUSH, LULU, I MUST OBSERVE MY SUSPECTS BEFORE I QUESTION THEM!
GOOD MORNING, TUBBY!
TICK-TOCK! TICK-TOCK
TICK-TOCK, GRANDDAUGHTER, TICK-TOCK!
TUBBY, WHY DID YOU HAVE TO SAY THAT?
I'M A GRAND-FATHER CLOCK, AREN'T I?
WILL YOU PLEASE TELL ME WHY YOU CAME OVER HERE IN THE FIRST PLACE?
YOU'RE IN TROUBLE, LULU! WHY DID YOU GET PUNISHED?
MY MOTHER SAID I SQUEEZED THE TOOTHPASTE TUBE IN THE MIDDLE AND IT SQUIRTED ON THE BATHROOM FLOOR!
I'D LIKE TO SEE THE SCENE OF THE CRIME!
SNIFF!
I THINK THE TUBE IS STILL IN THE BATHROOM!
MORNING, MR. MOPPET!
MORNING, TUBBY!

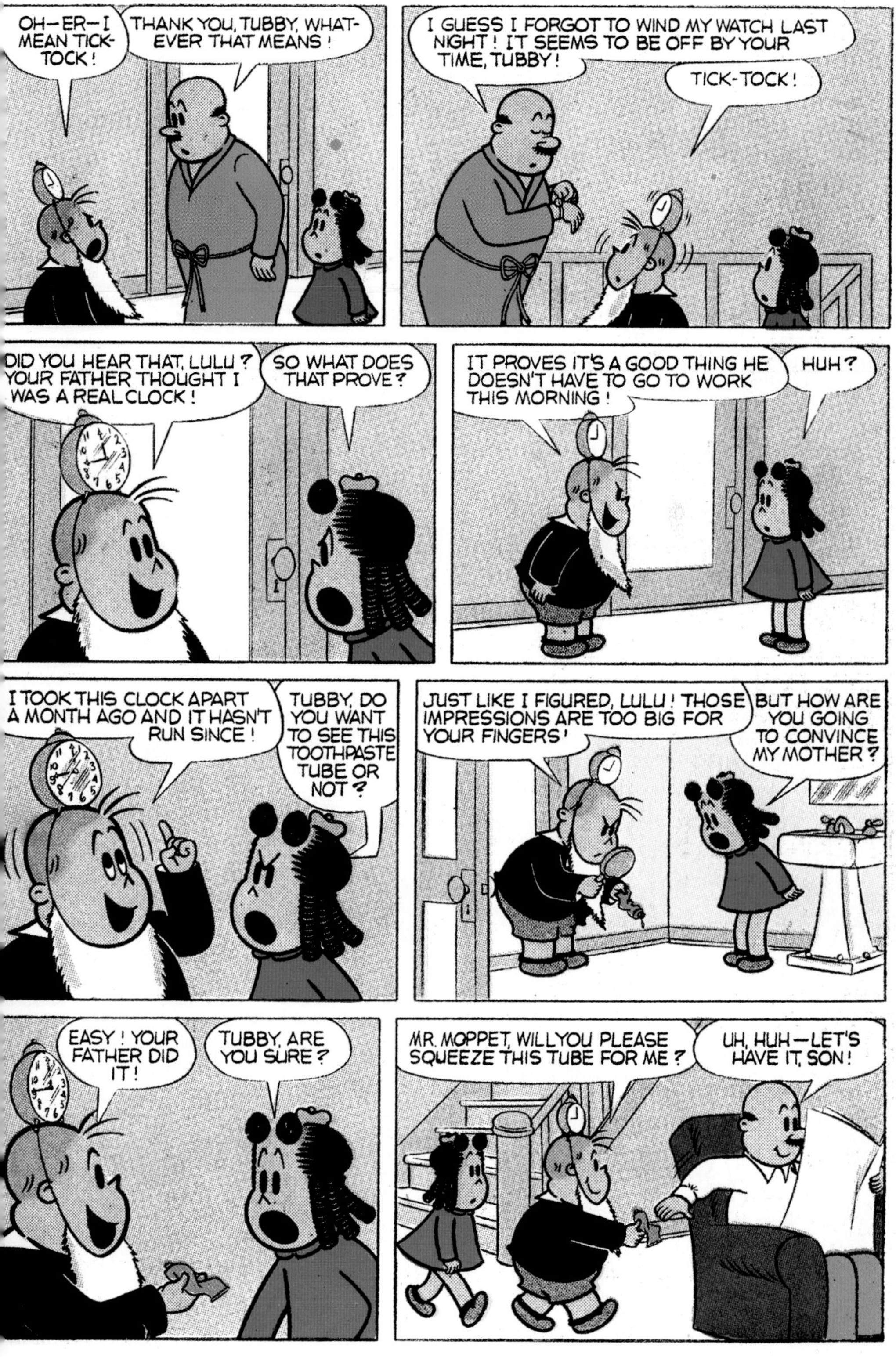

OH—ER—I MEAN TICK-TOCK!
THANK YOU, TUBBY, WHATEVER THAT MEANS!
I GUESS I FORGOT TO WIND MY WATCH LAST NIGHT! IT SEEMS TO BE OFF BY YOUR TIME, TUBBY!
TICK-TOCK!
DID YOU HEAR THAT, LULU? YOUR FATHER THOUGHT I WAS A REAL CLOCK!
SO WHAT DOES THAT PROVE?
IT PROVES IT'S A GOOD THING HE DOESN'T HAVE TO GO TO WORK THIS MORNING!
HUH?
I TOOK THIS CLOCK APART A MONTH AGO AND IT HASN'T RUN SINCE!
TUBBY, DO YOU WANT TO SEE THIS TOOTHPASTE TUBE OR NOT?
JUST LIKE I FIGURED, LULU! THOSE IMPRESSIONS ARE TOO BIG FOR YOUR FINGERS!
BUT HOW ARE YOU GOING TO CONVINCE MY MOTHER?
EASY! YOUR FATHER DID IT!
TUBBY, ARE YOU SURE?
MR. MOPPET, WILL YOU PLEASE SQUEEZE THIS TUBE FOR ME?
UH, HUH—LET'S HAVE IT, SON!

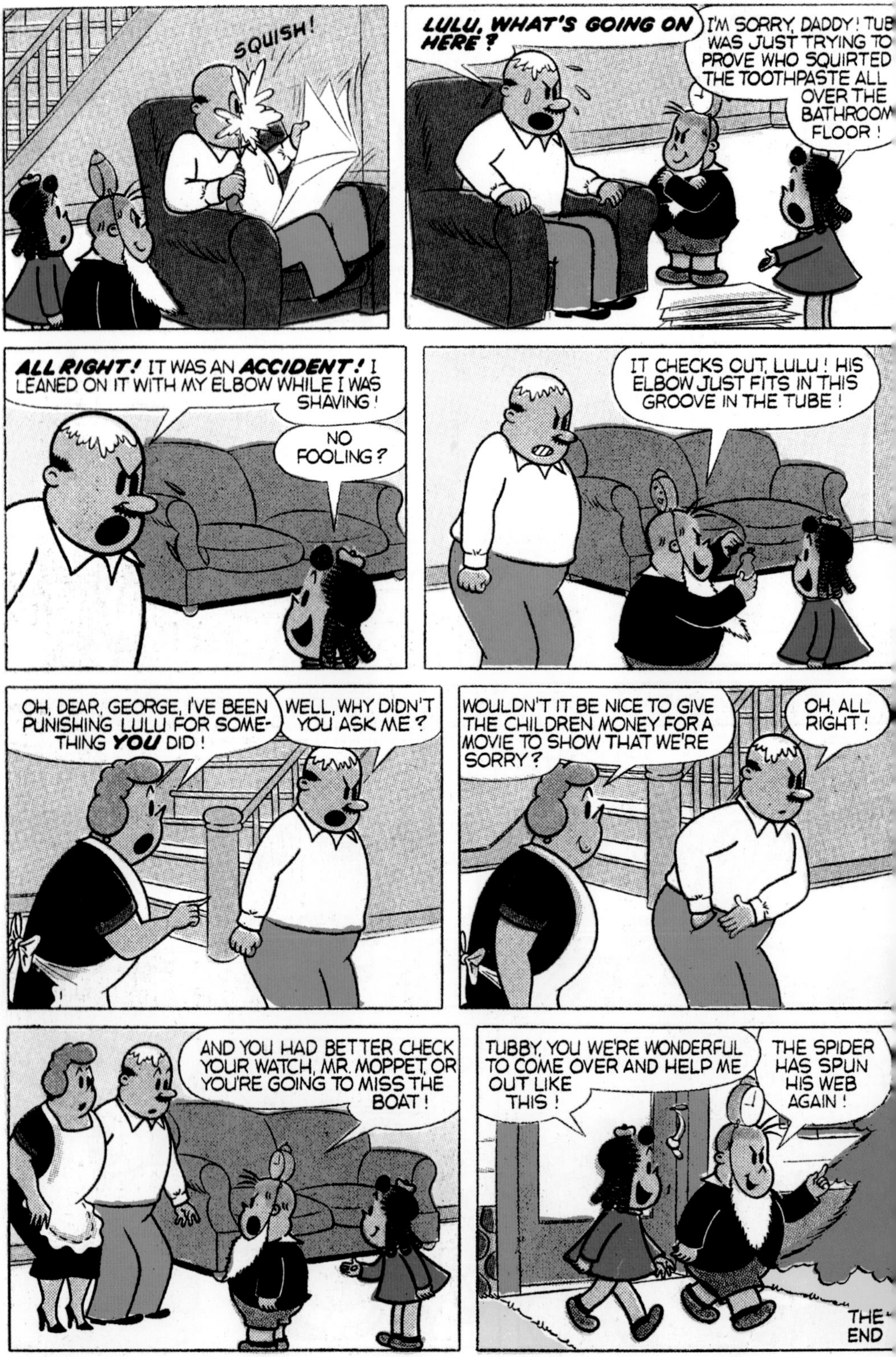
SQUISH!
LULU, WHAT'S GOING ON HERE?
I'M SORRY, DADDY! TUB WAS JUST TRYING TO PROVE WHO SQUIRTED THE TOOTHPASTE ALL OVER THE BATHROOM FLOOR!
ALL RIGHT! IT WAS AN ACCIDENT! I LEANED ON IT WITH MY ELBOW WHILE I WAS SHAVING!
NO FOOLING?
IT CHECKS OUT, LULU! HIS ELBOW JUST FITS IN THIS GROOVE IN THE TUBE!
OH, DEAR, GEORGE, I'VE BEEN PUNISHING LULU FOR SOME-THING YOU DID!
WELL, WHY DIDN'T YOU ASK ME?
WOULDN'T IT BE NICE TO GIVE THE CHILDREN MONEY FOR A MOVIE TO SHOW THAT WE'RE SORRY?
OH, ALL RIGHT!
AND YOU HAD BETTER CHECK YOUR WATCH, MR. MOPPET, OR YOU'RE GOING TO MISS THE BOAT!
TUBBY, YOU WE'RE WONDERFUL TO COME OVER AND HELP ME OUT LIKE THIS!
THE SPIDER HAS SPUN HIS WEB AGAIN!
THE END

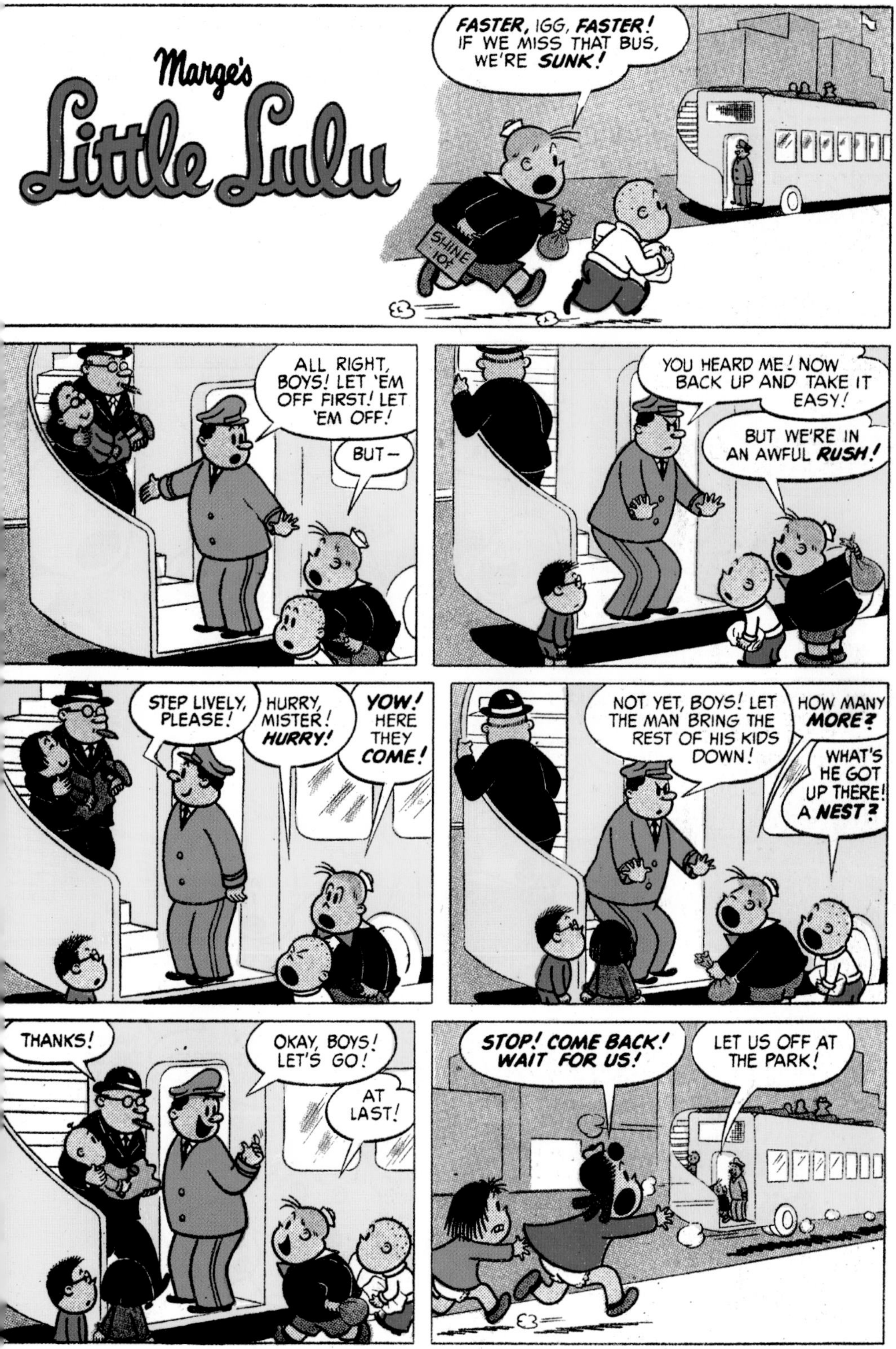
Marge's
Little Lulu
FASTER, IGG, FASTER! IF WE MISS THAT BUS, WE'RE SUNK!
SHINE 10¢
ALL RIGHT, BOYS! LET 'EM OFF FIRST! LET 'EM OFF!
BUT--
YOU HEARD ME! NOW BACK UP AND TAKE IT EASY!
BUT WE'RE IN AN AWFUL RUSH!
STEP LIVELY, PLEASE!
HURRY, MISTER! HURRY!
YOW! HERE THEY COME!
NOT YET, BOYS! LET THE MAN BRING THE REST OF HIS KIDS DOWN!
HOW MANY MORE?
WHAT'S HE GOT UP THERE! A NEST?
THANKS!
OKAY, BOYS! LET'S GO!
AT LAST!
STOP! COME BACK! WAIT FOR US!
LET US OFF AT THE PARK!

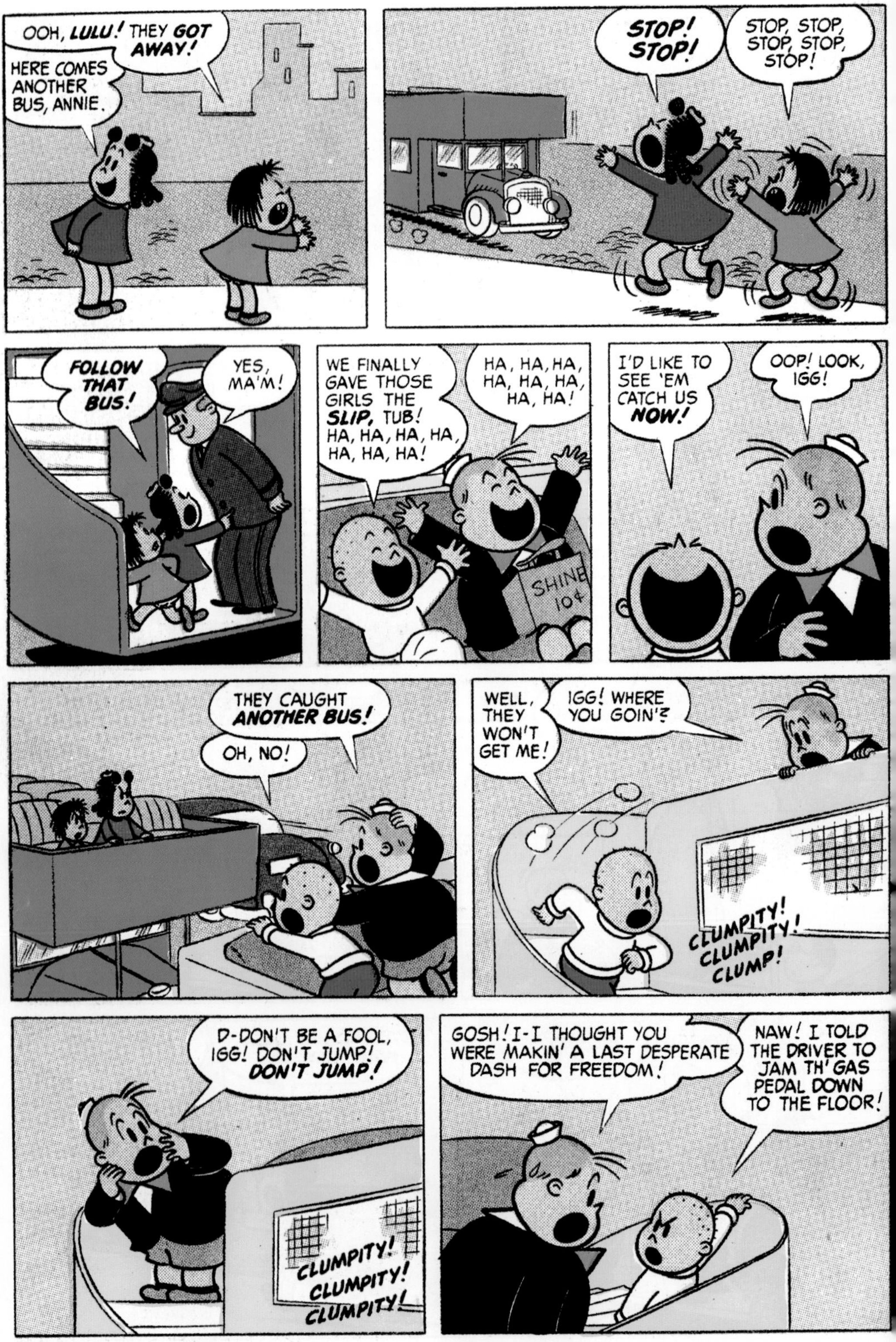

OOH, LULU! THEY GOT AWAY!
HERE COMES ANOTHER BUS, ANNIE.
STOP! STOP!
STOP, STOP, STOP, STOP, STOP!
FOLLOW THAT BUS!
YES, MA'M!
WE FINALLY GAVE THOSE GIRLS THE SLIP, TUB! HA, HA, HA, HA, HA, HA, HA!
HA, HA, HA, HA, HA, HA, HA, HA!
SHINE 10¢
I'D LIKE TO SEE 'EM CATCH US NOW!
OOP! LOOK, IGG!
THEY CAUGHT ANOTHER BUS!
OH, NO!
WELL, THEY WON'T GET ME!
IGG! WHERE YOU GOIN'?
CLUMPITY! CLUMPITY! CLUMP!
D-DON'T BE A FOOL, IGG! DON'T JUMP! DON'T JUMP!
CLUMPITY! CLUMPITY! CLUMPITY!
GOSH! I-I THOUGHT YOU WERE MAKIN' A LAST DESPERATE DASH FOR FREEDOM!
NAW! I TOLD THE DRIVER TO JAM TH' GAS PEDAL DOWN TO THE FLOOR!

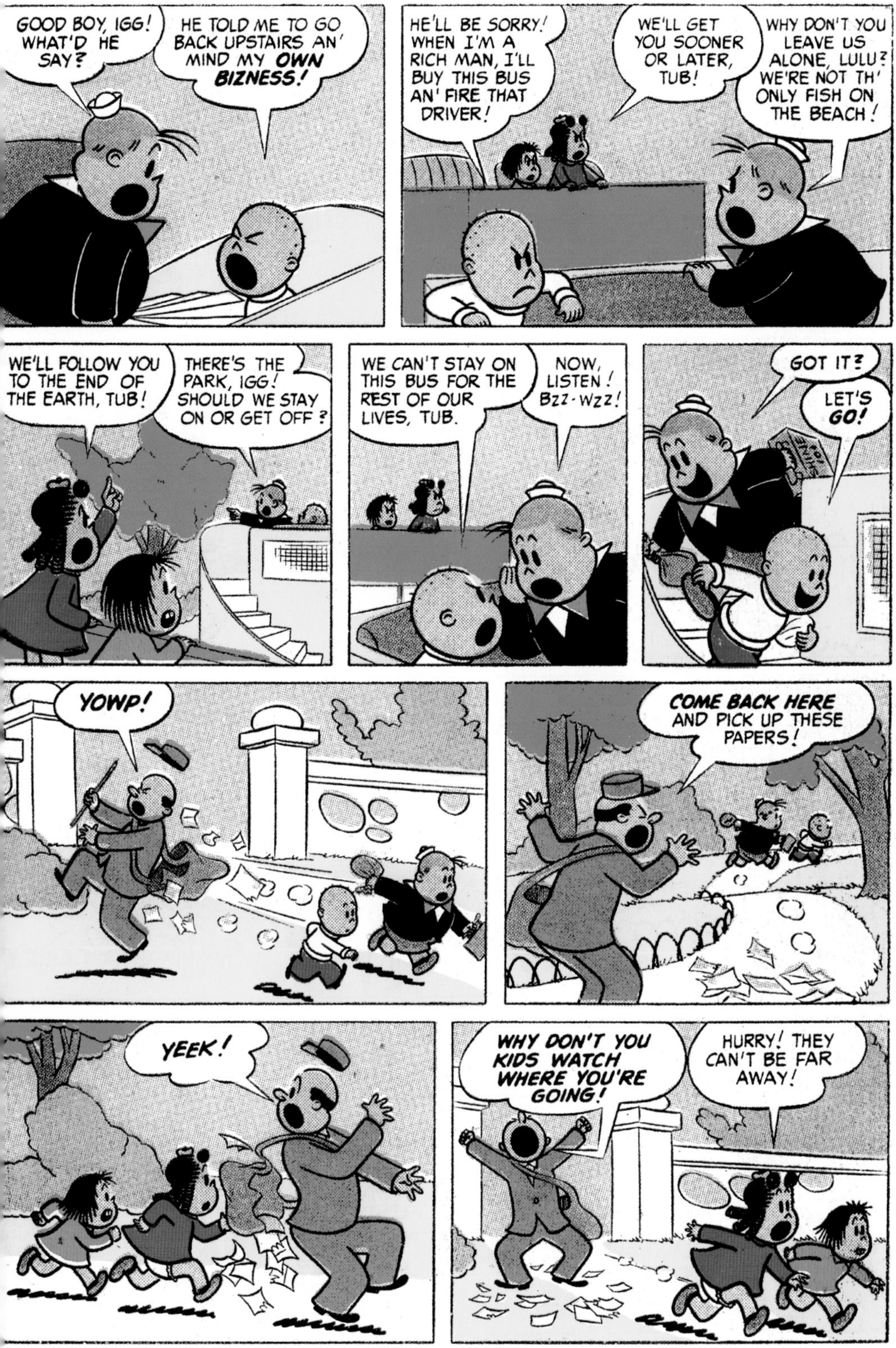
GOOD BOY, IGG! WHAT'D HE SAY?
HE TOLD ME TO GO BACK UPSTAIRS AN' MIND MY OWN BIZNESS!
HE'LL BE SORRY! WHEN I'M A RICH MAN, I'LL BUY THIS BUS AN' FIRE THAT DRIVER!
WE'LL GET YOU SOONER OR LATER, TUB!
WHY DON'T YOU LEAVE US ALONE, LULU? WE'RE NOT TH' ONLY FISH ON THE BEACH!
WE'LL FOLLOW YOU TO THE END OF THE EARTH, TUB!
THERE'S THE PARK, IGG! SHOULD WE STAY ON OR GET OFF?
WE CAN'T STAY ON THIS BUS FOR THE REST OF OUR LIVES, TUB.
NOW, LISTEN! BZZ-WZZ!
GOT IT?
LET'S GO!
YOWP!
COME BACK HERE AND PICK UP THESE PAPERS!
YEEK!
WHY DON'T YOU KIDS WATCH WHERE YOU'RE GOING!
HURRY! THEY CAN'T BE FAR AWAY!

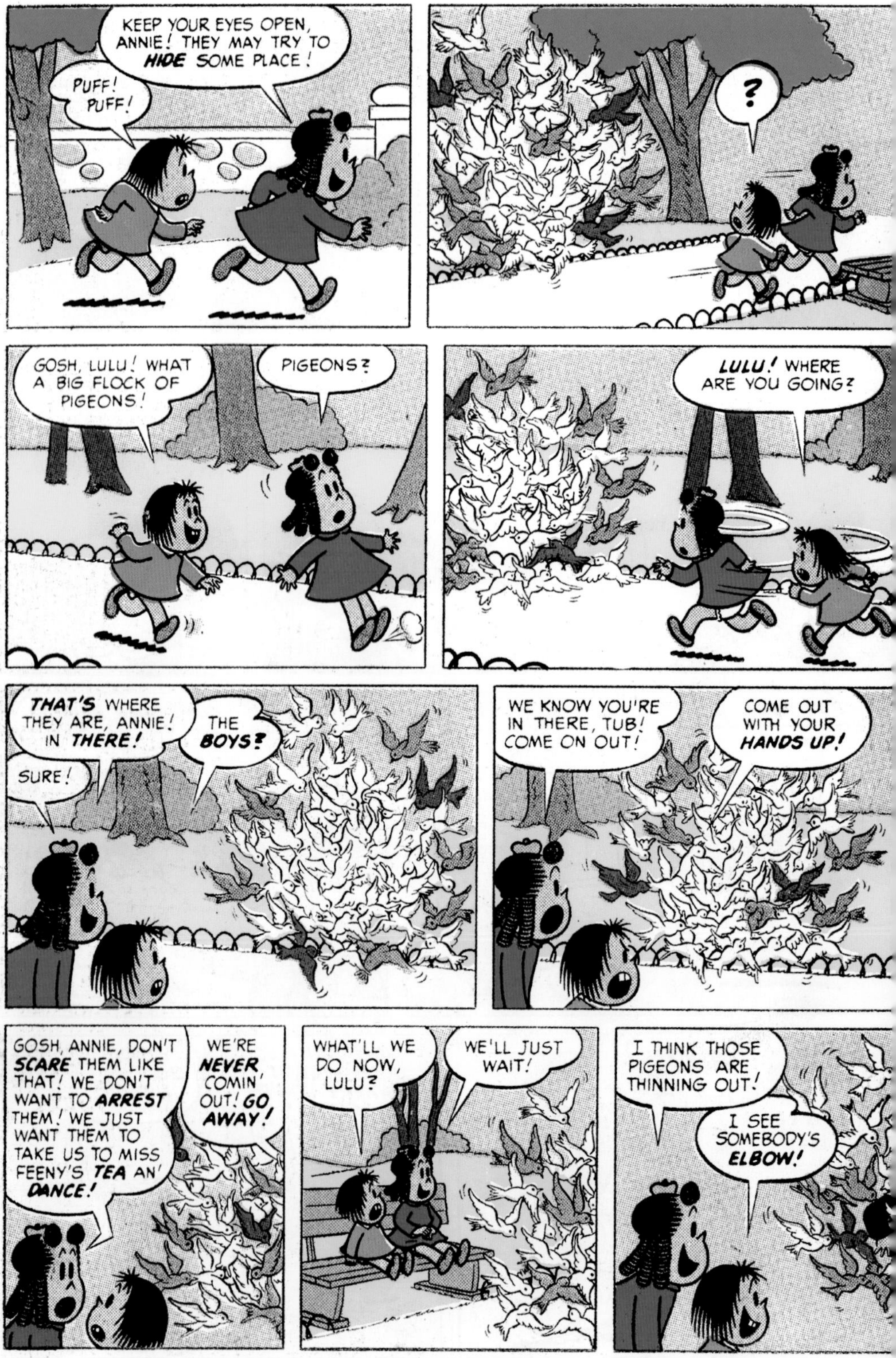
KEEP YOUR EYES OPEN, ANNIE! THEY MAY TRY TO HIDE SOME PLACE!
PUFF! PUFF!
?
GOSH, LULU! WHAT A BIG FLOCK OF PIGEONS!
PIGEONS?
LULU! WHERE ARE YOU GOING?
THAT'S WHERE THEY ARE, ANNIE! IN THERE!
THE BOYS?
SURE!
WE KNOW YOU'RE IN THERE, TUB! COME ON OUT!
COME OUT WITH YOUR HANDS UP!
GOSH, ANNIE, DON'T SCARE THEM LIKE THAT! WE DON'T WANT TO ARREST THEM! WE JUST WANT THEM TO TAKE US TO MISS FEENY'S TEA AN' DANCE!
WE'RE NEVER COMIN' OUT! GO AWAY!
WHAT'LL WE DO NOW, LULU?
WE'LL JUST WAIT!
I THINK THOSE PIGEONS ARE THINNING OUT!
I SEE SOMEBODY'S ELBOW!

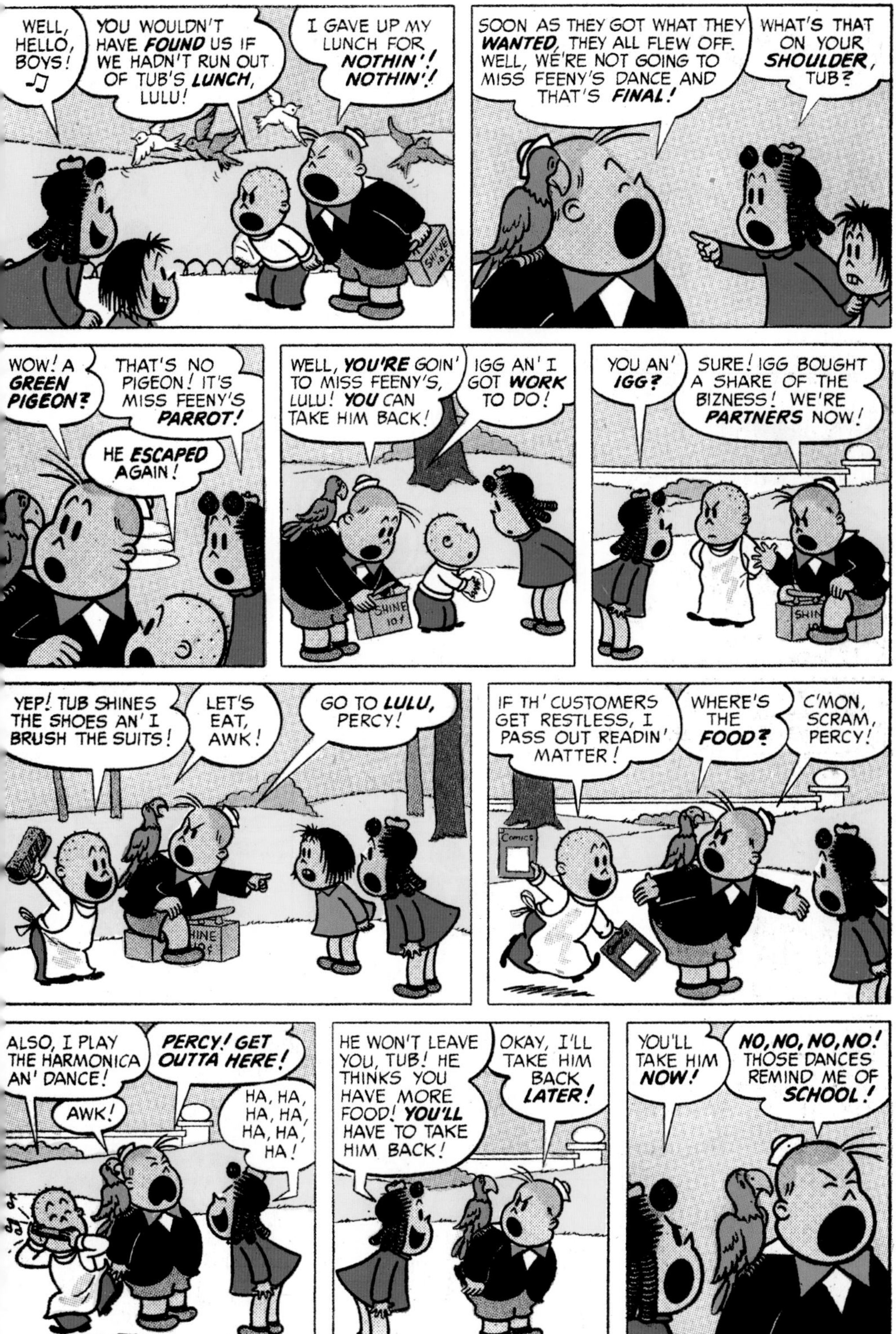
WELL, HELLO, BOYS! ♫
YOU WOULDN'T HAVE FOUND US IF WE HADN'T RUN OUT OF TUB'S LUNCH, LULU!
I GAVE UP MY LUNCH FOR NOTHIN'! NOTHIN'!
SOON AS THEY GOT WHAT THEY WANTED, THEY ALL FLEW OFF. WELL, WE'RE NOT GOING TO MISS FEENY'S DANCE AND THAT'S FINAL!
WHAT'S THAT ON YOUR SHOULDER, TUB?
SHINE 10¢
WOW! A GREEN PIGEON?
THAT'S NO PIGEON! IT'S MISS FEENY'S PARROT!
HE ESCAPED AGAIN!
WELL, YOU'RE GOIN' TO MISS FEENY'S, LULU! YOU CAN TAKE HIM BACK!
IGG AN' I GOT WORK TO DO!
SHINE 10¢
YOU AN' IGG?
SURE! IGG BOUGHT A SHARE OF THE BIZNESS! WE'RE PARTNERS NOW!
YEP! TUB SHINES THE SHOES AN' I BRUSH THE SUITS!
LET'S EAT, AWK!
GO TO LULU, PERCY!
IF TH' CUSTOMERS GET RESTLESS, I PASS OUT READIN' MATTER!
WHERE'S THE FOOD?
C'MON, SCRAM, PERCY!
Comics
ALSO, I PLAY THE HARMONICA AN' DANCE!
PERCY! GET OUTTA HERE!
AWK!
HA, HA, HA, HA, HA, HA, HA!
HE WON'T LEAVE YOU, TUB! HE THINKS YOU HAVE MORE FOOD! YOU'LL HAVE TO TAKE HIM BACK!
OKAY, I'LL TAKE HIM BACK LATER!
YOU'LL TAKE HIM NOW!
NO, NO, NO, NO! THOSE DANCES REMIND ME OF SCHOOL!

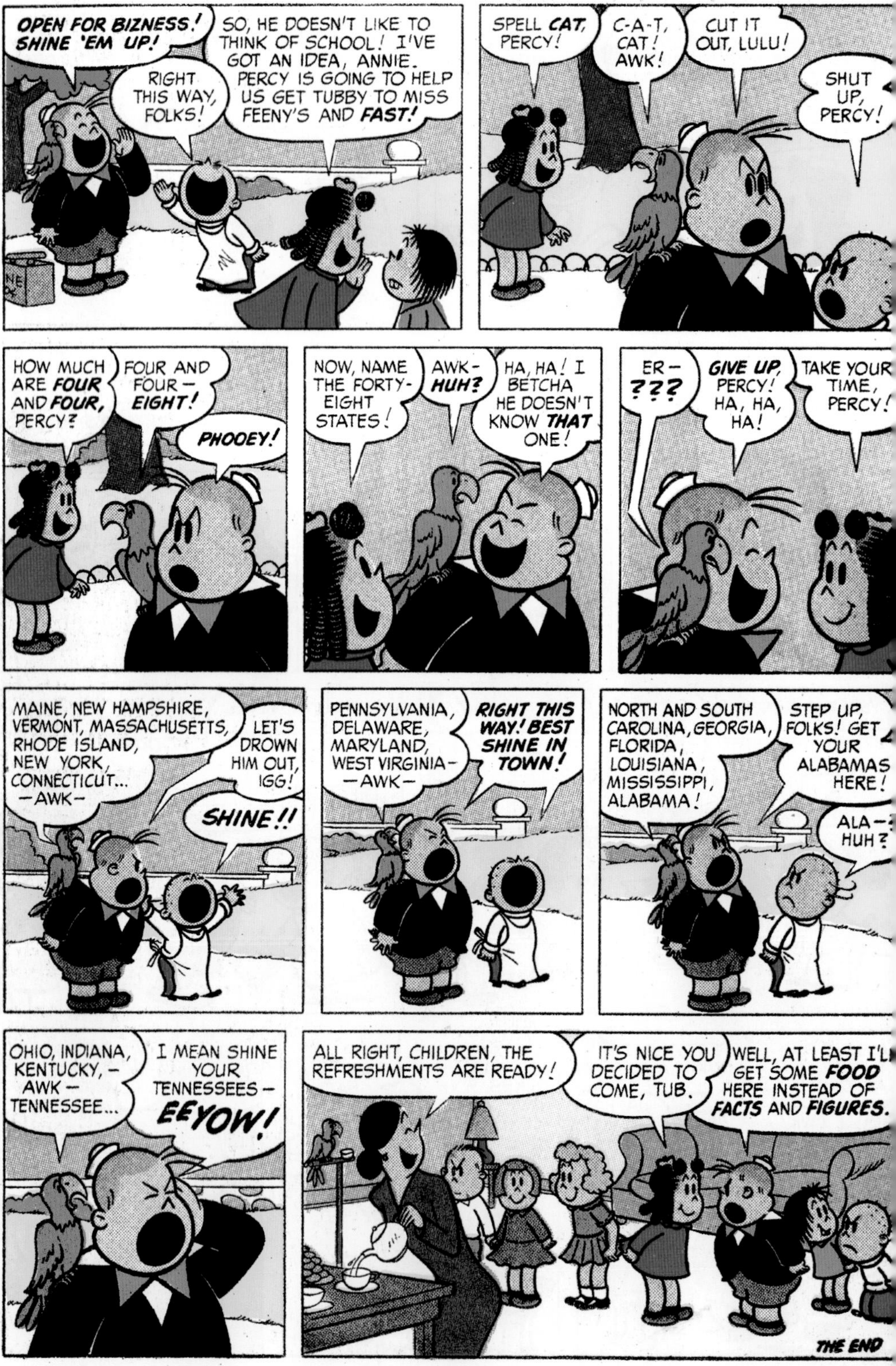
OPEN FOR BIZNESS! SHINE 'EM UP!
RIGHT THIS WAY, FOLKS!
SO, HE DOESN'T LIKE TO THINK OF SCHOOL! I'VE GOT AN IDEA, ANNIE. PERCY IS GOING TO HELP US GET TUBBY TO MISS FEENY'S AND FAST!
SPELL CAT, PERCY!
C-A-T, CAT! AWK!
CUT IT OUT, LULU!
SHUT UP, PERCY!
HOW MUCH ARE FOUR AND FOUR, PERCY?
FOUR AND FOUR— EIGHT!
PHOOEY!
NOW, NAME THE FORTY-EIGHT STATES!
AWK- HUH?
HA, HA! I BETCHA HE DOESN'T KNOW THAT ONE!
ER— ???
GIVE UP, PERCY! HA, HA, HA!
TAKE YOUR TIME, PERCY!
MAINE, NEW HAMPSHIRE, VERMONT, MASSACHUSETTS, RHODE ISLAND, NEW YORK, CONNECTICUT... —AWK—
LET'S DROWN HIM OUT, IGG!
SHINE!!
PENNSYLVANIA, DELAWARE, MARYLAND, WEST VIRGINIA— —AWK—
RIGHT THIS WAY! BEST SHINE IN TOWN!
NORTH AND SOUTH CAROLINA, GEORGIA, FLORIDA, LOUISIANA, MISSISSIPPI, ALABAMA!
STEP UP, FOLKS! GET YOUR ALABAMAS HERE!
ALA— HUH?
OHIO, INDIANA, KENTUCKY, —AWK— TENNESSEE...
I MEAN SHINE YOUR TENNESSEES— EEYOW!
ALL RIGHT, CHILDREN, THE REFRESHMENTS ARE READY!
IT'S NICE YOU DECIDED TO COME, TUB.
WELL, AT LEAST I'LL GET SOME FOOD HERE INSTEAD OF FACTS AND FIGURES.
THE END

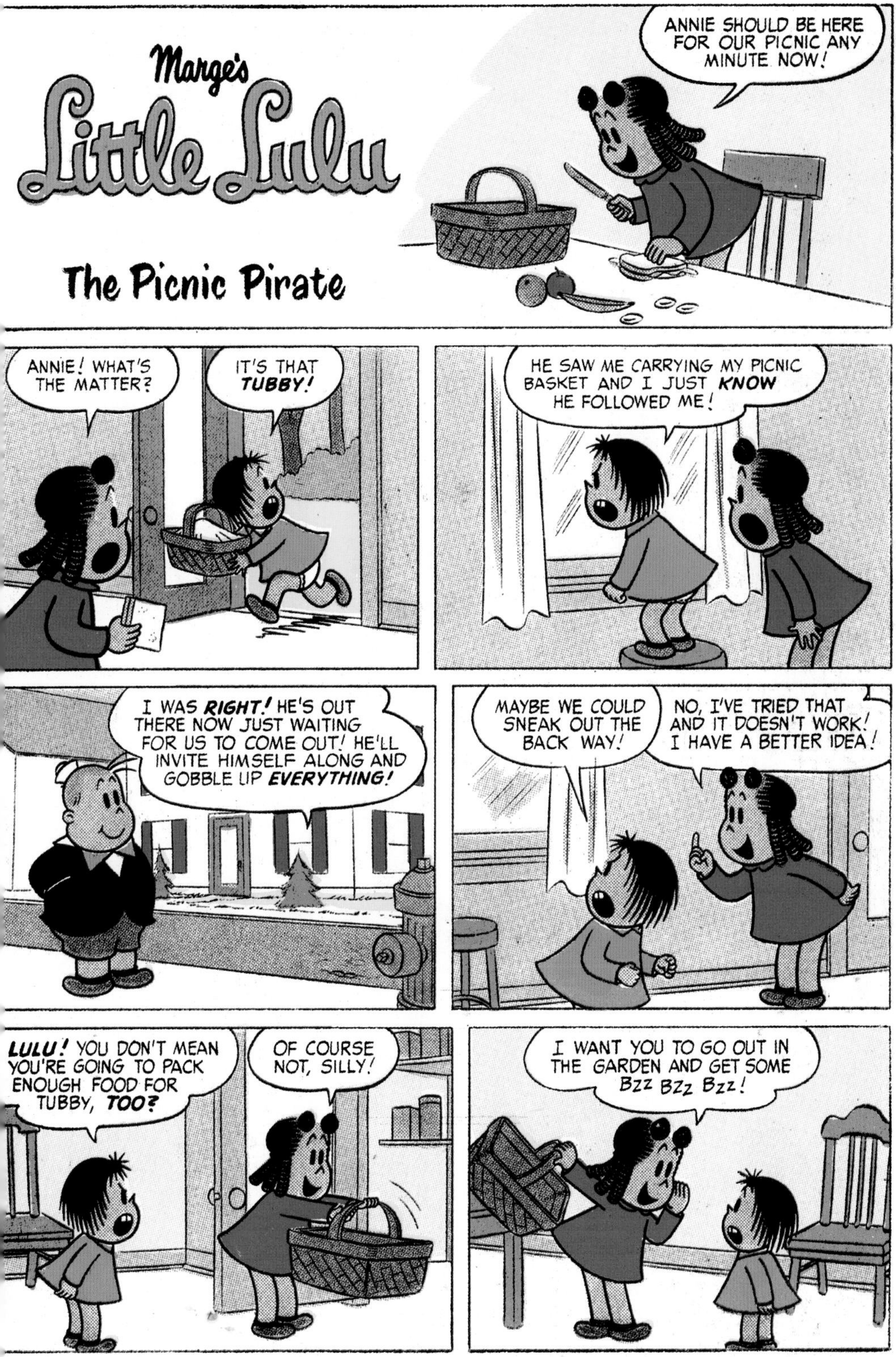
Marge's
Little Lulu
The Picnic Pirate
ANNIE SHOULD BE HERE FOR OUR PICNIC ANY MINUTE NOW!
ANNIE! WHAT'S THE MATTER?
IT'S THAT TUBBY!
HE SAW ME CARRYING MY PICNIC BASKET AND I JUST KNOW HE FOLLOWED ME!
I WAS RIGHT! HE'S OUT THERE NOW JUST WAITING FOR US TO COME OUT! HE'LL INVITE HIMSELF ALONG AND GOBBLE UP EVERYTHING!
MAYBE WE COULD SNEAK OUT THE BACK WAY!
NO, I'VE TRIED THAT AND IT DOESN'T WORK! I HAVE A BETTER IDEA!
LULU! YOU DON'T MEAN YOU'RE GOING TO PACK ENOUGH FOOD FOR TUBBY, TOO?
OF COURSE NOT, SILLY!
I WANT YOU TO GO OUT IN THE GARDEN AND GET SOME Bzz Bzz Bzz!

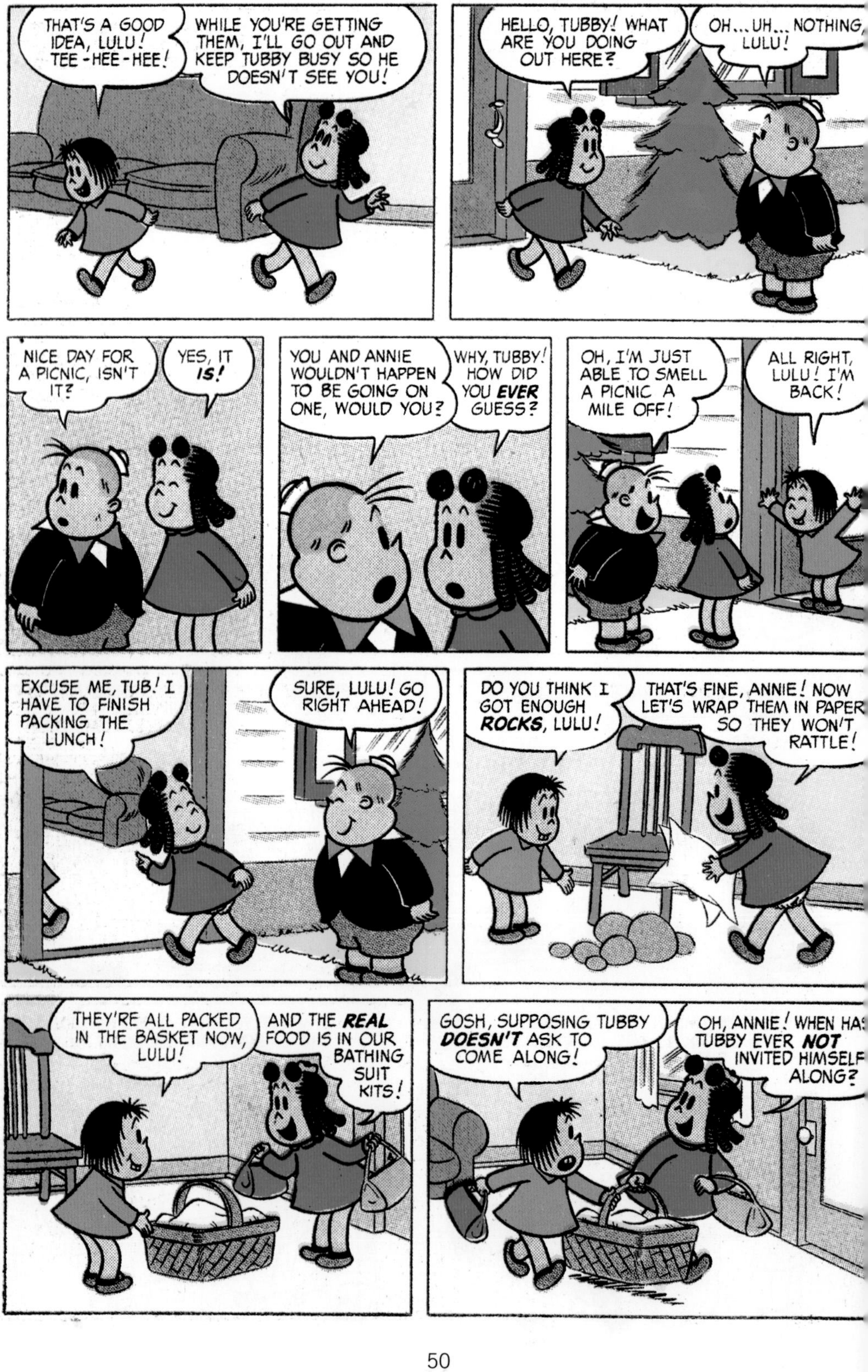
THAT'S A GOOD IDEA, LULU! TEE-HEE-HEE!
WHILE YOU'RE GETTING THEM, I'LL GO OUT AND KEEP TUBBY BUSY SO HE DOESN'T SEE YOU!
HELLO, TUBBY! WHAT ARE YOU DOING OUT HERE?
OH... UH... NOTHING, LULU!
NICE DAY FOR A PICNIC, ISN'T IT?
YES, IT **IS**!
YOU AND ANNIE WOULDN'T HAPPEN TO BE GOING ON ONE, WOULD YOU?
WHY, TUBBY! HOW DID YOU **EVER** GUESS?
OH, I'M JUST ABLE TO SMELL A PICNIC A MILE OFF!
ALL RIGHT, LULU! I'M BACK!
EXCUSE ME, TUB! I HAVE TO FINISH PACKING THE LUNCH!
SURE, LULU! GO RIGHT AHEAD!
DO YOU THINK I GOT ENOUGH **ROCKS**, LULU!
THAT'S FINE, ANNIE! NOW LET'S WRAP THEM IN PAPER SO THEY WON'T RATTLE!
THEY'RE ALL PACKED IN THE BASKET NOW, LULU!
AND THE **REAL** FOOD IS IN OUR BATHING SUIT KITS!
GOSH, SUPPOSING TUBBY **DOESN'T** ASK TO COME ALONG!
OH, ANNIE! WHEN HAS TUBBY EVER **NOT** INVITED HIMSELF ALONG?

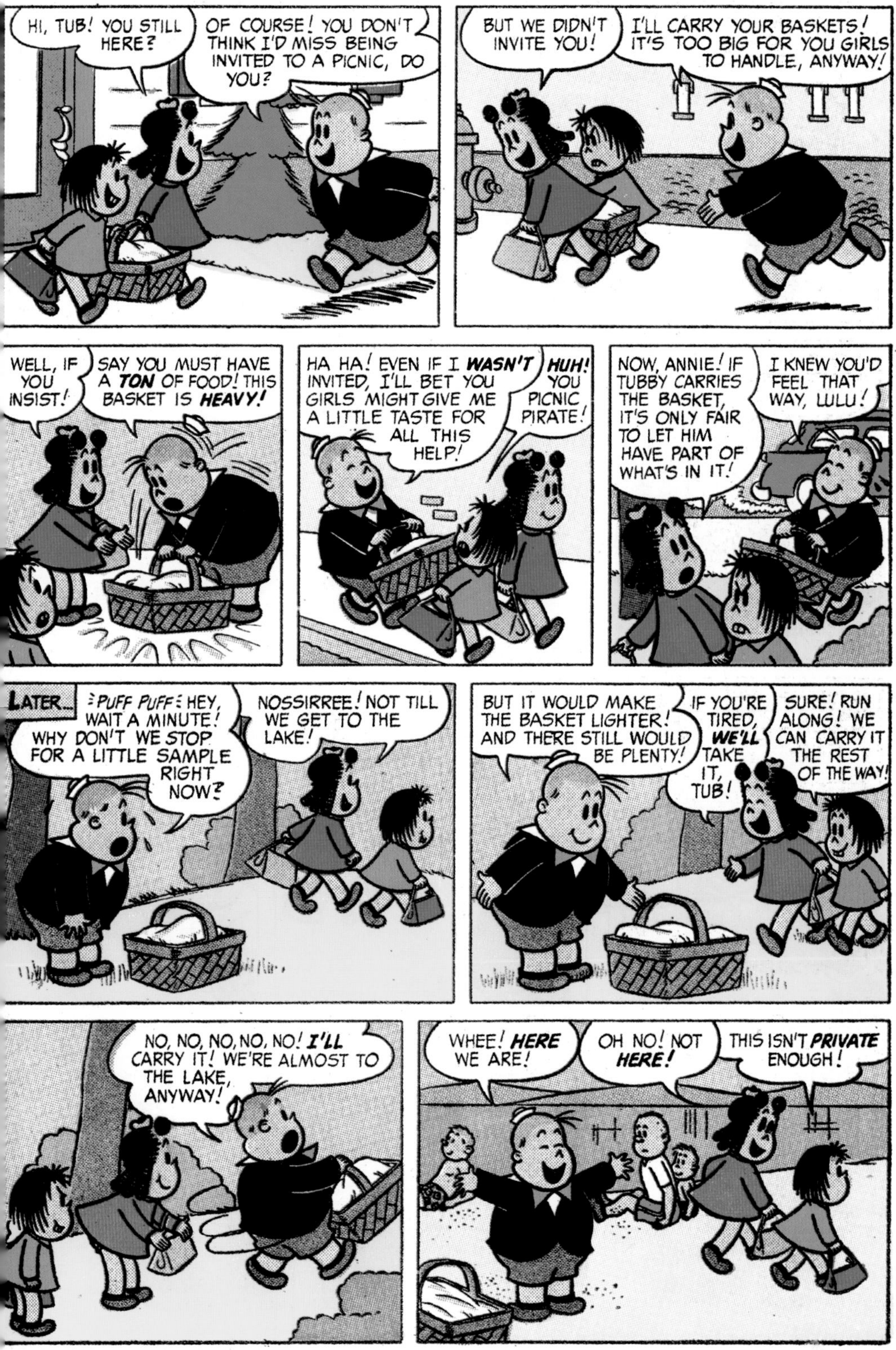
HI, TUB! YOU STILL HERE?
OF COURSE! YOU DON'T THINK I'D MISS BEING INVITED TO A PICNIC, DO YOU?
BUT WE DIDN'T INVITE YOU!
I'LL CARRY YOUR BASKETS! IT'S TOO BIG FOR YOU GIRLS TO HANDLE, ANYWAY!
WELL, IF YOU INSIST!
SAY YOU MUST HAVE A TON OF FOOD! THIS BASKET IS HEAVY!
HA HA! EVEN IF I WASN'T INVITED, I'LL BET YOU GIRLS MIGHT GIVE ME A LITTLE TASTE FOR ALL THIS HELP!
HUH! YOU PICNIC PIRATE!
NOW, ANNIE! IF TUBBY CARRIES THE BASKET, IT'S ONLY FAIR TO LET HIM HAVE PART OF WHAT'S IN IT!
I KNEW YOU'D FEEL THAT WAY, LULU!
LATER...
PUFF PUFF HEY, WAIT A MINUTE! WHY DON'T WE STOP FOR A LITTLE SAMPLE RIGHT NOW?
NOSSIRREE! NOT TILL WE GET TO THE LAKE!
BUT IT WOULD MAKE THE BASKET LIGHTER! AND THERE STILL WOULD BE PLENTY!
IF YOU'RE TIRED, WE'LL TAKE IT, TUB!
SURE! RUN ALONG! WE CAN CARRY IT THE REST OF THE WAY!
NO, NO, NO, NO, NO! I'LL CARRY IT! WE'RE ALMOST TO THE LAKE, ANYWAY!
WHEE! HERE WE ARE!
OH NO! NOT HERE!
THIS ISN'T PRIVATE ENOUGH!

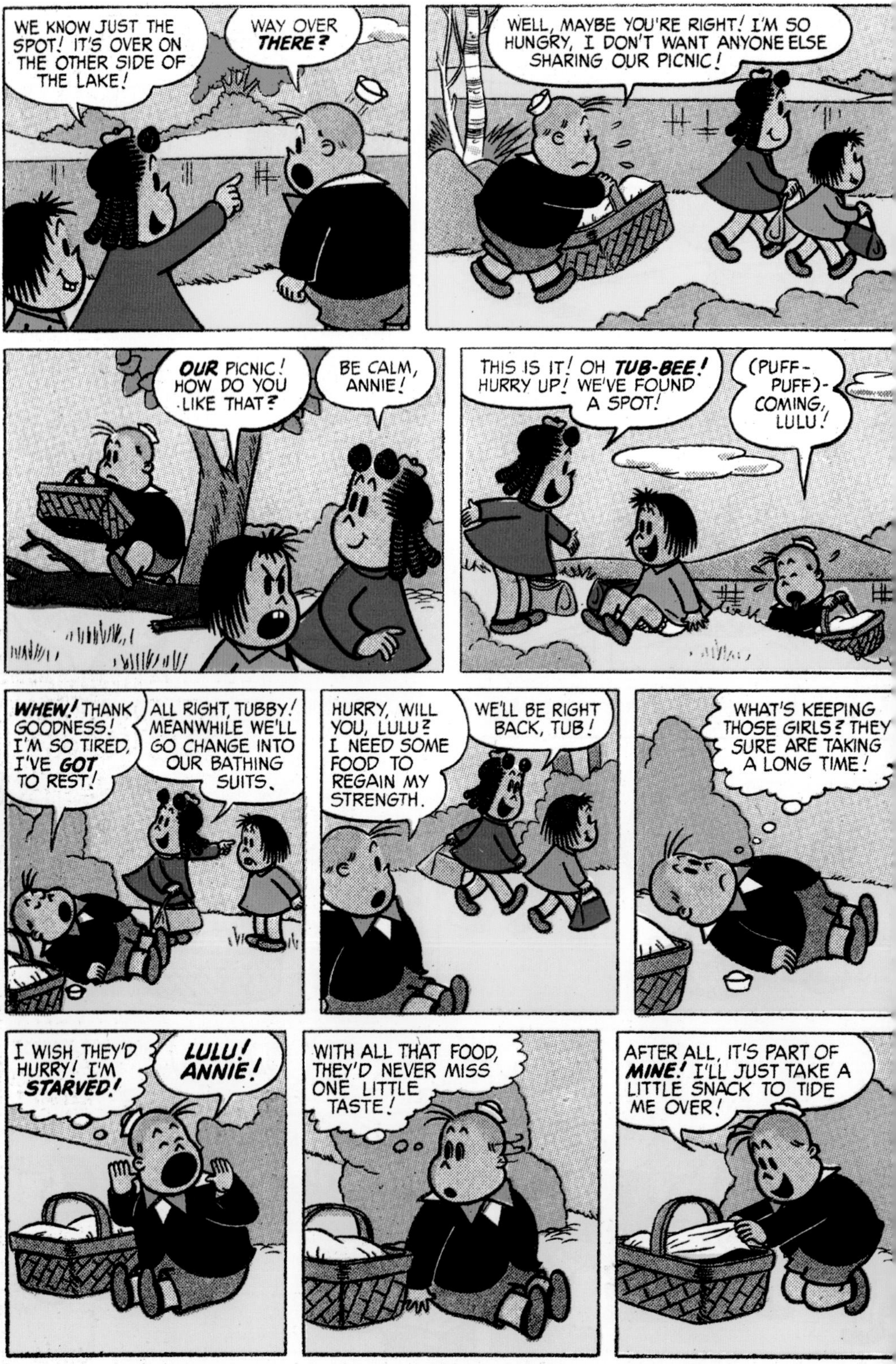
WE KNOW JUST THE SPOT! IT'S OVER ON THE OTHER SIDE OF THE LAKE!
WAY OVER THERE?
WELL, MAYBE YOU'RE RIGHT! I'M SO HUNGRY, I DON'T WANT ANYONE ELSE SHARING OUR PICNIC!
OUR PICNIC! HOW DO YOU LIKE THAT?
BE CALM, ANNIE!
THIS IS IT! OH TUB-BEE! HURRY UP! WE'VE FOUND A SPOT!
(PUFF-PUFF)- COMING, LULU!
WHEW! THANK GOODNESS! I'M SO TIRED, I'VE GOT TO REST!
ALL RIGHT, TUBBY! MEANWHILE WE'LL GO CHANGE INTO OUR BATHING SUITS.
HURRY, WILL YOU, LULU? I NEED SOME FOOD TO REGAIN MY STRENGTH.
WE'LL BE RIGHT BACK, TUB!
WHAT'S KEEPING THOSE GIRLS? THEY SURE ARE TAKING A LONG TIME!
I WISH THEY'D HURRY! I'M STARVED!
LULU! ANNIE!
WITH ALL THAT FOOD, THEY'D NEVER MISS ONE LITTLE TASTE!
AFTER ALL, IT'S PART OF MINE! I'LL JUST TAKE A LITTLE SNACK TO TIDE ME OVER!

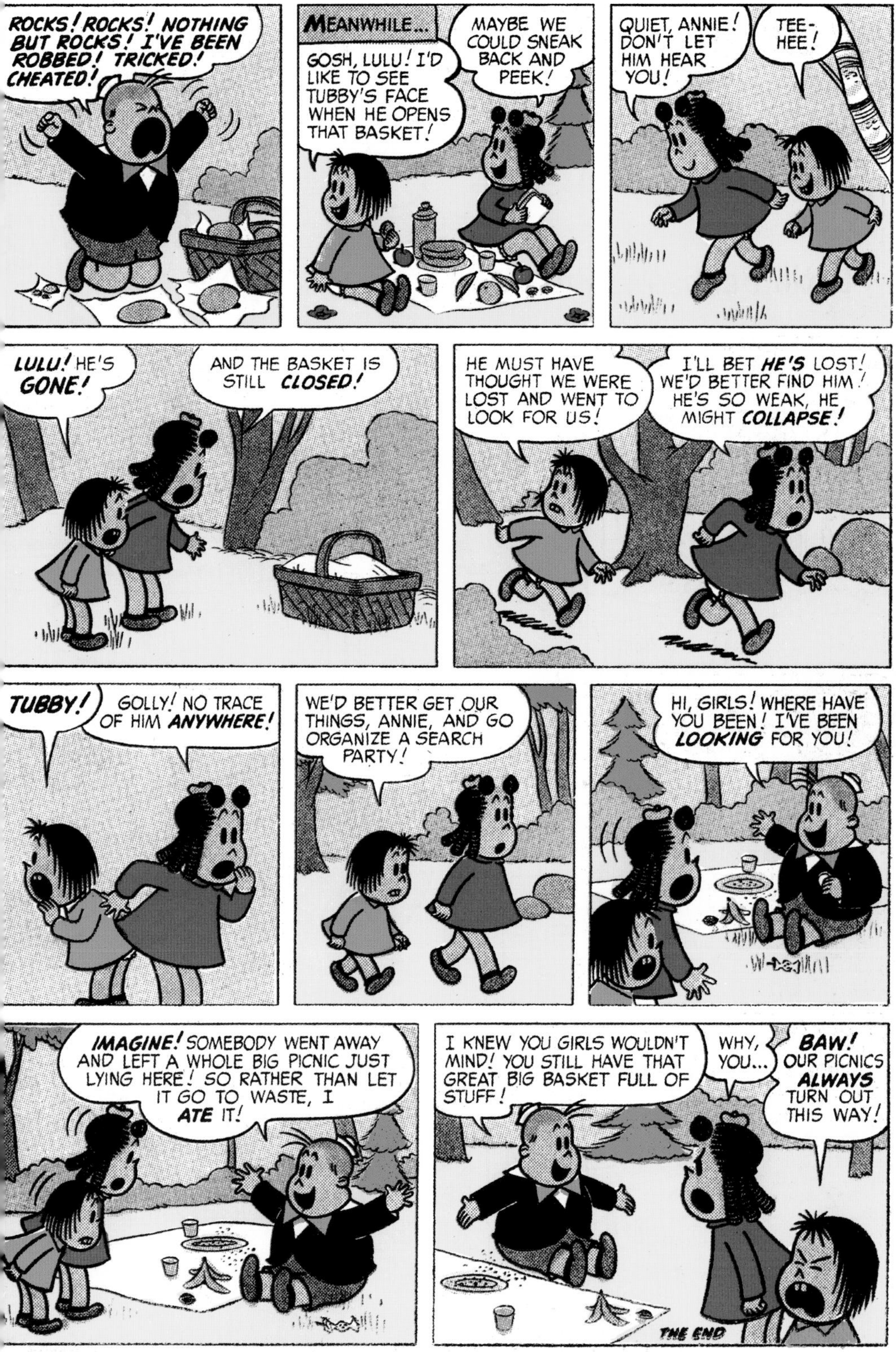
ROCKS! ROCKS! NOTHING BUT ROCKS! I'VE BEEN ROBBED! TRICKED! CHEATED!
MEANWHILE...
GOSH, LULU! I'D LIKE TO SEE TUBBY'S FACE WHEN HE OPENS THAT BASKET!
MAYBE WE COULD SNEAK BACK AND PEEK!
QUIET, ANNIE! DON'T LET HIM HEAR YOU!
TEE-HEE!
LULU! HE'S GONE!
AND THE BASKET IS STILL CLOSED!
HE MUST HAVE THOUGHT WE WERE LOST AND WENT TO LOOK FOR US!
I'LL BET HE'S LOST! WE'D BETTER FIND HIM! HE'S SO WEAK, HE MIGHT COLLAPSE!
TUBBY!
GOLLY! NO TRACE OF HIM ANYWHERE!
WE'D BETTER GET OUR THINGS, ANNIE, AND GO ORGANIZE A SEARCH PARTY!
HI, GIRLS! WHERE HAVE YOU BEEN! I'VE BEEN LOOKING FOR YOU!
IMAGINE! SOMEBODY WENT AWAY AND LEFT A WHOLE BIG PICNIC JUST LYING HERE! SO RATHER THAN LET IT GO TO WASTE, I ATE IT!
I KNEW YOU GIRLS WOULDN'T MIND! YOU STILL HAVE THAT GREAT BIG BASKET FULL OF STUFF!
WHY, YOU...
BAW! OUR PICNICS ALWAYS TURN OUT THIS WAY!
THE END

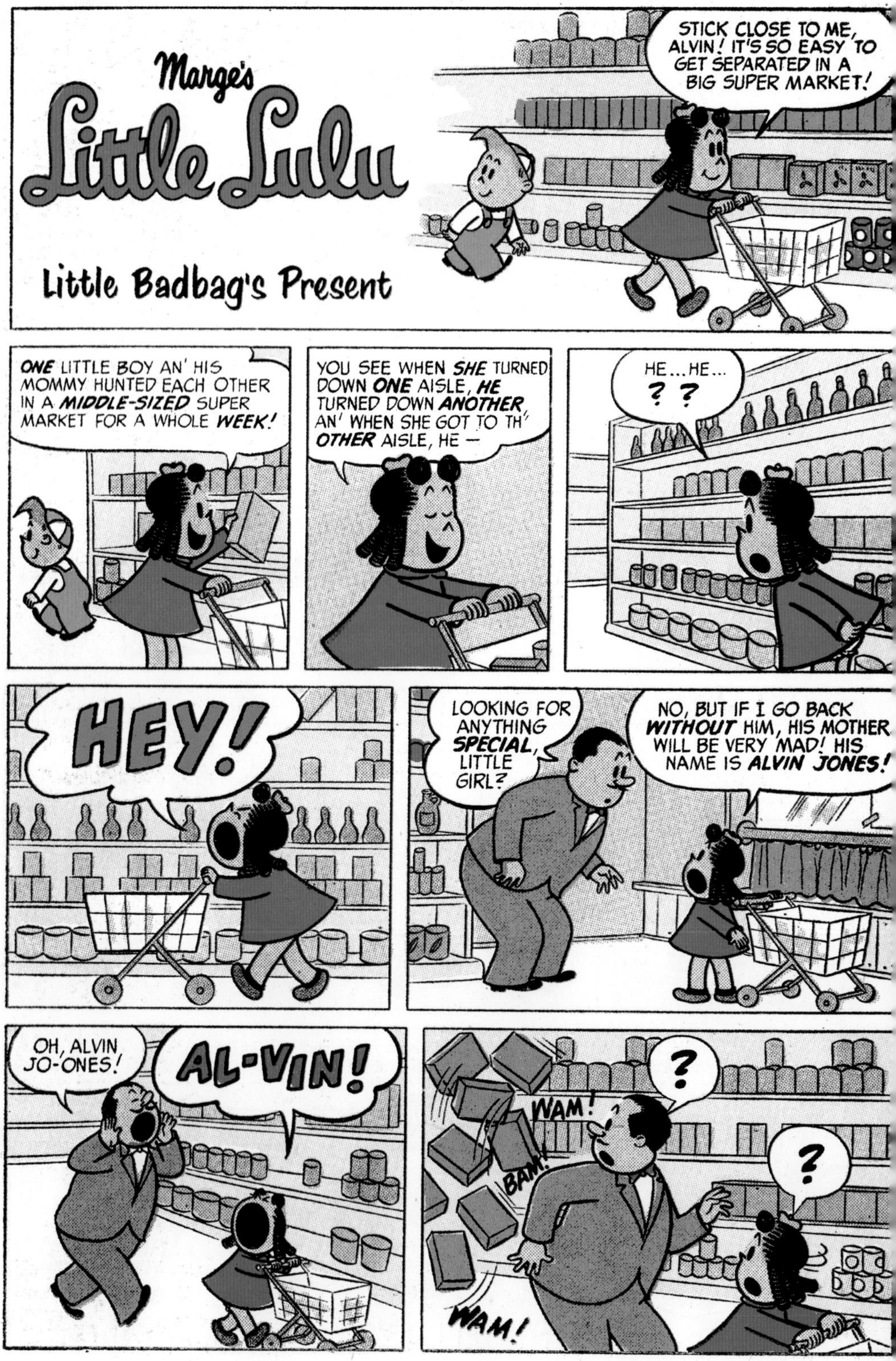
Marge's
Little Lulu
Little Badbag's Present
STICK CLOSE TO ME, ALVIN! IT'S SO EASY TO GET SEPARATED IN A BIG SUPER MARKET!
ONE LITTLE BOY AN' HIS MOMMY HUNTED EACH OTHER IN A MIDDLE-SIZED SUPER MARKET FOR A WHOLE WEEK!
YOU SEE WHEN SHE TURNED DOWN ONE AISLE, HE TURNED DOWN ANOTHER, AN' WHEN SHE GOT TO TH' OTHER AISLE, HE —
HE...HE...
? ?
HEY!
LOOKING FOR ANYTHING SPECIAL, LITTLE GIRL?
NO, BUT IF I GO BACK WITHOUT HIM, HIS MOTHER WILL BE VERY MAD! HIS NAME IS ALVIN JONES!
OH, ALVIN JO-ONES!
AL-VIN!
WAM!
BAM!
WAM!
?
?

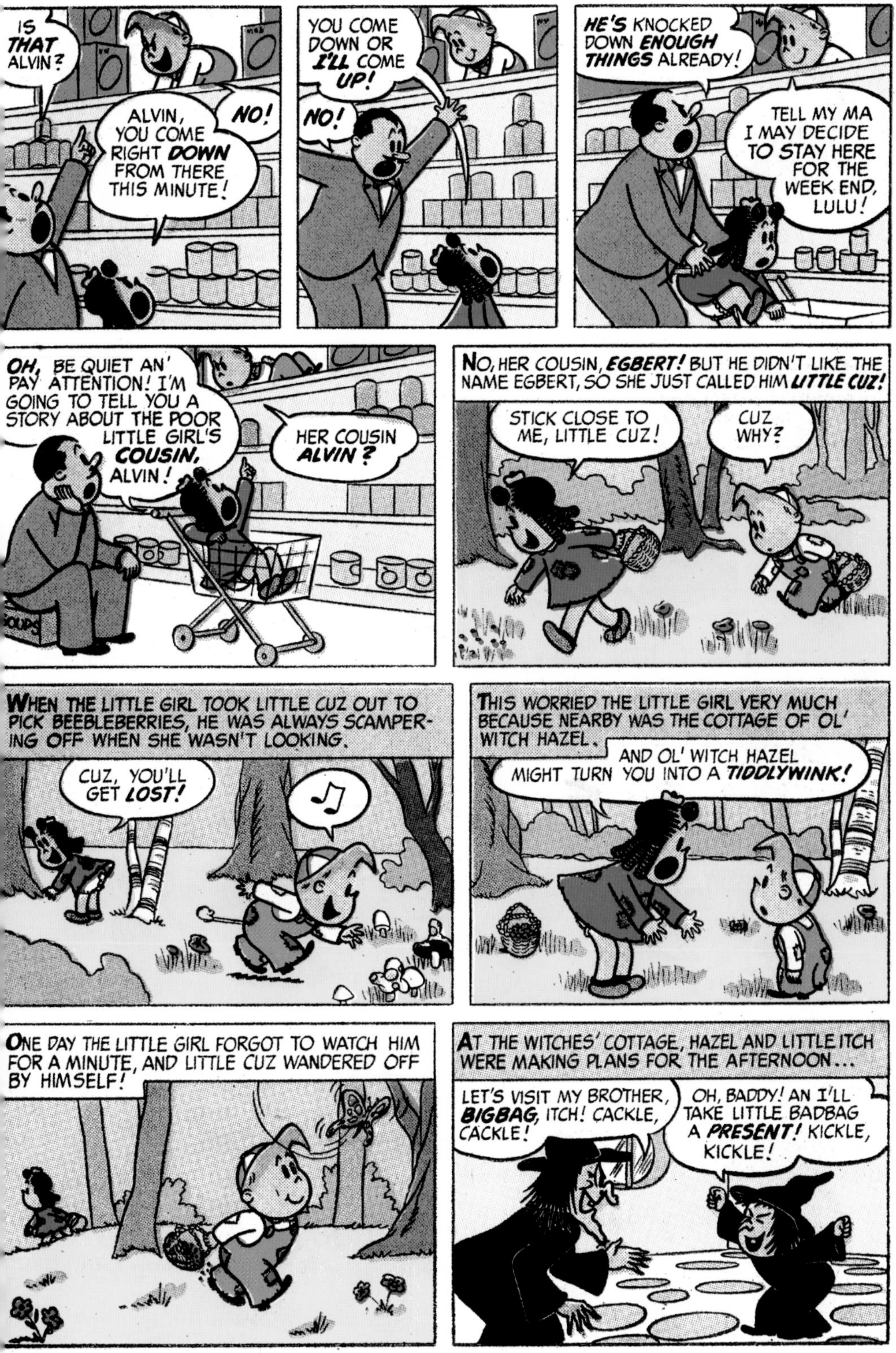
IS THAT ALVIN?
ALVIN, YOU COME RIGHT DOWN FROM THERE THIS MINUTE!
NO!
YOU COME DOWN OR I'LL COME UP!
NO!
HE'S KNOCKED DOWN ENOUGH THINGS ALREADY!
TELL MY MA I MAY DECIDE TO STAY HERE FOR THE WEEK END, LULU!
OH, BE QUIET AN' PAY ATTENTION! I'M GOING TO TELL YOU A STORY ABOUT THE POOR LITTLE GIRL'S COUSIN, ALVIN!
HER COUSIN ALVIN?
SOUPS
NO, HER COUSIN, EGBERT! BUT HE DIDN'T LIKE THE NAME EGBERT, SO SHE JUST CALLED HIM LITTLE CUZ!
STICK CLOSE TO ME, LITTLE CUZ!
CUZ WHY?
WHEN THE LITTLE GIRL TOOK LITTLE CUZ OUT TO PICK BEEBLEBERRIES, HE WAS ALWAYS SCAMPERING OFF WHEN SHE WASN'T LOOKING.
CUZ, YOU'LL GET LOST!
THIS WORRIED THE LITTLE GIRL VERY MUCH, BECAUSE NEARBY WAS THE COTTAGE OF OL' WITCH HAZEL.
AND OL' WITCH HAZEL MIGHT TURN YOU INTO A TIDDLYWINK!
ONE DAY THE LITTLE GIRL FORGOT TO WATCH HIM FOR A MINUTE, AND LITTLE CUZ WANDERED OFF BY HIMSELF!
AT THE WITCHES' COTTAGE, HAZEL AND LITTLE ITCH WERE MAKING PLANS FOR THE AFTERNOON...
LET'S VISIT MY BROTHER, BIGBAG, ITCH! CACKLE, CACKLE!
OH, BADDY! AN I'LL TAKE LITTLE BADBAG A PRESENT! KICKLE, KICKLE!

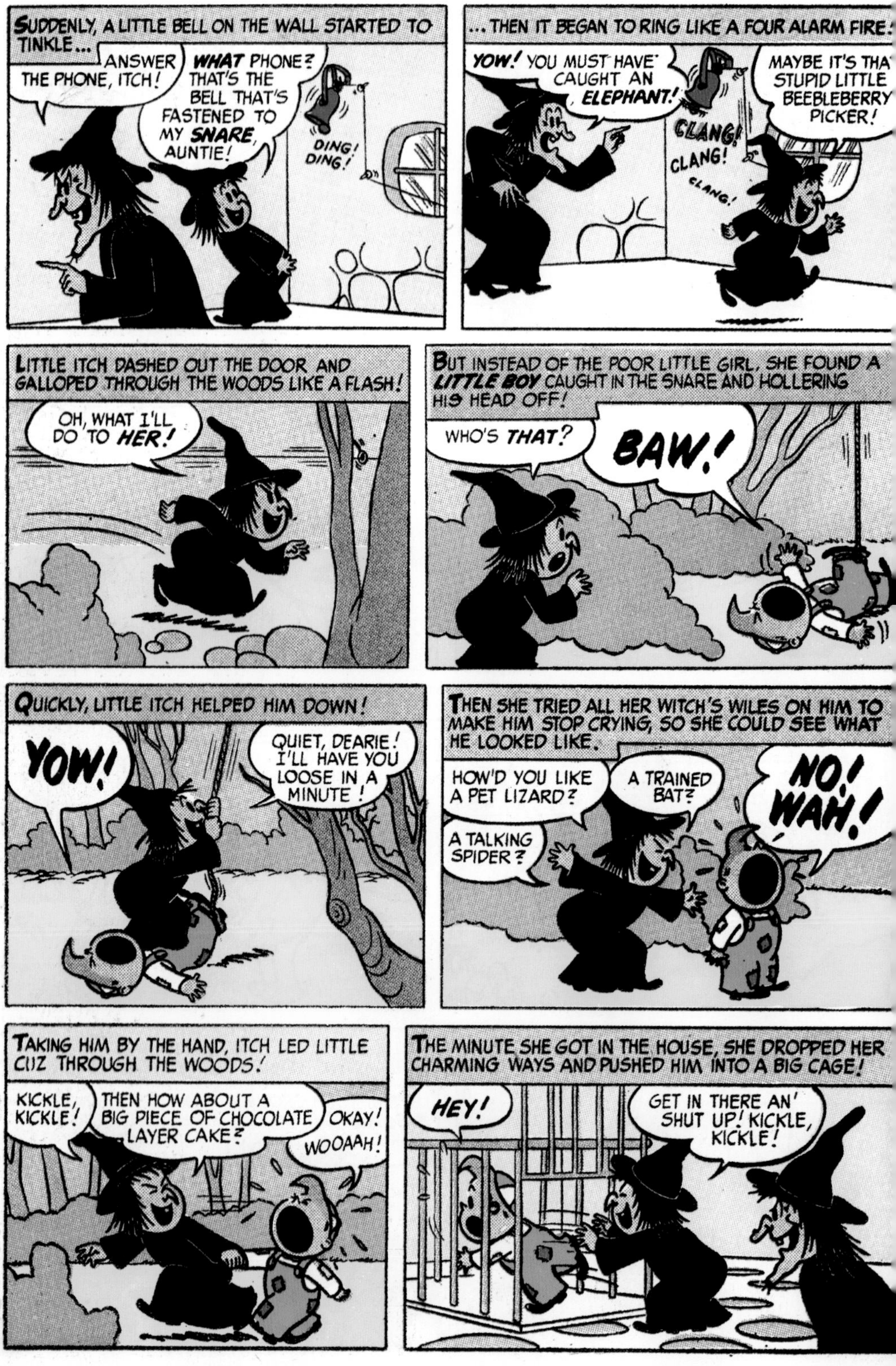
SUDDENLY, A LITTLE BELL ON THE WALL STARTED TO TINKLE...
ANSWER THE PHONE, ITCH!
WHAT PHONE? THAT'S THE BELL THAT'S FASTENED TO MY SNARE, AUNTIE!
DING! DING!
...THEN IT BEGAN TO RING LIKE A FOUR ALARM FIRE!
YOW! YOU MUST HAVE CAUGHT AN ELEPHANT!
CLANG! CLANG! CLANG!
MAYBE IT'S THAT STUPID LITTLE BEEBLEBERRY PICKER!
LITTLE ITCH DASHED OUT THE DOOR AND GALLOPED THROUGH THE WOODS LIKE A FLASH!
OH, WHAT I'LL DO TO HER!
BUT INSTEAD OF THE POOR LITTLE GIRL, SHE FOUND A LITTLE BOY CAUGHT IN THE SNARE AND HOLLERING HIS HEAD OFF!
WHO'S THAT?
BAW!
QUICKLY, LITTLE ITCH HELPED HIM DOWN!
YOW!
QUIET, DEARIE! I'LL HAVE YOU LOOSE IN A MINUTE!
THEN SHE TRIED ALL HER WITCH'S WILES ON HIM TO MAKE HIM STOP CRYING, SO SHE COULD SEE WHAT HE LOOKED LIKE.
HOW'D YOU LIKE A PET LIZARD?
A TRAINED BAT?
A TALKING SPIDER?
NO! WAH!
TAKING HIM BY THE HAND, ITCH LED LITTLE CUZ THROUGH THE WOODS!
KICKLE, KICKLE!
THEN HOW ABOUT A BIG PIECE OF CHOCOLATE LAYER CAKE?
OKAY! WOOAAH!
THE MINUTE SHE GOT IN THE HOUSE, SHE DROPPED HER CHARMING WAYS AND PUSHED HIM INTO A BIG CAGE!
HEY!
GET IN THERE AN' SHUT UP! KICKLE, KICKLE!

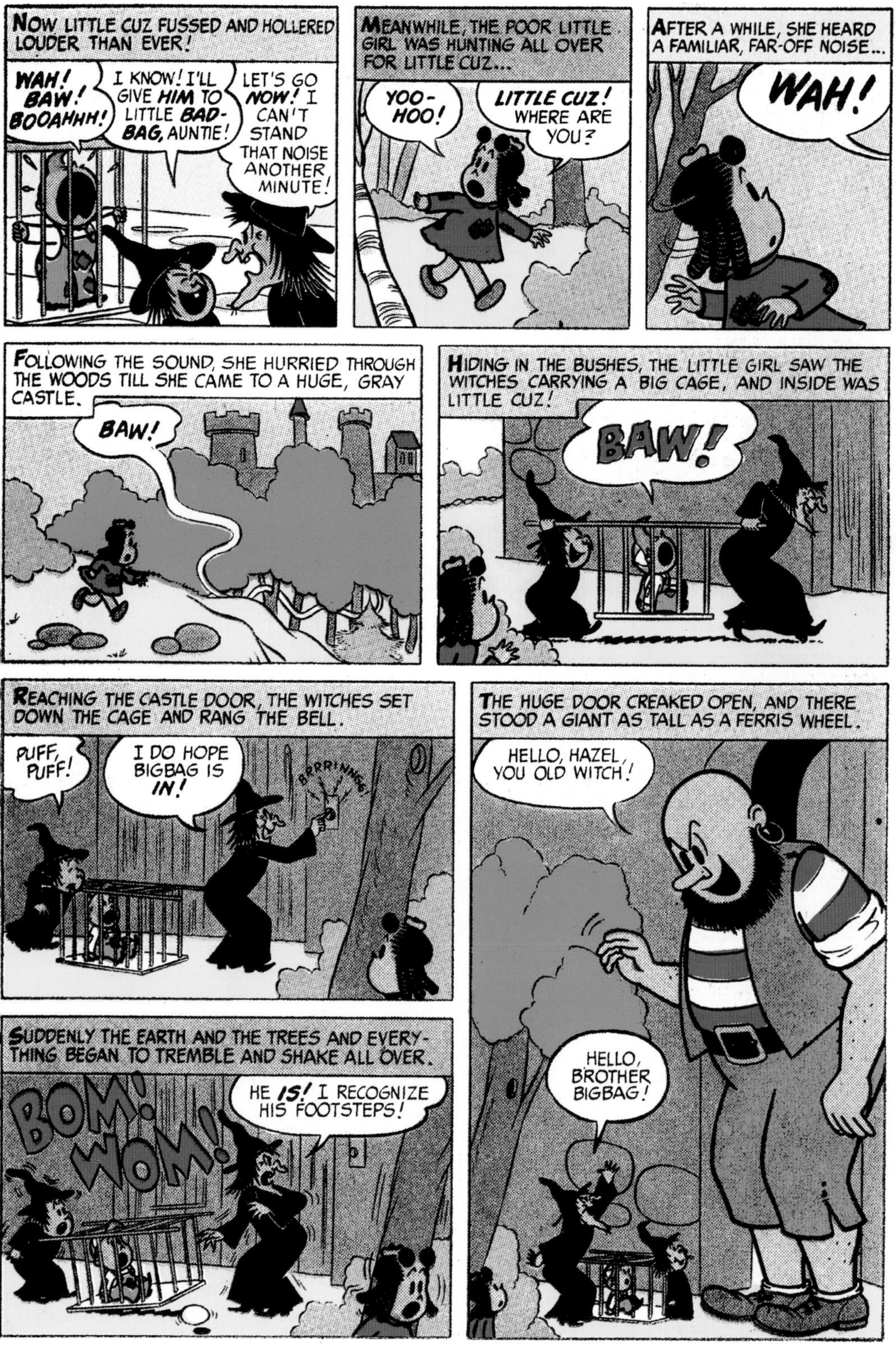
NOW LITTLE CUZ FUSSED AND HOLLERED LOUDER THAN EVER!
WAH! BAW! BOOAHHH!
I KNOW! I'LL GIVE HIM TO LITTLE BAD-BAG, AUNTIE!
LET'S GO NOW! I CAN'T STAND THAT NOISE ANOTHER MINUTE!
MEANWHILE, THE POOR LITTLE GIRL WAS HUNTING ALL OVER FOR LITTLE CUZ...
YOO-HOO!
LITTLE CUZ! WHERE ARE YOU?
AFTER A WHILE, SHE HEARD A FAMILIAR, FAR-OFF NOISE...
WAH!
FOLLOWING THE SOUND, SHE HURRIED THROUGH THE WOODS TILL SHE CAME TO A HUGE, GRAY CASTLE.
BAW!
HIDING IN THE BUSHES, THE LITTLE GIRL SAW THE WITCHES CARRYING A BIG CAGE, AND INSIDE WAS LITTLE CUZ!
BAW!
REACHING THE CASTLE DOOR, THE WITCHES SET DOWN THE CAGE AND RANG THE BELL.
PUFF, PUFF!
I DO HOPE BIGBAG IS IN!
SUDDENLY THE EARTH AND THE TREES AND EVERYTHING BEGAN TO TREMBLE AND SHAKE ALL OVER.
BOM! WOM!
HE IS! I RECOGNIZE HIS FOOTSTEPS!
THE HUGE DOOR CREAKED OPEN, AND THERE STOOD A GIANT AS TALL AS A FERRIS WHEEL.
HELLO, HAZEL, YOU OLD WITCH!
HELLO, BROTHER BIGBAG!

PICKING UP THE CAGE, THE WITCHES CARRIED IT INTO THE CASTLE.

WHAT'S *THAT?*

A LITTLE PRESENT FOR LITTLE *BADBAG!*

THEN THE GREAT DOOR BANGED SHUT BEHIND THEM.

BAM!

AW, YOU SHOULDN'T HAVE *DONE* IT!

BAW!

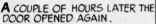

A COUPLE OF HOURS LATER THE DOOR OPENED AGAIN.

CREE-AKK!

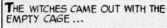

THE WITCHES CAME OUT WITH THE EMPTY CAGE ...

GOOD-BYE, BIGBAG! CACKLE, CACKLE!

... AND STARTED FOR HOME. THE POOR LITTLE GIRL WONDERED HOW SHE WOULD EVER GET INTO THE CASTLE TO RESCUE LITTLE CUZ.

OH, POOR LITTLE CUZ!

SUDDENLY SHE FELT A COLD DRAFT AT HER FEET. THE LITTLE GIRL LOOKED AROUND AND SAW A GIANT MOUSEHOLE IN THE WALL. (BEING A GIANT CASTLE, IT HAD GIANT MICE.)

CRAWLING INTO THE HOLE, THE LITTLE GIRL FOLLOWED A LONG TUNNEL UNTIL SHE SUDDENLY POPPED OUT INTO THE BANQUET HALL.

GUIDED BY LITTLE CUZ'S HOWLS, SHE RAN THROUGH THE HUGE CASTLE AND UP A LONG WINDING STAIR TO THE VERY TOP OF A HIGH TOWER ...

BAW! WAH! YOW! BAW!

BAW!

IN A BIRD CAGE SHE FOUND LITTLE CUZ, AND IN HIS PLAY PEN WAS LITTLE BADBAG... FAST ASLEEP!

WELL, IT'S ABOUT TIME!

58

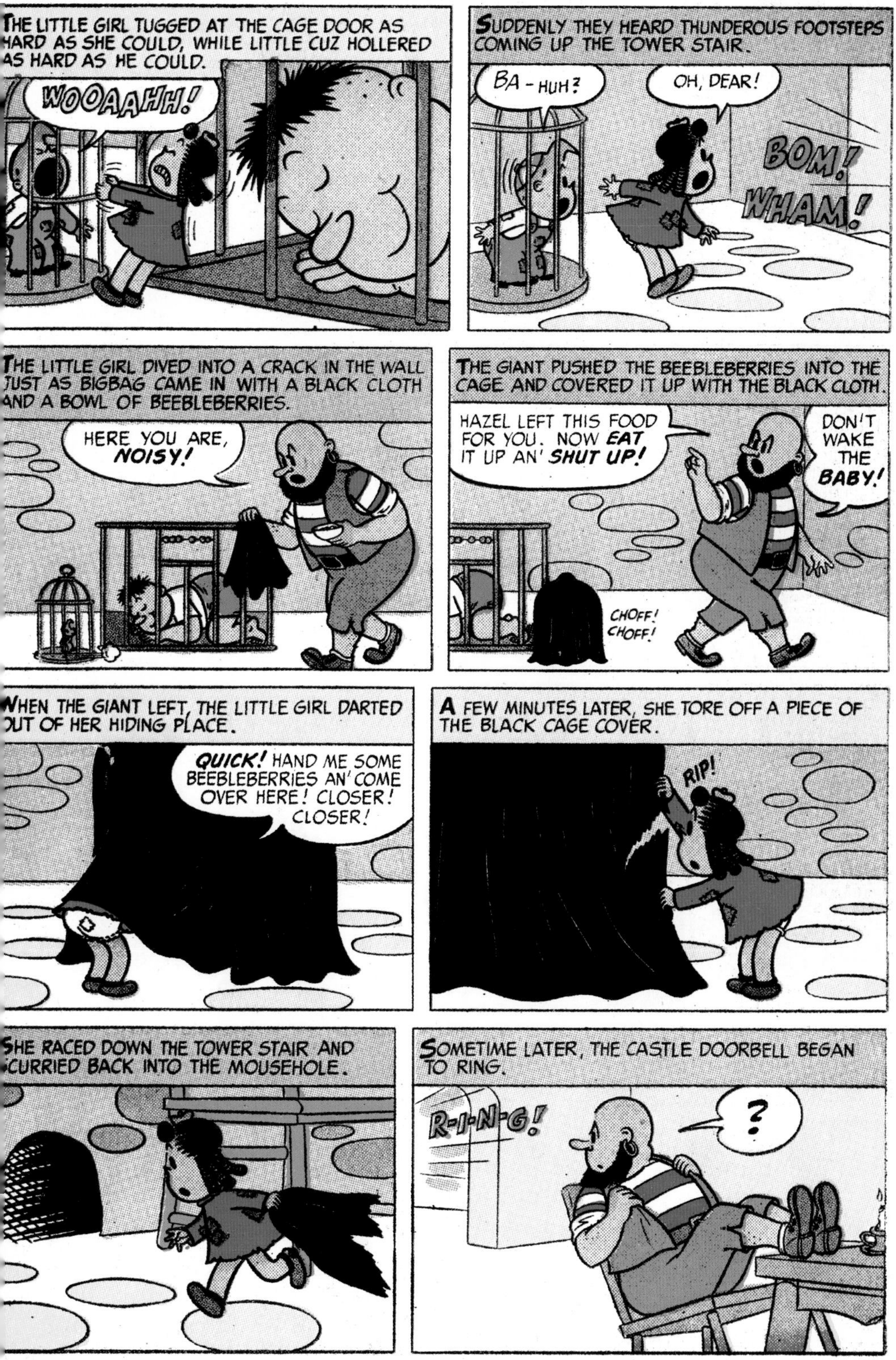
THE LITTLE GIRL TUGGED AT THE CAGE DOOR AS HARD AS SHE COULD, WHILE LITTLE CUZ HOLLERED AS HARD AS HE COULD.
WOOAAHH!
SUDDENLY THEY HEARD THUNDEROUS FOOTSTEPS COMING UP THE TOWER STAIR.
BA-HUH?
OH, DEAR!
BOM!
WHAM!
THE LITTLE GIRL DIVED INTO A CRACK IN THE WALL JUST AS BIGBAG CAME IN WITH A BLACK CLOTH AND A BOWL OF BEEBLEBERRIES.
HERE YOU ARE, NOISY!
THE GIANT PUSHED THE BEEBLEBERRIES INTO THE CAGE AND COVERED IT UP WITH THE BLACK CLOTH.
HAZEL LEFT THIS FOOD FOR YOU. NOW EAT IT UP AN' SHUT UP!
DON'T WAKE THE BABY!
CHOFF! CHOFF!
WHEN THE GIANT LEFT, THE LITTLE GIRL DARTED OUT OF HER HIDING PLACE.
QUICK! HAND ME SOME BEEBLEBERRIES AN' COME OVER HERE! CLOSER! CLOSER!
A FEW MINUTES LATER, SHE TORE OFF A PIECE OF THE BLACK CAGE COVER.
RIP!
SHE RACED DOWN THE TOWER STAIR AND SCURRIED BACK INTO THE MOUSEHOLE.
SOMETIME LATER, THE CASTLE DOORBELL BEGAN TO RING.
R-I-N-G!
?

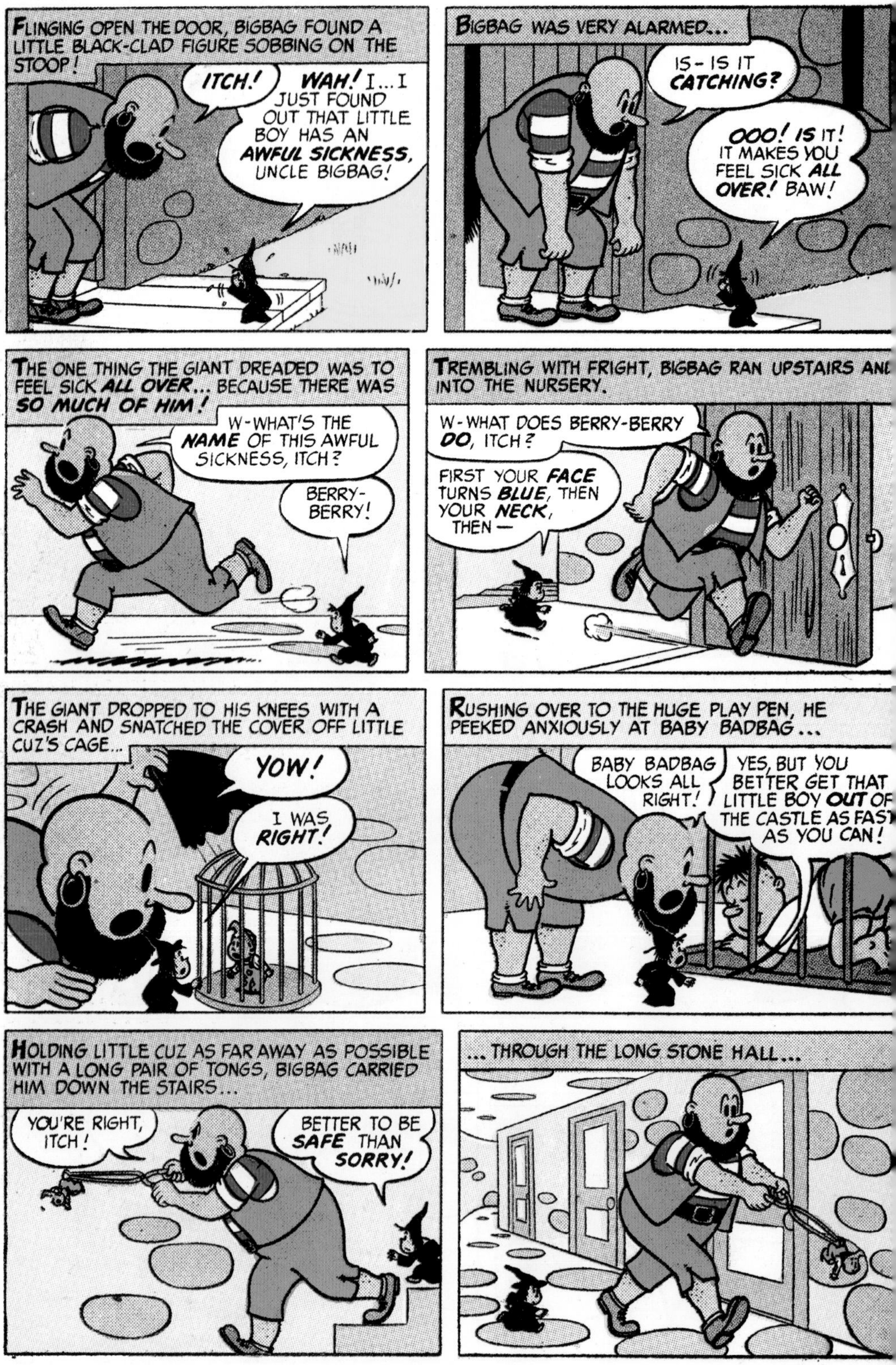
FLINGING OPEN THE DOOR, BIGBAG FOUND A LITTLE BLACK-CLAD FIGURE SOBBING ON THE STOOP!
ITCH!
WAH! I...I JUST FOUND OUT THAT LITTLE BOY HAS AN AWFUL SICKNESS, UNCLE BIGBAG!
BIGBAG WAS VERY ALARMED...
IS-IS IT CATCHING?
OOO! IS IT! IT MAKES YOU FEEL SICK ALL OVER! BAW!
THE ONE THING THE GIANT DREADED WAS TO FEEL SICK ALL OVER... BECAUSE THERE WAS SO MUCH OF HIM!
W-WHAT'S THE NAME OF THIS AWFUL SICKNESS, ITCH?
BERRY-BERRY!
TREMBLING WITH FRIGHT, BIGBAG RAN UPSTAIRS AND INTO THE NURSERY.
W-WHAT DOES BERRY-BERRY DO, ITCH?
FIRST YOUR FACE TURNS BLUE, THEN YOUR NECK, THEN—
THE GIANT DROPPED TO HIS KNEES WITH A CRASH AND SNATCHED THE COVER OFF LITTLE CUZ'S CAGE...
YOW!
I WAS RIGHT!
RUSHING OVER TO THE HUGE PLAY PEN, HE PEEKED ANXIOUSLY AT BABY BADBAG...
BABY BADBAG LOOKS ALL RIGHT!
YES, BUT YOU BETTER GET THAT LITTLE BOY OUT OF THE CASTLE AS FAST AS YOU CAN!
HOLDING LITTLE CUZ AS FAR AWAY AS POSSIBLE WITH A LONG PAIR OF TONGS, BIGBAG CARRIED HIM DOWN THE STAIRS...
YOU'RE RIGHT, ITCH!
BETTER TO BE SAFE THAN SORRY!
...THROUGH THE LONG STONE HALL...

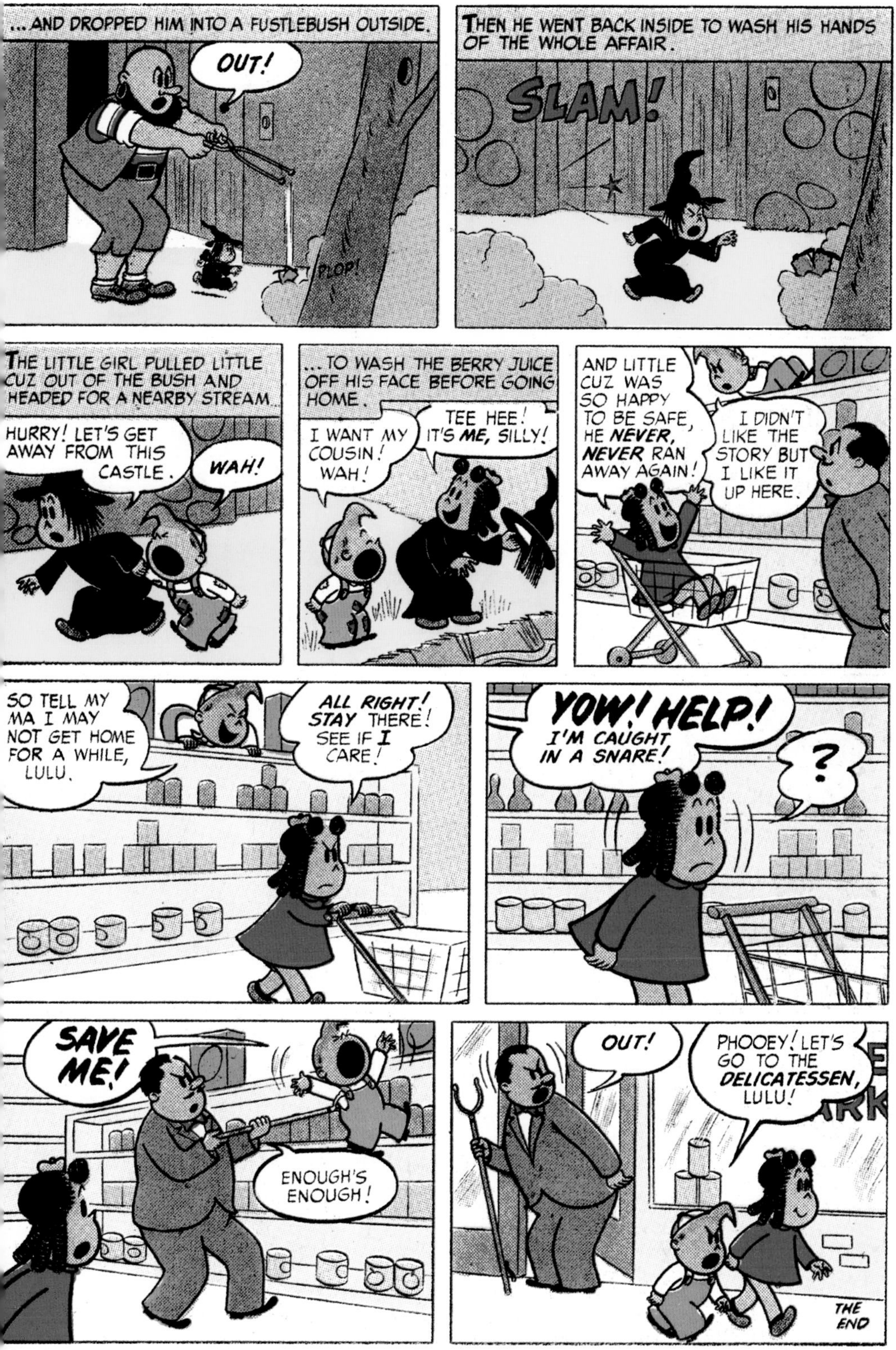
...AND DROPPED HIM INTO A FUSTLEBUSH OUTSIDE.
OUT!
PLOP!
THEN HE WENT BACK INSIDE TO WASH HIS HANDS OF THE WHOLE AFFAIR.
SLAM!
THE LITTLE GIRL PULLED LITTLE CUZ OUT OF THE BUSH AND HEADED FOR A NEARBY STREAM.
HURRY! LET'S GET AWAY FROM THIS CASTLE.
WAH!
...TO WASH THE BERRY JUICE OFF HIS FACE BEFORE GOING HOME.
I WANT MY COUSIN! WAH!
TEE HEE! IT'S ME, SILLY!
AND LITTLE CUZ WAS SO HAPPY TO BE SAFE, HE NEVER, NEVER RAN AWAY AGAIN!
I DIDN'T LIKE THE STORY BUT I LIKE IT UP HERE.
SO TELL MY MA I MAY NOT GET HOME FOR A WHILE, LULU.
ALL RIGHT! STAY THERE! SEE IF I CARE!
YOW! HELP! I'M CAUGHT IN A SNARE!
?
SAVE ME!
ENOUGH'S ENOUGH!
OUT!
PHOOEY! LET'S GO TO THE DELICATESSEN, LULU!
THE END

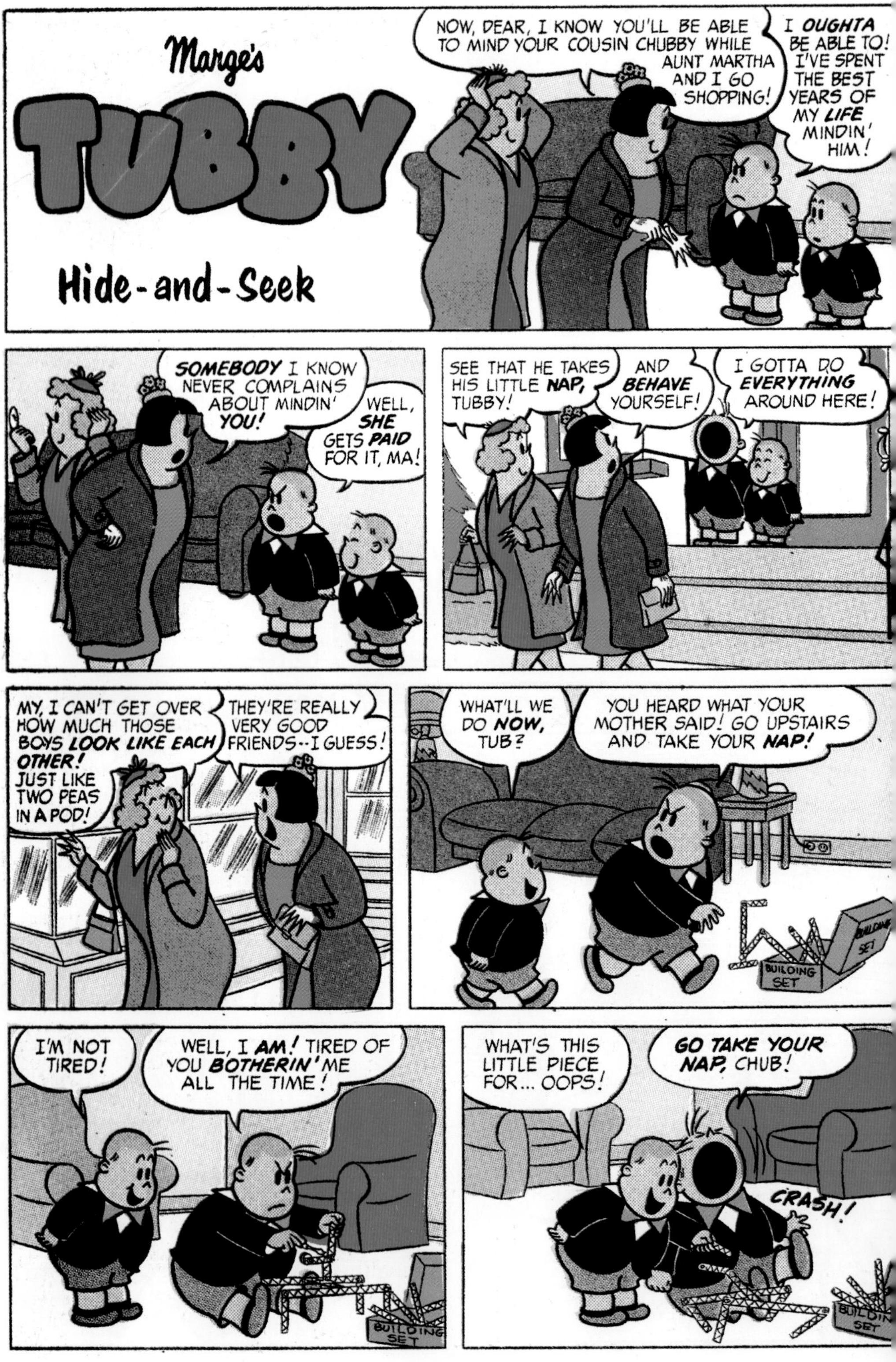
Marge's
TUBBY
Hide-and-Seek
NOW, DEAR, I KNOW YOU'LL BE ABLE TO MIND YOUR COUSIN CHUBBY WHILE AUNT MARTHA AND I GO SHOPPING!
I OUGHTA BE ABLE TO! I'VE SPENT THE BEST YEARS OF MY LIFE MINDIN' HIM!
SOMEBODY I KNOW NEVER COMPLAINS ABOUT MINDIN' YOU!
WELL, SHE GETS PAID FOR IT, MA!
SEE THAT HE TAKES HIS LITTLE NAP, TUBBY!
AND BEHAVE YOURSELF!
I GOTTA DO EVERYTHING AROUND HERE!
MY, I CAN'T GET OVER HOW MUCH THOSE BOYS LOOK LIKE EACH OTHER! JUST LIKE TWO PEAS IN A POD!
THEY'RE REALLY VERY GOOD FRIENDS--I GUESS!
WHAT'LL WE DO NOW, TUB?
YOU HEARD WHAT YOUR MOTHER SAID! GO UPSTAIRS AND TAKE YOUR NAP!
BUILDING SET
I'M NOT TIRED!
WELL, I AM! TIRED OF YOU BOTHERIN' ME ALL THE TIME!
BUILDING SET
WHAT'S THIS LITTLE PIECE FOR... OOPS!
GO TAKE YOUR NAP, CHUB!
CRASH!

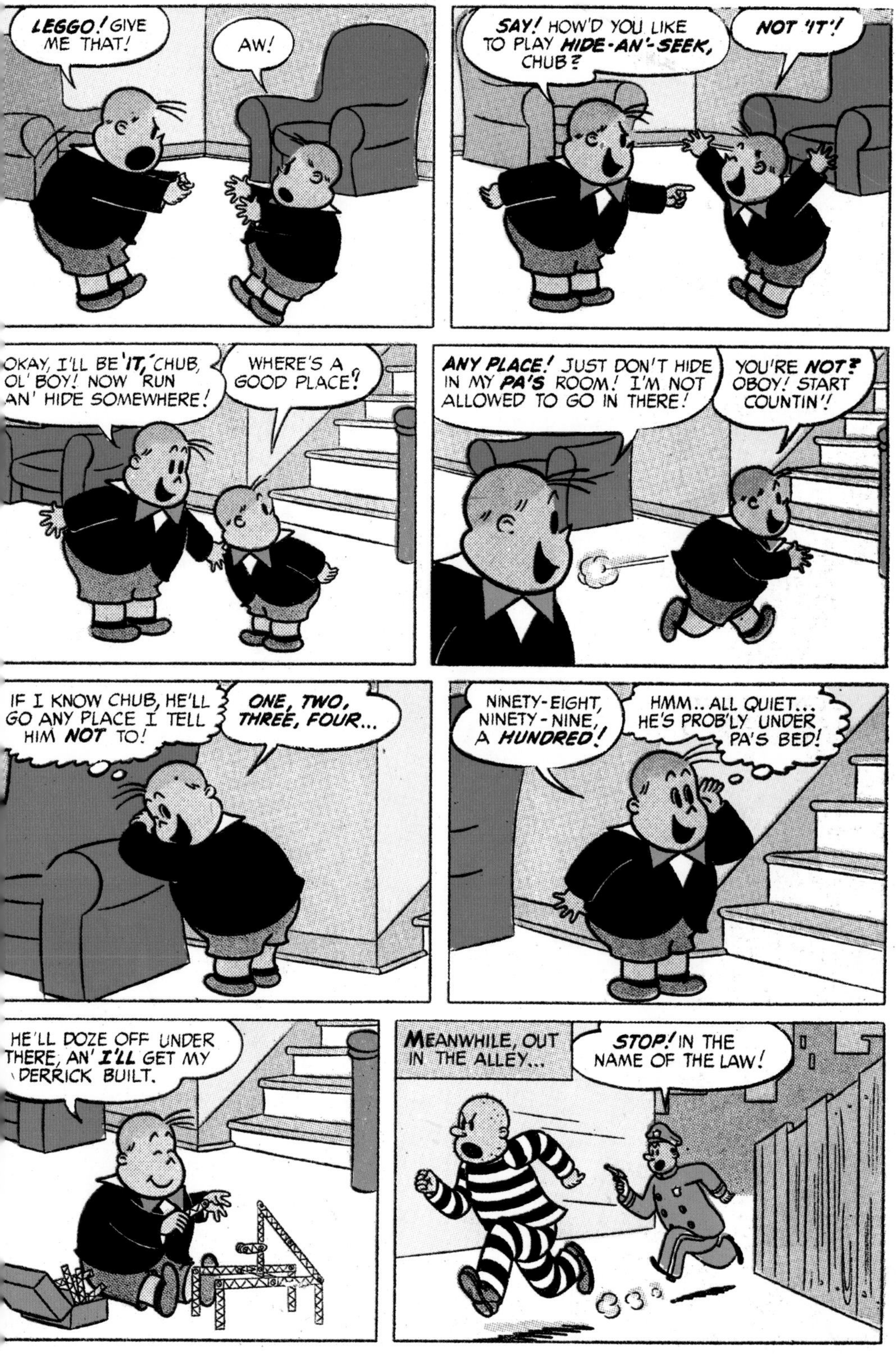
LEGGO! GIVE ME THAT!
AW!
SAY! HOW'D YOU LIKE TO PLAY HIDE-AN'-SEEK, CHUB?
NOT 'IT'!
OKAY, I'LL BE 'IT,' CHUB, OL' BOY! NOW RUN AN' HIDE SOMEWHERE!
WHERE'S A GOOD PLACE?
ANY PLACE! JUST DON'T HIDE IN MY PA'S ROOM! I'M NOT ALLOWED TO GO IN THERE!
YOU'RE NOT? OBOY! START COUNTIN'!
IF I KNOW CHUB, HE'LL GO ANY PLACE I TELL HIM NOT TO!
ONE, TWO, THREE, FOUR...
NINETY-EIGHT, NINETY-NINE, A HUNDRED!
HMM.. ALL QUIET... HE'S PROB'LY UNDER PA'S BED!
HE'LL DOZE OFF UNDER THERE, AN' I'LL GET MY DERRICK BUILT.
MEANWHILE, OUT IN THE ALLEY...
STOP! IN THE NAME OF THE LAW!

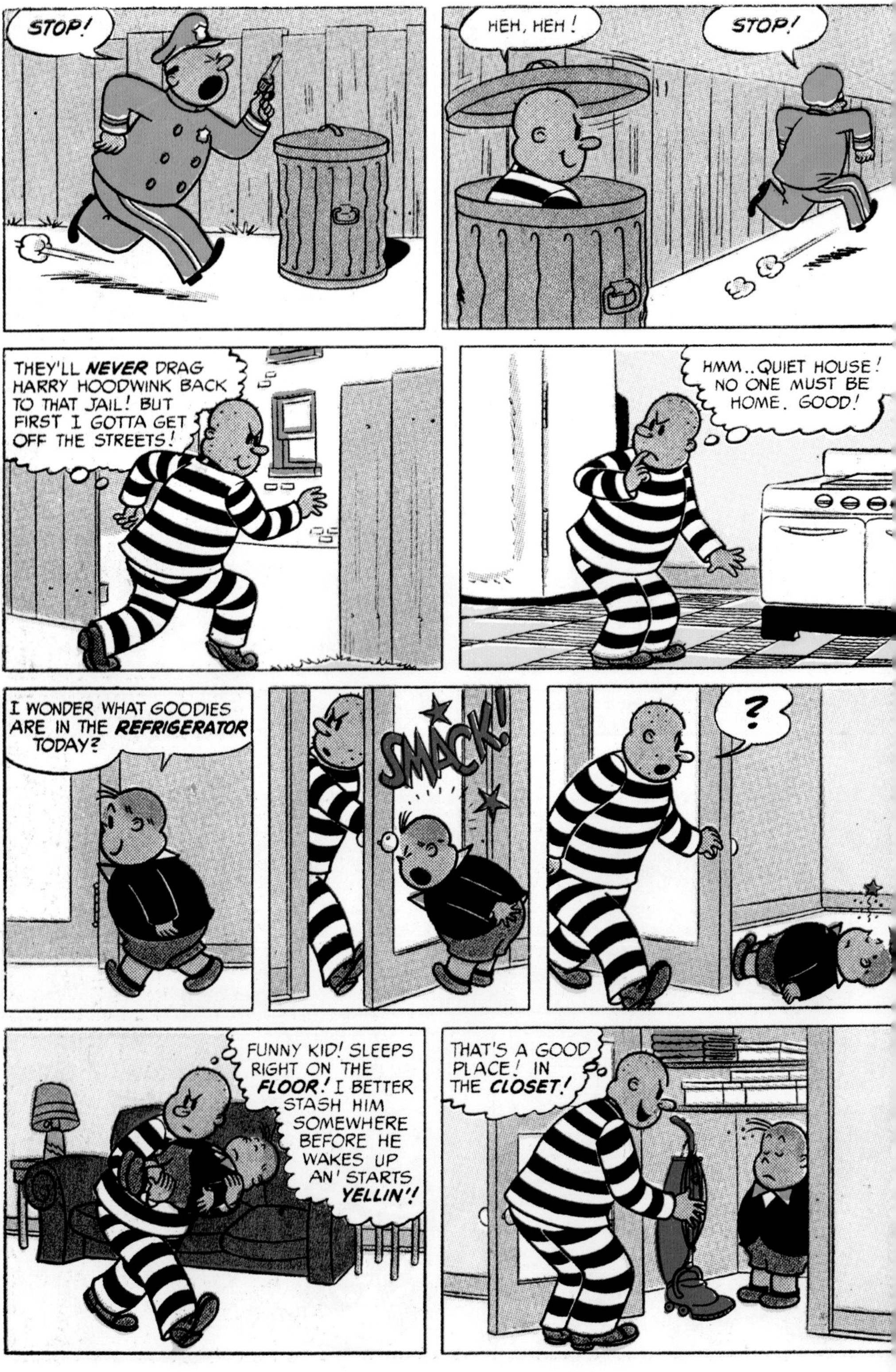
STOP!
HEH, HEH!
STOP!
THEY'LL NEVER DRAG HARRY HOODWINK BACK TO THAT JAIL! BUT FIRST I GOTTA GET OFF THE STREETS!
HMM..QUIET HOUSE! NO ONE MUST BE HOME. GOOD!
I WONDER WHAT GOODIES ARE IN THE REFRIGERATOR TODAY?
SMACK!
?
FUNNY KID! SLEEPS RIGHT ON THE FLOOR! I BETTER STASH HIM SOMEWHERE BEFORE HE WAKES UP AN' STARTS YELLIN'!
THAT'S A GOOD PLACE! IN THE CLOSET!

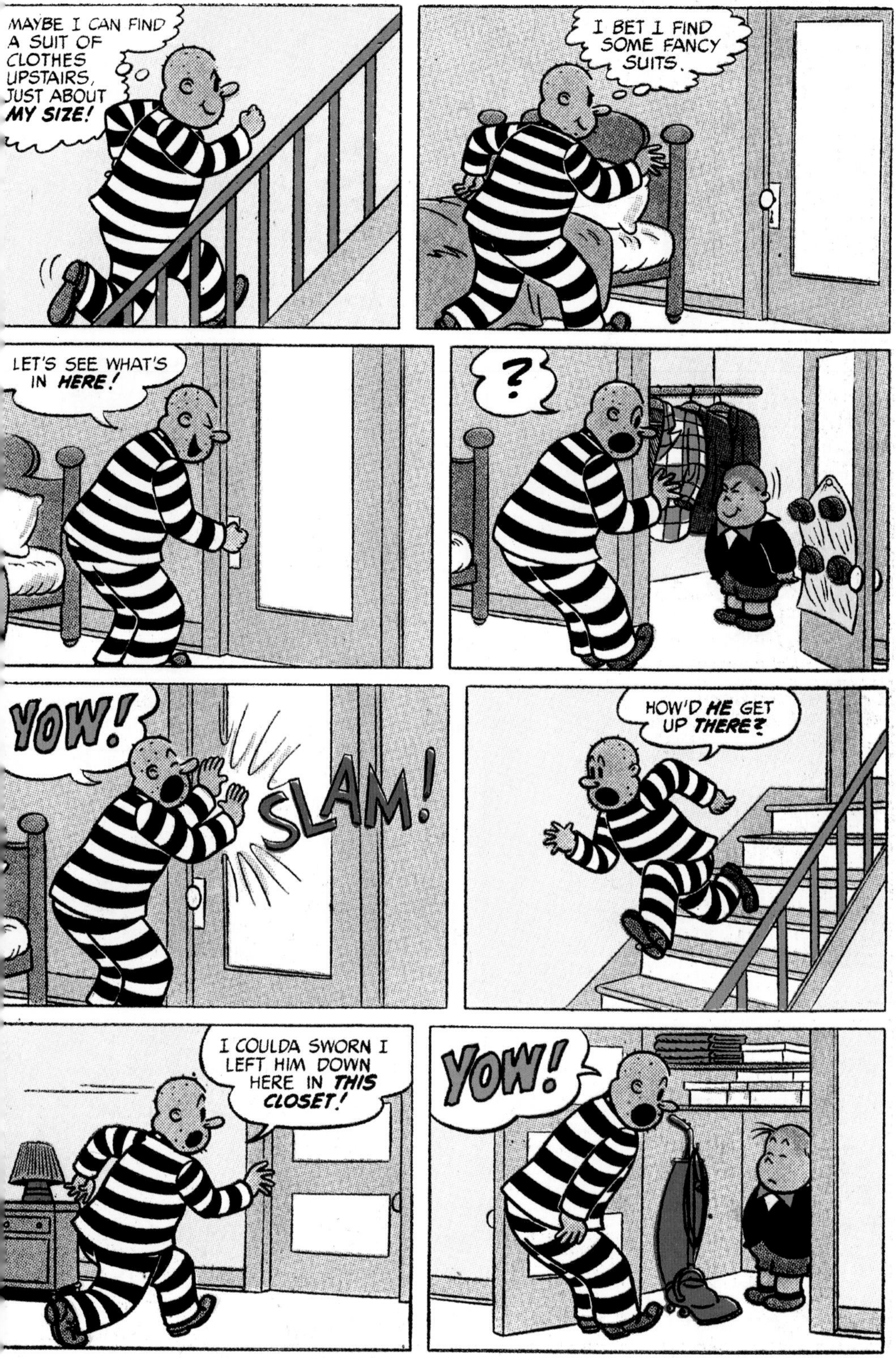
MAYBE I CAN FIND A SUIT OF CLOTHES UPSTAIRS, JUST ABOUT MY SIZE!
I BET I FIND SOME FANCY SUITS.
LET'S SEE WHAT'S IN HERE!
?
YOW!
SLAM!
HOW'D HE GET UP THERE?
I COULDA SWORN I LEFT HIM DOWN HERE IN THIS CLOSET!
YOW!

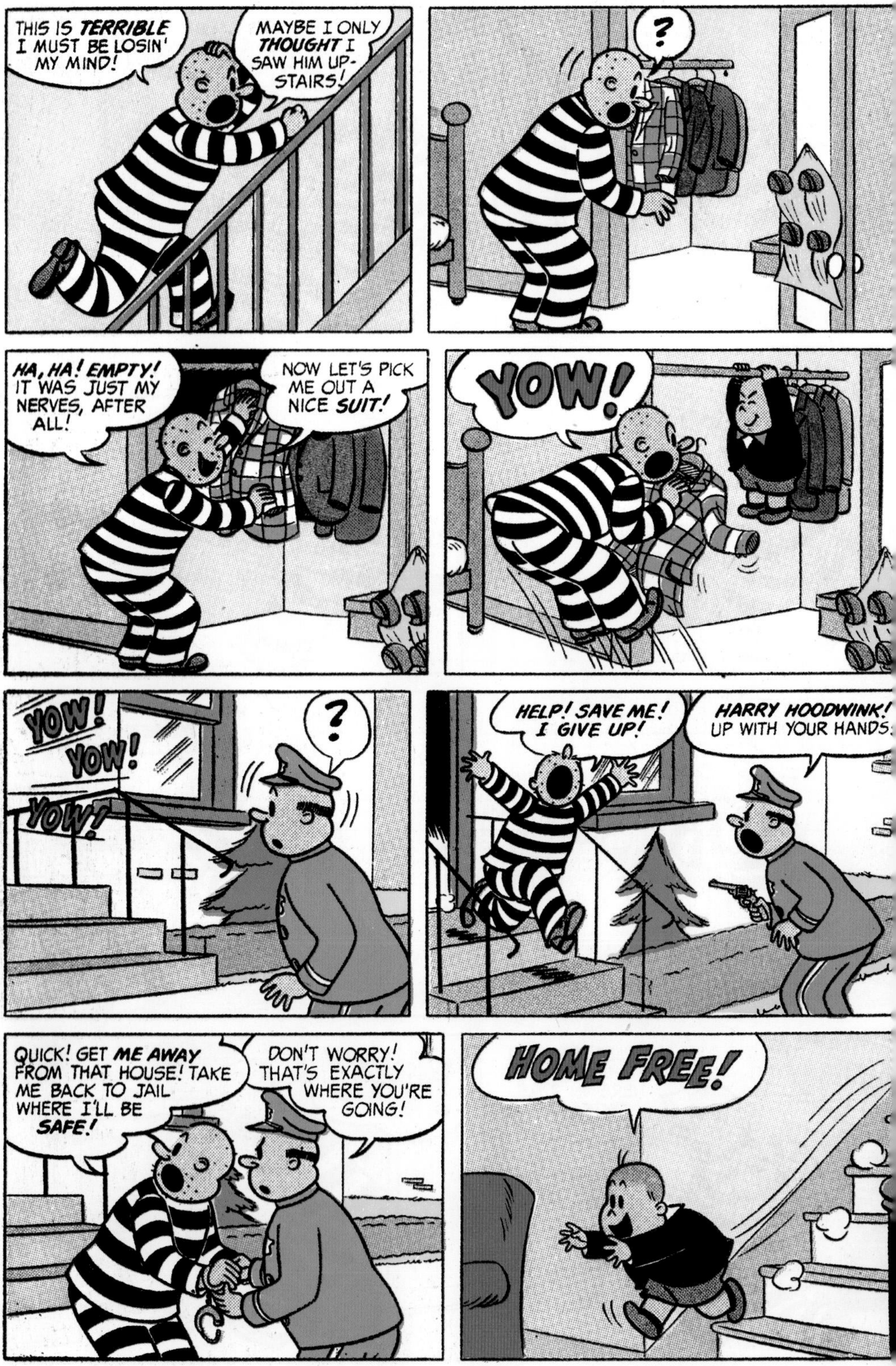
THIS IS TERRIBLE I MUST BE LOSIN' MY MIND!
MAYBE I ONLY THOUGHT I SAW HIM UP-STAIRS!
?
HA, HA! EMPTY! IT WAS JUST MY NERVES, AFTER ALL!
NOW LET'S PICK ME OUT A NICE SUIT!
YOW!
YOW! YOW! YOW!
?
HELP! SAVE ME! I GIVE UP!
HARRY HOODWINK! UP WITH YOUR HANDS!
QUICK! GET ME AWAY FROM THAT HOUSE! TAKE ME BACK TO JAIL WHERE I'LL BE SAFE!
DON'T WORRY! THAT'S EXACTLY WHERE YOU'RE GOING!
HOME FREE!

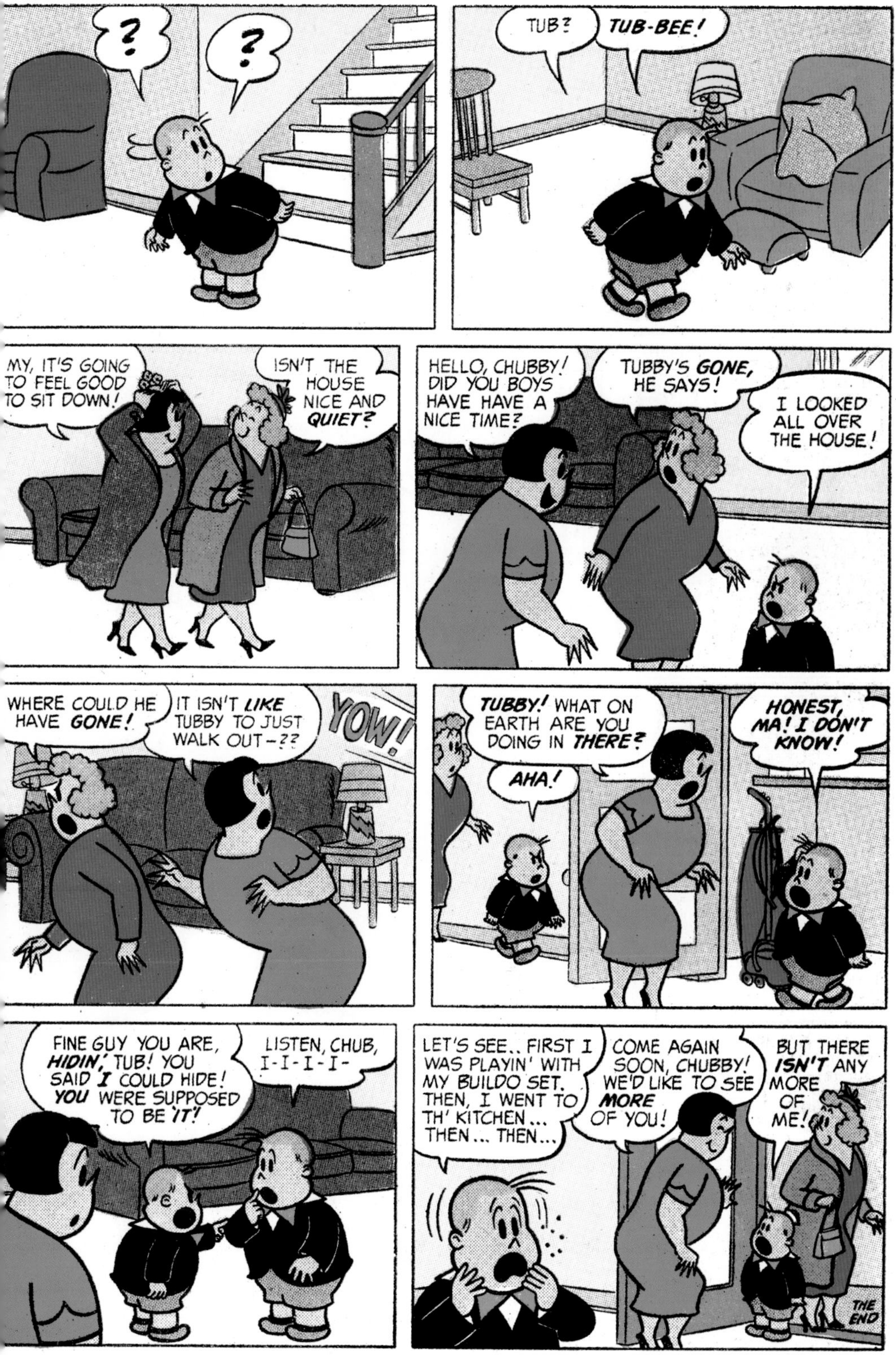
?
?
TUB?
TUB-BEE!
MY, IT'S GOING TO FEEL GOOD TO SIT DOWN!
ISN'T THE HOUSE NICE AND QUIET?
HELLO, CHUBBY! DID YOU BOYS HAVE HAVE A NICE TIME?
TUBBY'S GONE, HE SAYS!
I LOOKED ALL OVER THE HOUSE!
WHERE COULD HE HAVE GONE!
IT ISN'T LIKE TUBBY TO JUST WALK OUT-??
YOW!
TUBBY! WHAT ON EARTH ARE YOU DOING IN THERE?
AHA!
HONEST, MA! I DON'T KNOW!
FINE GUY YOU ARE, HIDIN,' TUB! YOU SAID I COULD HIDE! YOU WERE SUPPOSED TO BE 'IT'!
LISTEN, CHUB, I-I-I-I-
LET'S SEE.. FIRST I WAS PLAYIN' WITH MY BUILDO SET. THEN, I WENT TO TH' KITCHEN... THEN... THEN...
COME AGAIN SOON, CHUBBY! WE'D LIKE TO SEE MORE OF YOU!
BUT THERE ISN'T ANY MORE OF ME!
THE END

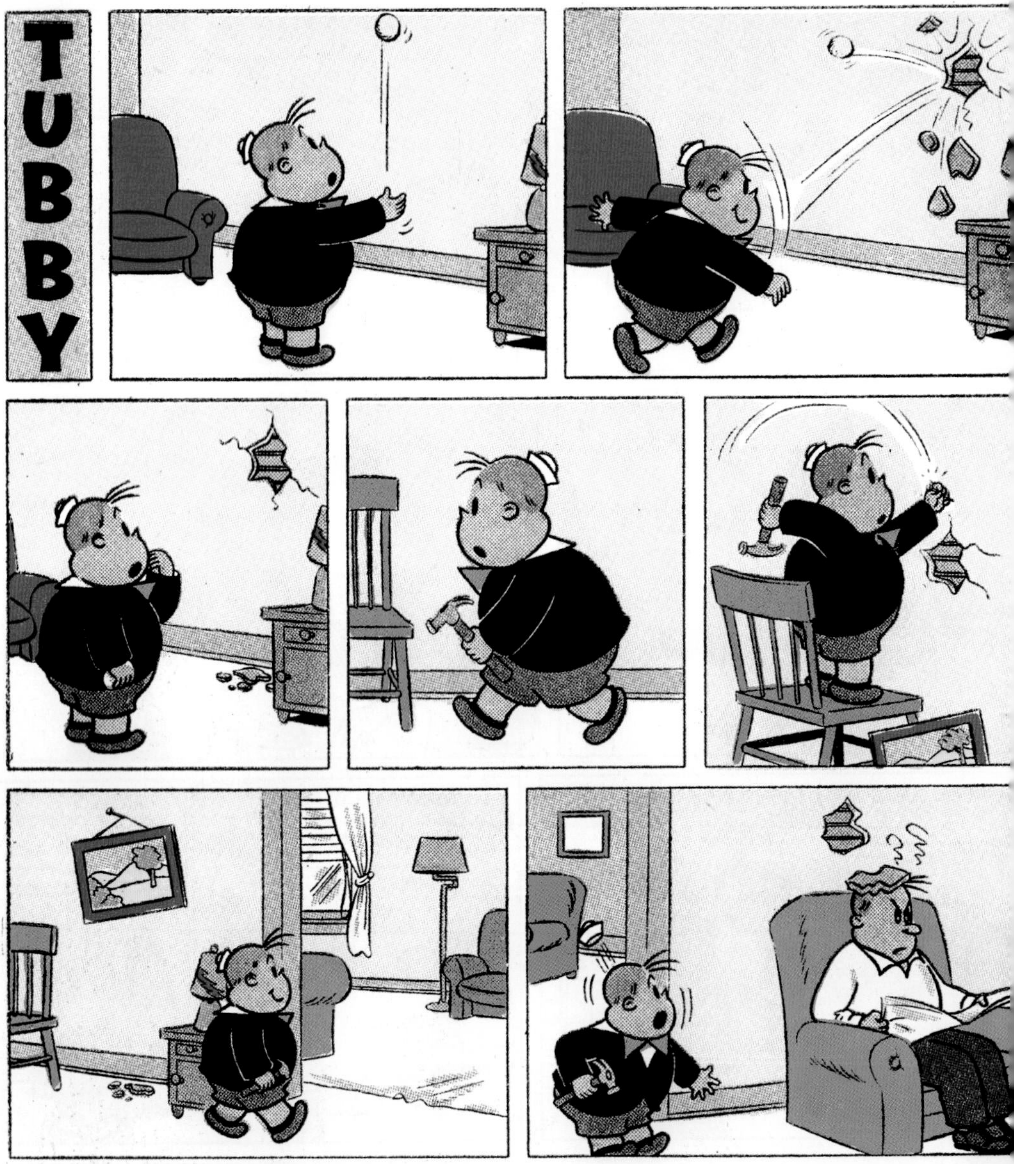
TUBBY

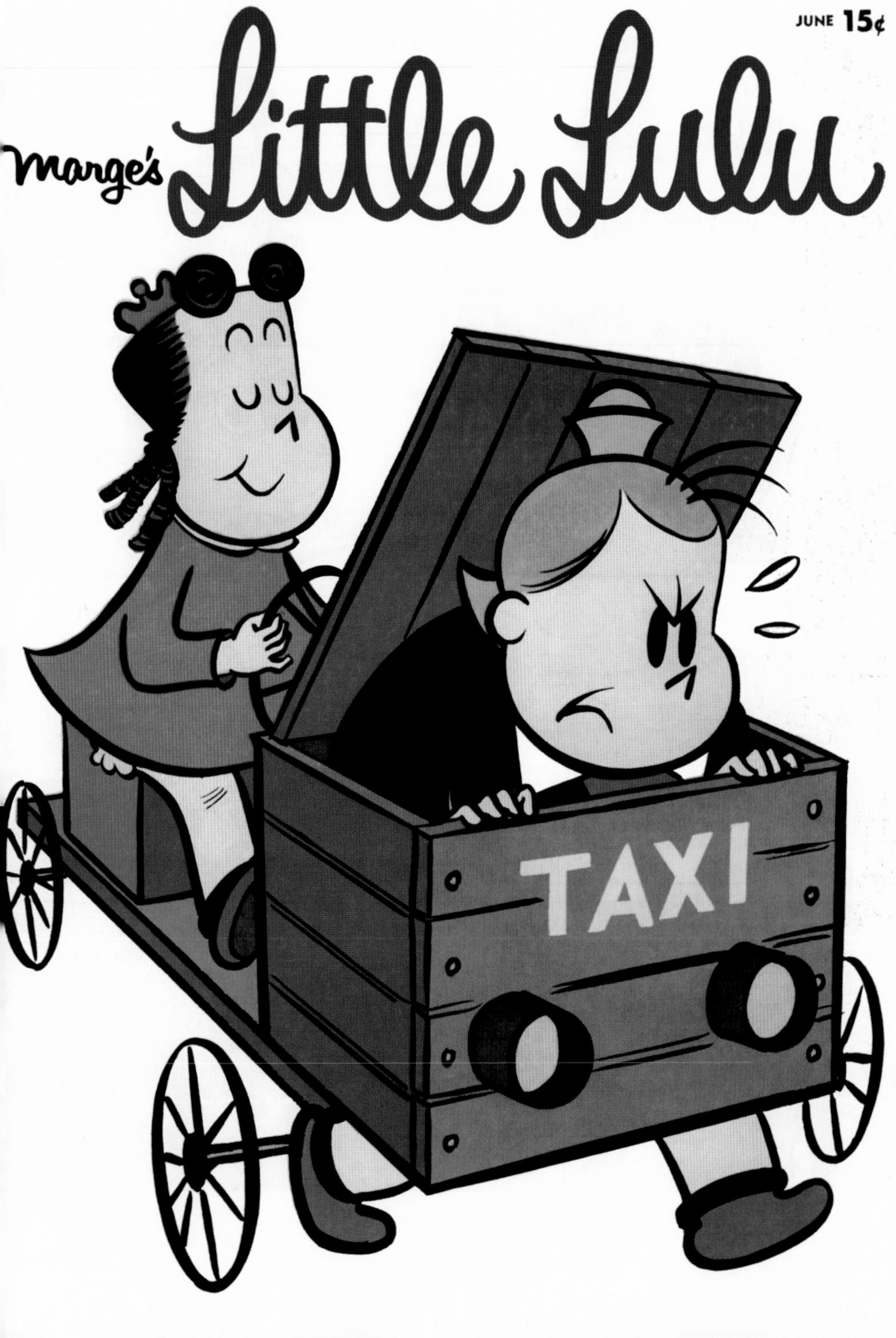

JUNE 15¢
Marge's Little Lulu
TAXI

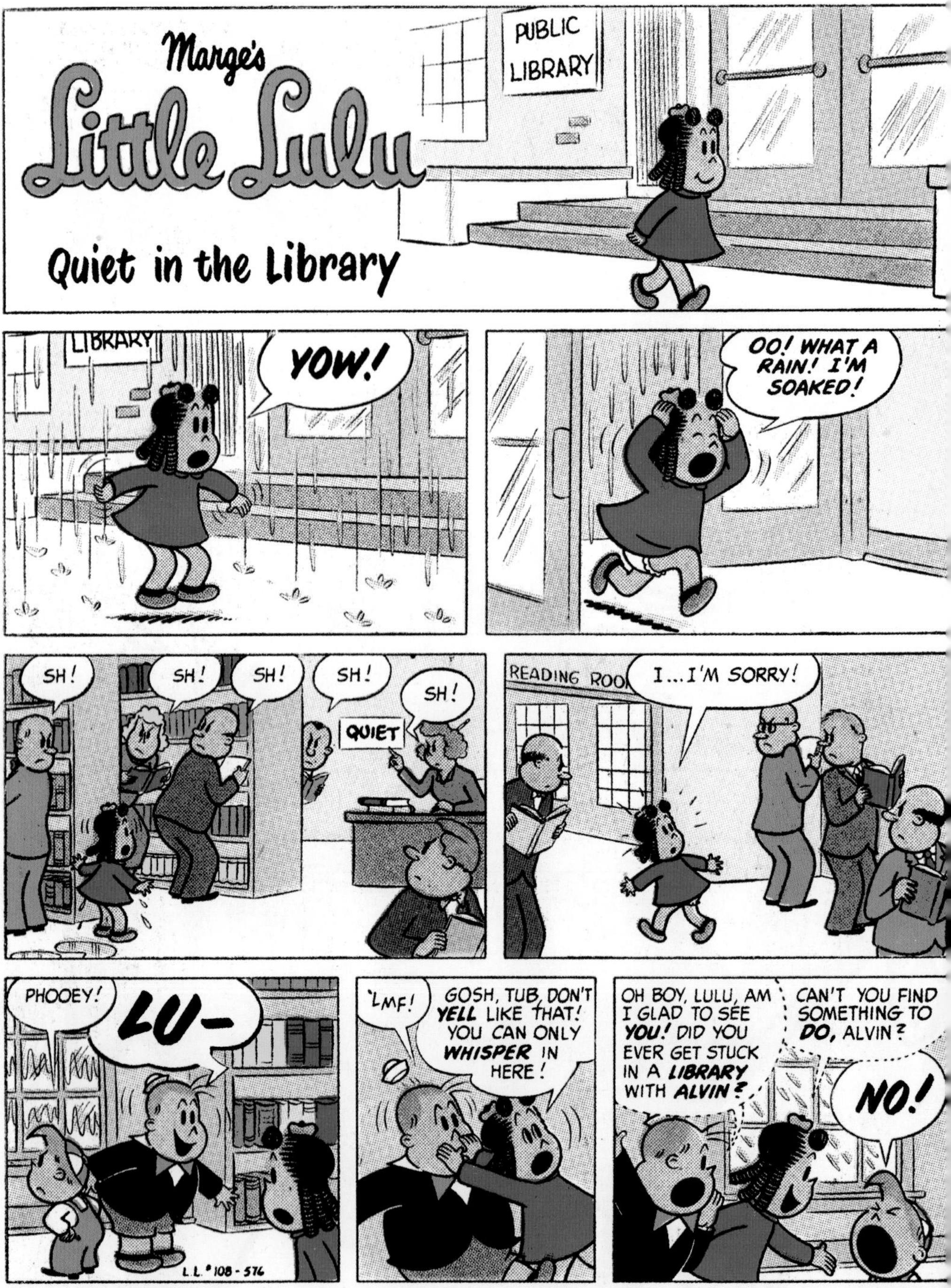
Marge's
Little Lulu
Quiet in the Library
PUBLIC LIBRARY
LIBRARY
YOW!
OO! WHAT A RAIN! I'M SOAKED!
SH!
SH!
SH!
SH!
QUIET
SH!
READING ROO
I...I'M SORRY!
PHOOEY!
LU-
L.L.°108-576
'LMF!
GOSH, TUB, DON'T YELL LIKE THAT! YOU CAN ONLY WHISPER IN HERE!
OH BOY, LULU, AM I GLAD TO SEE YOU! DID YOU EVER GET STUCK IN A LIBRARY WITH ALVIN?
CAN'T YOU FIND SOMETHING TO DO, ALVIN?
NO!

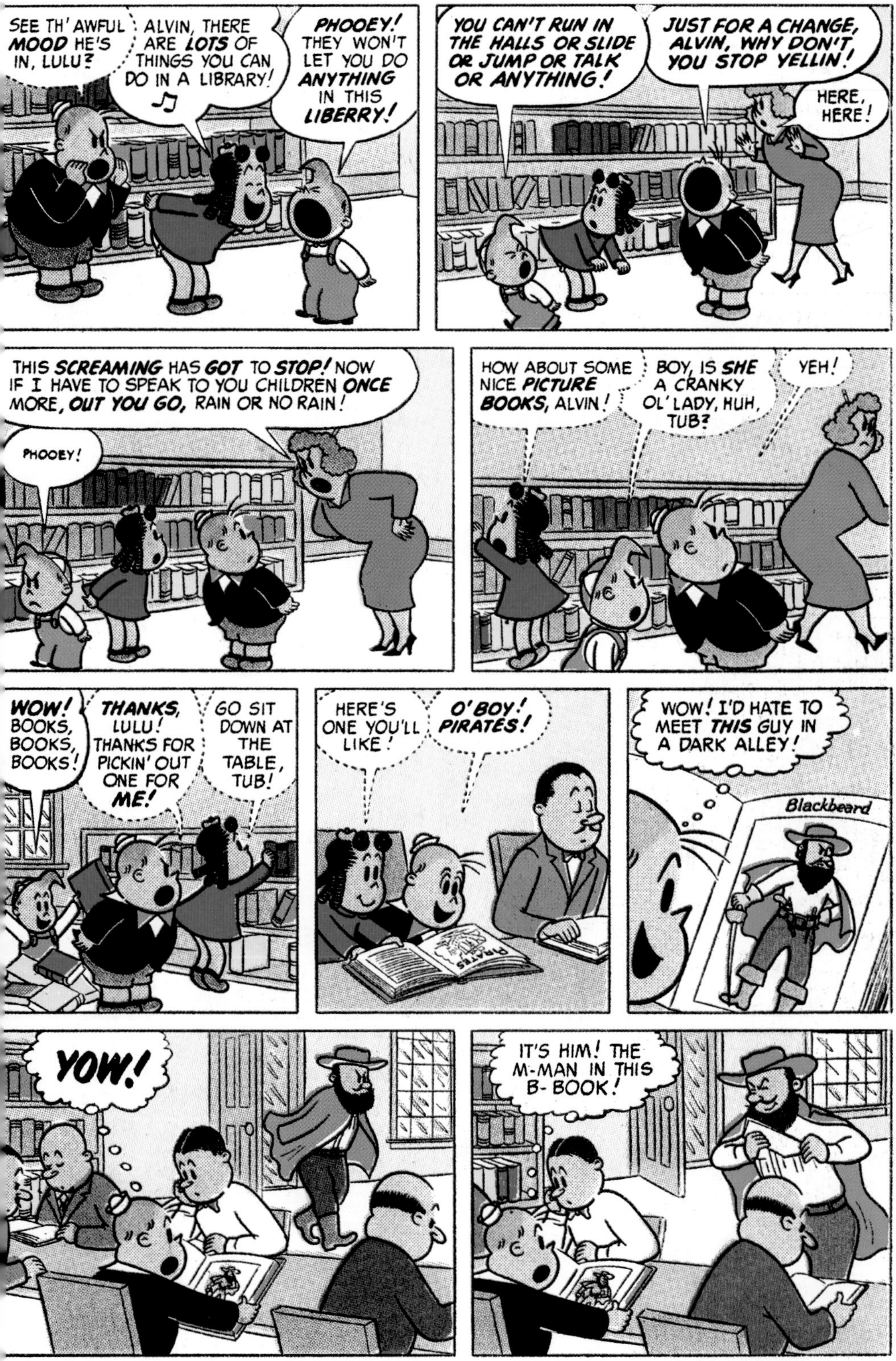
SEE TH' AWFUL MOOD HE'S IN, LULU?
ALVIN, THERE ARE LOTS OF THINGS YOU CAN DO IN A LIBRARY! ♫
PHOOEY! THEY WON'T LET YOU DO ANYTHING IN THIS LIBERRY!
YOU CAN'T RUN IN THE HALLS OR SLIDE OR JUMP OR TALK OR ANYTHING!
JUST FOR A CHANGE, ALVIN, WHY DON'T YOU STOP YELLIN'!
HERE, HERE!
THIS SCREAMING HAS GOT TO STOP! NOW IF I HAVE TO SPEAK TO YOU CHILDREN ONCE MORE, OUT YOU GO, RAIN OR NO RAIN!
PHOOEY!
HOW ABOUT SOME NICE PICTURE BOOKS, ALVIN!
BOY, IS SHE A CRANKY OL' LADY, HUH, TUB?
YEH!
WOW! BOOKS, BOOKS, BOOKS!
THANKS, LULU! THANKS FOR PICKIN' OUT ONE FOR ME!
GO SIT DOWN AT THE TABLE, TUB!
HERE'S ONE YOU'LL LIKE!
O'BOY! PIRATES!
PIRATES
WOW! I'D HATE TO MEET THIS GUY IN A DARK ALLEY!
Blackbeard
YOW!
IT'S HIM! THE M-MAN IN THIS B-BOOK!

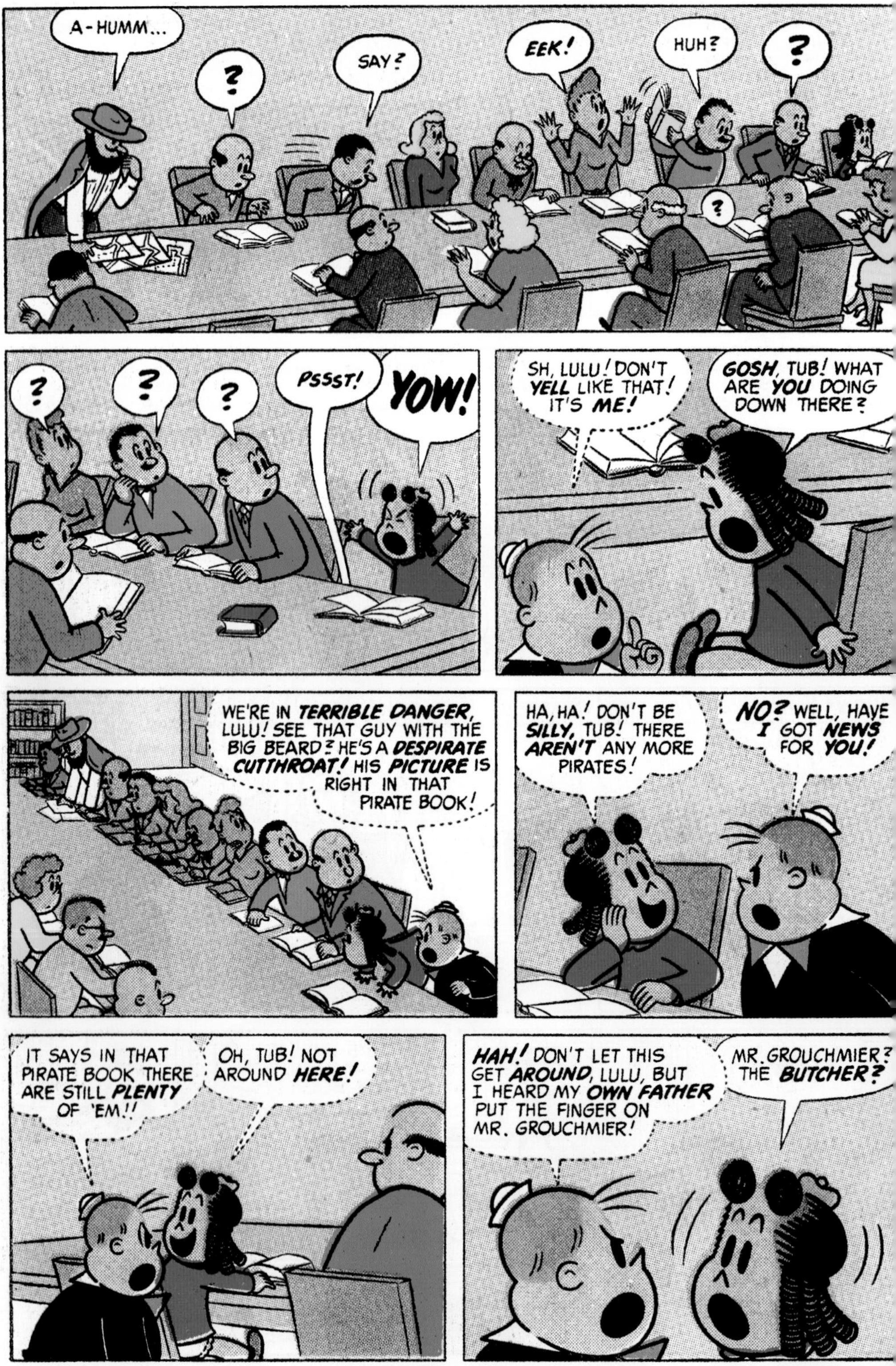
A-HUMM...
?
SAY?
EEK!
HUH?
?
?
?
?
?
PSSST!
YOW!
SH, LULU! DON'T YELL LIKE THAT! IT'S ME!
GOSH, TUB! WHAT ARE YOU DOING DOWN THERE?
WE'RE IN TERRIBLE DANGER, LULU! SEE THAT GUY WITH THE BIG BEARD? HE'S A DESPIRATE CUTTHROAT! HIS PICTURE IS RIGHT IN THAT PIRATE BOOK!
HA, HA! DON'T BE SILLY, TUB! THERE AREN'T ANY MORE PIRATES!
NO? WELL, HAVE I GOT NEWS FOR YOU!
IT SAYS IN THAT PIRATE BOOK THERE ARE STILL PLENTY OF 'EM!!
OH, TUB! NOT AROUND HERE!
HAH! DON'T LET THIS GET AROUND, LULU, BUT I HEARD MY OWN FATHER PUT THE FINGER ON MR. GROUCHMIER!
MR. GROUCHMIER? THE BUTCHER?

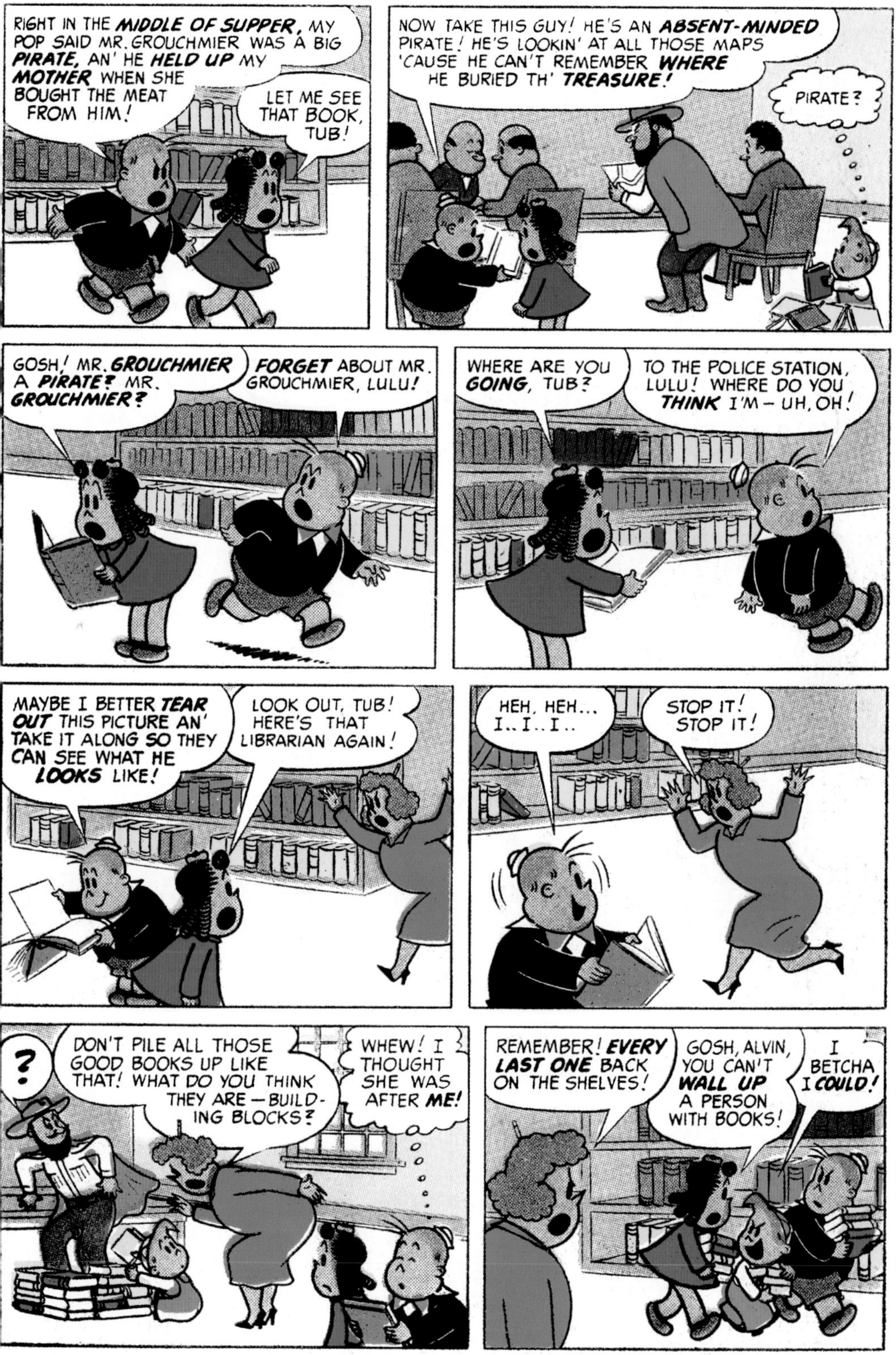
RIGHT IN THE MIDDLE OF SUPPER, MY POP SAID MR. GROUCHMIER WAS A BIG PIRATE, AN' HE HELD UP MY MOTHER WHEN SHE BOUGHT THE MEAT FROM HIM!
LET ME SEE THAT BOOK, TUB!
NOW TAKE THIS GUY! HE'S AN ABSENT-MINDED PIRATE! HE'S LOOKIN' AT ALL THOSE MAPS 'CAUSE HE CAN'T REMEMBER WHERE HE BURIED TH' TREASURE!
PIRATE?
GOSH! MR. GROUCHMIER A PIRATE? MR. GROUCHMIER?
FORGET ABOUT MR. GROUCHMIER, LULU!
WHERE ARE YOU GOING, TUB?
TO THE POLICE STATION, LULU! WHERE DO YOU THINK I'M — UH, OH!
MAYBE I BETTER TEAR OUT THIS PICTURE AN' TAKE IT ALONG SO THEY CAN SEE WHAT HE LOOKS LIKE!
LOOK OUT, TUB! HERE'S THAT LIBRARIAN AGAIN!
HEH, HEH... I..I..I..
STOP IT! STOP IT!
?
DON'T PILE ALL THOSE GOOD BOOKS UP LIKE THAT! WHAT DO YOU THINK THEY ARE — BUILD-ING BLOCKS?
WHEW! I THOUGHT SHE WAS AFTER ME!
REMEMBER! EVERY LAST ONE BACK ON THE SHELVES!
GOSH, ALVIN, YOU CAN'T WALL UP A PERSON WITH BOOKS!
I BETCHA I COULD!

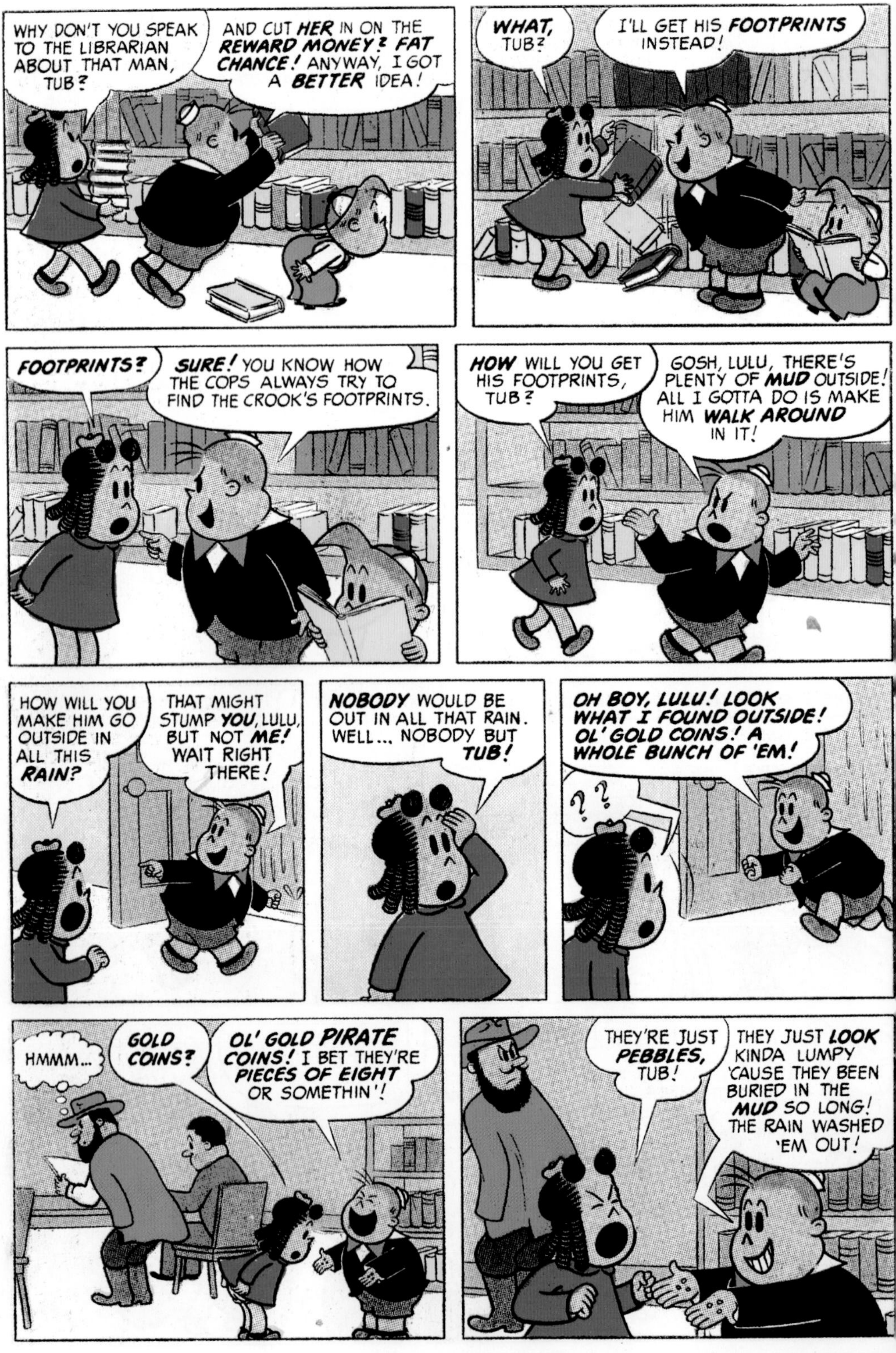
WHY DON'T YOU SPEAK TO THE LIBRARIAN ABOUT THAT MAN, TUB?
AND CUT HER IN ON THE REWARD MONEY? FAT CHANCE! ANYWAY, I GOT A BETTER IDEA!
WHAT, TUB?
I'LL GET HIS FOOTPRINTS INSTEAD!
FOOTPRINTS?
SURE! YOU KNOW HOW THE COPS ALWAYS TRY TO FIND THE CROOK'S FOOTPRINTS.
HOW WILL YOU GET HIS FOOTPRINTS, TUB?
GOSH, LULU, THERE'S PLENTY OF MUD OUTSIDE! ALL I GOTTA DO IS MAKE HIM WALK AROUND IN IT!
HOW WILL YOU MAKE HIM GO OUTSIDE IN ALL THIS RAIN?
THAT MIGHT STUMP YOU, LULU, BUT NOT ME! WAIT RIGHT THERE!
NOBODY WOULD BE OUT IN ALL THAT RAIN. WELL... NOBODY BUT TUB!
OH BOY, LULU! LOOK WHAT I FOUND OUTSIDE! OL' GOLD COINS! A WHOLE BUNCH OF 'EM!
HMMM...
GOLD COINS?
OL' GOLD PIRATE COINS! I BET THEY'RE PIECES OF EIGHT OR SOMETHIN'!
THEY'RE JUST PEBBLES, TUB!
THEY JUST LOOK KINDA LUMPY 'CAUSE THEY BEEN BURIED IN THE MUD SO LONG! THE RAIN WASHED 'EM OUT!

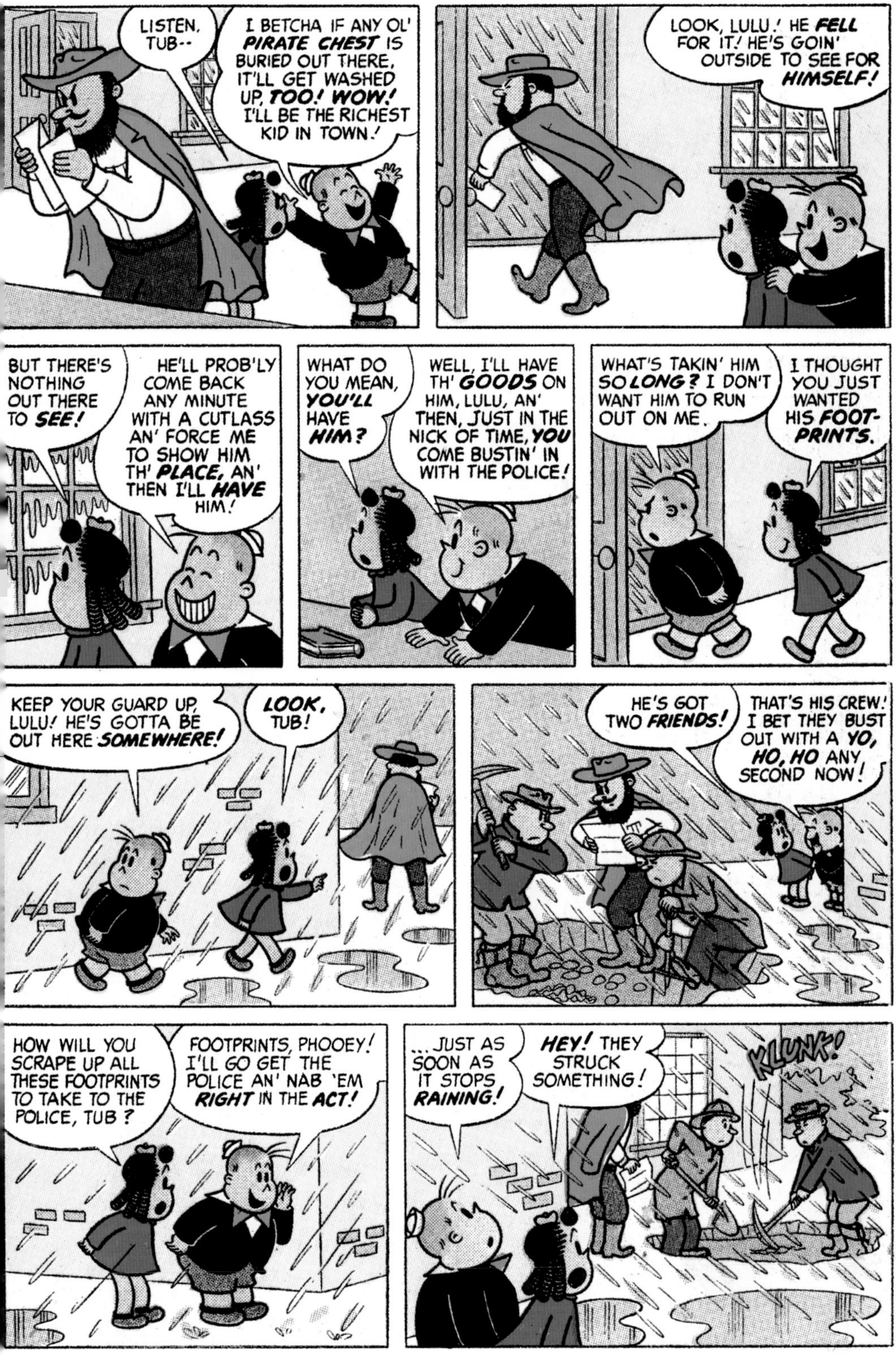
LISTEN, TUB--
I BETCHA IF ANY OL' PIRATE CHEST IS BURIED OUT THERE, IT'LL GET WASHED UP, TOO! WOW! I'LL BE THE RICHEST KID IN TOWN!
LOOK, LULU! HE FELL FOR IT! HE'S GOIN' OUTSIDE TO SEE FOR HIMSELF!
BUT THERE'S NOTHING OUT THERE TO SEE!
HE'LL PROB'LY COME BACK ANY MINUTE WITH A CUTLASS AN' FORCE ME TO SHOW HIM TH' PLACE, AN' THEN I'LL HAVE HIM!
WHAT DO YOU MEAN, YOU'LL HAVE HIM?
WELL, I'LL HAVE TH' GOODS ON HIM, LULU, AN' THEN, JUST IN THE NICK OF TIME, YOU COME BUSTIN' IN WITH THE POLICE!
WHAT'S TAKIN' HIM SO LONG? I DON'T WANT HIM TO RUN OUT ON ME.
I THOUGHT YOU JUST WANTED HIS FOOT-PRINTS.
KEEP YOUR GUARD UP, LULU! HE'S GOTTA BE OUT HERE SOMEWHERE!
LOOK, TUB!
HE'S GOT TWO FRIENDS!
THAT'S HIS CREW! I BET THEY BUST OUT WITH A YO, HO, HO ANY SECOND NOW!
HOW WILL YOU SCRAPE UP ALL THESE FOOTPRINTS TO TAKE TO THE POLICE, TUB?
FOOTPRINTS, PHOOEY! I'LL GO GET THE POLICE AN' NAB 'EM RIGHT IN THE ACT!
...JUST AS SOON AS IT STOPS RAINING!
HEY! THEY STRUCK SOMETHING!
KLUNK!

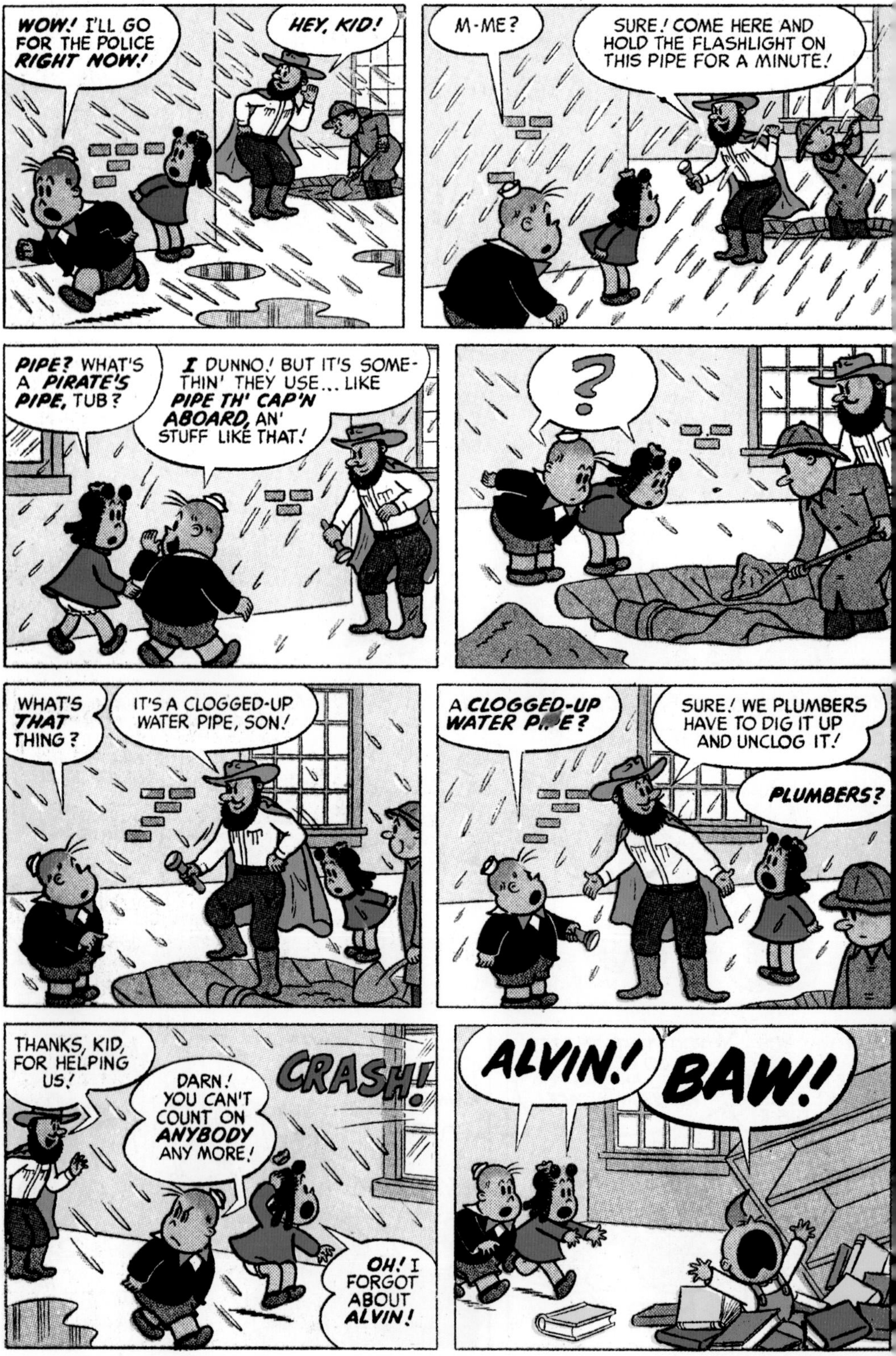
WOW! I'LL GO FOR THE POLICE RIGHT NOW!
HEY, KID!
M-ME?
SURE! COME HERE AND HOLD THE FLASHLIGHT ON THIS PIPE FOR A MINUTE!
PIPE? WHAT'S A PIRATE'S PIPE, TUB?
I DUNNO! BUT IT'S SOME-THIN' THEY USE... LIKE PIPE TH' CAP'N ABOARD, AN' STUFF LIKE THAT!
?
WHAT'S THAT THING?
IT'S A CLOGGED-UP WATER PIPE, SON!
A CLOGGED-UP WATER PIPE?
SURE! WE PLUMBERS HAVE TO DIG IT UP AND UNCLOG IT!
PLUMBERS?
THANKS, KID, FOR HELPING US!
DARN! YOU CAN'T COUNT ON ANYBODY ANY MORE!
CRASH!
OH! I FORGOT ABOUT ALVIN!
ALVIN!
BAW!

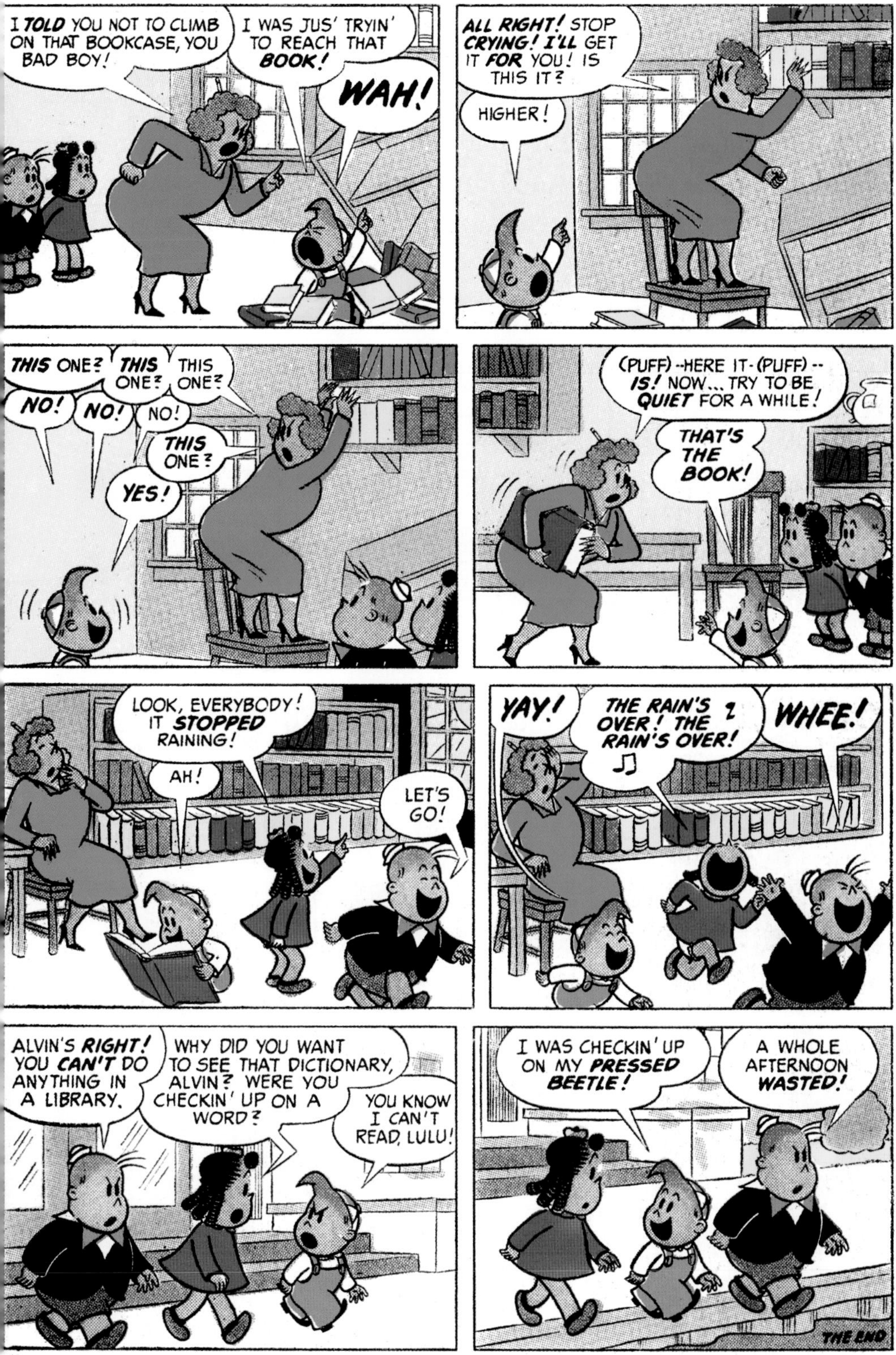
I **TOLD** YOU NOT TO CLIMB ON THAT BOOKCASE, YOU BAD BOY!
I WAS JUS' TRYIN' TO REACH THAT **BOOK**!
WAH!
ALL RIGHT! STOP **CRYING! I'LL** GET IT **FOR** YOU! IS THIS IT?
HIGHER!
THIS ONE?
NO!
THIS ONE?
NO!
THIS ONE?
NO!
THIS ONE?
YES!
(PUFF) --HERE IT- (PUFF) -- **IS!** NOW... TRY TO BE **QUIET** FOR A WHILE!
THAT'S THE BOOK!
LOOK, EVERYBODY! IT **STOPPED** RAINING!
AH!
LET'S GO!
YAY!
THE RAIN'S OVER! THE RAIN'S OVER!
WHEE!
ALVIN'S **RIGHT!** YOU **CAN'T** DO ANYTHING IN A LIBRARY.
WHY DID YOU WANT TO SEE THAT DICTIONARY, ALVIN? WERE YOU CHECKIN' UP ON A WORD?
YOU KNOW I CAN'T READ, LULU!
I WAS CHECKIN' UP ON MY **PRESSED BEETLE!**
A WHOLE AFTERNOON **WASTED!**
THE END

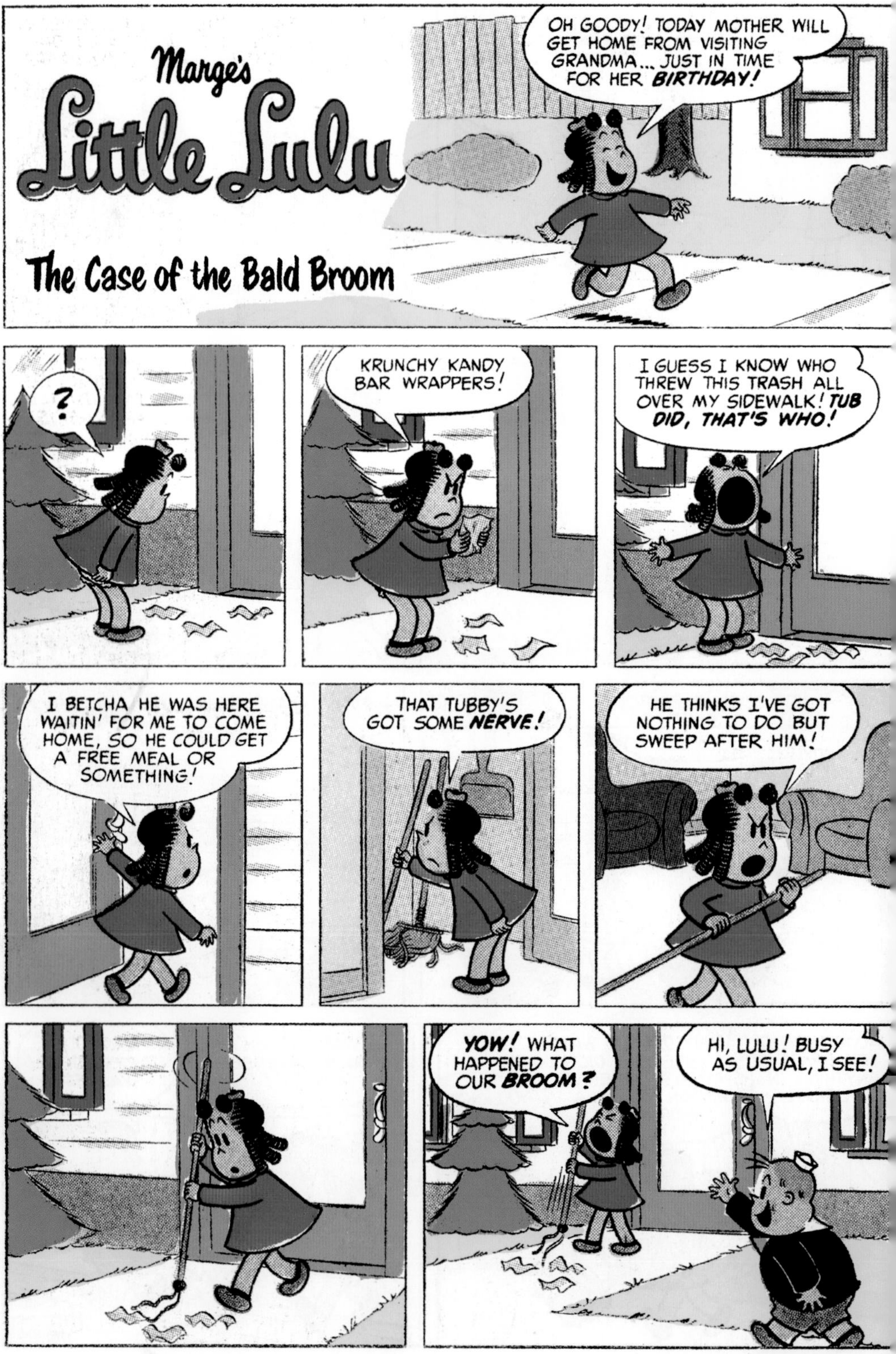
Marge's Little Lulu
The Case of the Bald Broom
OH GOODY! TODAY MOTHER WILL GET HOME FROM VISITING GRANDMA... JUST IN TIME FOR HER BIRTHDAY!
?
KRUNCHY KANDY BAR WRAPPERS!
I GUESS I KNOW WHO THREW THIS TRASH ALL OVER MY SIDEWALK! TUB DID, THAT'S WHO!
I BETCHA HE WAS HERE WAITIN' FOR ME TO COME HOME, SO HE COULD GET A FREE MEAL OR SOMETHING!
THAT TUBBY'S GOT SOME NERVE!
HE THINKS I'VE GOT NOTHING TO DO BUT SWEEP AFTER HIM!
YOW! WHAT HAPPENED TO OUR BROOM?
HI, LULU! BUSY AS USUAL, I SEE!

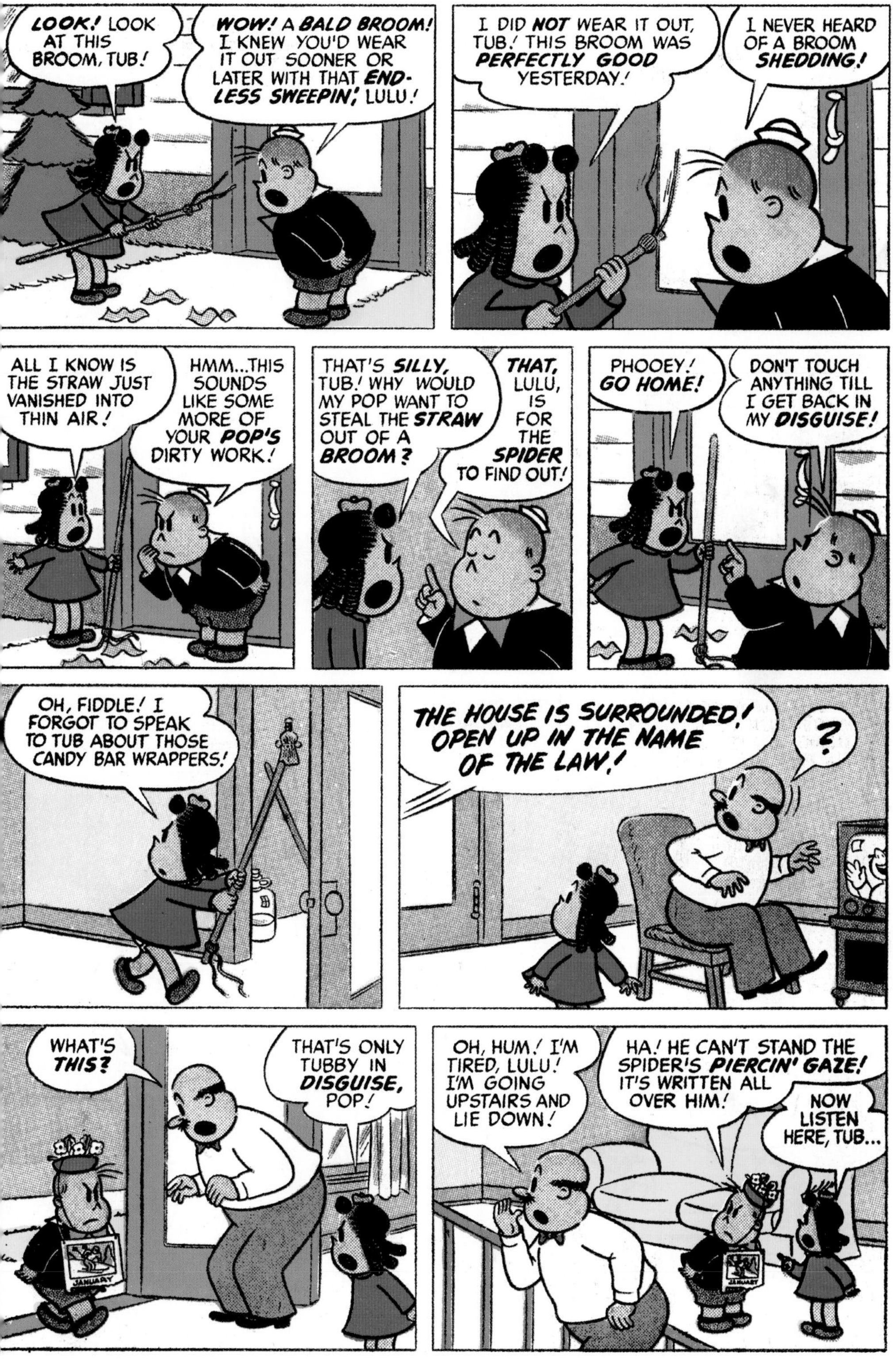
LOOK! LOOK AT THIS BROOM, TUB!
WOW! A BALD BROOM! I KNEW YOU'D WEAR IT OUT SOONER OR LATER WITH THAT ENDLESS SWEEPIN', LULU!
I DID NOT WEAR IT OUT, TUB! THIS BROOM WAS PERFECTLY GOOD YESTERDAY!
I NEVER HEARD OF A BROOM SHEDDING!
ALL I KNOW IS THE STRAW JUST VANISHED INTO THIN AIR!
HMM...THIS SOUNDS LIKE SOME MORE OF YOUR POP'S DIRTY WORK!
THAT'S SILLY, TUB! WHY WOULD MY POP WANT TO STEAL THE STRAW OUT OF A BROOM?
THAT, LULU, IS FOR THE SPIDER TO FIND OUT!
PHOOEY! GO HOME!
DON'T TOUCH ANYTHING TILL I GET BACK IN MY DISGUISE!
OH, FIDDLE! I FORGOT TO SPEAK TO TUB ABOUT THOSE CANDY BAR WRAPPERS!
THE HOUSE IS SURROUNDED! OPEN UP IN THE NAME OF THE LAW!
?
WHAT'S THIS?
THAT'S ONLY TUBBY IN DISGUISE, POP!
OH, HUM! I'M TIRED, LULU! I'M GOING UPSTAIRS AND LIE DOWN!
HA! HE CAN'T STAND THE SPIDER'S PIERCIN' GAZE! IT'S WRITTEN ALL OVER HIM!
NOW LISTEN HERE, TUB...

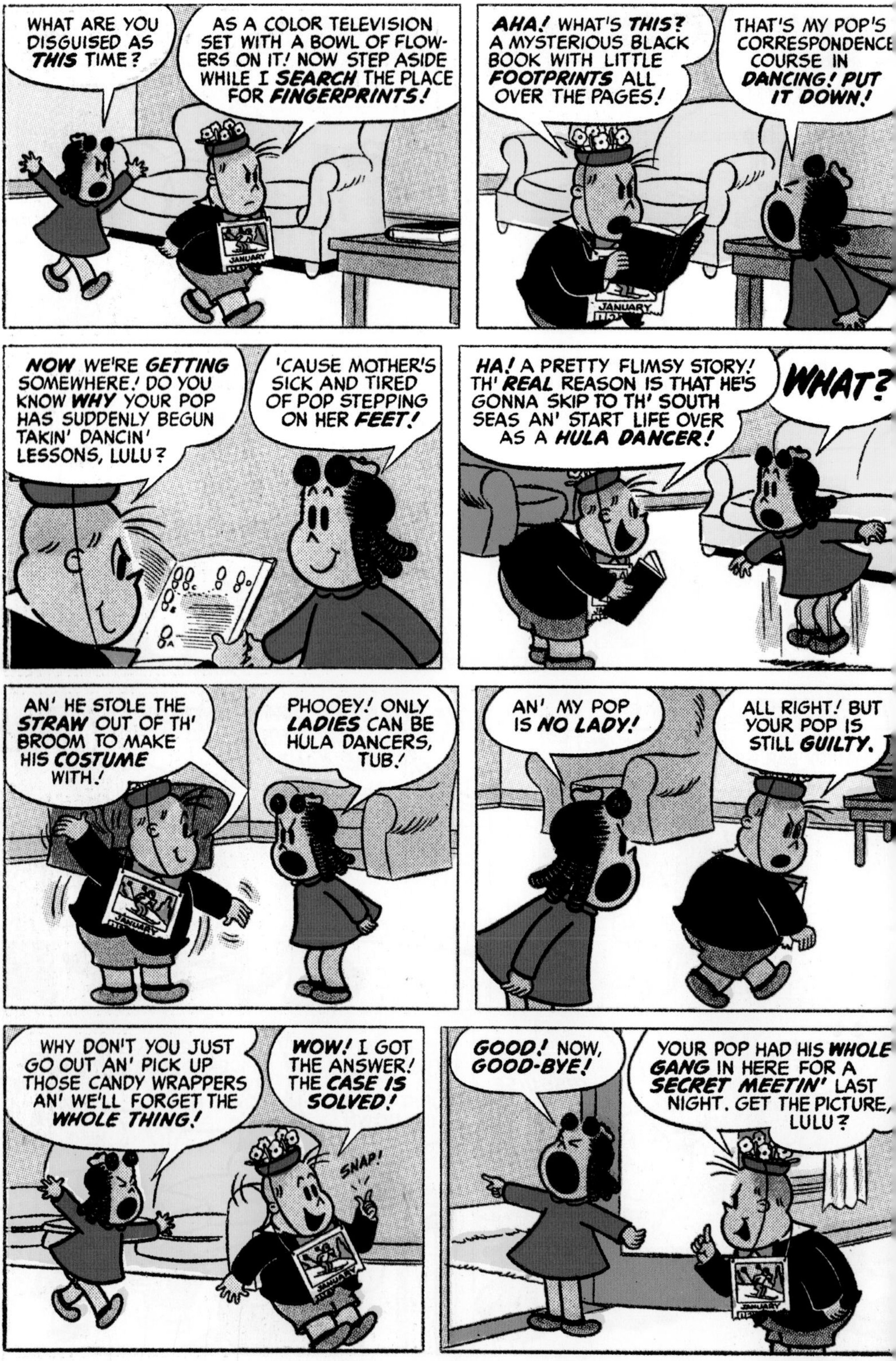
WHAT ARE YOU DISGUISED AS THIS TIME?
AS A COLOR TELEVISION SET WITH A BOWL OF FLOWERS ON IT! NOW STEP ASIDE WHILE I SEARCH THE PLACE FOR FINGERPRINTS!
JANUARY
AHA! WHAT'S THIS? A MYSTERIOUS BLACK BOOK WITH LITTLE FOOTPRINTS ALL OVER THE PAGES!
THAT'S MY POP'S CORRESPONDENCE COURSE IN DANCING! PUT IT DOWN!
JANUARY
NOW WE'RE GETTING SOMEWHERE! DO YOU KNOW WHY YOUR POP HAS SUDDENLY BEGUN TAKIN' DANCIN' LESSONS, LULU?
'CAUSE MOTHER'S SICK AND TIRED OF POP STEPPING ON HER FEET!
HA! A PRETTY FLIMSY STORY! TH' REAL REASON IS THAT HE'S GONNA SKIP TO TH' SOUTH SEAS AN' START LIFE OVER AS A HULA DANCER!
WHAT?
AN' HE STOLE THE STRAW OUT OF TH' BROOM TO MAKE HIS COSTUME WITH!
PHOOEY! ONLY LADIES CAN BE HULA DANCERS, TUB!
JANUARY
AN' MY POP IS NO LADY!
ALL RIGHT! BUT YOUR POP IS STILL GUILTY.
WHY DON'T YOU JUST GO OUT AN' PICK UP THOSE CANDY WRAPPERS AN' WE'LL FORGET THE WHOLE THING!
WOW! I GOT THE ANSWER! THE CASE IS SOLVED!
SNAP!
JANUARY
GOOD! NOW, GOOD-BYE!
YOUR POP HAD HIS WHOLE GANG IN HERE FOR A SECRET MEETIN' LAST NIGHT. GET THE PICTURE, LULU?
JANUARY

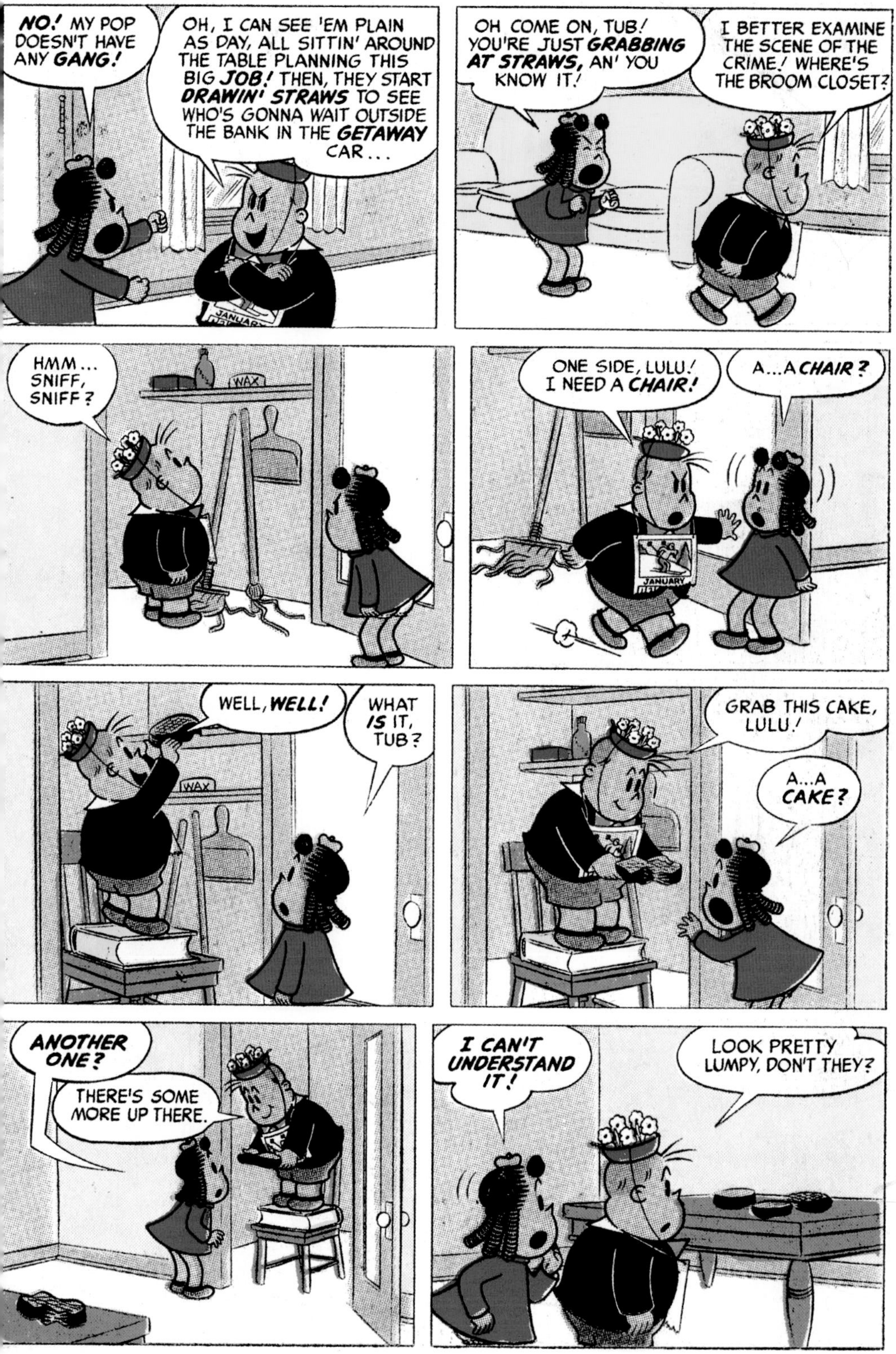
NO! MY POP DOESN'T HAVE ANY GANG!
OH, I CAN SEE 'EM PLAIN AS DAY, ALL SITTIN' AROUND THE TABLE PLANNING THIS BIG JOB! THEN, THEY START DRAWIN' STRAWS TO SEE WHO'S GONNA WAIT OUTSIDE THE BANK IN THE GETAWAY CAR...
OH COME ON, TUB! YOU'RE JUST GRABBING AT STRAWS, AN' YOU KNOW IT!
I BETTER EXAMINE THE SCENE OF THE CRIME! WHERE'S THE BROOM CLOSET?
HMM... SNIFF, SNIFF?
WAX
ONE SIDE, LULU! I NEED A CHAIR!
A...A CHAIR?
JANUARY
WELL, WELL!
WHAT IS IT, TUB?
WAX
GRAB THIS CAKE, LULU!
A...A CAKE?
ANOTHER ONE?
THERE'S SOME MORE UP THERE.
I CAN'T UNDERSTAND IT!
LOOK PRETTY LUMPY, DON'T THEY?

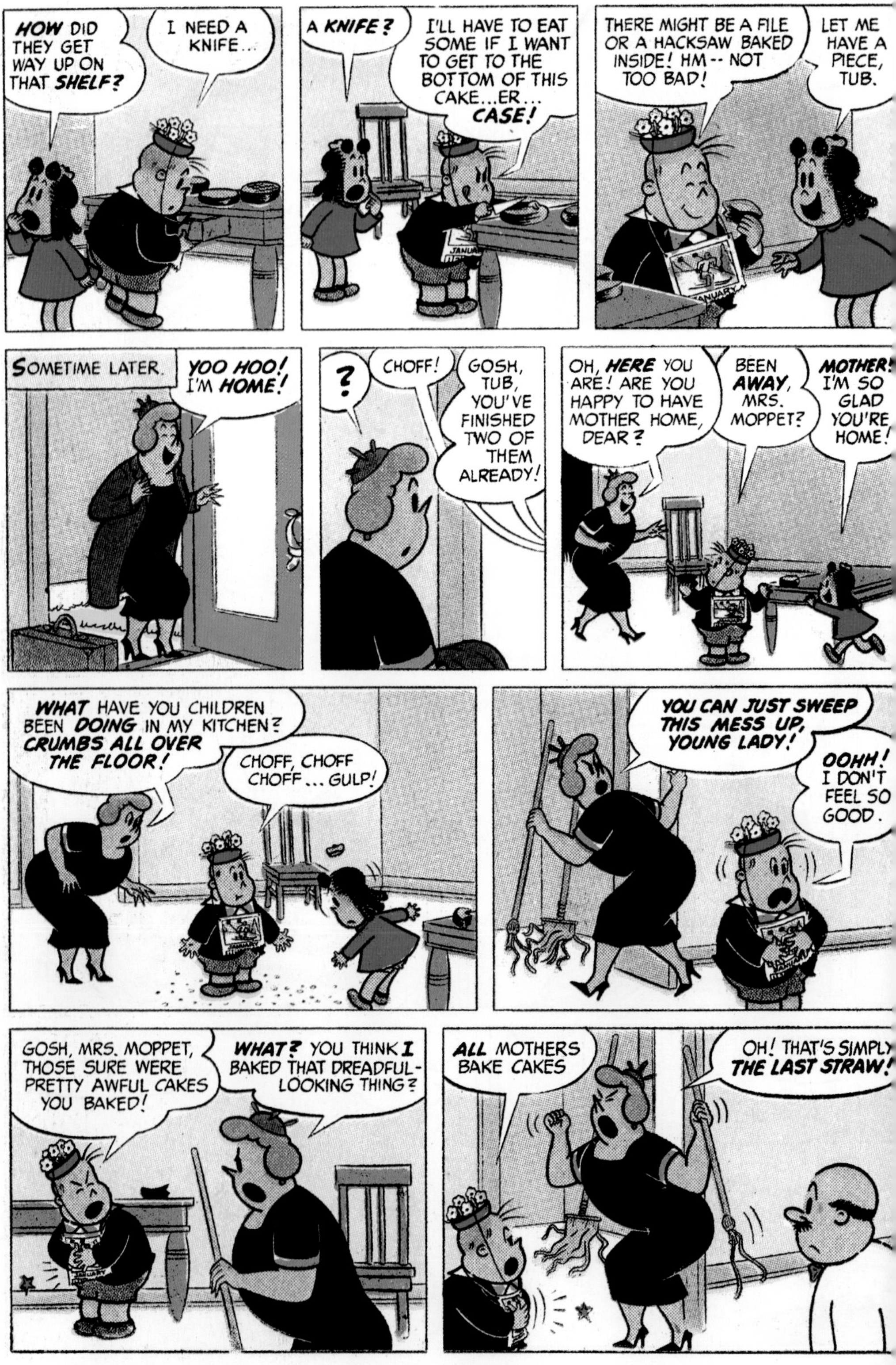

HOW DID THEY GET WAY UP ON THAT SHELF?
I NEED A KNIFE...
A KNIFE?
I'LL HAVE TO EAT SOME IF I WANT TO GET TO THE BOTTOM OF THIS CAKE...ER... CASE!
THERE MIGHT BE A FILE OR A HACKSAW BAKED INSIDE! HM -- NOT TOO BAD!
LET ME HAVE A PIECE, TUB.
SOMETIME LATER.
YOO HOO! I'M HOME!
?
CHOFF!
GOSH, TUB, YOU'VE FINISHED TWO OF THEM ALREADY!
OH, HERE YOU ARE! ARE YOU HAPPY TO HAVE MOTHER HOME, DEAR?
BEEN AWAY, MRS. MOPPET?
MOTHER! I'M SO GLAD YOU'RE HOME!
WHAT HAVE YOU CHILDREN BEEN DOING IN MY KITCHEN? CRUMBS ALL OVER THE FLOOR!
CHOFF, CHOFF CHOFF ... GULP!
YOU CAN JUST SWEEP THIS MESS UP, YOUNG LADY!
OOHH! I DON'T FEEL SO GOOD.
GOSH, MRS. MOPPET, THOSE SURE WERE PRETTY AWFUL CAKES YOU BAKED!
WHAT? YOU THINK I BAKED THAT DREADFUL-LOOKING THING?
ALL MOTHERS BAKE CAKES
OH! THAT'S SIMPLY THE LAST STRAW!

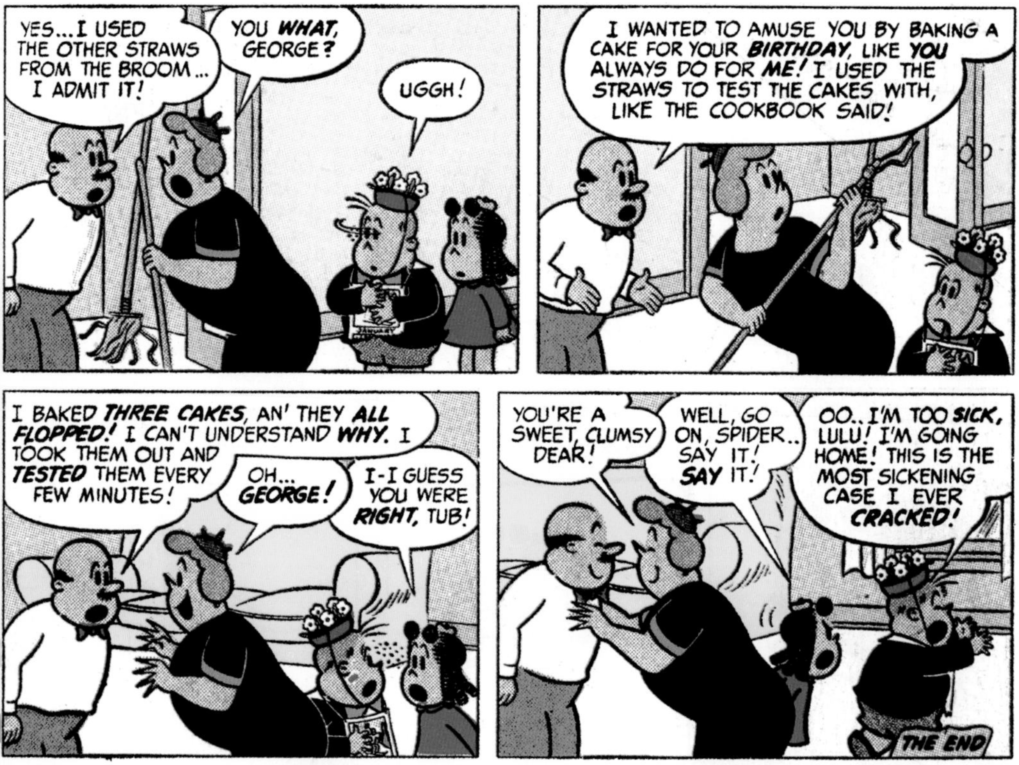
YES...I USED THE OTHER STRAWS FROM THE BROOM... I ADMIT IT!
YOU WHAT, GEORGE?
UGGH!
I WANTED TO AMUSE YOU BY BAKING A CAKE FOR YOUR BIRTHDAY, LIKE YOU ALWAYS DO FOR ME! I USED THE STRAWS TO TEST THE CAKES WITH, LIKE THE COOKBOOK SAID!
I BAKED THREE CAKES, AN' THEY ALL FLOPPED! I CAN'T UNDERSTAND WHY. I TOOK THEM OUT AND TESTED THEM EVERY FEW MINUTES!
OH... GEORGE!
I-I GUESS YOU WERE RIGHT, TUB!
YOU'RE A SWEET, CLUMSY DEAR!
WELL, GO ON, SPIDER.. SAY IT! SAY IT!
OO.. I'M TOO SICK, LULU! I'M GOING HOME! THIS IS THE MOST SICKENING CASE I EVER CRACKED!
THE END

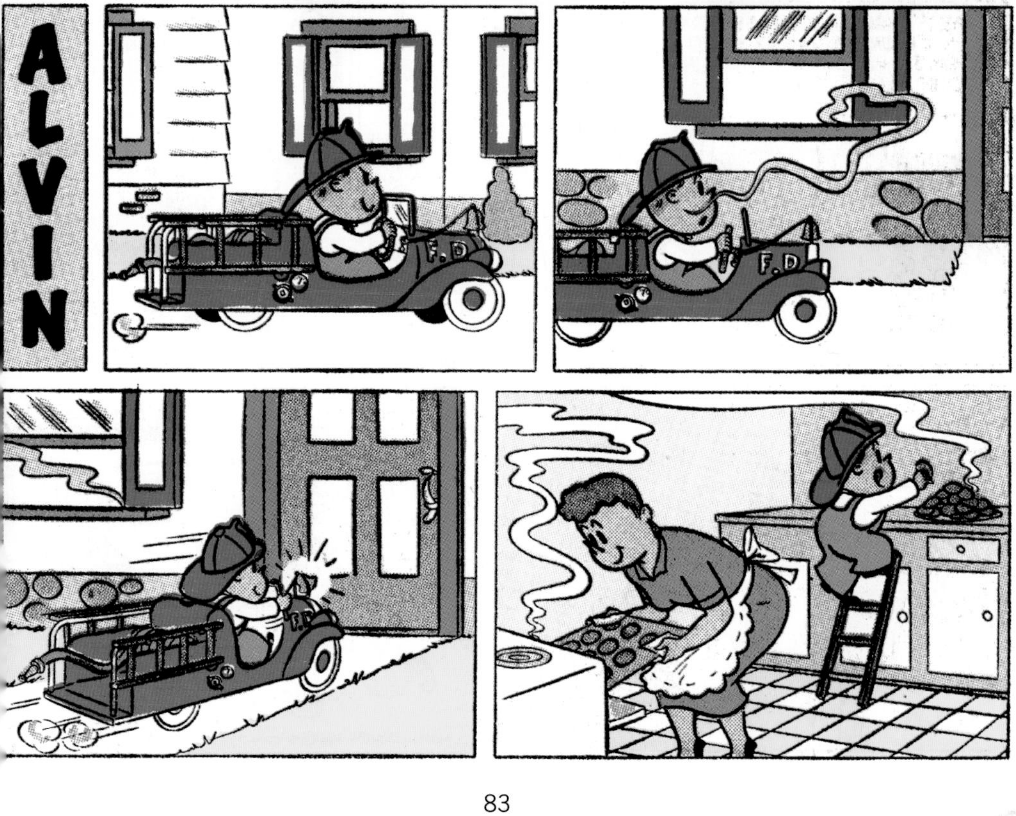
ALVIN
F.D.

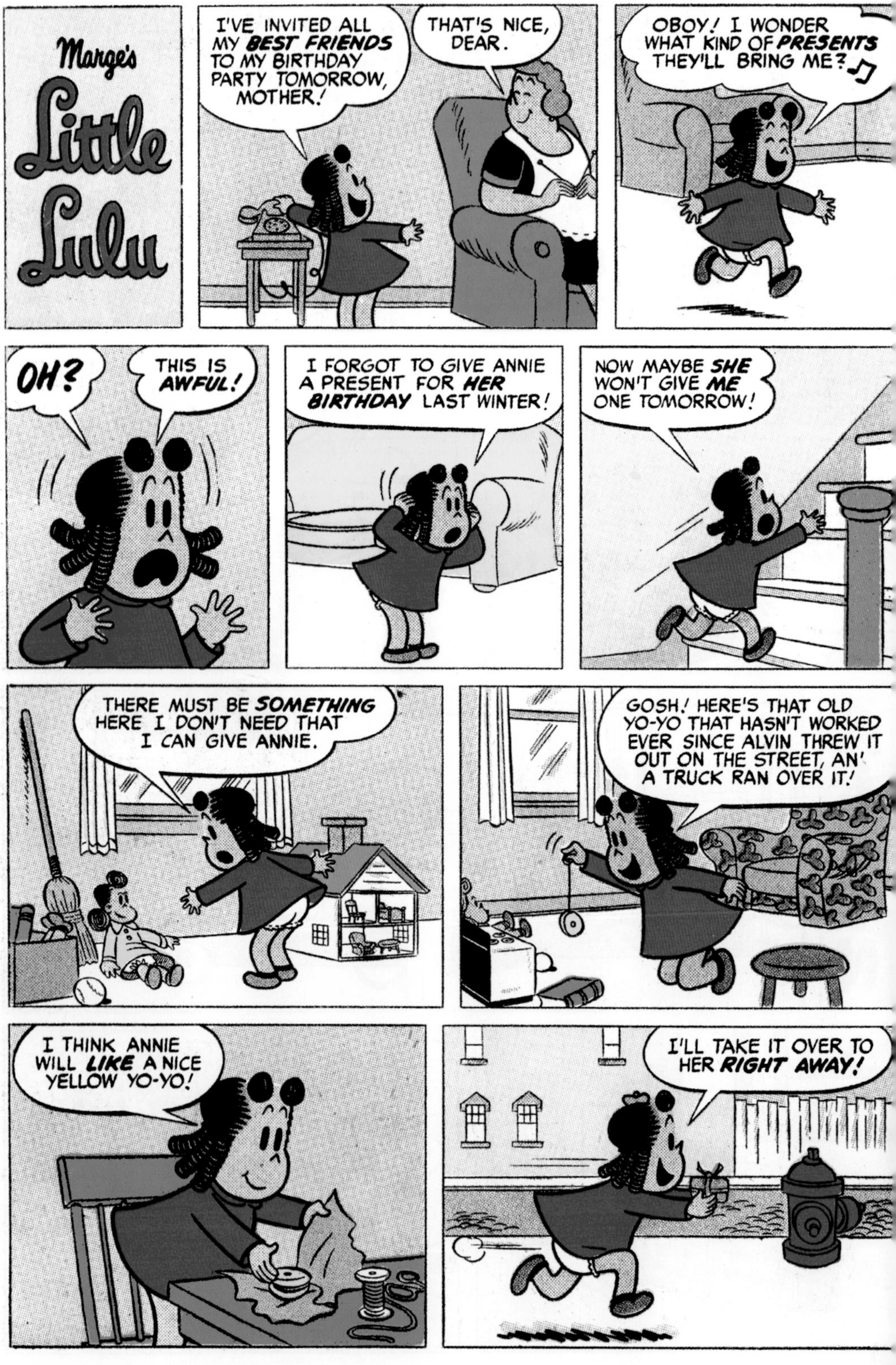
Marge's Little Lulu
I'VE INVITED ALL MY BEST FRIENDS TO MY BIRTHDAY PARTY TOMORROW, MOTHER!
THAT'S NICE, DEAR.
OBOY! I WONDER WHAT KIND OF PRESENTS THEY'LL BRING ME?
OH?
THIS IS AWFUL!
I FORGOT TO GIVE ANNIE A PRESENT FOR HER BIRTHDAY LAST WINTER!
NOW MAYBE SHE WON'T GIVE ME ONE TOMORROW!
THERE MUST BE SOMETHING HERE I DON'T NEED THAT I CAN GIVE ANNIE.
GOSH! HERE'S THAT OLD YO-YO THAT HASN'T WORKED EVER SINCE ALVIN THREW IT OUT ON THE STREET, AN' A TRUCK RAN OVER IT!
I THINK ANNIE WILL LIKE A NICE YELLOW YO-YO!
I'LL TAKE IT OVER TO HER RIGHT AWAY!

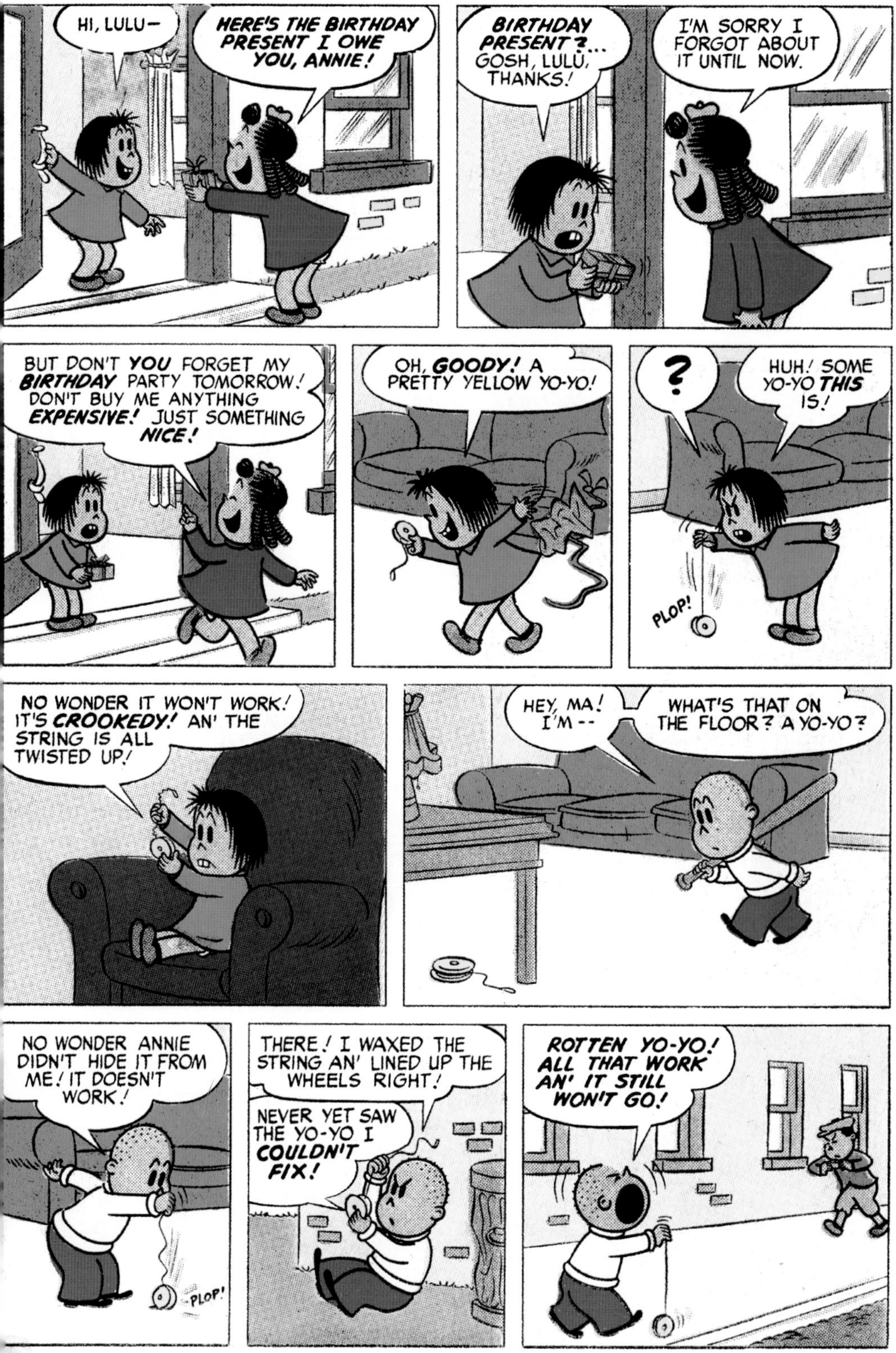
HI, LULU—
HERE'S THE BIRTHDAY PRESENT I OWE YOU, ANNIE!
BIRTHDAY PRESENT?... GOSH, LULU, THANKS!
I'M SORRY I FORGOT ABOUT IT UNTIL NOW.
BUT DON'T YOU FORGET MY BIRTHDAY PARTY TOMORROW! DON'T BUY ME ANYTHING EXPENSIVE! JUST SOMETHING NICE!
OH, GOODY! A PRETTY YELLOW YO-YO!
?
HUH! SOME YO-YO THIS IS!
PLOP!
NO WONDER IT WON'T WORK! IT'S CROOKEDY! AN' THE STRING IS ALL TWISTED UP!
HEY, MA! I'M --
WHAT'S THAT ON THE FLOOR? A YO-YO?
NO WONDER ANNIE DIDN'T HIDE IT FROM ME! IT DOESN'T WORK!
PLOP!
THERE! I WAXED THE STRING AN' LINED UP THE WHEELS RIGHT!
NEVER YET SAW THE YO-YO I COULDN'T FIX!
ROTTEN YO-YO! ALL THAT WORK AN' IT STILL WON'T GO!

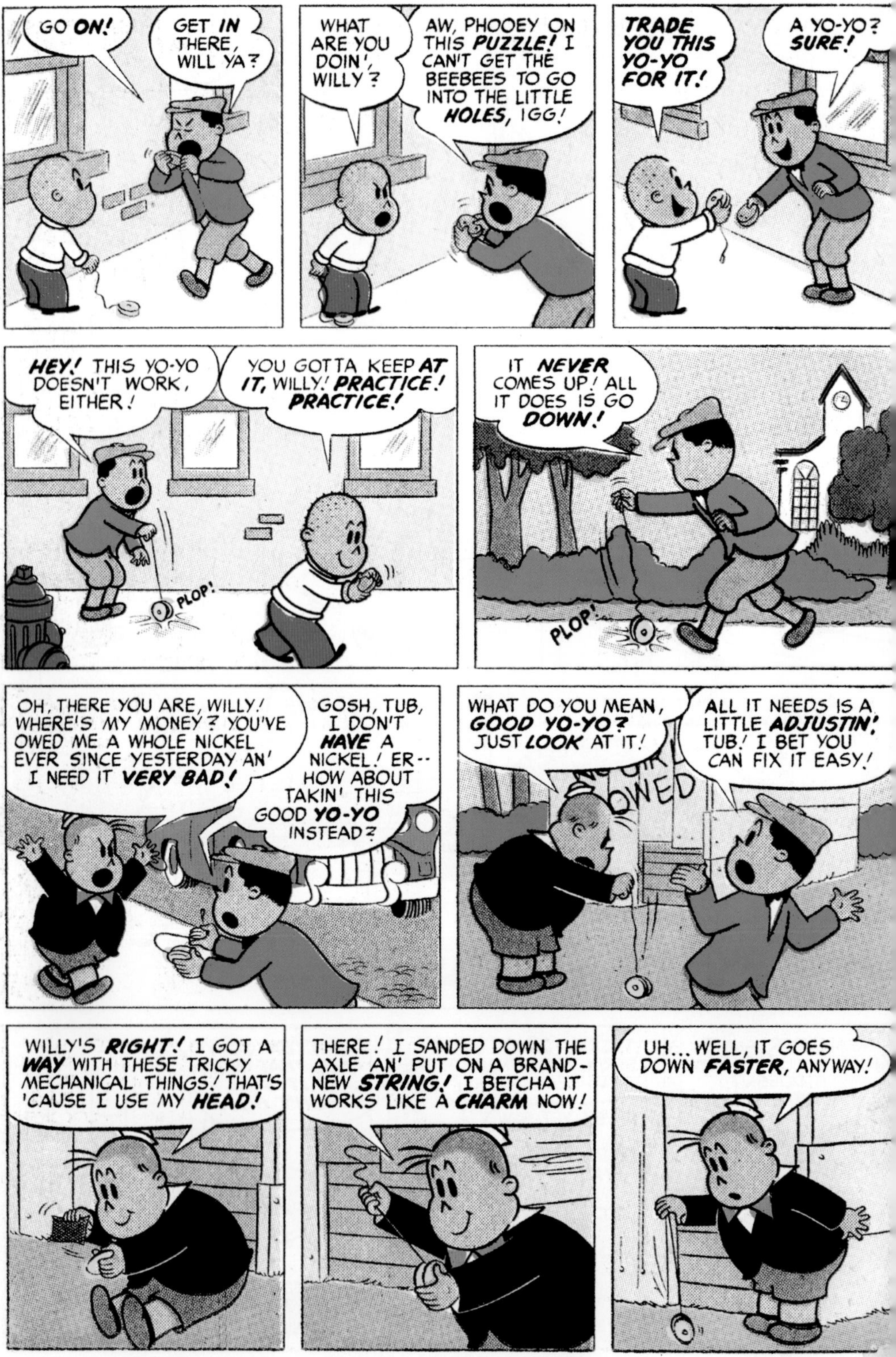
GO ON!
GET IN THERE, WILL YA?
WHAT ARE YOU DOIN', WILLY?
AW, PHOOEY ON THIS PUZZLE! I CAN'T GET THE BEEBEES TO GO INTO THE LITTLE HOLES, IGG!
TRADE YOU THIS YO-YO FOR IT!
A YO-YO? SURE!
HEY! THIS YO-YO DOESN'T WORK, EITHER!
YOU GOTTA KEEP AT IT, WILLY! PRACTICE! PRACTICE!
PLOP!
IT NEVER COMES UP! ALL IT DOES IS GO DOWN!
PLOP!
OH, THERE YOU ARE, WILLY! WHERE'S MY MONEY? YOU'VE OWED ME A WHOLE NICKEL EVER SINCE YESTERDAY AN' I NEED IT VERY BAD!
GOSH, TUB, I DON'T HAVE A NICKEL! ER-- HOW ABOUT TAKIN' THIS GOOD YO-YO INSTEAD?
WHAT DO YOU MEAN, GOOD YO-YO? JUST LOOK AT IT!
ALL IT NEEDS IS A LITTLE ADJUSTIN'! TUB! I BET YOU CAN FIX IT EASY!
WILLY'S RIGHT! I GOT A WAY WITH THESE TRICKY MECHANICAL THINGS! THAT'S 'CAUSE I USE MY HEAD!
THERE! I SANDED DOWN THE AXLE AN' PUT ON A BRAND-NEW STRING! I BETCHA IT WORKS LIKE A CHARM NOW!
UH... WELL, IT GOES DOWN FASTER, ANYWAY!

THE NEXT DAY...
OH, THAT MUST BE ANOTHER GUEST, LULU!
COMING! ♫
HERE, LULU! HOW SOON DO WE EAT?
A PRESENT? FOR ME? OH, THANK YOU, TUBBY!
GOLLY, I WONDER WHAT IT CAN BE?
I CAN HARDLY WAIT TO SEE IT!
IT'S A...
YOW!
THAT AWFUL YO-YO AGAIN! HOW DID YOU GET IT?
POCK!
OW! OW! WHAT'S THE MATTER WITH YOU, LULU? THAT'S A GOOD YO-YO!
IT IS NOT! IT'S A TERRIBLE YO-YO! I SHOULD KNOW. WATCH!
HUH?... IT... IT WORKS!
IT WORKS GOOD, LULU!
ZIP!
ZIP!
ZIP!
WOW!
GOSH, IT WOULDN'T DO ANYTHING BEFORE!
I'LL KEEP IT, TUB! HOW DID YOU FIX IT?
WELL- UH...
HE USED HIS HEAD, LULU! THAT'S WHAT MADE IT WORK!
HOW DOES YOUR HEAD WORK NOW, TUB?
THE END

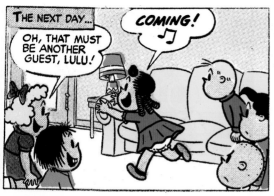

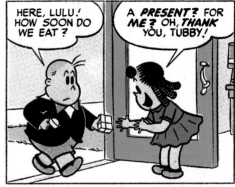

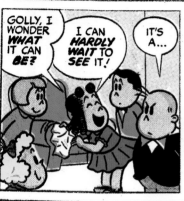

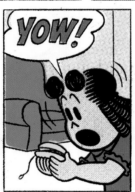

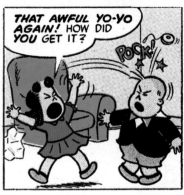

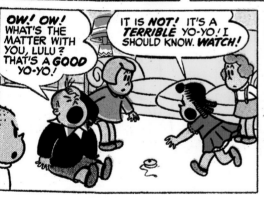

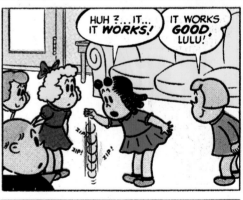

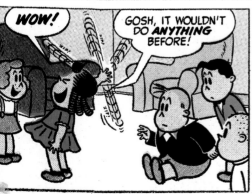

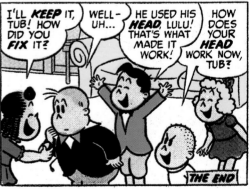

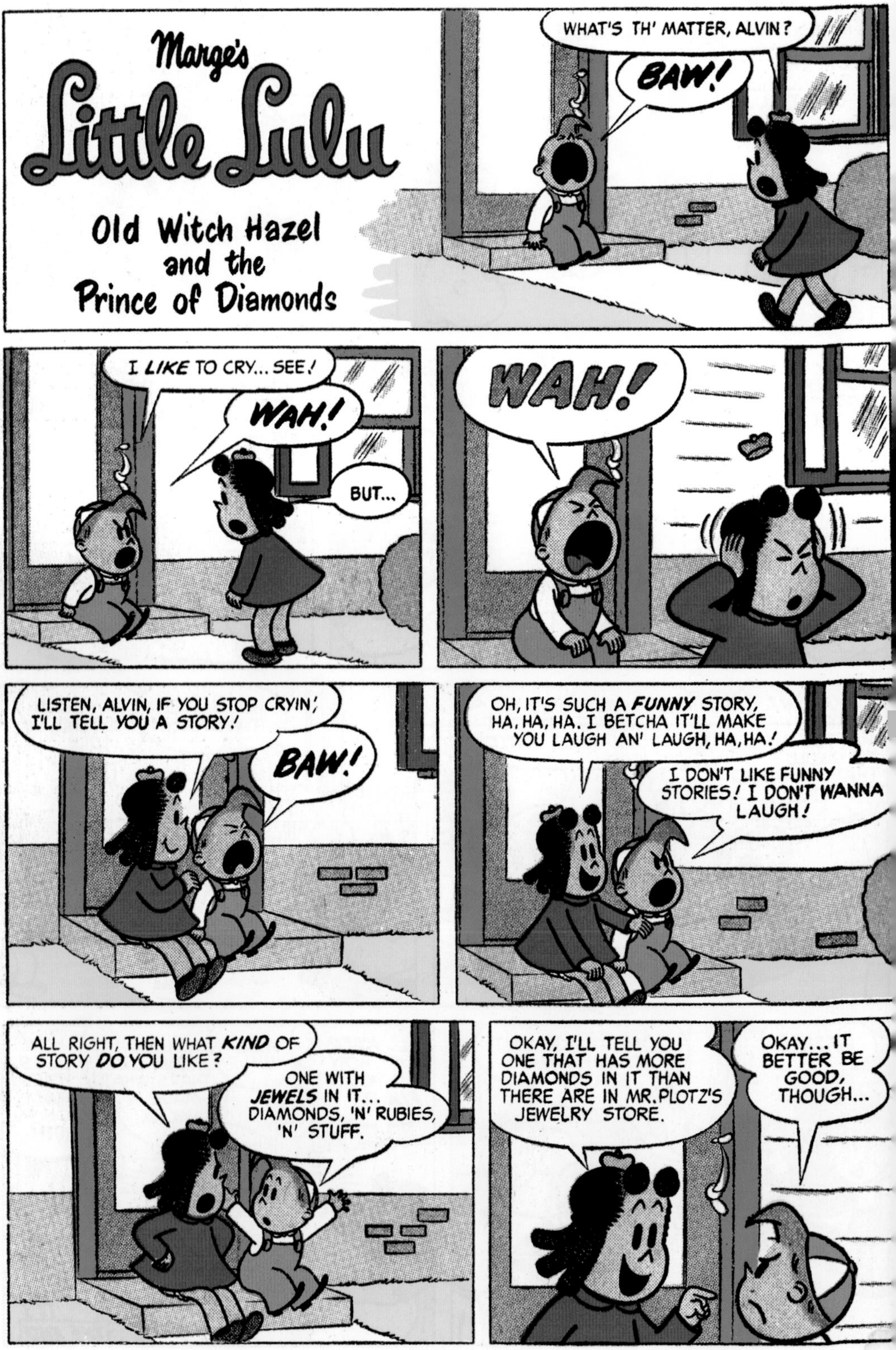
Marge's
Little Lulu
Old Witch Hazel
and the
Prince of Diamonds
WHAT'S TH' MATTER, ALVIN?
BAW!
I LIKE TO CRY... SEE!
WAH!
BUT...
WAH!
LISTEN, ALVIN, IF YOU STOP CRYIN', I'LL TELL YOU A STORY!
BAW!
OH, IT'S SUCH A FUNNY STORY, HA, HA, HA. I BETCHA IT'LL MAKE YOU LAUGH AN' LAUGH, HA, HA!
I DON'T LIKE FUNNY STORIES! I DON'T WANNA LAUGH!
ALL RIGHT, THEN WHAT KIND OF STORY DO YOU LIKE?
ONE WITH JEWELS IN IT... DIAMONDS, 'N' RUBIES, 'N' STUFF.
OKAY, I'LL TELL YOU ONE THAT HAS MORE DIAMONDS IN IT THAN THERE ARE IN MR. PLOTZ'S JEWELRY STORE.
OKAY... IT BETTER BE GOOD, THOUGH...

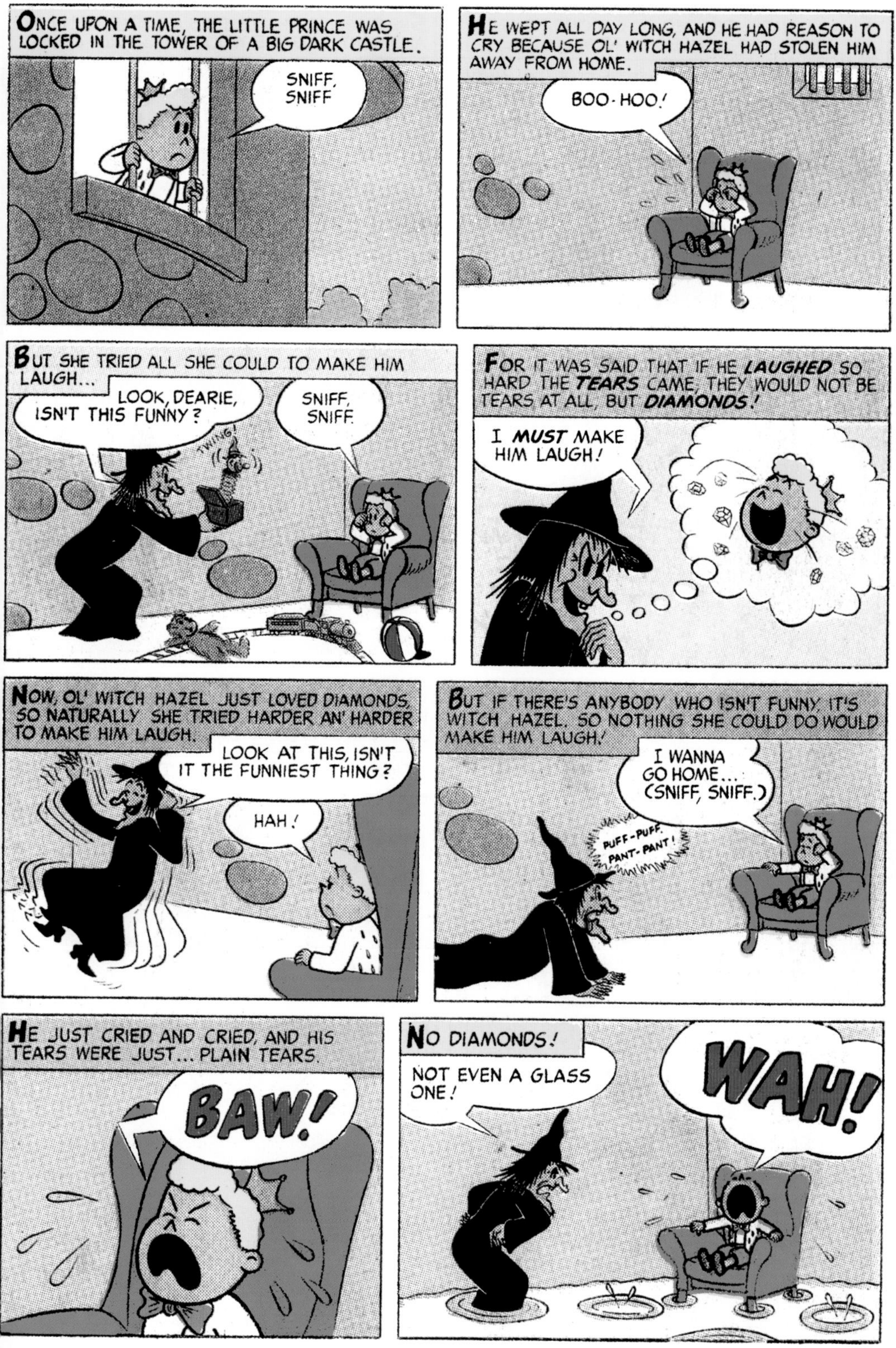
ONCE UPON A TIME, THE LITTLE PRINCE WAS LOCKED IN THE TOWER OF A BIG DARK CASTLE.
SNIFF, SNIFF
HE WEPT ALL DAY LONG, AND HE HAD REASON TO CRY BECAUSE OL' WITCH HAZEL HAD STOLEN HIM AWAY FROM HOME.
BOO-HOO!
BUT SHE TRIED ALL SHE COULD TO MAKE HIM LAUGH...
LOOK, DEARIE, ISN'T THIS FUNNY?
TWING!
SNIFF, SNIFF
FOR IT WAS SAID THAT IF HE LAUGHED SO HARD THE TEARS CAME, THEY WOULD NOT BE TEARS AT ALL, BUT DIAMONDS!
I MUST MAKE HIM LAUGH!
NOW, OL' WITCH HAZEL JUST LOVED DIAMONDS, SO NATURALLY SHE TRIED HARDER AN' HARDER TO MAKE HIM LAUGH.
LOOK AT THIS, ISN'T IT THE FUNNIEST THING?
HAH!
BUT IF THERE'S ANYBODY WHO ISN'T FUNNY IT'S WITCH HAZEL. SO NOTHING SHE COULD DO WOULD MAKE HIM LAUGH!
I WANNA GO HOME... (SNIFF, SNIFF.)
PUFF-PUFF PANT-PANT!
HE JUST CRIED AND CRIED, AND HIS TEARS WERE JUST... PLAIN TEARS.
BAW!
NO DIAMONDS!
NOT EVEN A GLASS ONE!
WAH!

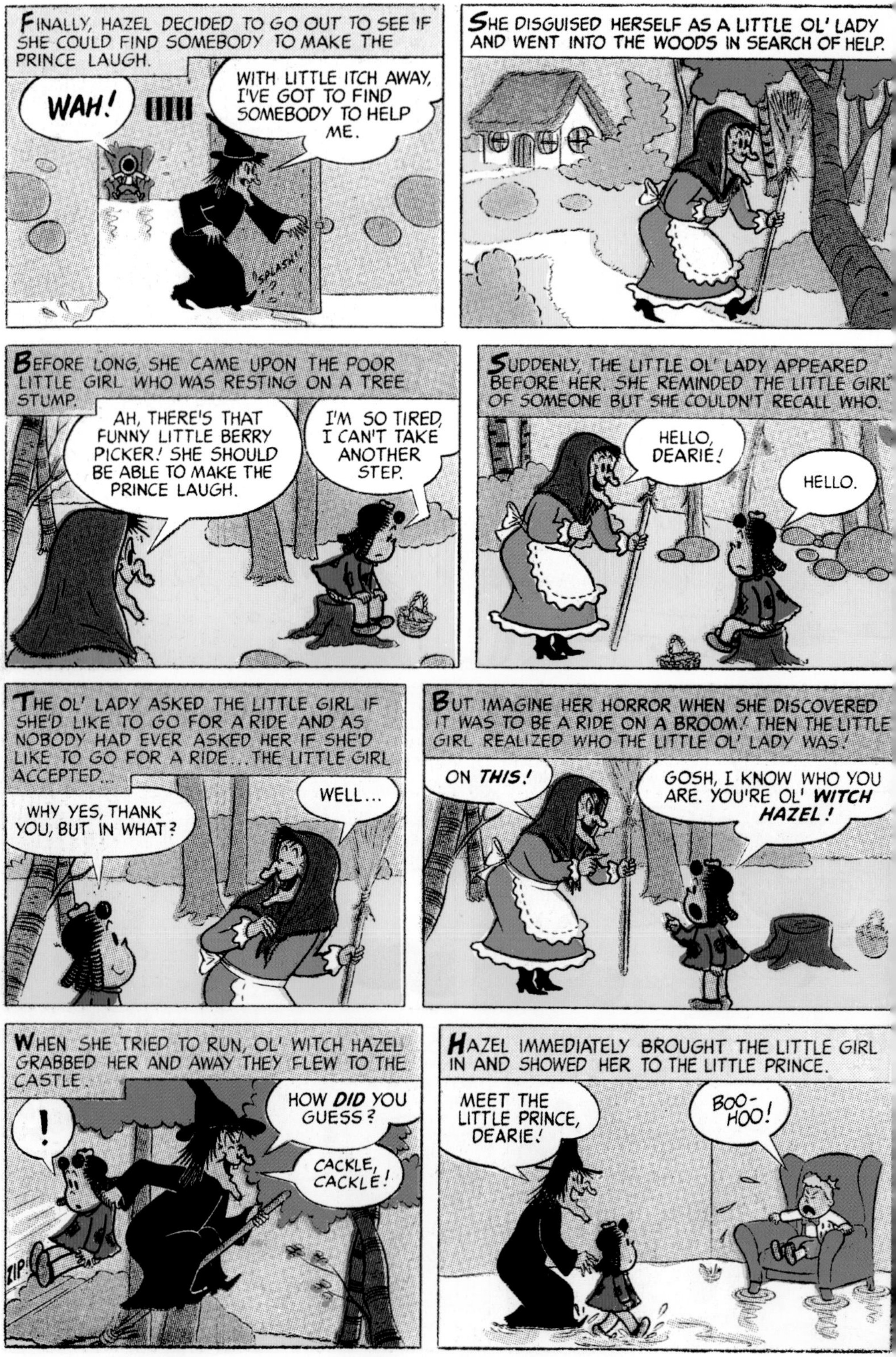
FINALLY, HAZEL DECIDED TO GO OUT TO SEE IF SHE COULD FIND SOMEBODY TO MAKE THE PRINCE LAUGH.
WAH!
WITH LITTLE ITCH AWAY, I'VE GOT TO FIND SOMEBODY TO HELP ME.
SPLASH!
SHE DISGUISED HERSELF AS A LITTLE OL' LADY AND WENT INTO THE WOODS IN SEARCH OF HELP.
BEFORE LONG, SHE CAME UPON THE POOR LITTLE GIRL WHO WAS RESTING ON A TREE STUMP.
AH, THERE'S THAT FUNNY LITTLE BERRY PICKER! SHE SHOULD BE ABLE TO MAKE THE PRINCE LAUGH.
I'M SO TIRED, I CAN'T TAKE ANOTHER STEP.
SUDDENLY, THE LITTLE OL' LADY APPEARED BEFORE HER. SHE REMINDED THE LITTLE GIRL OF SOMEONE BUT SHE COULDN'T RECALL WHO.
HELLO, DEARIE!
HELLO.
THE OL' LADY ASKED THE LITTLE GIRL IF SHE'D LIKE TO GO FOR A RIDE AND AS NOBODY HAD EVER ASKED HER IF SHE'D LIKE TO GO FOR A RIDE... THE LITTLE GIRL ACCEPTED...
WHY YES, THANK YOU, BUT IN WHAT?
WELL...
BUT IMAGINE HER HORROR WHEN SHE DISCOVERED IT WAS TO BE A RIDE ON A BROOM! THEN THE LITTLE GIRL REALIZED WHO THE LITTLE OL' LADY WAS!
ON THIS!
GOSH, I KNOW WHO YOU ARE. YOU'RE OL' WITCH HAZEL!
WHEN SHE TRIED TO RUN, OL' WITCH HAZEL GRABBED HER AND AWAY THEY FLEW TO THE CASTLE.
!
HOW DID YOU GUESS?
CACKLE, CACKLE!
ZIP!
HAZEL IMMEDIATELY BROUGHT THE LITTLE GIRL IN AND SHOWED HER TO THE LITTLE PRINCE.
MEET THE LITTLE PRINCE, DEARIE!
BOO-HOO!

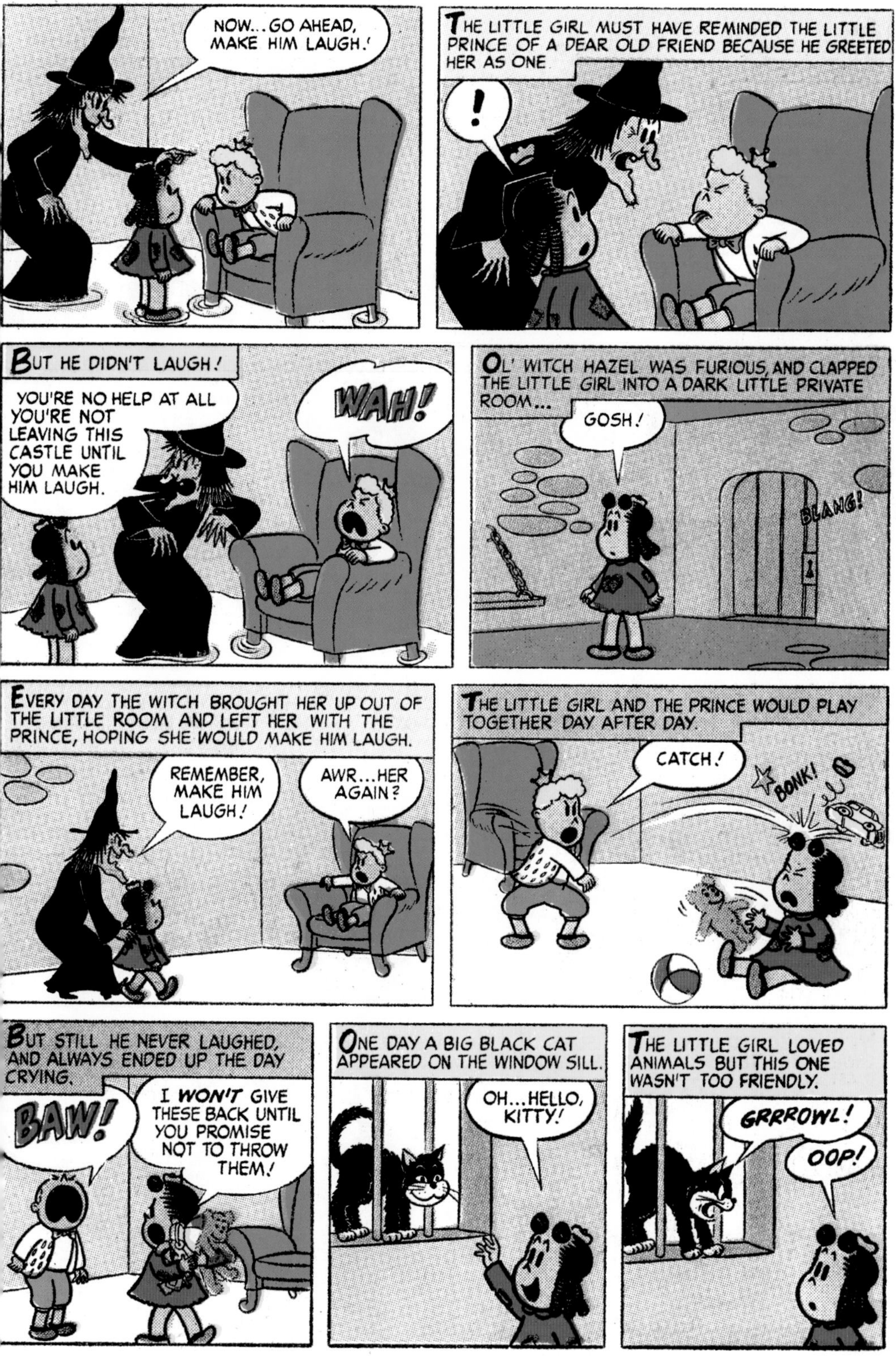
NOW...GO AHEAD, MAKE HIM LAUGH!
THE LITTLE GIRL MUST HAVE REMINDED THE LITTLE PRINCE OF A DEAR OLD FRIEND BECAUSE HE GREETED HER AS ONE.
!
BUT HE DIDN'T LAUGH!
YOU'RE NO HELP AT ALL YOU'RE NOT LEAVING THIS CASTLE UNTIL YOU MAKE HIM LAUGH.
WAH!
OL' WITCH HAZEL WAS FURIOUS, AND CLAPPED THE LITTLE GIRL INTO A DARK LITTLE PRIVATE ROOM...
GOSH!
BLANG!
EVERY DAY THE WITCH BROUGHT HER UP OUT OF THE LITTLE ROOM AND LEFT HER WITH THE PRINCE, HOPING SHE WOULD MAKE HIM LAUGH.
REMEMBER, MAKE HIM LAUGH!
AWR...HER AGAIN?
THE LITTLE GIRL AND THE PRINCE WOULD PLAY TOGETHER DAY AFTER DAY.
CATCH!
BONK!
BUT STILL HE NEVER LAUGHED, AND ALWAYS ENDED UP THE DAY CRYING.
BAW!
I WON'T GIVE THESE BACK UNTIL YOU PROMISE NOT TO THROW THEM!
ONE DAY A BIG BLACK CAT APPEARED ON THE WINDOW SILL.
OH...HELLO, KITTY!
THE LITTLE GIRL LOVED ANIMALS BUT THIS ONE WASN'T TOO FRIENDLY.
GRRROWL!
OOP!

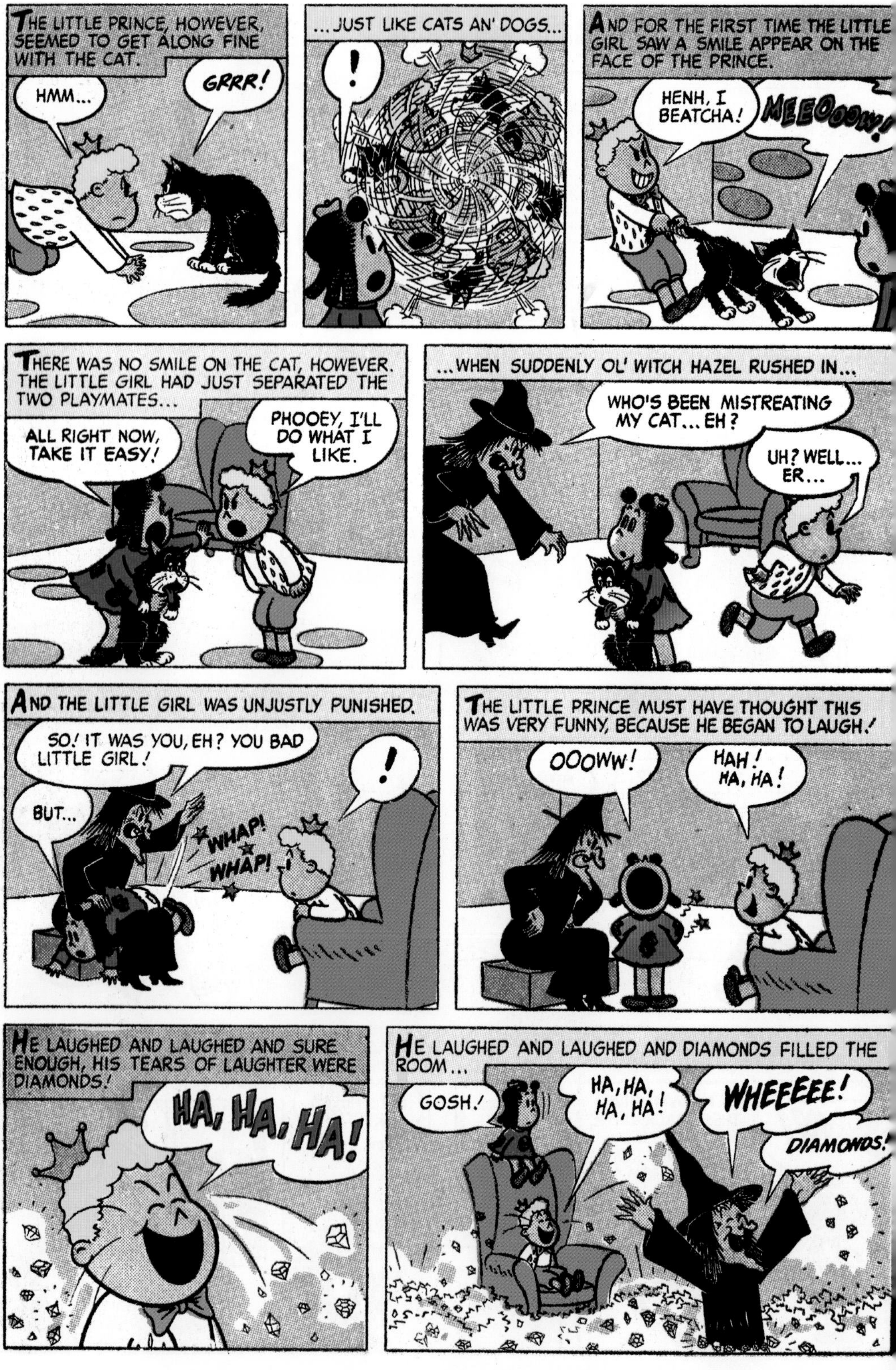
THE LITTLE PRINCE, HOWEVER, SEEMED TO GET ALONG FINE WITH THE CAT.
HMM...
GRRR!
...JUST LIKE CATS AN' DOGS...
!
AND FOR THE FIRST TIME THE LITTLE GIRL SAW A SMILE APPEAR ON THE FACE OF THE PRINCE.
HENH, I BEATCHA!
MEEOoow!
THERE WAS NO SMILE ON THE CAT, HOWEVER. THE LITTLE GIRL HAD JUST SEPARATED THE TWO PLAYMATES...
ALL RIGHT NOW, TAKE IT EASY!
PHOOEY, I'LL DO WHAT I LIKE.
...WHEN SUDDENLY OL' WITCH HAZEL RUSHED IN...
WHO'S BEEN MISTREATING MY CAT... EH?
UH? WELL... ER...
AND THE LITTLE GIRL WAS UNJUSTLY PUNISHED.
SO! IT WAS YOU, EH? YOU BAD LITTLE GIRL!
BUT...
!
WHAP!
WHAP!
THE LITTLE PRINCE MUST HAVE THOUGHT THIS WAS VERY FUNNY, BECAUSE HE BEGAN TO LAUGH!
OOOWW!
HAH! HA, HA!
HE LAUGHED AND LAUGHED AND SURE ENOUGH, HIS TEARS OF LAUGHTER WERE DIAMONDS!
HA, HA, HA!
HE LAUGHED AND LAUGHED AND DIAMONDS FILLED THE ROOM...
GOSH!
HA, HA, HA, HA!
WHEEEEE!
DIAMONDS!

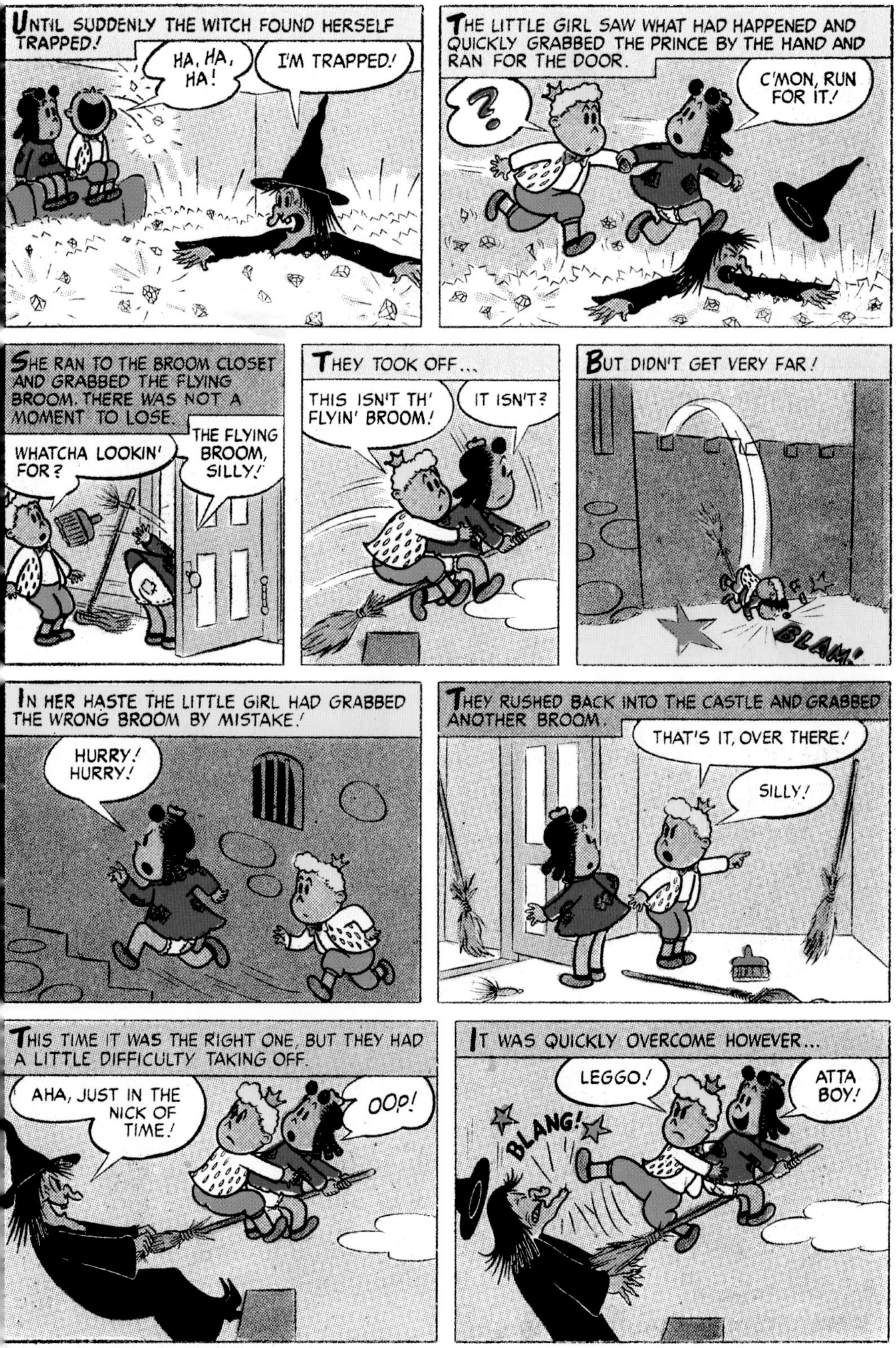
UNTIL SUDDENLY THE WITCH FOUND HERSELF TRAPPED!
HA, HA, HA!
I'M TRAPPED!
THE LITTLE GIRL SAW WHAT HAD HAPPENED AND QUICKLY GRABBED THE PRINCE BY THE HAND AND RAN FOR THE DOOR.
?
C'MON, RUN FOR IT!
SHE RAN TO THE BROOM CLOSET AND GRABBED THE FLYING BROOM. THERE WAS NOT A MOMENT TO LOSE.
WHATCHA LOOKIN' FOR?
THE FLYING BROOM, SILLY!
THEY TOOK OFF...
THIS ISN'T TH' FLYIN' BROOM!
IT ISN'T?
BUT DIDN'T GET VERY FAR!
BLAM!
IN HER HASTE THE LITTLE GIRL HAD GRABBED THE WRONG BROOM BY MISTAKE!
HURRY! HURRY!
THEY RUSHED BACK INTO THE CASTLE AND GRABBED ANOTHER BROOM.
THAT'S IT, OVER THERE!
SILLY!
THIS TIME IT WAS THE RIGHT ONE, BUT THEY HAD A LITTLE DIFFICULTY TAKING OFF.
AHA, JUST IN THE NICK OF TIME!
OOP!
IT WAS QUICKLY OVERCOME HOWEVER...
LEGGO!
ATTA BOY!
BLANG!

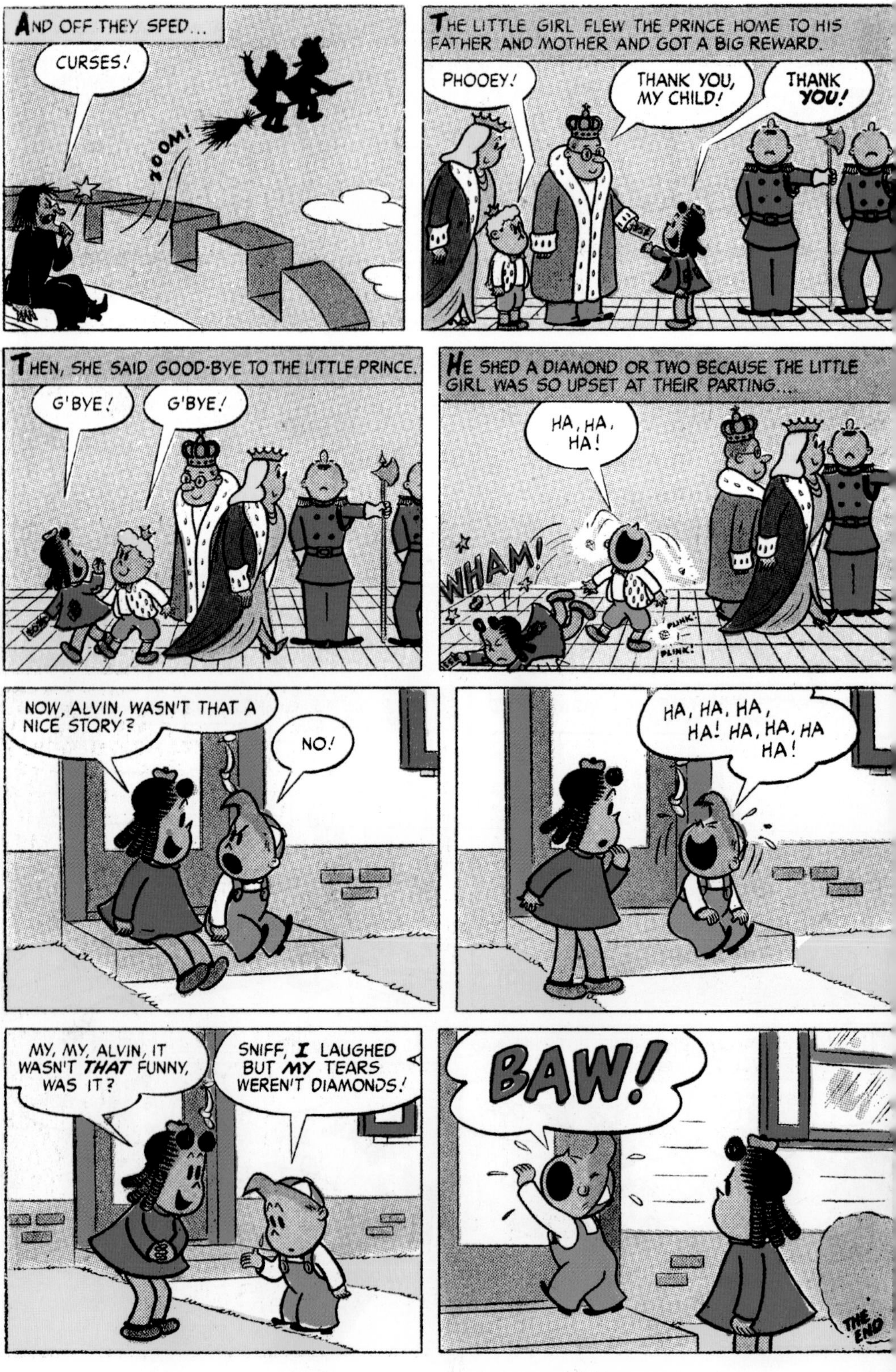
AND OFF THEY SPED...
CURSES!
ZOOM!
THE LITTLE GIRL FLEW THE PRINCE HOME TO HIS FATHER AND MOTHER AND GOT A BIG REWARD.
PHOOEY!
THANK YOU, MY CHILD!
THANK YOU!
THEN, SHE SAID GOOD-BYE TO THE LITTLE PRINCE.
G'BYE!
G'BYE!
HE SHED A DIAMOND OR TWO BECAUSE THE LITTLE GIRL WAS SO UPSET AT THEIR PARTING...
HA, HA, HA!
WHAM!
PLINK!
PLINK!
NOW, ALVIN, WASN'T THAT A NICE STORY?
NO!
HA, HA, HA, HA! HA, HA, HA HA!
MY, MY, ALVIN, IT WASN'T THAT FUNNY, WAS IT?
SNIFF, I LAUGHED BUT MY TEARS WEREN'T DIAMONDS!
BAW!
THE END

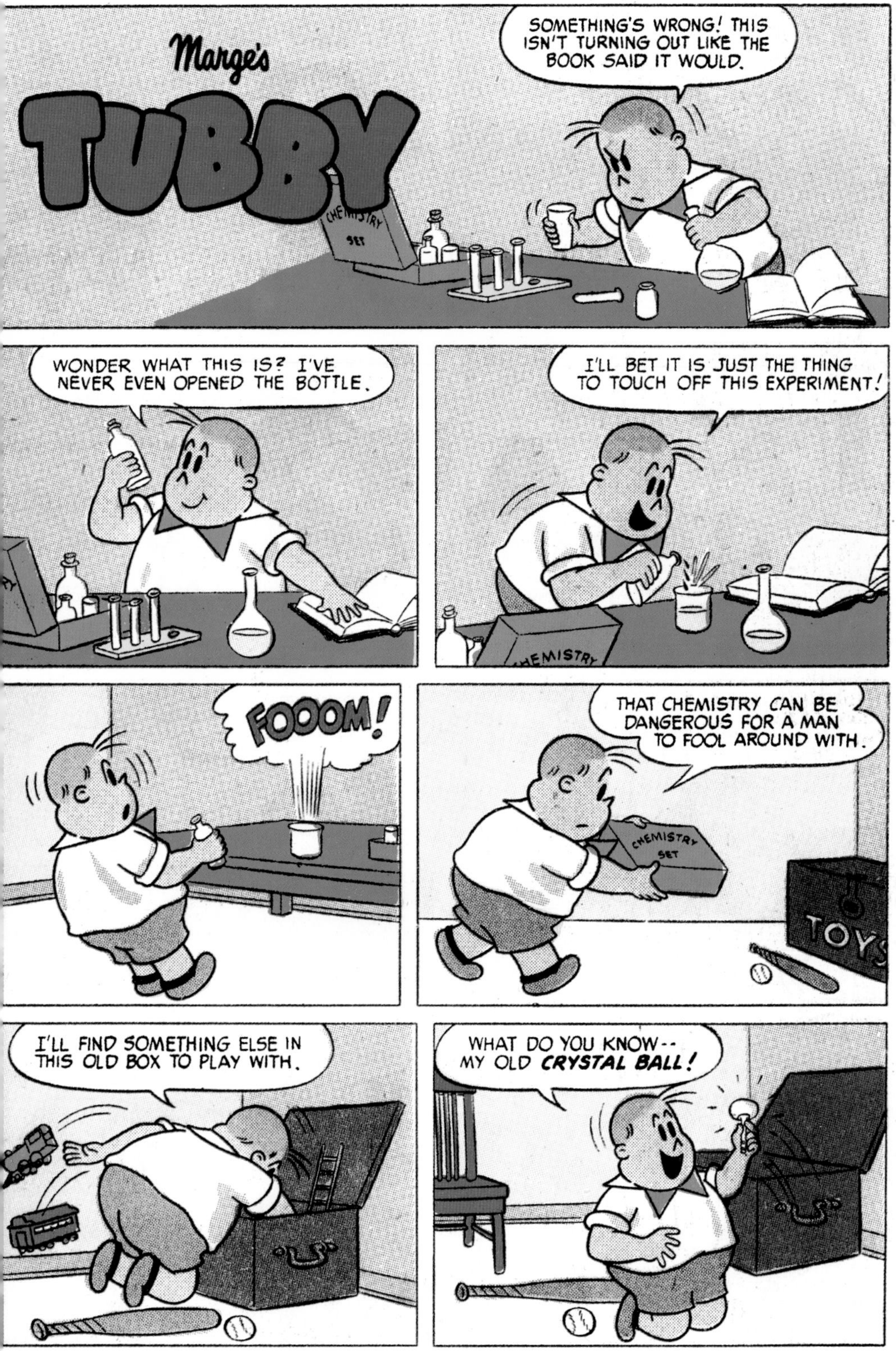
Marge's
TUBBY
SOMETHING'S WRONG! THIS ISN'T TURNING OUT LIKE THE BOOK SAID IT WOULD.
CHEMISTRY SET
WONDER WHAT THIS IS? I'VE NEVER EVEN OPENED THE BOTTLE.
I'LL BET IT IS JUST THE THING TO TOUCH OFF THIS EXPERIMENT!
CHEMISTRY
FOOOM!
THAT CHEMISTRY CAN BE DANGEROUS FOR A MAN TO FOOL AROUND WITH.
CHEMISTRY SET
TOYS
I'LL FIND SOMETHING ELSE IN THIS OLD BOX TO PLAY WITH.
WHAT DO YOU KNOW-- MY OLD CRYSTAL BALL!

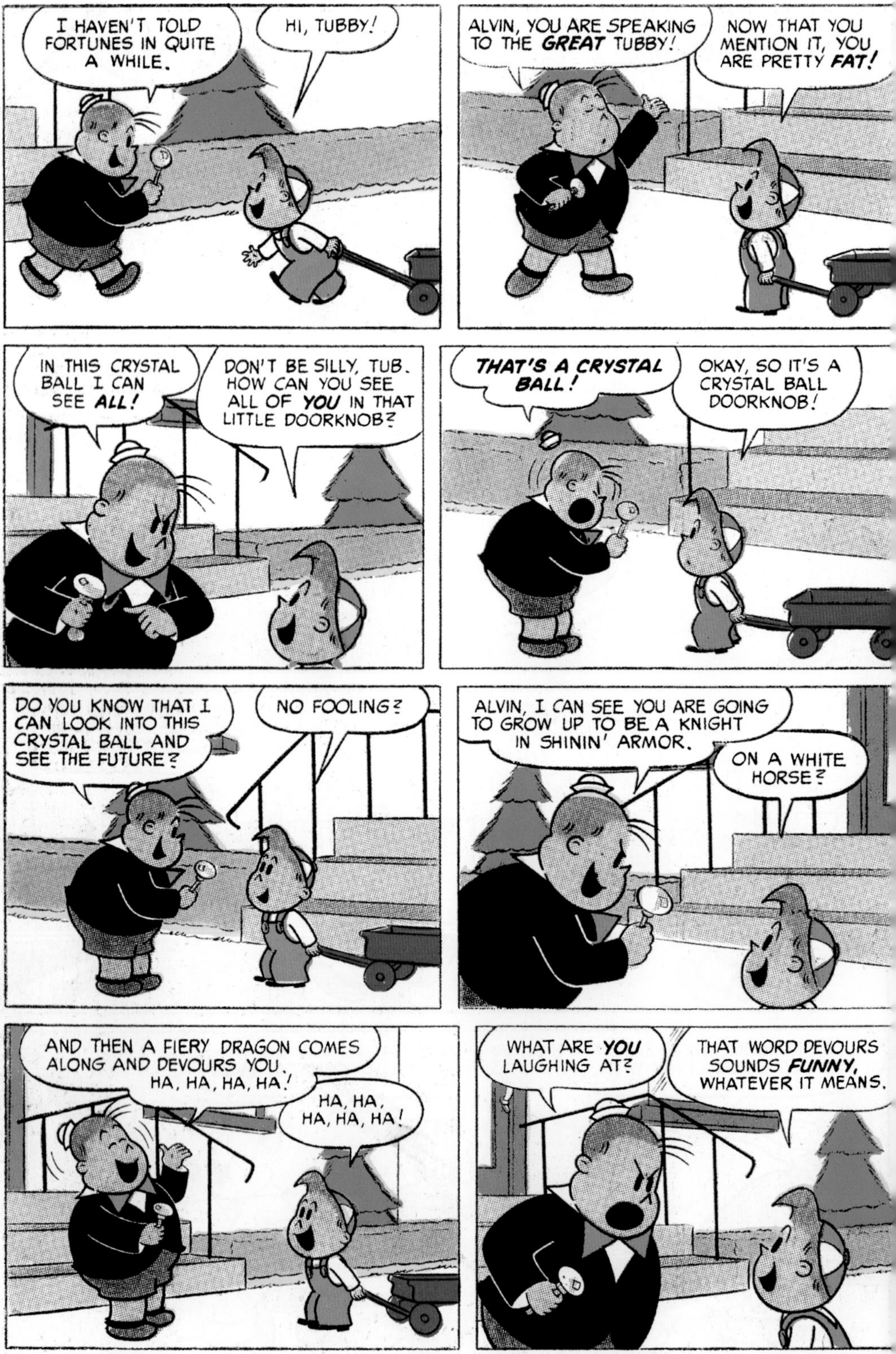
I HAVEN'T TOLD FORTUNES IN QUITE A WHILE.
HI, TUBBY!
ALVIN, YOU ARE SPEAKING TO THE GREAT TUBBY!
NOW THAT YOU MENTION IT, YOU ARE PRETTY FAT!
IN THIS CRYSTAL BALL I CAN SEE ALL!
DON'T BE SILLY, TUB. HOW CAN YOU SEE ALL OF YOU IN THAT LITTLE DOORKNOB?
THAT'S A CRYSTAL BALL!
OKAY, SO IT'S A CRYSTAL BALL DOORKNOB!
DO YOU KNOW THAT I CAN LOOK INTO THIS CRYSTAL BALL AND SEE THE FUTURE?
NO FOOLING?
ALVIN, I CAN SEE YOU ARE GOING TO GROW UP TO BE A KNIGHT IN SHININ' ARMOR.
ON A WHITE HORSE?
AND THEN A FIERY DRAGON COMES ALONG AND DEVOURS YOU. HA, HA, HA, HA!
HA, HA, HA, HA, HA!
WHAT ARE YOU LAUGHING AT?
THAT WORD DEVOURS SOUNDS FUNNY, WHATEVER IT MEANS.

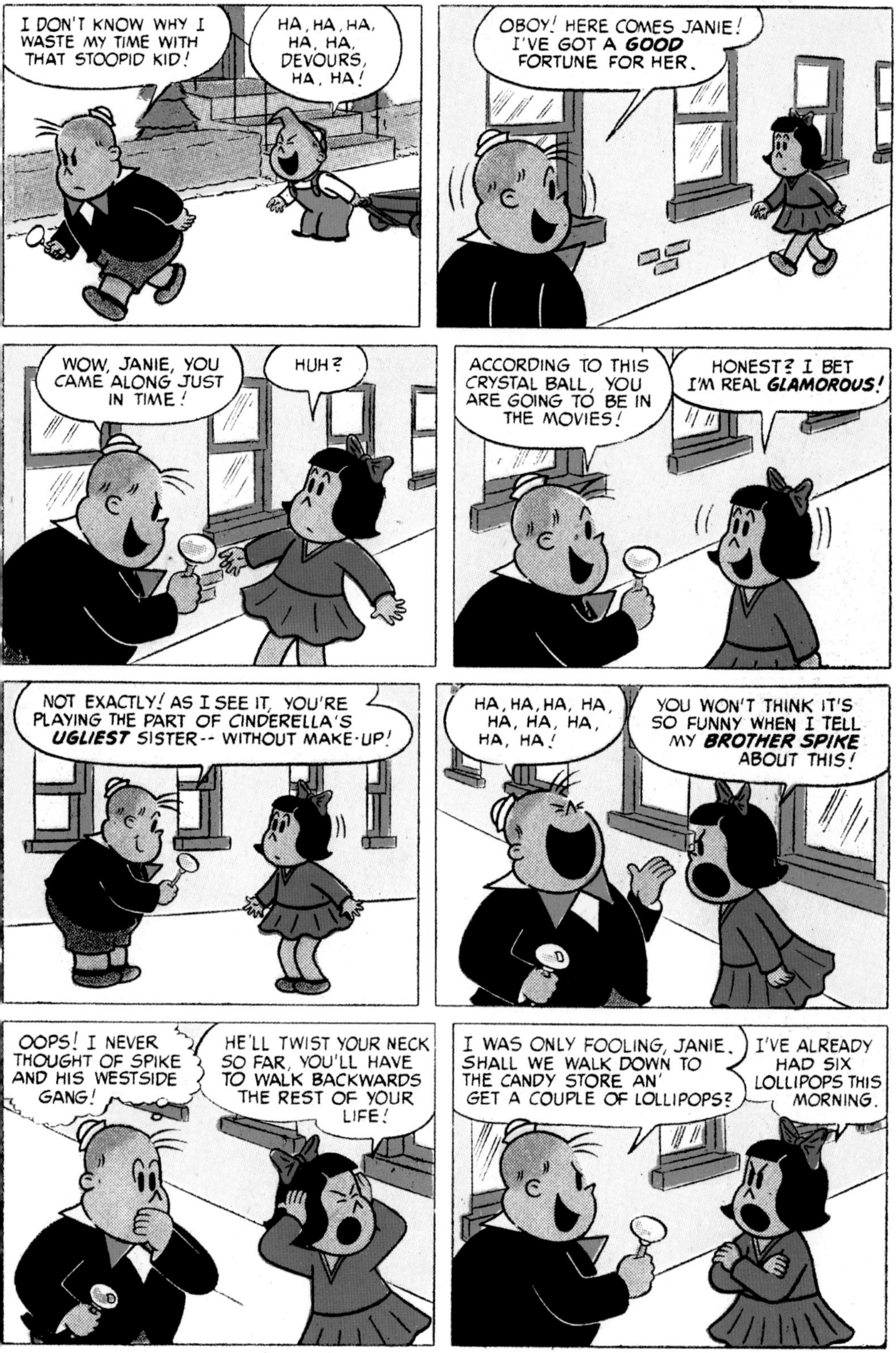
I DON'T KNOW WHY I WASTE MY TIME WITH THAT STOOPID KID!
HA, HA, HA, HA, HA, DEVOURS, HA, HA!
OBOY! HERE COMES JANIE! I'VE GOT A GOOD FORTUNE FOR HER.
WOW, JANIE, YOU CAME ALONG JUST IN TIME!
HUH?
ACCORDING TO THIS CRYSTAL BALL, YOU ARE GOING TO BE IN THE MOVIES!
HONEST? I BET I'M REAL GLAMOROUS!
NOT EXACTLY! AS I SEE IT, YOU'RE PLAYING THE PART OF CINDERELLA'S UGLIEST SISTER-- WITHOUT MAKE-UP!
HA, HA, HA, HA, HA, HA, HA, HA, HA!
YOU WON'T THINK IT'S SO FUNNY WHEN I TELL MY BROTHER SPIKE ABOUT THIS!
OOPS! I NEVER THOUGHT OF SPIKE AND HIS WESTSIDE GANG!
HE'LL TWIST YOUR NECK SO FAR, YOU'LL HAVE TO WALK BACKWARDS THE REST OF YOUR LIFE!
I WAS ONLY FOOLING, JANIE. SHALL WE WALK DOWN TO THE CANDY STORE AN' GET A COUPLE OF LOLLIPOPS?
I'VE ALREADY HAD SIX LOLLIPOPS THIS MORNING.

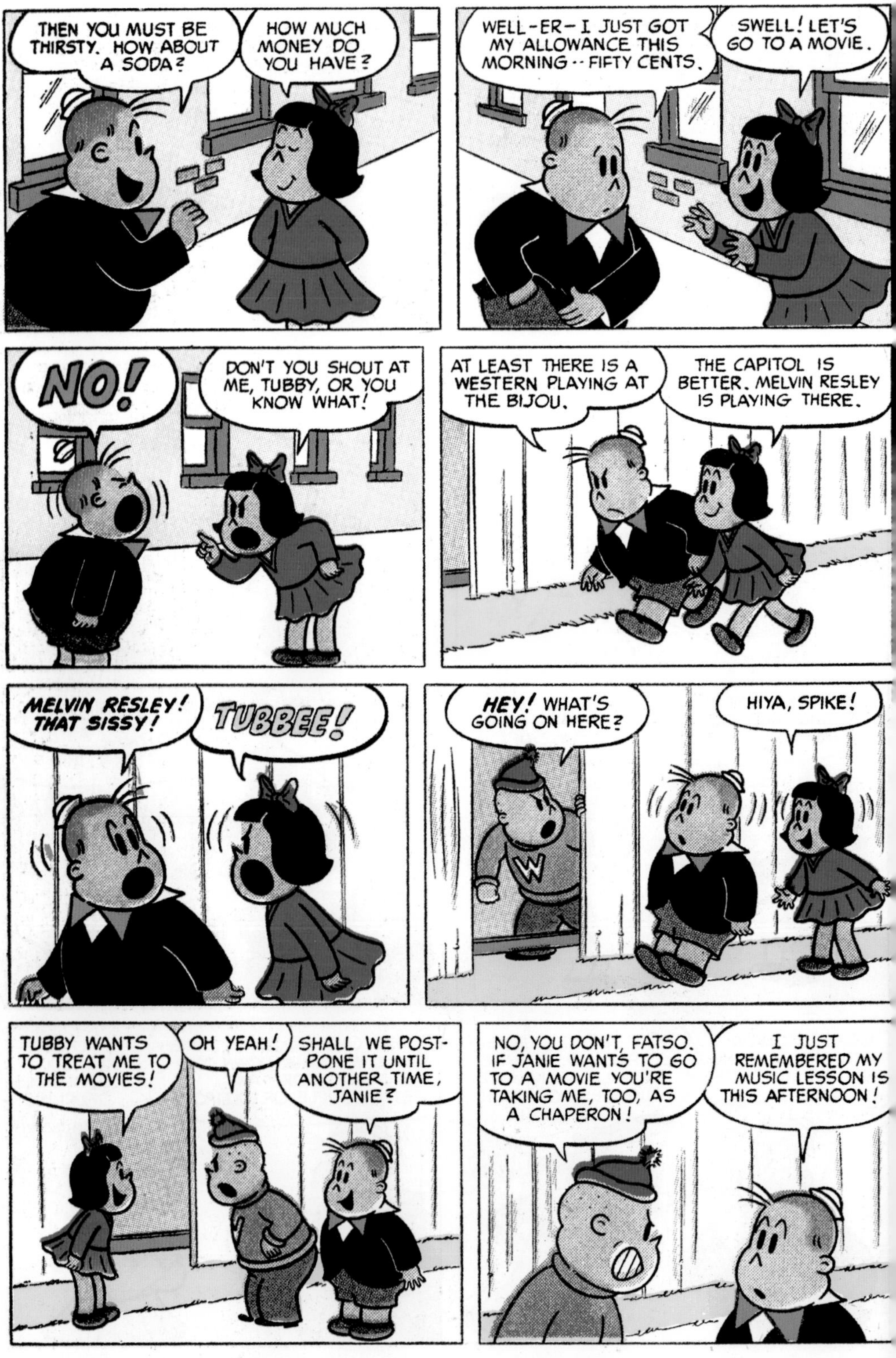
THEN YOU MUST BE THIRSTY. HOW ABOUT A SODA?
HOW MUCH MONEY DO YOU HAVE?
WELL-ER-I JUST GOT MY ALLOWANCE THIS MORNING -- FIFTY CENTS.
SWELL! LET'S GO TO A MOVIE.
NO!
DON'T YOU SHOUT AT ME, TUBBY, OR YOU KNOW WHAT!
AT LEAST THERE IS A WESTERN PLAYING AT THE BIJOU.
THE CAPITOL IS BETTER. MELVIN RESLEY IS PLAYING THERE.
MELVIN RESLEY! THAT SISSY!
TUBBEE!
HEY! WHAT'S GOING ON HERE?
HIYA, SPIKE!
TUBBY WANTS TO TREAT ME TO THE MOVIES!
OH YEAH!
SHALL WE POSTPONE IT UNTIL ANOTHER TIME, JANIE?
NO, YOU DON'T, FATSO. IF JANIE WANTS TO GO TO A MOVIE YOU'RE TAKING ME, TOO, AS A CHAPERON!
I JUST REMEMBERED MY MUSIC LESSON IS THIS AFTERNOON!

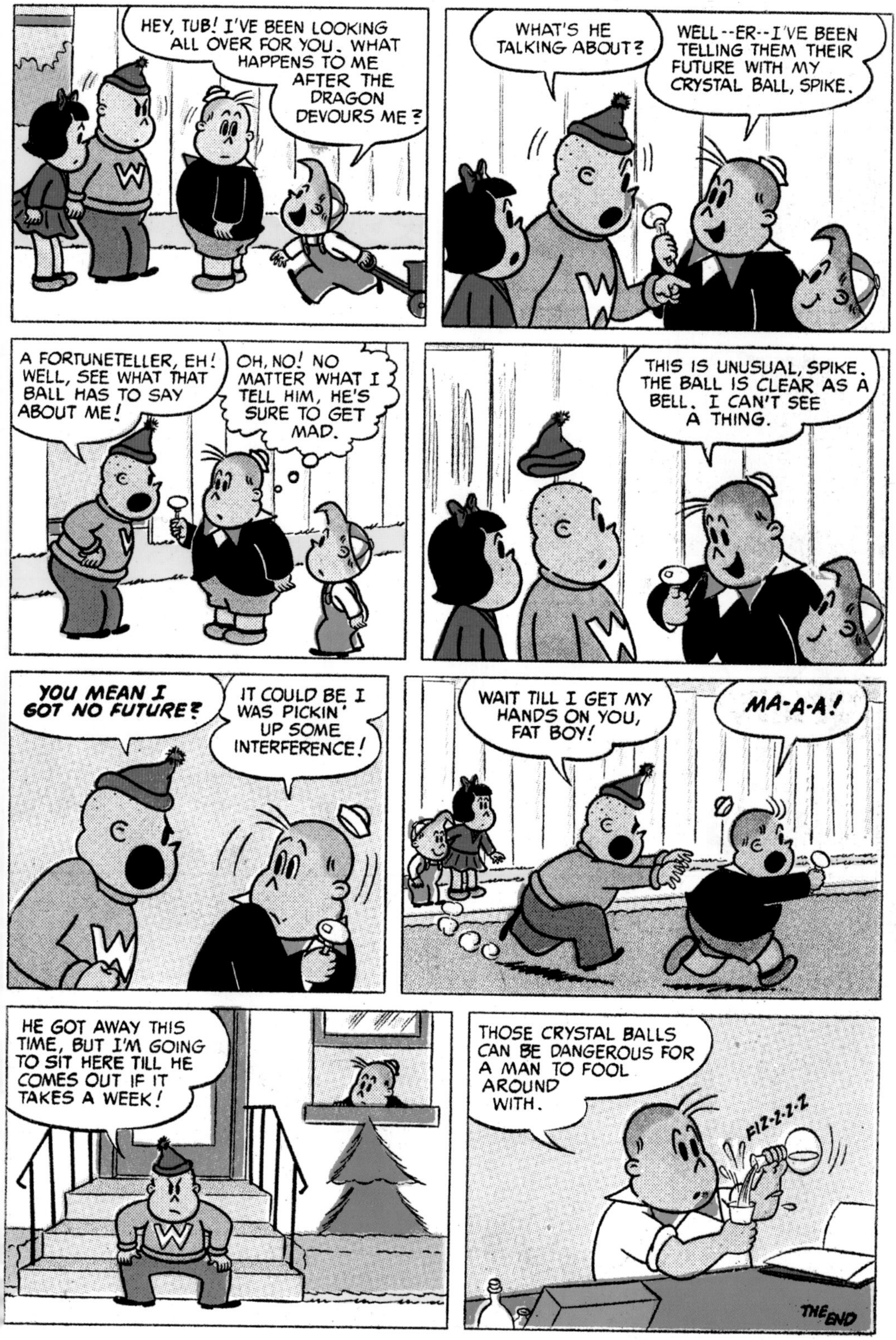
HEY, TUB! I'VE BEEN LOOKING ALL OVER FOR YOU. WHAT HAPPENS TO ME AFTER THE DRAGON DEVOURS ME?
WHAT'S HE TALKING ABOUT?
WELL--ER--I'VE BEEN TELLING THEM THEIR FUTURE WITH MY CRYSTAL BALL, SPIKE.
A FORTUNETELLER, EH! WELL, SEE WHAT THAT BALL HAS TO SAY ABOUT ME!
OH, NO! NO MATTER WHAT I TELL HIM, HE'S SURE TO GET MAD.
THIS IS UNUSUAL, SPIKE. THE BALL IS CLEAR AS A BELL. I CAN'T SEE A THING.
YOU MEAN I GOT NO FUTURE?
IT COULD BE I WAS PICKIN' UP SOME INTERFERENCE!
WAIT TILL I GET MY HANDS ON YOU, FAT BOY!
MA-A-A!
HE GOT AWAY THIS TIME, BUT I'M GOING TO SIT HERE TILL HE COMES OUT IF IT TAKES A WEEK!
THOSE CRYSTAL BALLS CAN BE DANGEROUS FOR A MAN TO FOOL AROUND WITH.
FIZ-Z-Z-Z
THE END

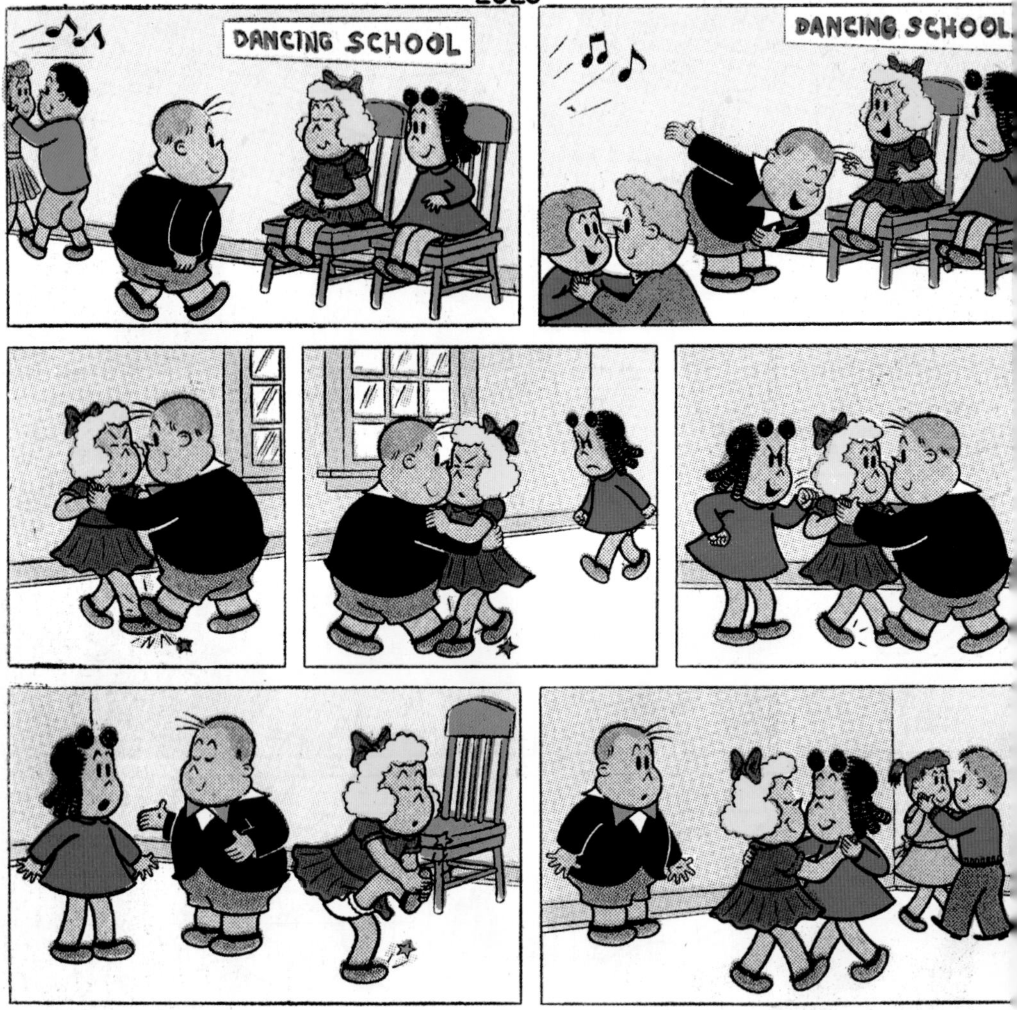
DANCING SCHOOL
DANCING SCHOOL

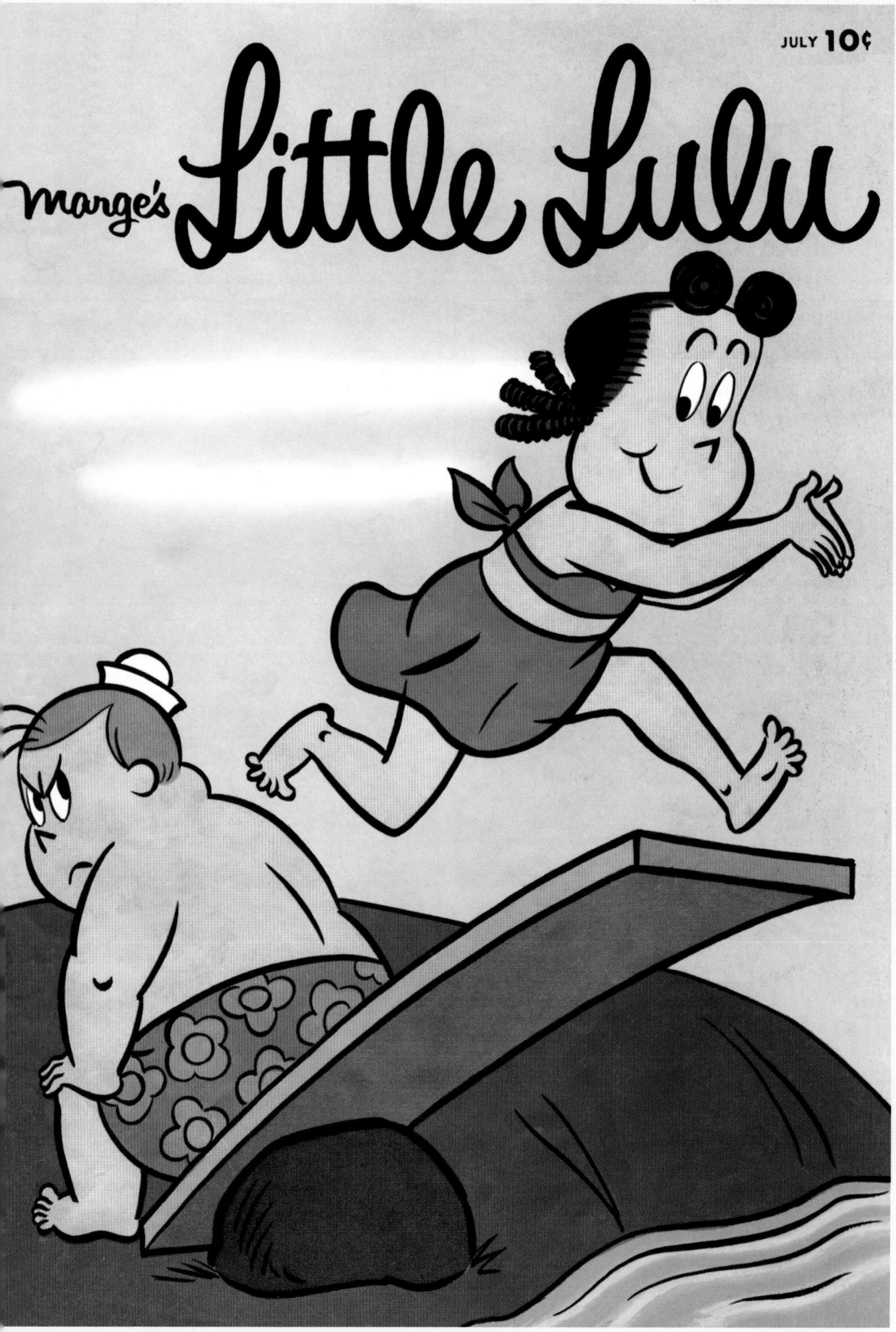
JULY 10¢
Marge's Little Lulu

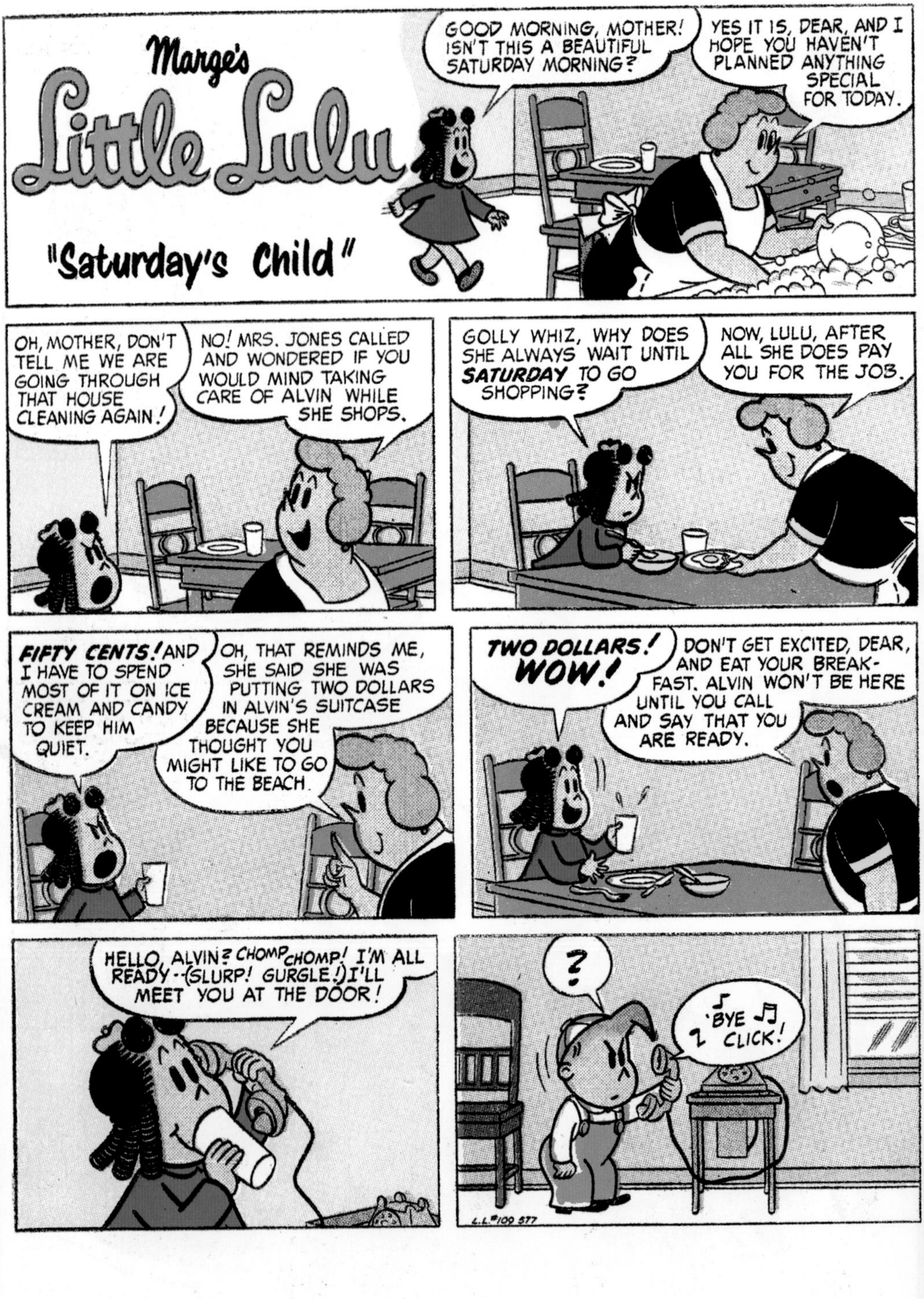
Marge's
Little Lulu
"Saturday's Child"
GOOD MORNING, MOTHER! ISN'T THIS A BEAUTIFUL SATURDAY MORNING?
YES IT IS, DEAR, AND I HOPE YOU HAVEN'T PLANNED ANYTHING SPECIAL FOR TODAY.
OH, MOTHER, DON'T TELL ME WE ARE GOING THROUGH THAT HOUSE CLEANING AGAIN!
NO! MRS. JONES CALLED AND WONDERED IF YOU WOULD MIND TAKING CARE OF ALVIN WHILE SHE SHOPS.
GOLLY WHIZ, WHY DOES SHE ALWAYS WAIT UNTIL SATURDAY TO GO SHOPPING?
NOW, LULU, AFTER ALL SHE DOES PAY YOU FOR THE JOB.
FIFTY CENTS! AND I HAVE TO SPEND MOST OF IT ON ICE CREAM AND CANDY TO KEEP HIM QUIET.
OH, THAT REMINDS ME, SHE SAID SHE WAS PUTTING TWO DOLLARS IN ALVIN'S SUITCASE BECAUSE SHE THOUGHT YOU MIGHT LIKE TO GO TO THE BEACH.
TWO DOLLARS! WOW!
DON'T GET EXCITED, DEAR, AND EAT YOUR BREAK-FAST. ALVIN WON'T BE HERE UNTIL YOU CALL AND SAY THAT YOU ARE READY.
HELLO, ALVIN? CHOMP CHOMP! I'M ALL READY--(SLURP! GURGLE!) I'LL MEET YOU AT THE DOOR!
?
'BYE CLICK!
L.L. #109 577

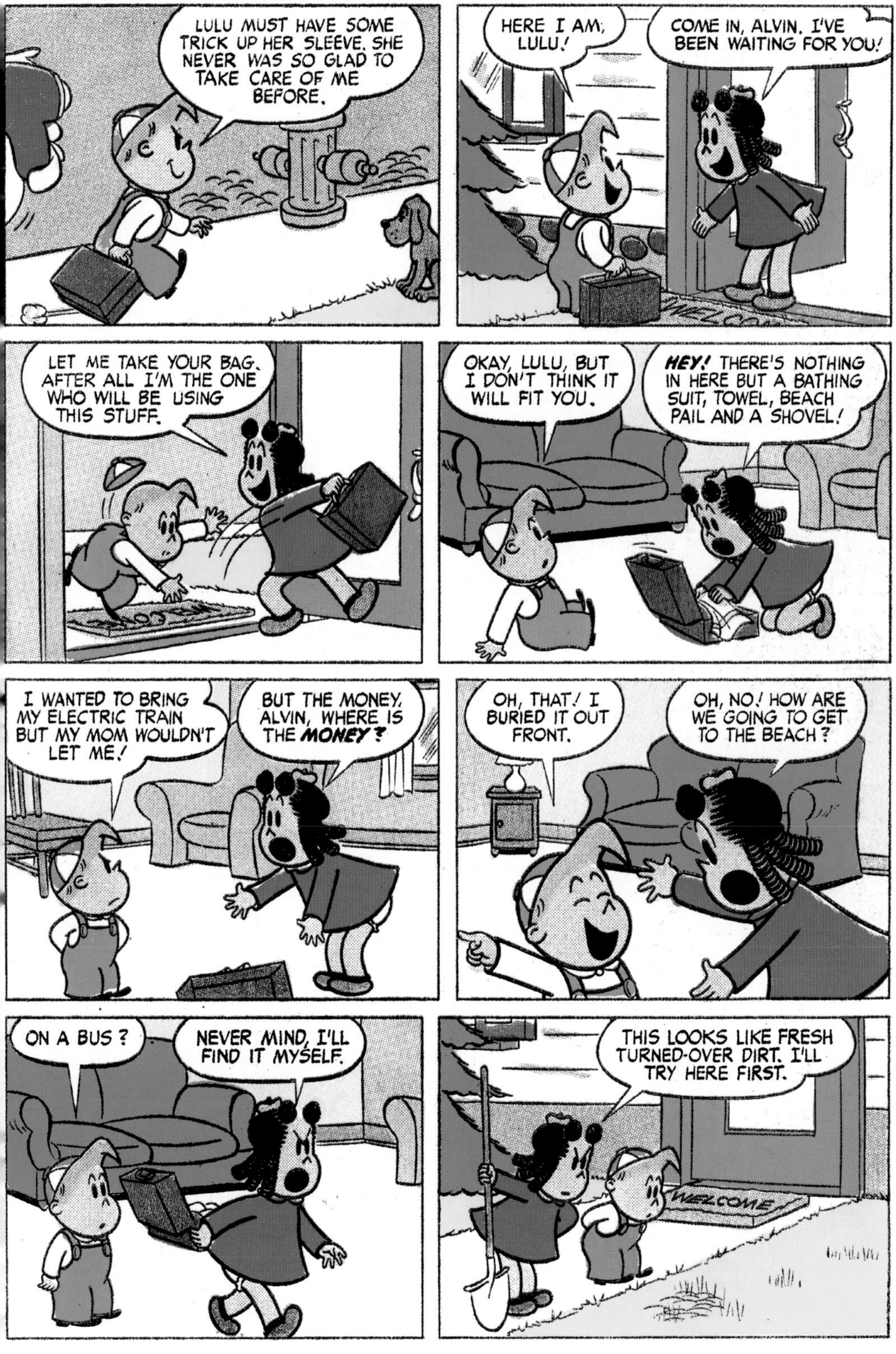
LULU MUST HAVE SOME TRICK UP HER SLEEVE. SHE NEVER WAS SO GLAD TO TAKE CARE OF ME BEFORE.
HERE I AM, LULU!
COME IN, ALVIN. I'VE BEEN WAITING FOR YOU!
WELCOME
LET ME TAKE YOUR BAG. AFTER ALL I'M THE ONE WHO WILL BE USING THIS STUFF.
OKAY, LULU, BUT I DON'T THINK IT WILL FIT YOU.
HEY! THERE'S NOTHING IN HERE BUT A BATHING SUIT, TOWEL, BEACH PAIL AND A SHOVEL!
I WANTED TO BRING MY ELECTRIC TRAIN BUT MY MOM WOULDN'T LET ME!
BUT THE MONEY, ALVIN, WHERE IS THE MONEY?
OH, THAT! I BURIED IT OUT FRONT.
OH, NO! HOW ARE WE GOING TO GET TO THE BEACH?
ON A BUS?
NEVER MIND, I'LL FIND IT MYSELF.
THIS LOOKS LIKE FRESH TURNED-OVER DIRT. I'LL TRY HERE FIRST.
WELCOME

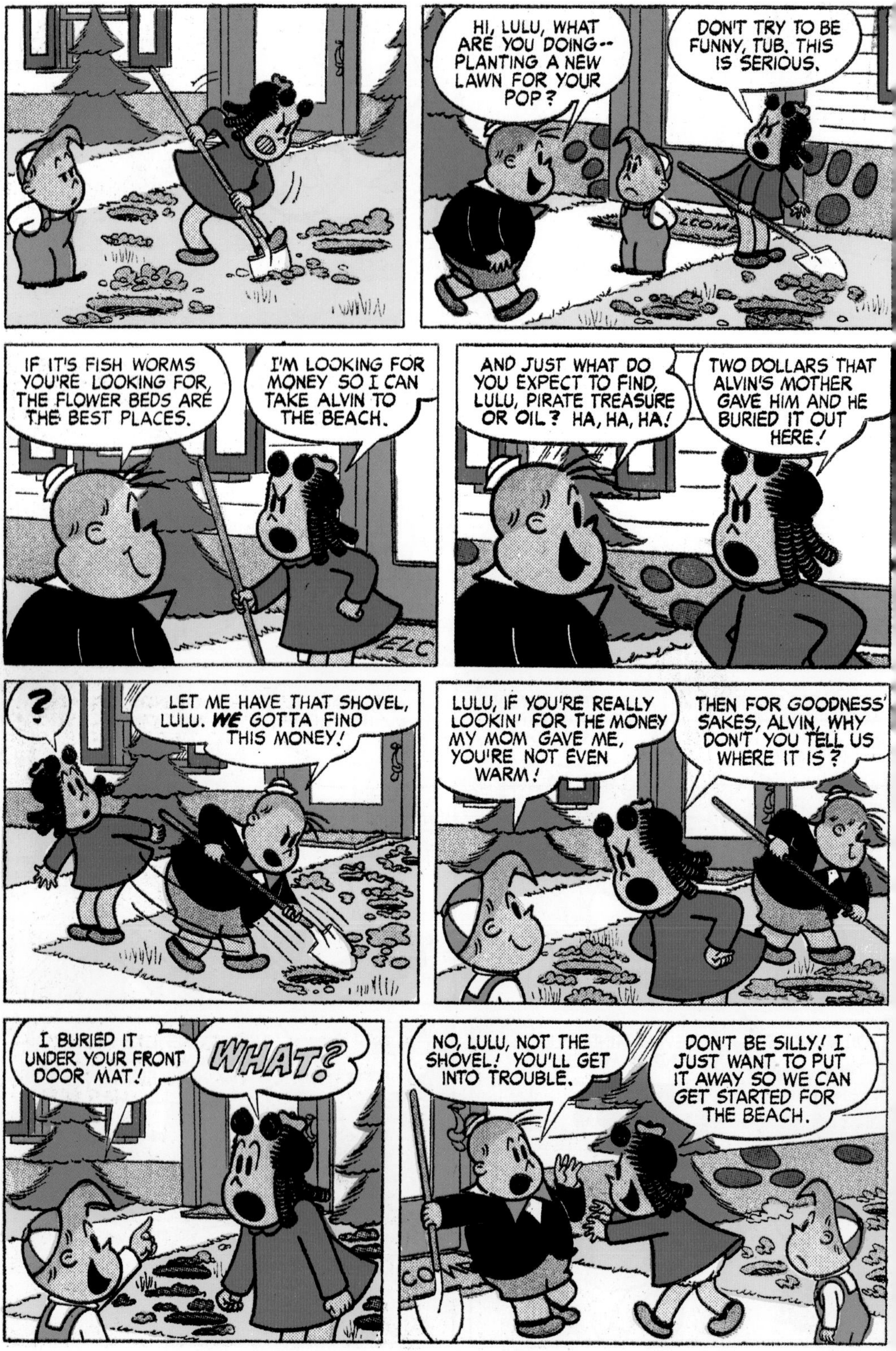

HI, LULU, WHAT ARE YOU DOING-- PLANTING A NEW LAWN FOR YOUR POP?
DON'T TRY TO BE FUNNY, TUB. THIS IS SERIOUS.
IF IT'S FISH WORMS YOU'RE LOOKING FOR, THE FLOWER BEDS ARE THE BEST PLACES.
I'M LOOKING FOR MONEY SO I CAN TAKE ALVIN TO THE BEACH.
AND JUST WHAT DO YOU EXPECT TO FIND, LULU, PIRATE TREASURE OR OIL? HA, HA, HA!
TWO DOLLARS THAT ALVIN'S MOTHER GAVE HIM AND HE BURIED IT OUT HERE!
?
LET ME HAVE THAT SHOVEL, LULU. WE GOTTA FIND THIS MONEY!
LULU, IF YOU'RE REALLY LOOKIN' FOR THE MONEY MY MOM GAVE ME, YOU'RE NOT EVEN WARM!
THEN FOR GOODNESS' SAKES, ALVIN, WHY DON'T YOU TELL US WHERE IT IS?
I BURIED IT UNDER YOUR FRONT DOOR MAT!
WHAT?
NO, LULU, NOT THE SHOVEL! YOU'LL GET INTO TROUBLE.
DON'T BE SILLY! I JUST WANT TO PUT IT AWAY SO WE CAN GET STARTED FOR THE BEACH.

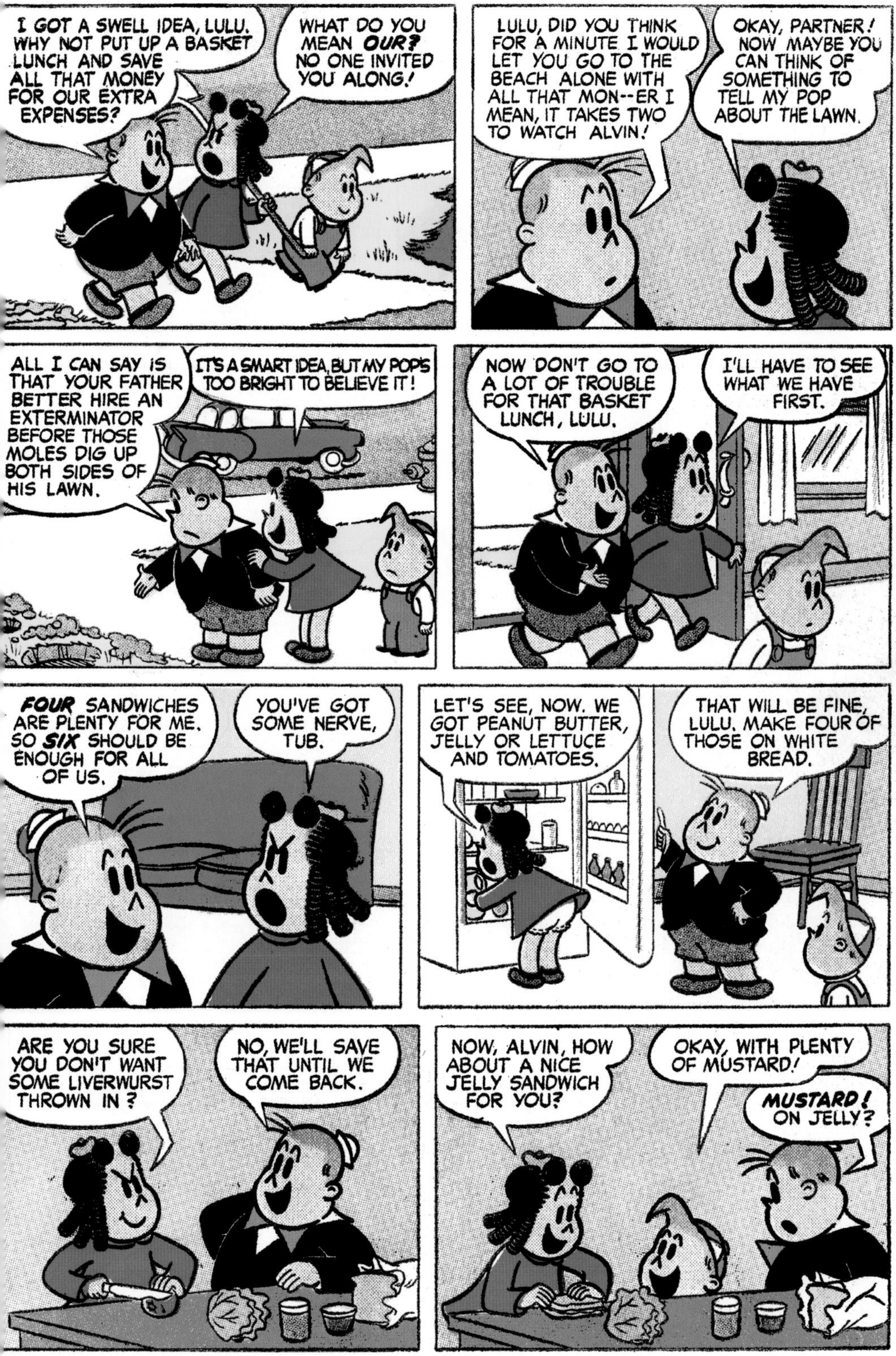

I GOT A SWELL IDEA, LULU. WHY NOT PUT UP A BASKET LUNCH AND SAVE ALL THAT MONEY FOR OUR EXTRA EXPENSES?
WHAT DO YOU MEAN OUR? NO ONE INVITED YOU ALONG!
LULU, DID YOU THINK FOR A MINUTE I WOULD LET YOU GO TO THE BEACH ALONE WITH ALL THAT MON--ER I MEAN, IT TAKES TWO TO WATCH ALVIN!
OKAY, PARTNER! NOW MAYBE YOU CAN THINK OF SOMETHING TO TELL MY POP ABOUT THE LAWN.
ALL I CAN SAY IS THAT YOUR FATHER BETTER HIRE AN EXTERMINATOR BEFORE THOSE MOLES DIG UP BOTH SIDES OF HIS LAWN.
IT'S A SMART IDEA, BUT MY POP'S TOO BRIGHT TO BELIEVE IT!
NOW DON'T GO TO A LOT OF TROUBLE FOR THAT BASKET LUNCH, LULU.
I'LL HAVE TO SEE WHAT WE HAVE FIRST.
FOUR SANDWICHES ARE PLENTY FOR ME. SO SIX SHOULD BE ENOUGH FOR ALL OF US.
YOU'VE GOT SOME NERVE, TUB.
LET'S SEE, NOW. WE GOT PEANUT BUTTER, JELLY OR LETTUCE AND TOMATOES.
THAT WILL BE FINE, LULU. MAKE FOUR OF THOSE ON WHITE BREAD.
ARE YOU SURE YOU DON'T WANT SOME LIVERWURST THROWN IN?
NO, WE'LL SAVE THAT UNTIL WE COME BACK.
NOW, ALVIN, HOW ABOUT A NICE JELLY SANDWICH FOR YOU?
OKAY, WITH PLENTY OF MUSTARD!
MUSTARD! ON JELLY?

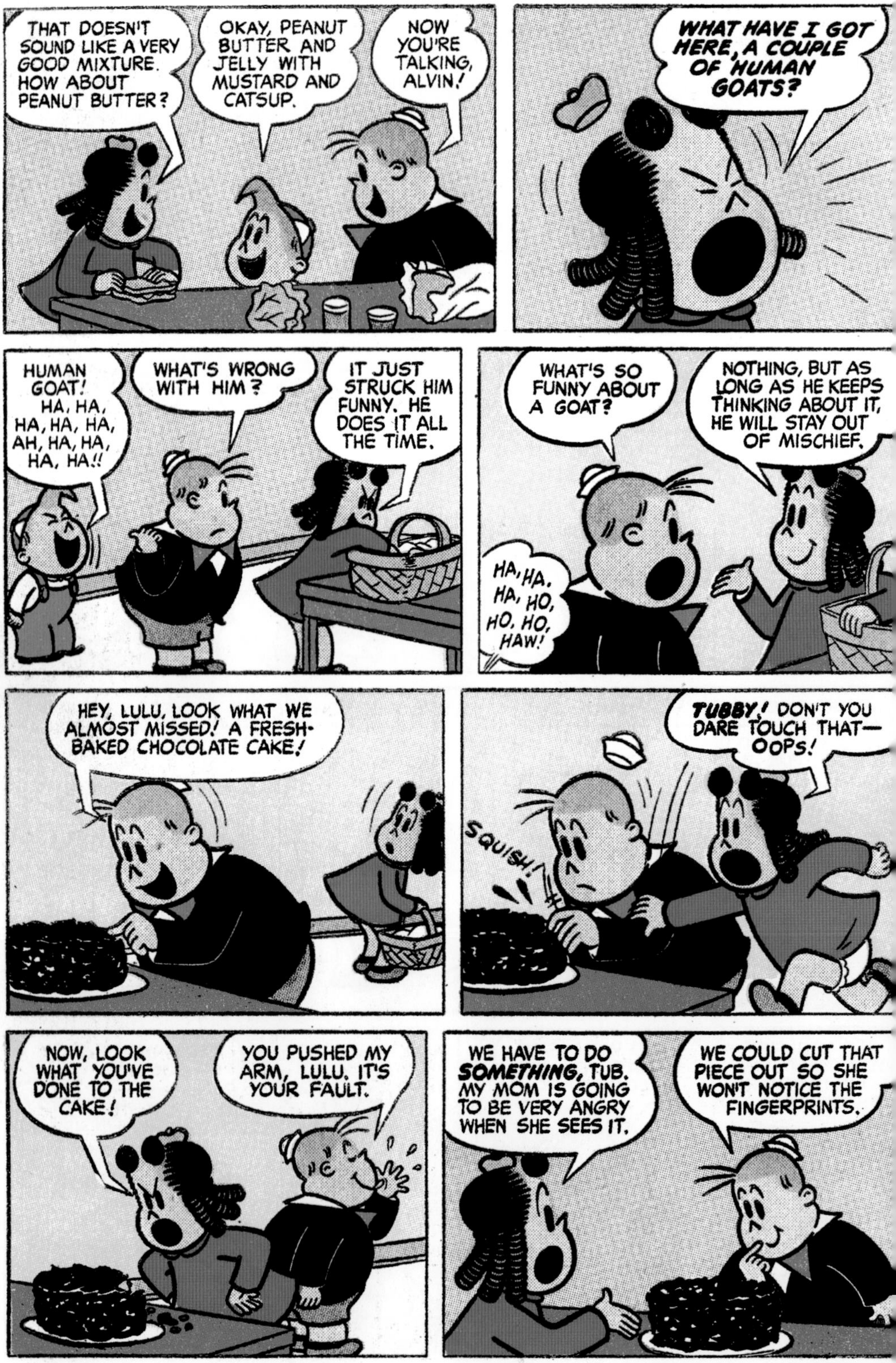
THAT DOESN'T SOUND LIKE A VERY GOOD MIXTURE. HOW ABOUT PEANUT BUTTER?
OKAY, PEANUT BUTTER AND JELLY WITH MUSTARD AND CATSUP.
NOW YOU'RE TALKING, ALVIN!
WHAT HAVE I GOT HERE, A COUPLE OF HUMAN GOATS?
HUMAN GOAT! HA, HA, HA, HA, HA, AH, HA, HA, HA, HA!!
WHAT'S WRONG WITH HIM?
IT JUST STRUCK HIM FUNNY. HE DOES IT ALL THE TIME.
WHAT'S SO FUNNY ABOUT A GOAT?
NOTHING, BUT AS LONG AS HE KEEPS THINKING ABOUT IT, HE WILL STAY OUT OF MISCHIEF.
HA, HA, HA, HO, HO, HO, HAW!
HEY, LULU, LOOK WHAT WE ALMOST MISSED! A FRESH-BAKED CHOCOLATE CAKE!
TUBBY! DON'T YOU DARE TOUCH THAT— OOPS!
SQUISH!
NOW, LOOK WHAT YOU'VE DONE TO THE CAKE!
YOU PUSHED MY ARM, LULU. IT'S YOUR FAULT.
WE HAVE TO DO SOMETHING, TUB. MY MOM IS GOING TO BE VERY ANGRY WHEN SHE SEES IT.
WE COULD CUT THAT PIECE OUT SO SHE WON'T NOTICE THE FINGERPRINTS.

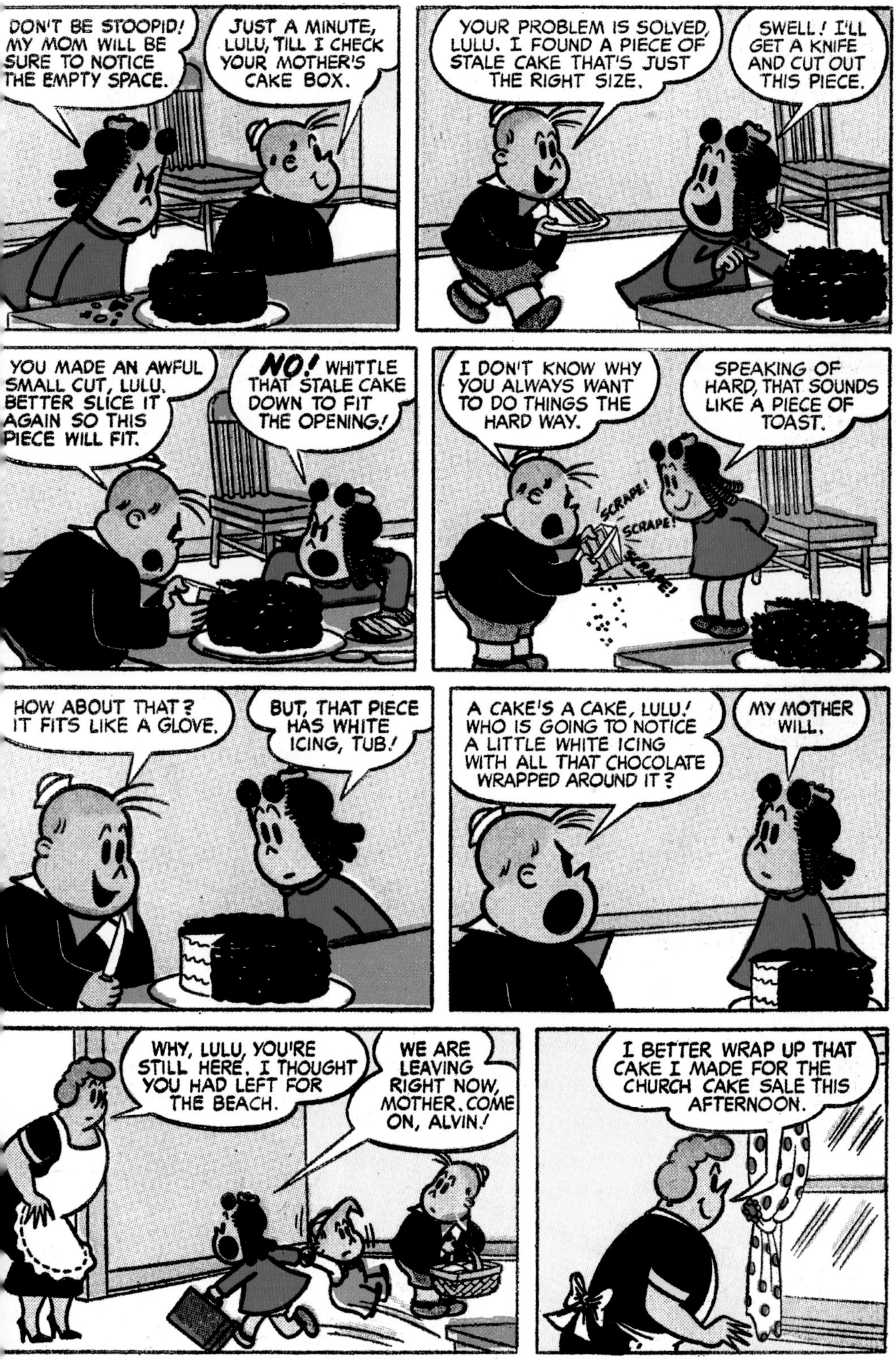
DON'T BE STOOPID! MY MOM WILL BE SURE TO NOTICE THE EMPTY SPACE.
JUST A MINUTE, LULU, TILL I CHECK YOUR MOTHER'S CAKE BOX.
YOUR PROBLEM IS SOLVED, LULU. I FOUND A PIECE OF STALE CAKE THAT'S JUST THE RIGHT SIZE.
SWELL! I'LL GET A KNIFE AND CUT OUT THIS PIECE.
YOU MADE AN AWFUL SMALL CUT, LULU. BETTER SLICE IT AGAIN SO THIS PIECE WILL FIT.
NO! WHITTLE THAT STALE CAKE DOWN TO FIT THE OPENING!
I DON'T KNOW WHY YOU ALWAYS WANT TO DO THINGS THE HARD WAY.
SPEAKING OF HARD, THAT SOUNDS LIKE A PIECE OF TOAST.
SCRAPE!
SCRAPE!
SCRAPE!
HOW ABOUT THAT? IT FITS LIKE A GLOVE.
BUT, THAT PIECE HAS WHITE ICING, TUB!
A CAKE'S A CAKE, LULU! WHO IS GOING TO NOTICE A LITTLE WHITE ICING WITH ALL THAT CHOCOLATE WRAPPED AROUND IT?
MY MOTHER WILL.
WHY, LULU, YOU'RE STILL HERE. I THOUGHT YOU HAD LEFT FOR THE BEACH.
WE ARE LEAVING RIGHT NOW, MOTHER. COME ON, ALVIN!
I BETTER WRAP UP THAT CAKE I MADE FOR THE CHURCH CAKE SALE THIS AFTERNOON.

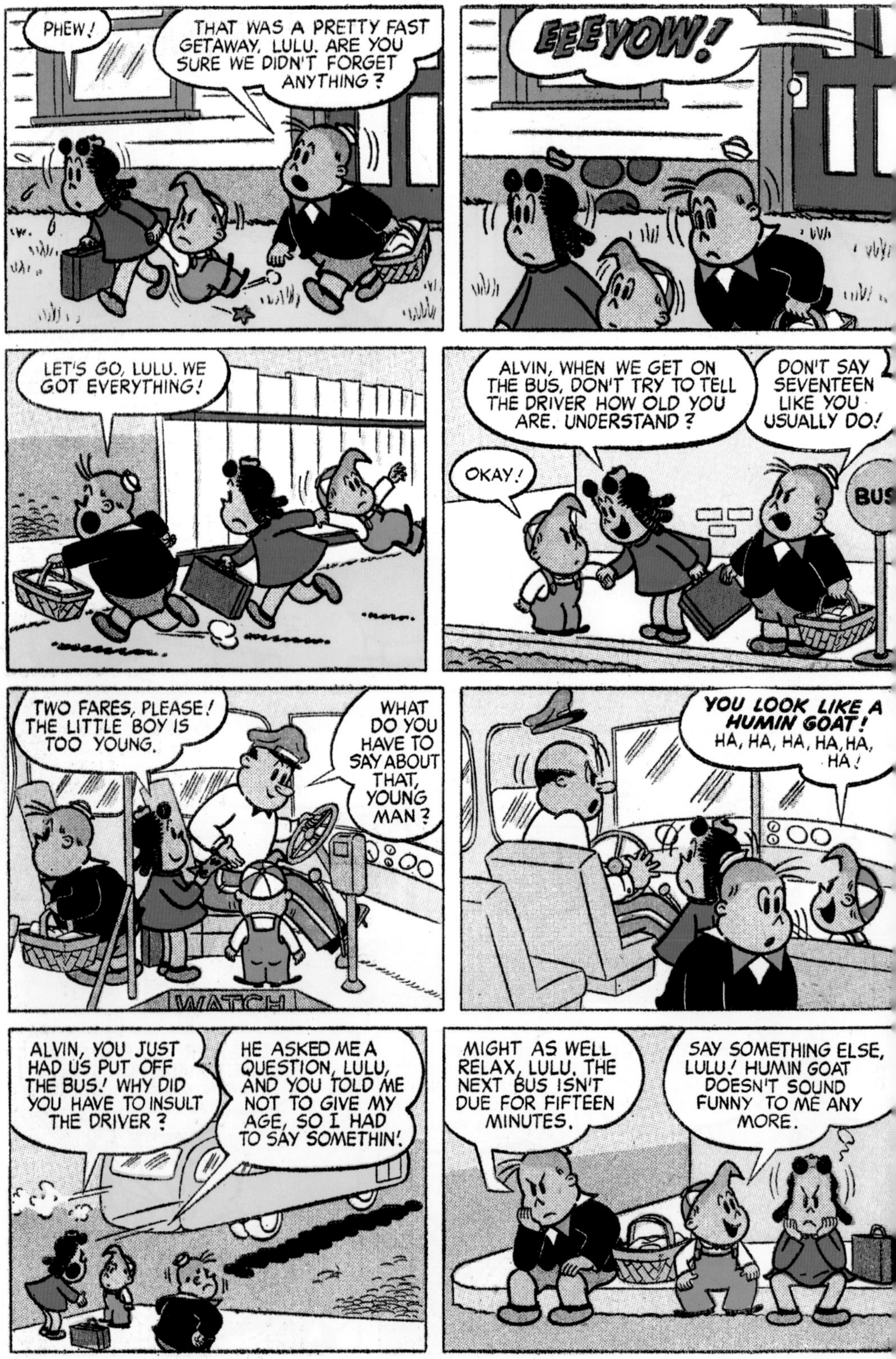
PHEW!
THAT WAS A PRETTY FAST GETAWAY, LULU. ARE YOU SURE WE DIDN'T FORGET ANYTHING?
EEEYOW!
LET'S GO, LULU. WE GOT EVERYTHING!
ALVIN, WHEN WE GET ON THE BUS, DON'T TRY TO TELL THE DRIVER HOW OLD YOU ARE. UNDERSTAND?
DON'T SAY SEVENTEEN LIKE YOU USUALLY DO!
OKAY!
BUS
TWO FARES, PLEASE! THE LITTLE BOY IS TOO YOUNG.
WHAT DO YOU HAVE TO SAY ABOUT THAT, YOUNG MAN?
WATCH
YOU LOOK LIKE A HUMIN GOAT! HA, HA, HA, HA, HA, HA!
ALVIN, YOU JUST HAD US PUT OFF THE BUS! WHY DID YOU HAVE TO INSULT THE DRIVER?
HE ASKED ME A QUESTION, LULU, AND YOU TOLD ME NOT TO GIVE MY AGE, SO I HAD TO SAY SOMETHIN'.
MIGHT AS WELL RELAX, LULU. THE NEXT BUS ISN'T DUE FOR FIFTEEN MINUTES.
SAY SOMETHING ELSE, LULU! HUMIN GOAT DOESN'T SOUND FUNNY TO ME ANY MORE.

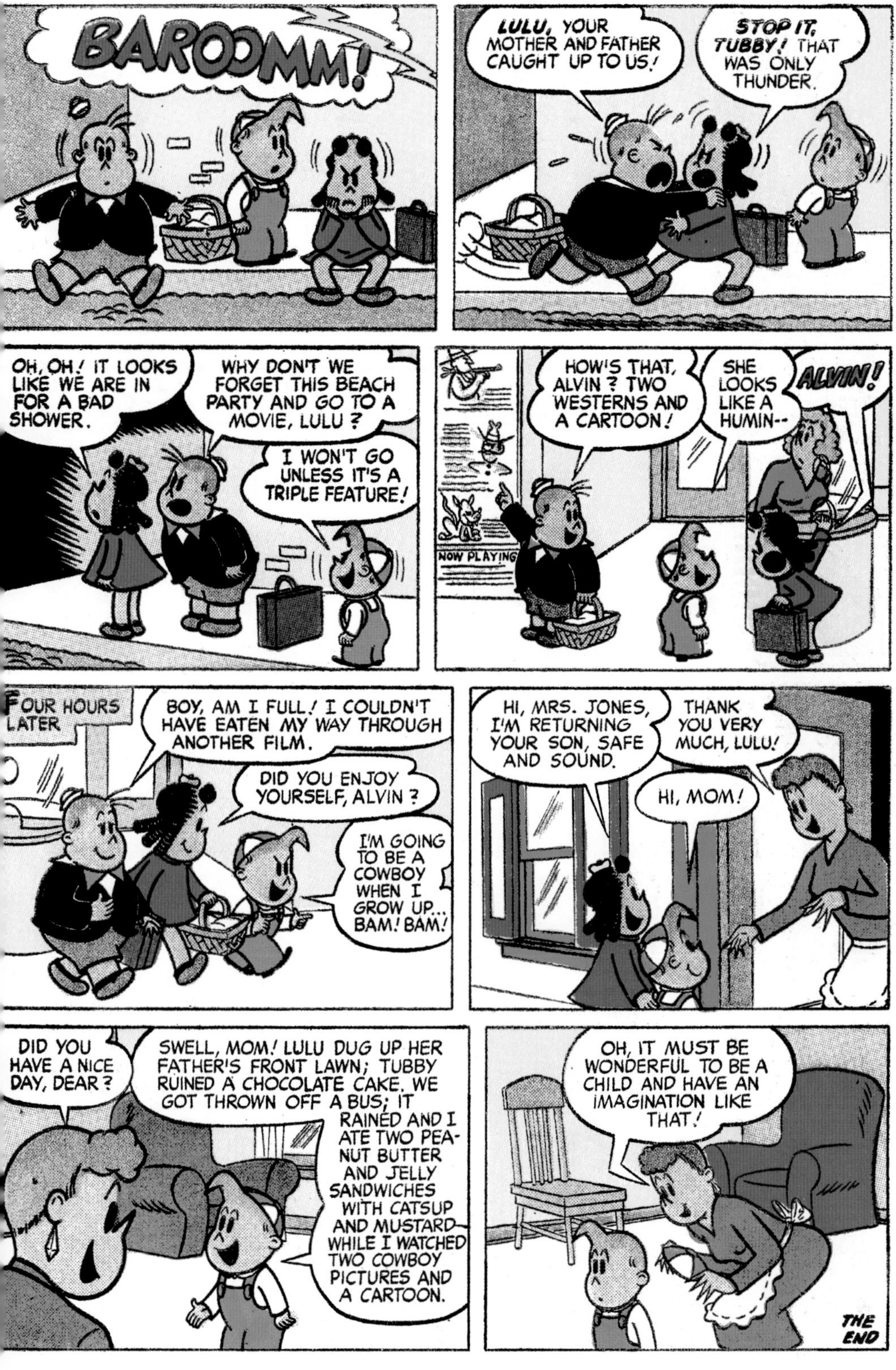
BAROOMM!
LULU, YOUR MOTHER AND FATHER CAUGHT UP TO US!
STOP IT, TUBBY! THAT WAS ONLY THUNDER.
OH, OH! IT LOOKS LIKE WE ARE IN FOR A BAD SHOWER.
WHY DON'T WE FORGET THIS BEACH PARTY AND GO TO A MOVIE, LULU?
I WON'T GO UNLESS IT'S A TRIPLE FEATURE!
NOW PLAYING
HOW'S THAT, ALVIN? TWO WESTERNS AND A CARTOON!
SHE LOOKS LIKE A HUMIN--
ALVIN!
FOUR HOURS LATER
BOY, AM I FULL! I COULDN'T HAVE EATEN MY WAY THROUGH ANOTHER FILM.
DID YOU ENJOY YOURSELF, ALVIN?
I'M GOING TO BE A COWBOY WHEN I GROW UP... BAM! BAM!
HI, MRS. JONES, I'M RETURNING YOUR SON, SAFE AND SOUND.
THANK YOU VERY MUCH, LULU!
HI, MOM!
DID YOU HAVE A NICE DAY, DEAR?
SWELL, MOM! LULU DUG UP HER FATHER'S FRONT LAWN; TUBBY RUINED A CHOCOLATE CAKE. WE GOT THROWN OFF A BUS; IT RAINED AND I ATE TWO PEA-NUT BUTTER AND JELLY SANDWICHES WITH CATSUP AND MUSTARD WHILE I WATCHED TWO COWBOY PICTURES AND A CARTOON.
OH, IT MUST BE WONDERFUL TO BE A CHILD AND HAVE AN IMAGINATION LIKE THAT!
THE END

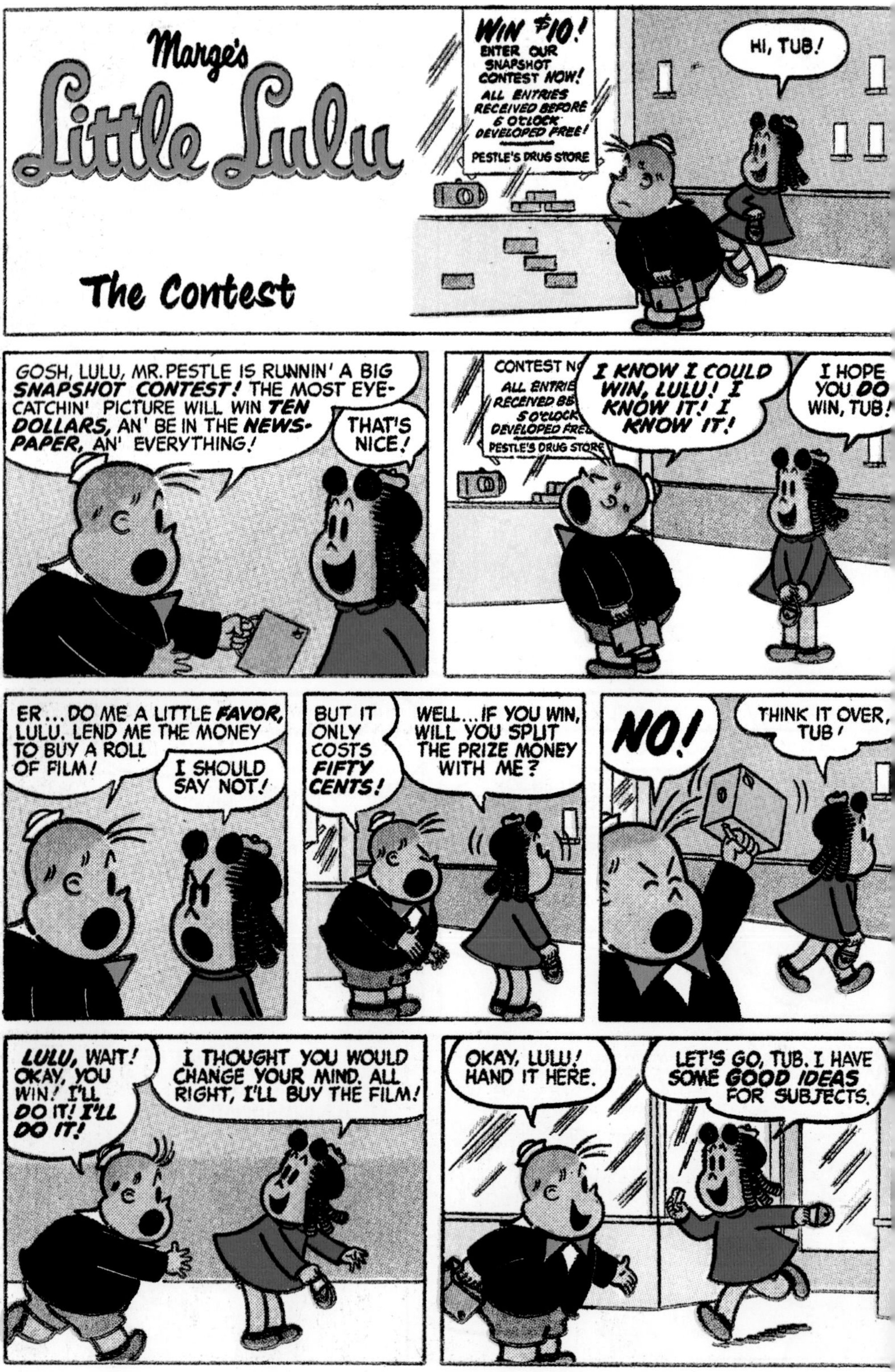
Marge's Little Lulu
The Contest
WIN $10! ENTER OUR SNAPSHOT CONTEST NOW! ALL ENTRIES RECEIVED BEFORE 6 O'CLOCK DEVELOPED FREE! PESTLE'S DRUG STORE
HI, TUB!
GOSH, LULU, MR. PESTLE IS RUNNIN' A BIG SNAPSHOT CONTEST! THE MOST EYE-CATCHIN' PICTURE WILL WIN TEN DOLLARS, AN' BE IN THE NEWSPAPER, AN' EVERYTHING!
THAT'S NICE!
I KNOW I COULD WIN, LULU! I KNOW IT! I KNOW IT!
I HOPE YOU DO WIN, TUB!
ER... DO ME A LITTLE FAVOR, LULU. LEND ME THE MONEY TO BUY A ROLL OF FILM!
I SHOULD SAY NOT!
BUT IT ONLY COSTS FIFTY CENTS!
WELL... IF YOU WIN, WILL YOU SPLIT THE PRIZE MONEY WITH ME?
NO!
THINK IT OVER, TUB!
LULU, WAIT! OKAY, YOU WIN! I'LL DO IT! I'LL DO IT!
I THOUGHT YOU WOULD CHANGE YOUR MIND. ALL RIGHT, I'LL BUY THE FILM!
OKAY, LULU! HAND IT HERE.
LET'S GO, TUB. I HAVE SOME GOOD IDEAS FOR SUBJECTS.

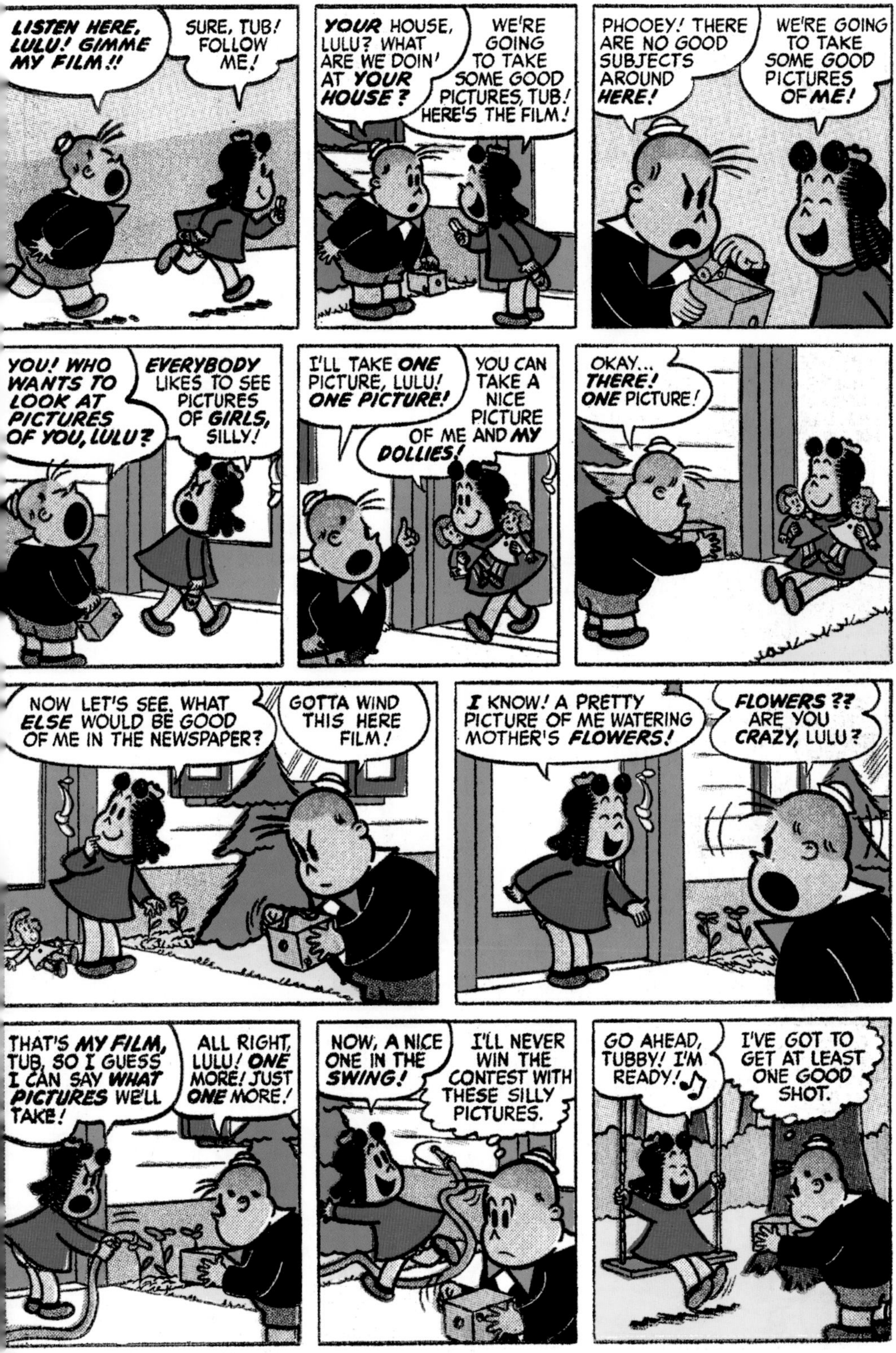
LISTEN HERE, LULU! GIMME MY FILM!!
SURE, TUB! FOLLOW ME!
YOUR HOUSE, LULU? WHAT ARE WE DOIN' AT YOUR HOUSE?
WE'RE GOING TO TAKE SOME GOOD PICTURES, TUB! HERE'S THE FILM!
PHOOEY! THERE ARE NO GOOD SUBJECTS AROUND HERE!
WE'RE GOING TO TAKE SOME GOOD PICTURES OF ME!
YOU! WHO WANTS TO LOOK AT PICTURES OF YOU, LULU?
EVERYBODY LIKES TO SEE PICTURES OF GIRLS, SILLY!
I'LL TAKE ONE PICTURE, LULU! ONE PICTURE!
YOU CAN TAKE A NICE PICTURE OF ME AND MY DOLLIES!
OKAY... THERE! ONE PICTURE!
NOW LET'S SEE. WHAT ELSE WOULD BE GOOD OF ME IN THE NEWSPAPER?
GOTTA WIND THIS HERE FILM!
I KNOW! A PRETTY PICTURE OF ME WATERING MOTHER'S FLOWERS!
FLOWERS?? ARE YOU CRAZY, LULU?
THAT'S MY FILM, TUB, SO I GUESS I CAN SAY WHAT PICTURES WE'LL TAKE!
ALL RIGHT, LULU! ONE MORE! JUST ONE MORE!
NOW, A NICE ONE IN THE SWING!
I'LL NEVER WIN THE CONTEST WITH THESE SILLY PICTURES.
GO AHEAD, TUBBY! I'M READY!
I'VE GOT TO GET AT LEAST ONE GOOD SHOT.

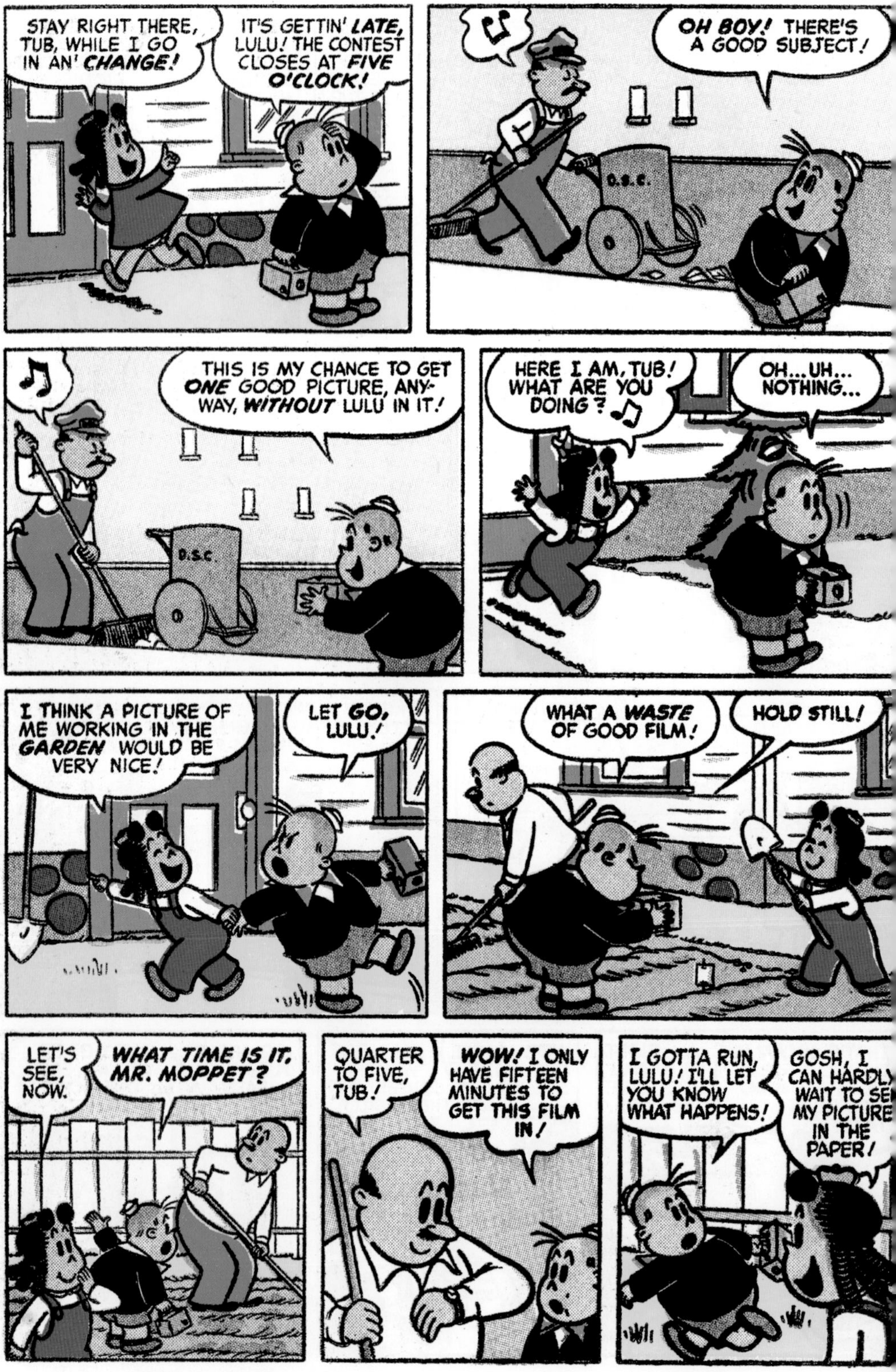
STAY RIGHT THERE, TUB, WHILE I GO IN AN' CHANGE!
IT'S GETTIN' LATE, LULU! THE CONTEST CLOSES AT FIVE O'CLOCK!
OH BOY! THERE'S A GOOD SUBJECT!
D.S.C.
THIS IS MY CHANCE TO GET ONE GOOD PICTURE, ANY-WAY, WITHOUT LULU IN IT!
D.S.C.
HERE I AM, TUB! WHAT ARE YOU DOING?
OH...UH... NOTHING...
I THINK A PICTURE OF ME WORKING IN THE GARDEN WOULD BE VERY NICE!
LET GO, LULU!
WHAT A WASTE OF GOOD FILM!
HOLD STILL!
LET'S SEE, NOW.
WHAT TIME IS IT, MR. MOPPET?
QUARTER TO FIVE, TUB!
WOW! I ONLY HAVE FIFTEEN MINUTES TO GET THIS FILM IN!
I GOTTA RUN, LULU! I'LL LET YOU KNOW WHAT HAPPENS!
GOSH, I CAN HARDLY WAIT TO SEE MY PICTURE IN THE PAPER!

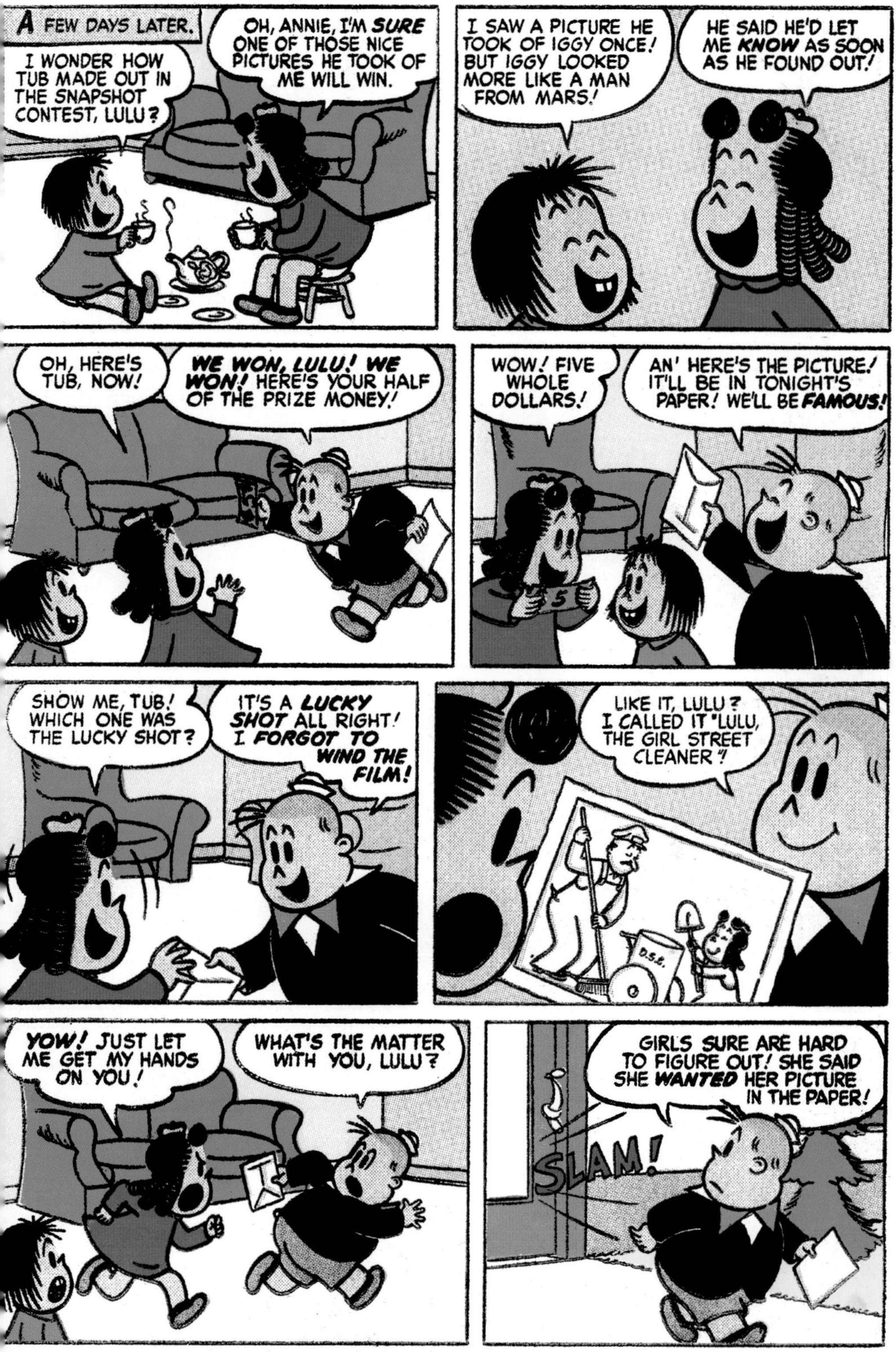
A FEW DAYS LATER.
I WONDER HOW TUB MADE OUT IN THE SNAPSHOT CONTEST, LULU?
OH, ANNIE, I'M SURE ONE OF THOSE NICE PICTURES HE TOOK OF ME WILL WIN.
I SAW A PICTURE HE TOOK OF IGGY ONCE! BUT IGGY LOOKED MORE LIKE A MAN FROM MARS!
HE SAID HE'D LET ME KNOW AS SOON AS HE FOUND OUT!
OH, HERE'S TUB, NOW!
WE WON, LULU! WE WON! HERE'S YOUR HALF OF THE PRIZE MONEY!
WOW! FIVE WHOLE DOLLARS!
AN' HERE'S THE PICTURE! IT'LL BE IN TONIGHT'S PAPER! WE'LL BE FAMOUS!
SHOW ME, TUB! WHICH ONE WAS THE LUCKY SHOT?
IT'S A LUCKY SHOT ALL RIGHT! I FORGOT TO WIND THE FILM!
LIKE IT, LULU? I CALLED IT "LULU, THE GIRL STREET CLEANER"!
YOW! JUST LET ME GET MY HANDS ON YOU!
WHAT'S THE MATTER WITH YOU, LULU?
GIRLS SURE ARE HARD TO FIGURE OUT! SHE SAID SHE WANTED HER PICTURE IN THE PAPER!
SLAM!

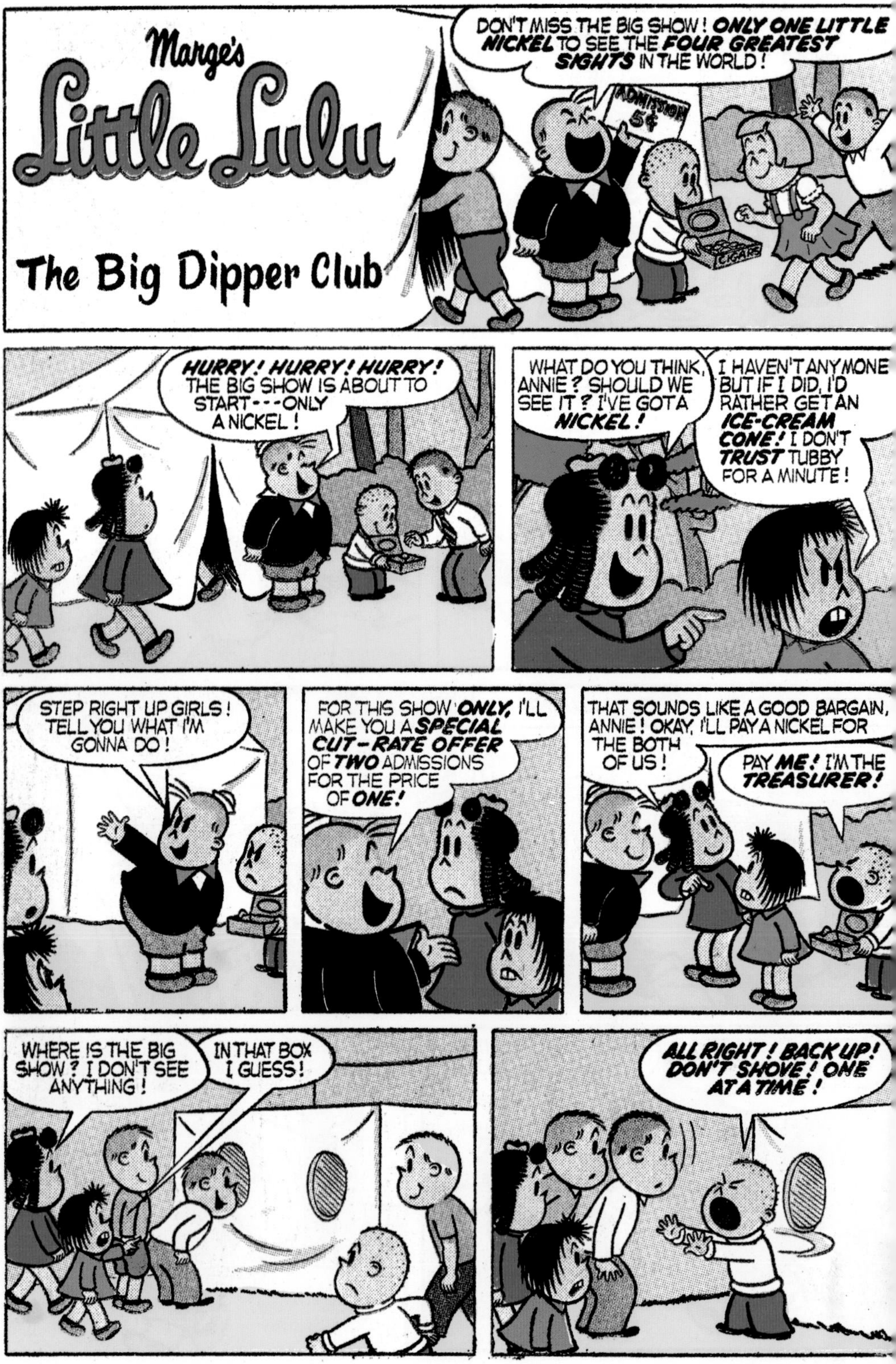
Marge's
Little Lulu
The Big Dipper Club
DON'T MISS THE BIG SHOW! ONLY ONE LITTLE NICKEL TO SEE THE FOUR GREATEST SIGHTS IN THE WORLD!
ADMISSION 5¢
CIGARS
HURRY! HURRY! HURRY! THE BIG SHOW IS ABOUT TO START---ONLY A NICKEL!
WHAT DO YOU THINK, ANNIE? SHOULD WE SEE IT? I'VE GOT A NICKEL!
I HAVEN'T ANY MONE BUT IF I DID, I'D RATHER GET AN ICE-CREAM CONE! I DON'T TRUST TUBBY FOR A MINUTE!
STEP RIGHT UP GIRLS! TELL YOU WHAT I'M GONNA DO!
FOR THIS SHOW ONLY, I'LL MAKE YOU A SPECIAL CUT-RATE OFFER OF TWO ADMISSIONS FOR THE PRICE OF ONE!
THAT SOUNDS LIKE A GOOD BARGAIN, ANNIE! OKAY, I'LL PAY A NICKEL FOR THE BOTH OF US!
PAY ME! I'M THE TREASURER!
WHERE IS THE BIG SHOW? I DON'T SEE ANYTHING!
IN THAT BOX I GUESS!
ALL RIGHT! BACK UP! DON'T SHOVE! ONE AT A TIME!

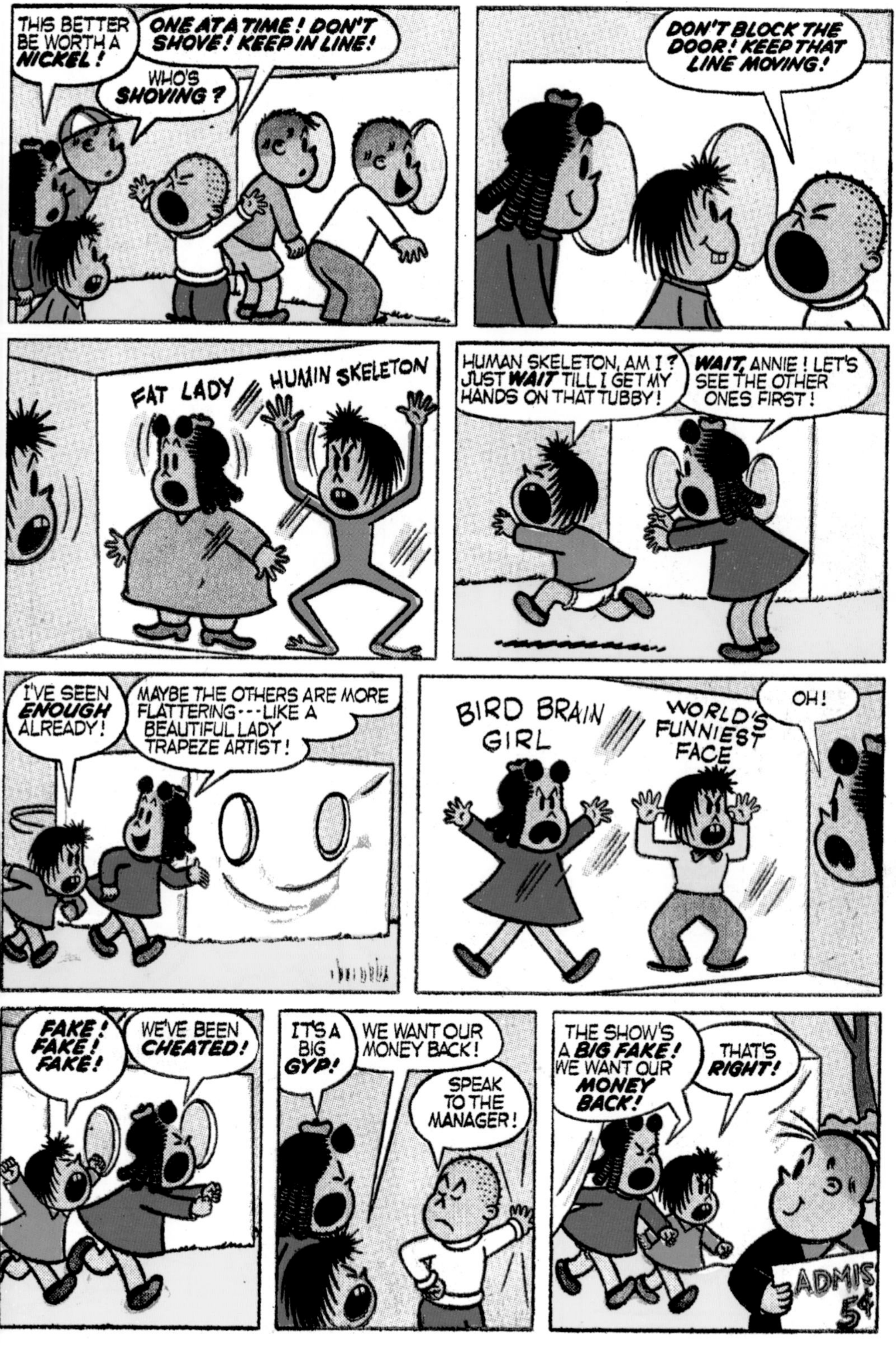

THIS BETTER BE WORTH A NICKEL!
ONE AT A TIME! DON'T SHOVE! KEEP IN LINE!
WHO'S SHOVING?
DON'T BLOCK THE DOOR! KEEP THAT LINE MOVING!
FAT LADY
HUMIN SKELETON
HUMAN SKELETON, AM I? JUST WAIT TILL I GET MY HANDS ON THAT TUBBY!
WAIT, ANNIE! LET'S SEE THE OTHER ONES FIRST!
I'VE SEEN ENOUGH ALREADY!
MAYBE THE OTHERS ARE MORE FLATTERING---LIKE A BEAUTIFUL LADY TRAPEZE ARTIST!
BIRD BRAIN GIRL
WORLD'S FUNNIEST FACE
OH!
FAKE! FAKE! FAKE!
WE'VE BEEN CHEATED!
IT'S A BIG GYP!
WE WANT OUR MONEY BACK!
SPEAK TO THE MANAGER!
THE SHOW'S A BIG FAKE! WE WANT OUR MONEY BACK!
THAT'S RIGHT!
ADMIS 5¢

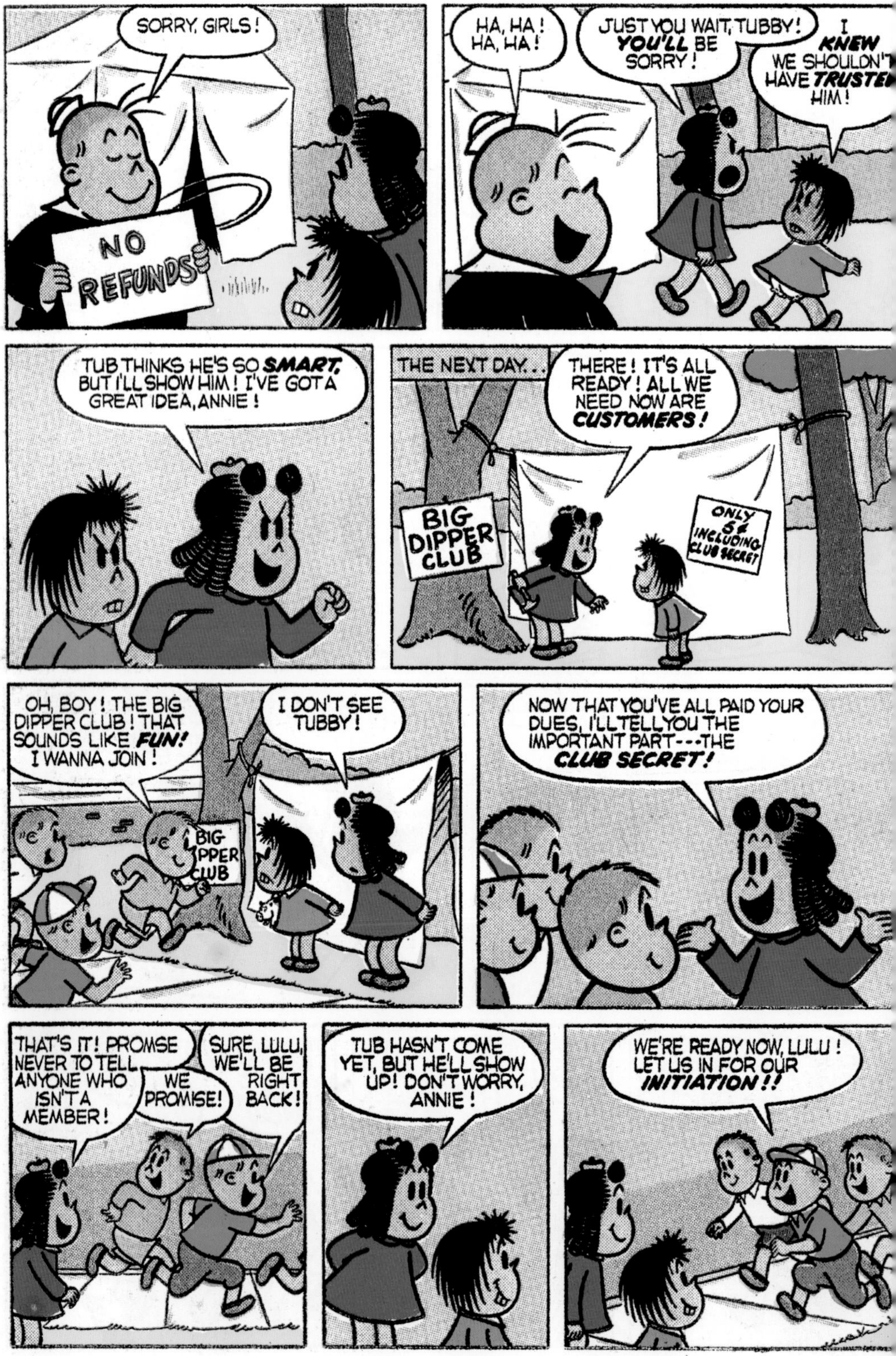
SORRY, GIRLS!
NO REFUNDS
HA, HA! HA, HA!
JUST YOU WAIT, TUBBY! YOU'LL BE SORRY!
I KNEW WE SHOULDN'T HAVE TRUSTED HIM!
TUB THINKS HE'S SO SMART, BUT I'LL SHOW HIM! I'VE GOT A GREAT IDEA, ANNIE!
THE NEXT DAY...
THERE! IT'S ALL READY! ALL WE NEED NOW ARE CUSTOMERS!
BIG DIPPER CLUB
ONLY 5¢ INCLUDING CLUB SECRET
OH, BOY! THE BIG DIPPER CLUB! THAT SOUNDS LIKE FUN! I WANNA JOIN!
I DON'T SEE TUBBY!
NOW THAT YOU'VE ALL PAID YOUR DUES, I'LL TELL YOU THE IMPORTANT PART---THE CLUB SECRET!
THAT'S IT! PROMSE NEVER TO TELL ANYONE WHO ISN'T A MEMBER!
WE PROMISE!
SURE, LULU, WE'LL BE RIGHT BACK!
TUB HASN'T COME YET, BUT HE'LL SHOW UP! DON'T WORRY, ANNIE!
WE'RE READY NOW, LULU! LET US IN FOR OUR INITIATION!!

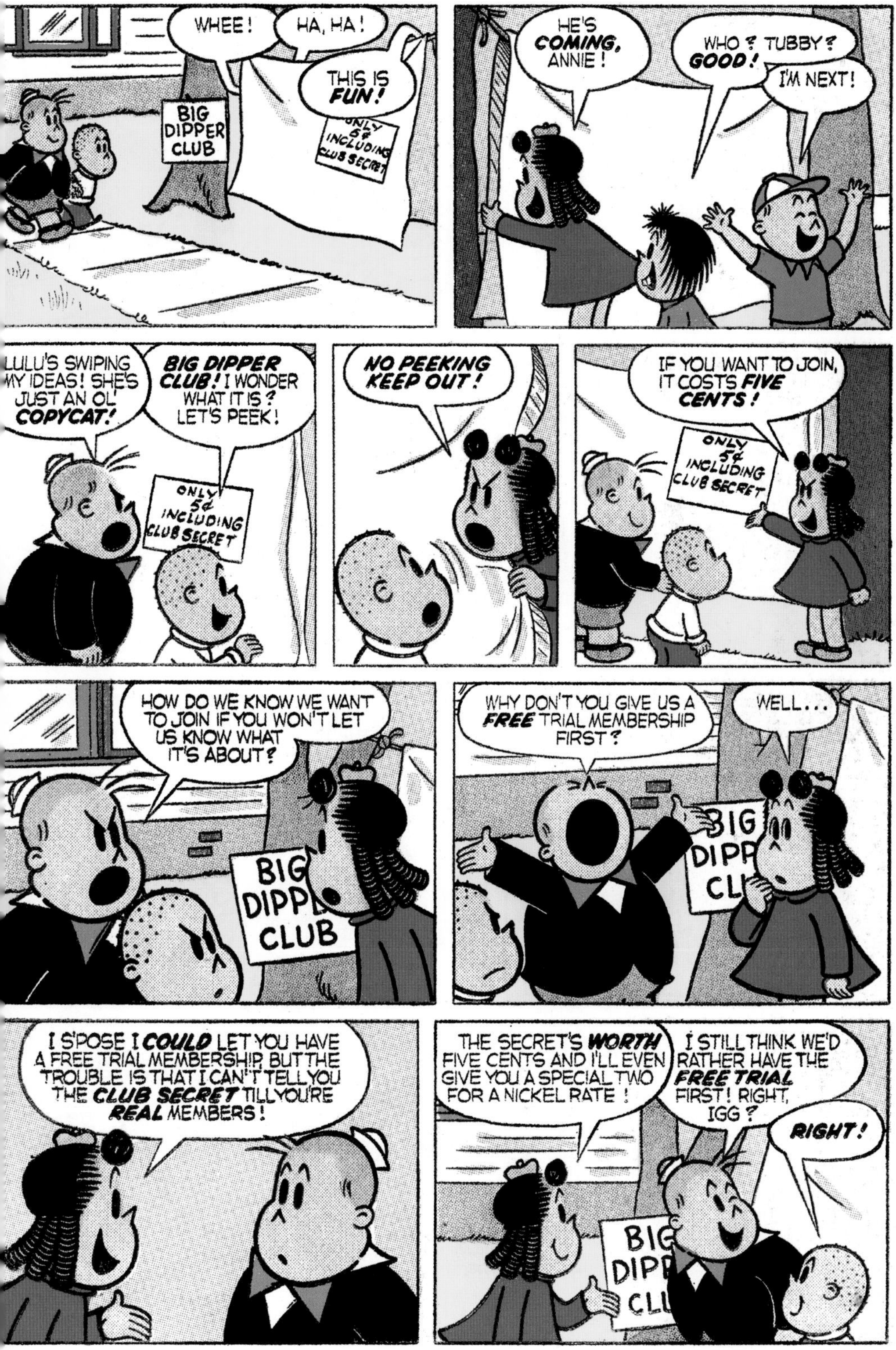
WHEE!
HA, HA!
THIS IS FUN!
BIG DIPPER CLUB
ONLY 5¢ INCLUDING CLUB SECRET
HE'S COMING, ANNIE!
WHO? TUBBY? GOOD!
I'M NEXT!
LULU'S SWIPING MY IDEAS! SHE'S JUST AN OL' COPYCAT!
BIG DIPPER CLUB! I WONDER WHAT IT IS? LET'S PEEK!
ONLY 5¢ INCLUDING CLUB SECRET
NO PEEKING KEEP OUT!
IF YOU WANT TO JOIN, IT COSTS FIVE CENTS!
ONLY 5¢ INCLUDING CLUB SECRET
HOW DO WE KNOW WE WANT TO JOIN IF YOU WON'T LET US KNOW WHAT IT'S ABOUT?
BIG DIPP CLUB
WHY DON'T YOU GIVE US A FREE TRIAL MEMBERSHIP FIRST?
WELL...
BIG DIPP CL
I S'POSE I COULD LET YOU HAVE A FREE TRIAL MEMBERSHIP, BUT THE TROUBLE IS THAT I CAN'T TELL YOU THE CLUB SECRET TILL YOU'RE REAL MEMBERS!
THE SECRET'S WORTH FIVE CENTS AND I'LL EVEN GIVE YOU A SPECIAL TWO FOR A NICKEL RATE!
I STILL THINK WE'D RATHER HAVE THE FREE TRIAL FIRST! RIGHT, IGG?
RIGHT!
BIG DIPP CLU

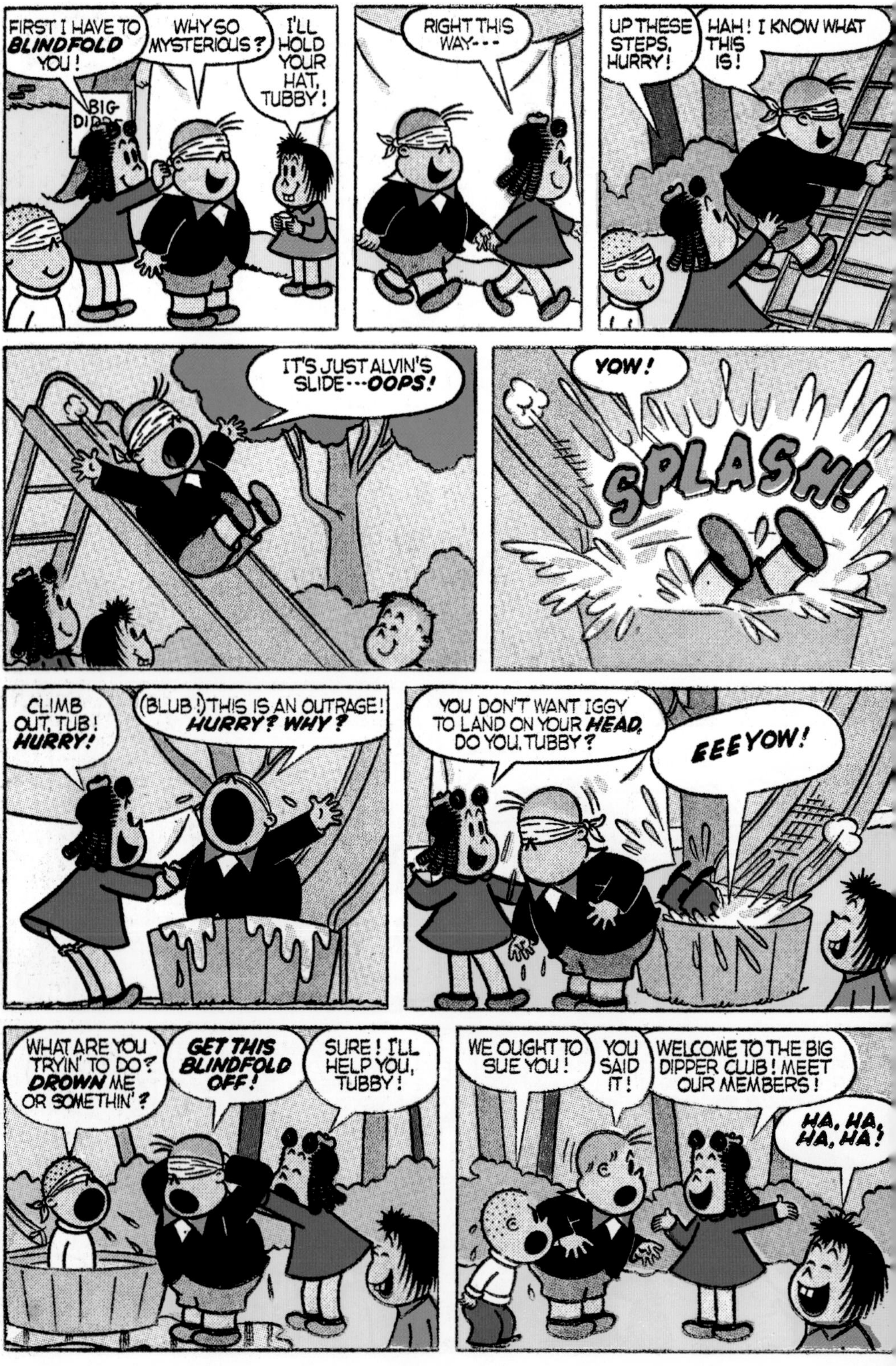
FIRST I HAVE TO BLINDFOLD YOU!
WHY SO MYSTERIOUS?
I'LL HOLD YOUR HAT, TUBBY!
RIGHT THIS WAY---
UP THESE STEPS, HURRY!
HAH! I KNOW WHAT THIS IS!
IT'S JUST ALVIN'S SLIDE---OOPS!
YOW!
SPLASH!
CLIMB OUT, TUB! HURRY!
(BLUB!) THIS IS AN OUTRAGE! HURRY? WHY?
YOU DON'T WANT IGGY TO LAND ON YOUR HEAD, DO YOU, TUBBY?
EEEYOW!
WHAT ARE YOU TRYIN' TO DO? DROWN ME OR SOMETHIN'?
GET THIS BLINDFOLD OFF!
SURE! I'LL HELP YOU, TUBBY!
WE OUGHT TO SUE YOU!
YOU SAID IT!
WELCOME TO THE BIG DIPPER CLUB! MEET OUR MEMBERS!
HA, HA, HA, HA!

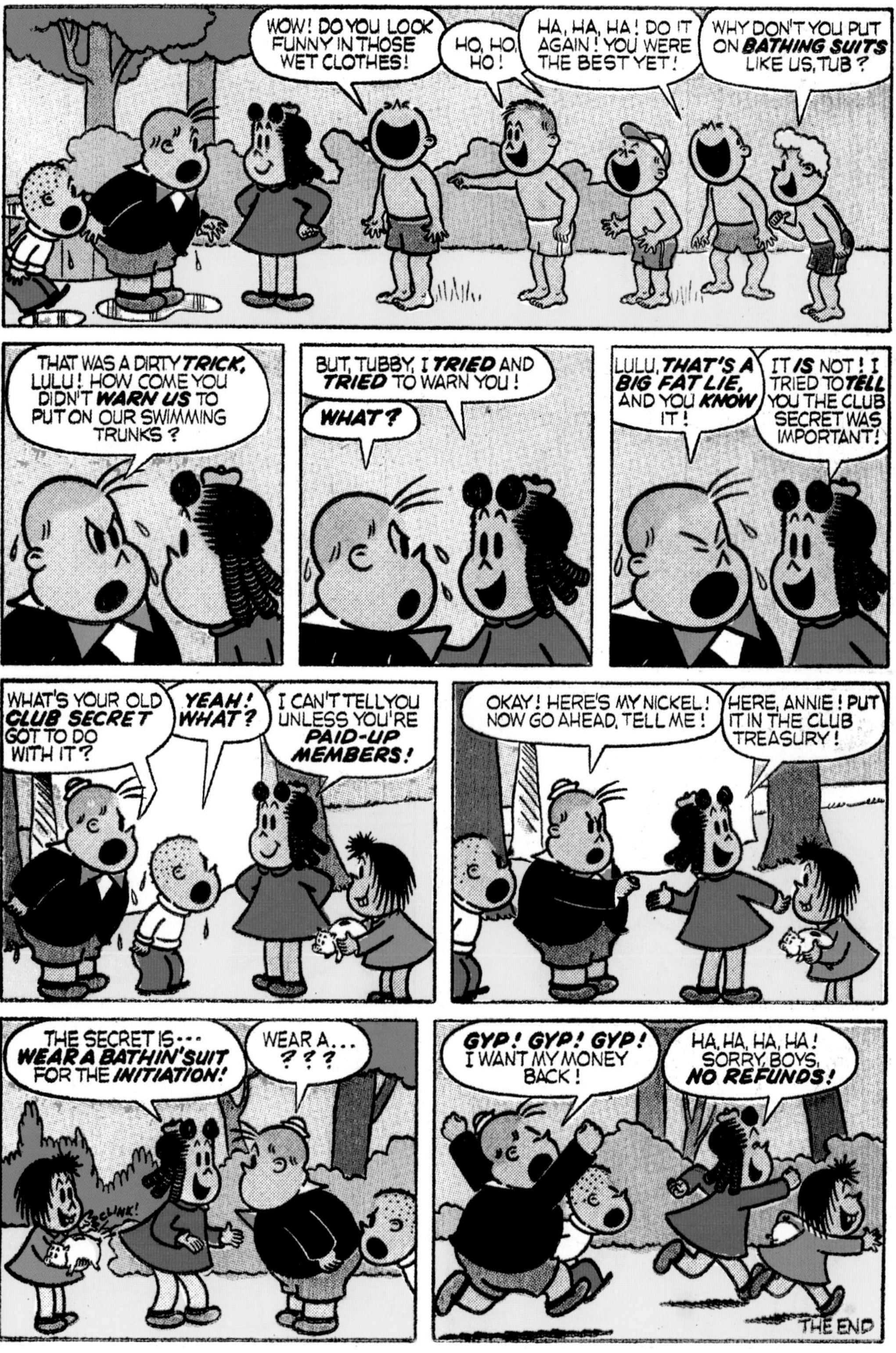
WOW! DO YOU LOOK FUNNY IN THOSE WET CLOTHES!
HO, HO, HO!
HA, HA, HA! DO IT AGAIN! YOU WERE THE BEST YET!
WHY DON'T YOU PUT ON BATHING SUITS LIKE US, TUB?
THAT WAS A DIRTY TRICK, LULU! HOW COME YOU DIDN'T WARN US TO PUT ON OUR SWIMMING TRUNKS?
BUT, TUBBY, I TRIED AND TRIED TO WARN YOU!
WHAT?
LULU, THAT'S A BIG FAT LIE, AND YOU KNOW IT!
IT IS NOT! I TRIED TO TELL YOU THE CLUB SECRET WAS IMPORTANT!
WHAT'S YOUR OLD CLUB SECRET GOT TO DO WITH IT?
YEAH! WHAT?
I CAN'T TELL YOU UNLESS YOU'RE PAID-UP MEMBERS!
OKAY! HERE'S MY NICKEL! NOW GO AHEAD, TELL ME!
HERE, ANNIE! PUT IT IN THE CLUB TREASURY!
THE SECRET IS··· WEAR A BATHIN' SUIT FOR THE INITIATION!
WEAR A... ???
CLINK!
GYP! GYP! GYP! I WANT MY MONEY BACK!
HA, HA, HA, HA! SORRY, BOYS, NO REFUNDS!
THE END

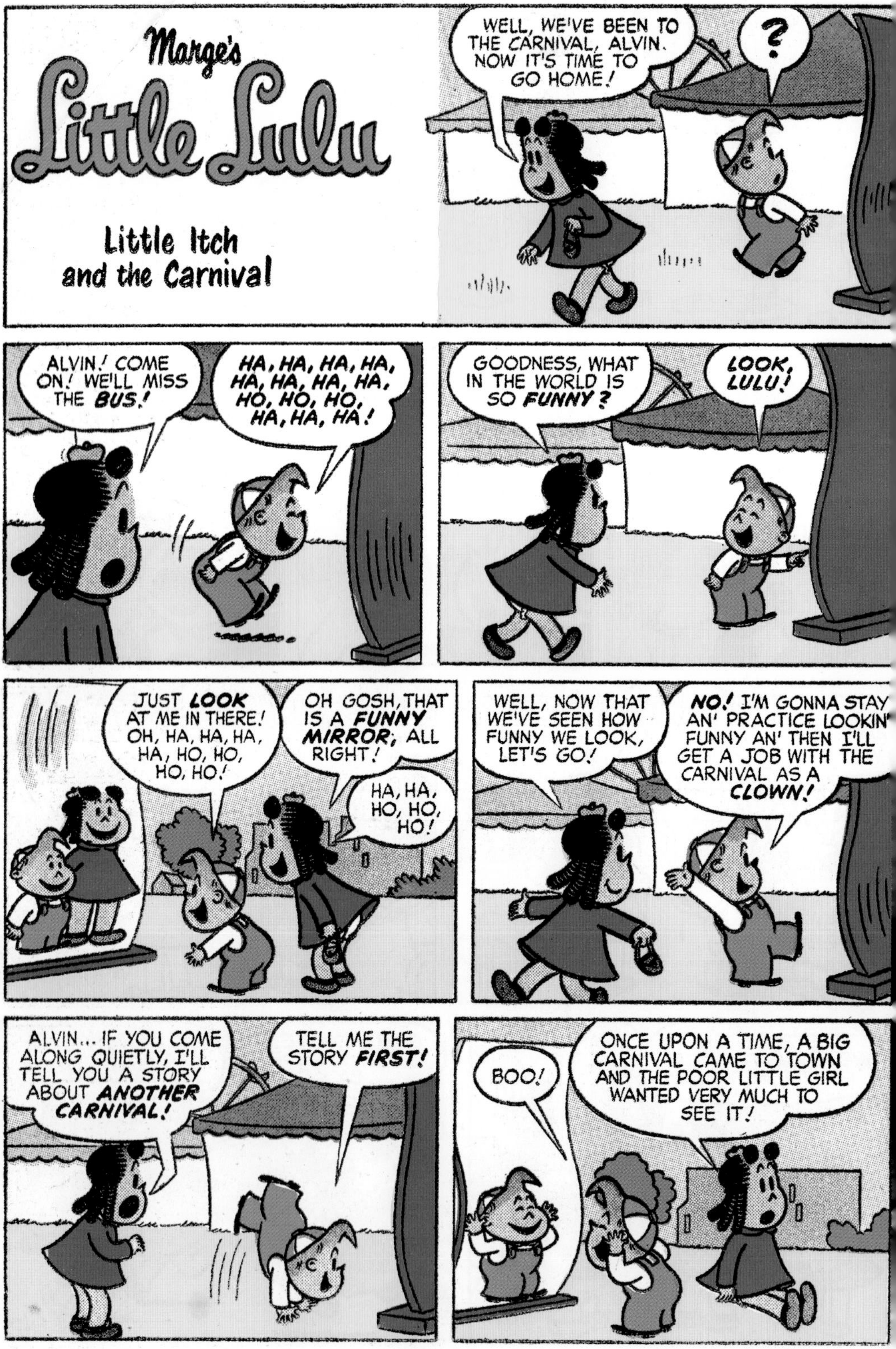

Marge's
Little Lulu
Little Itch and the Carnival
WELL, WE'VE BEEN TO THE CARNIVAL, ALVIN. NOW IT'S TIME TO GO HOME!
?
ALVIN! COME ON! WE'LL MISS THE BUS!
HA, HA, HA, HA, HA, HA, HA, HA, HO, HO, HO, HA, HA, HA!
GOODNESS, WHAT IN THE WORLD IS SO FUNNY?
LOOK, LULU!
JUST LOOK AT ME IN THERE! OH, HA, HA, HA, HA, HO, HO, HO, HO!
OH GOSH, THAT IS A FUNNY MIRROR; ALL RIGHT!
HA, HA, HO, HO, HO!
WELL, NOW THAT WE'VE SEEN HOW FUNNY WE LOOK, LET'S GO!
NO! I'M GONNA STAY AN' PRACTICE LOOKIN' FUNNY AN' THEN I'LL GET A JOB WITH THE CARNIVAL AS A CLOWN!
ALVIN... IF YOU COME ALONG QUIETLY, I'LL TELL YOU A STORY ABOUT ANOTHER CARNIVAL!
TELL ME THE STORY FIRST!
BOO!
ONCE UPON A TIME, A BIG CARNIVAL CAME TO TOWN AND THE POOR LITTLE GIRL WANTED VERY MUCH TO SEE IT!

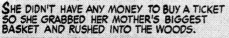

SHE DIDN'T HAVE ANY MONEY TO BUY A TICKET SO SHE GRABBED HER MOTHER'S BIGGEST BASKET AND RUSHED INTO THE WOODS.

I'LL PICK A LOT OF NICE *BEEBLEBERRIES* TO SELL AND BUY A TICKET WITH THE MONEY!

COMING TO A DENSE PATCH OF BEEBLEBERRIES, SHE STOOPED OVER AND BEGAN SCOOPING THEM UP WITH BOTH HANDS.

THIS IS MY LUCKY DAY! THERE ARE ENOUGH BEEBLEBERRIES HERE TO FILL A MILLION BASKETS.

SHE WAS SO BUSY STOOPING AND PICKING AND PICKING AND STOOPING THAT SHE DIDN'T NOTICE LITTLE ITCH COME SCRAMBLING OUT OF THE BUSHES.

HEY!

LITTLE ITCH HAD SPENT A BUSY MORNING TURNING THINGS INTO OTHER THINGS, AND WANTED TO RELAX!

LET'S PLAY SOME *GAMES!*

I'M TOO *BUSY!* I HAVE NO TIME FOR GAMES TODAY.

LITTLE ITCH *DIDN'T LIKE* BEING TURNED DOWN.

WHY NOT?

I HAVE TO SELL THESE BEEBLE-BERRIES SO I CAN BUY A TICKET TO THE GAY CARNIVAL THAT IS PLAYING OUTSIDE OF TOWN.

WHEN LITTLE ITCH HEARD ABOUT THE CARNIVAL, SHE FORGOT ALL ABOUT PLAYING GAMES!

I'VE NEVER BEEN TO A REAL CARNIVAL BEFORE IN ALL MY WHOLE LIFE!

I'LL SHOW YOU HOW TO CHANGE BEEBLE-BERRIES INTO MONEY THE *EASY WAY!*

WITH ONE WAVE OF HER MAGIC WAND, SHE TURNED THE BASKET OF BEEBLEBERRIES INTO A BASKET OF BRIGHT, SHINY DIMES!

BLDOXXLE!

YOW! DIMES!

THE LITTLE GIRL WAS SO HAPPY AND EXCITED, SHE DIDN'T SEE LITTLE ITCH SNATCH AWAY THE BASKET.

OH, *THANK* YOU, LITTLE ITCH! *NOW* I CAN GO TO THE CARNIVAL!

YOU MEAN NOW *I* CAN GO TO THE CARNIVAL! KICKLE, KICKLE!

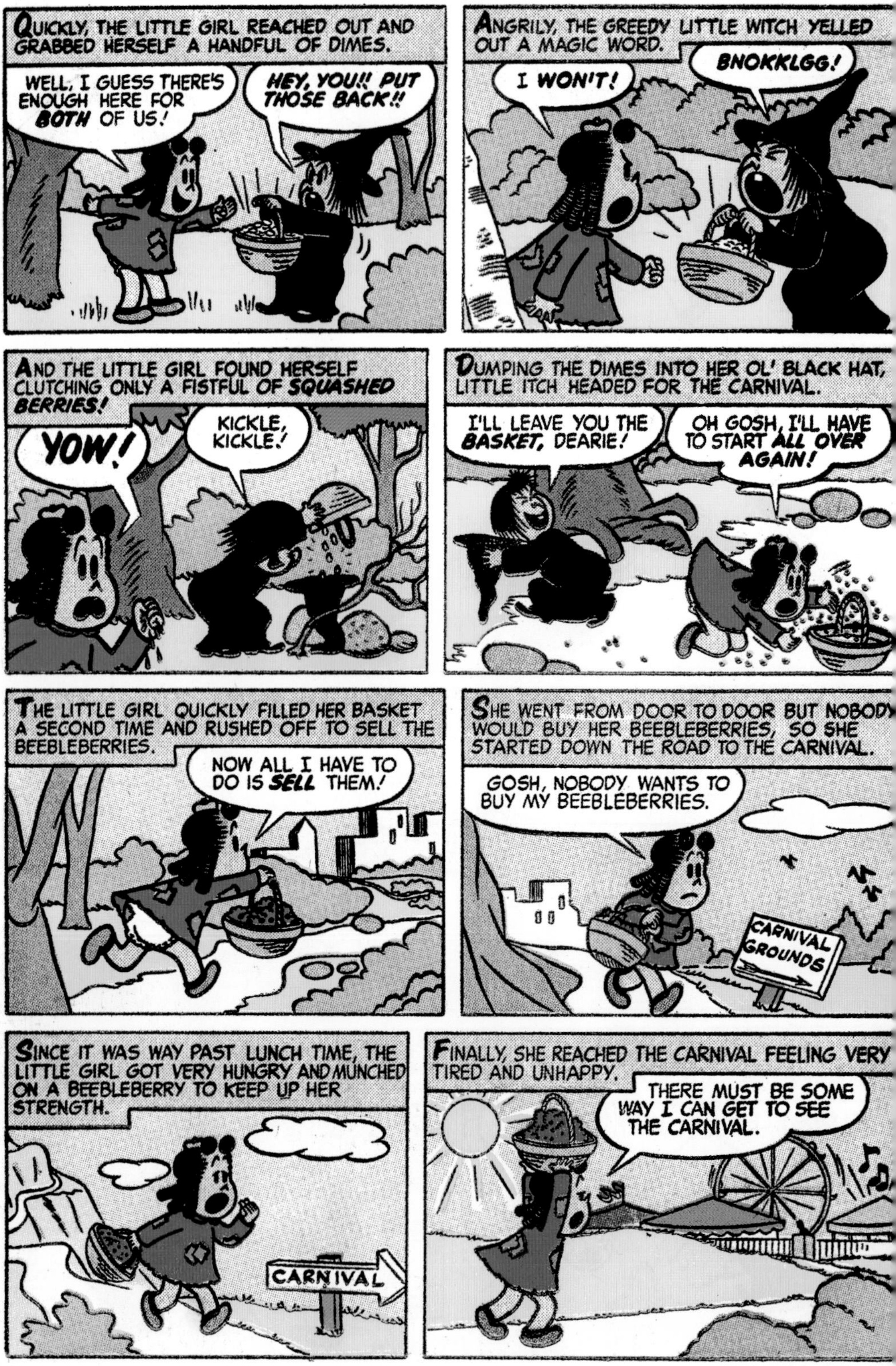
QUICKLY, THE LITTLE GIRL REACHED OUT AND GRABBED HERSELF A HANDFUL OF DIMES.
WELL, I GUESS THERE'S ENOUGH HERE FOR BOTH OF US!
HEY, YOU!! PUT THOSE BACK!!
ANGRILY, THE GREEDY LITTLE WITCH YELLED OUT A MAGIC WORD.
I WON'T!
BNOKKLGG!
AND THE LITTLE GIRL FOUND HERSELF CLUTCHING ONLY A FISTFUL OF SQUASHED BERRIES!
YOW!
KICKLE, KICKLE!
DUMPING THE DIMES INTO HER OL' BLACK HAT, LITTLE ITCH HEADED FOR THE CARNIVAL.
I'LL LEAVE YOU THE BASKET, DEARIE!
OH GOSH, I'LL HAVE TO START ALL OVER AGAIN!
THE LITTLE GIRL QUICKLY FILLED HER BASKET A SECOND TIME AND RUSHED OFF TO SELL THE BEEBLEBERRIES.
NOW ALL I HAVE TO DO IS SELL THEM!
SHE WENT FROM DOOR TO DOOR BUT NOBODY WOULD BUY HER BEEBLEBERRIES, SO SHE STARTED DOWN THE ROAD TO THE CARNIVAL.
GOSH, NOBODY WANTS TO BUY MY BEEBLEBERRIES.
CARNIVAL GROUNDS
SINCE IT WAS WAY PAST LUNCH TIME, THE LITTLE GIRL GOT VERY HUNGRY AND MUNCHED ON A BEEBLEBERRY TO KEEP UP HER STRENGTH.
CARNIVAL
FINALLY, SHE REACHED THE CARNIVAL FEELING VERY TIRED AND UNHAPPY.
THERE MUST BE SOME WAY I CAN GET TO SEE THE CARNIVAL.

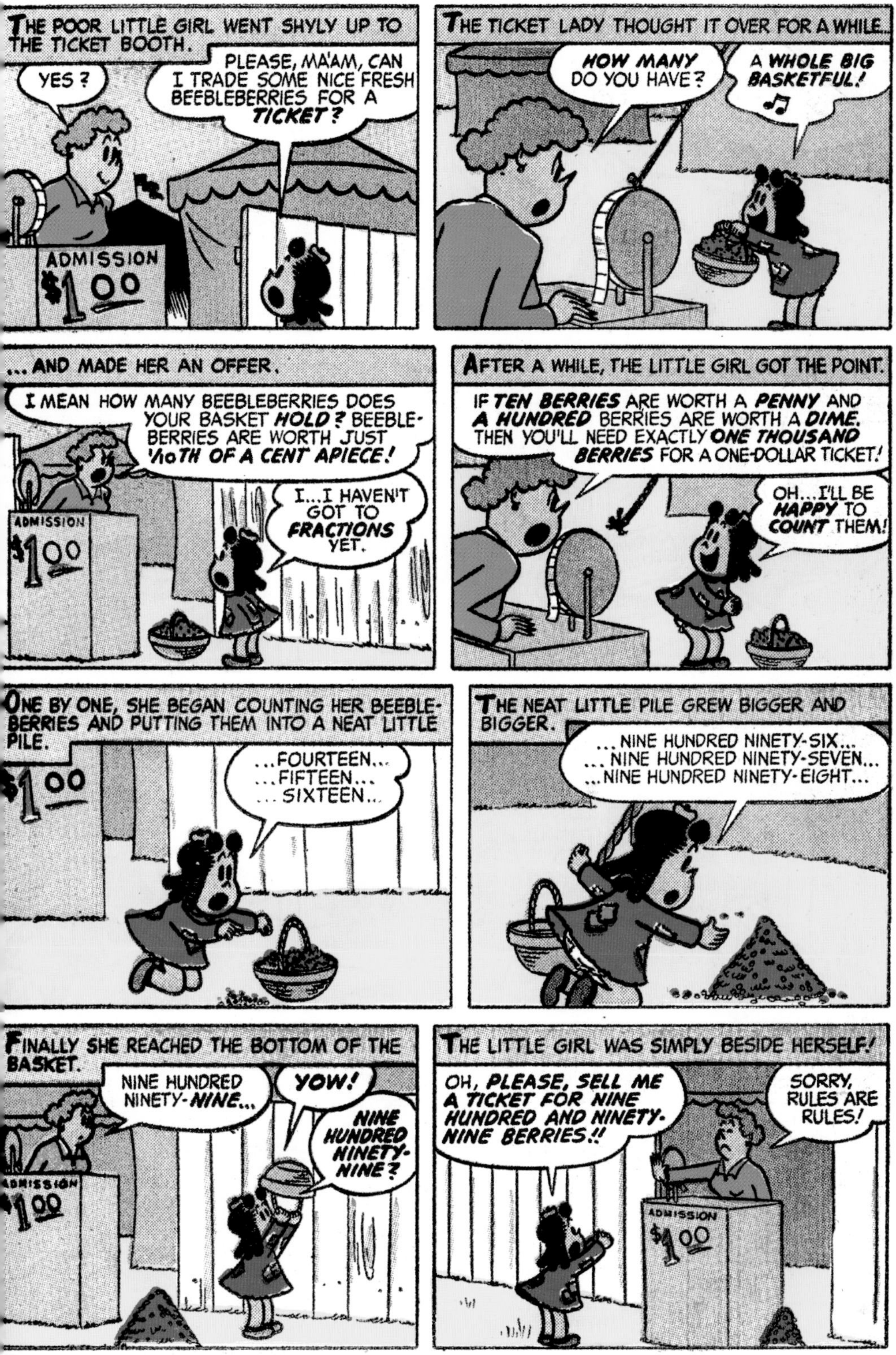
THE POOR LITTLE GIRL WENT SHYLY UP TO THE TICKET BOOTH.
YES?
PLEASE, MA'AM, CAN I TRADE SOME NICE FRESH BEEBLEBERRIES FOR A TICKET?
ADMISSION $1.00
THE TICKET LADY THOUGHT IT OVER FOR A WHILE...
HOW MANY DO YOU HAVE?
A WHOLE BIG BASKETFUL! ♫
...AND MADE HER AN OFFER.
I MEAN HOW MANY BEEBLEBERRIES DOES YOUR BASKET HOLD? BEEBLEBERRIES ARE WORTH JUST 1/10TH OF A CENT APIECE!
ADMISSION $1.00
I...I HAVEN'T GOT TO FRACTIONS YET.
AFTER A WHILE, THE LITTLE GIRL GOT THE POINT.
IF TEN BERRIES ARE WORTH A PENNY AND A HUNDRED BERRIES ARE WORTH A DIME, THEN YOU'LL NEED EXACTLY ONE THOUSAND BERRIES FOR A ONE-DOLLAR TICKET!
OH...I'LL BE HAPPY TO COUNT THEM!
ONE BY ONE, SHE BEGAN COUNTING HER BEEBLEBERRIES AND PUTTING THEM INTO A NEAT LITTLE PILE.
$1.00
...FOURTEEN... ...FIFTEEN... ...SIXTEEN...
THE NEAT LITTLE PILE GREW BIGGER AND BIGGER.
...NINE HUNDRED NINETY-SIX... ...NINE HUNDRED NINETY-SEVEN... ...NINE HUNDRED NINETY-EIGHT...
FINALLY SHE REACHED THE BOTTOM OF THE BASKET.
NINE HUNDRED NINETY-NINE...
YOW!
NINE HUNDRED NINETY-NINE?
ADMISSION $1.00
THE LITTLE GIRL WAS SIMPLY BESIDE HERSELF!
OH, PLEASE, SELL ME A TICKET FOR NINE HUNDRED AND NINETY-NINE BERRIES!!
SORRY, RULES ARE RULES!
ADMISSION $1.00

HER HEARTBROKEN HOWLS ATTRACTED THE ATTENTION OF LITTLE ITCH WHO WAS ROAMING AROUND INSIDE THE GATE.

BAW!

OH, IF ONLY I HADN'T EATEN THAT *ONE* *BEEBLEBERRY!*

HELLO, STOOPID!

EVEN AFTER SEEING THE WHOLE CARNIVAL *TWICE*, ITCH WAS STILL LOADED WITH MONEY!

PLEASE, LITTLE ITCH! PLEASE TURN JUST *ONE DIME* BACK INTO A BEEBLEBERRY!

WHAT? TURN A WHOLE DIME INTO A CHEAP BEEBLE-BERRY ONLY WORTH 1/10TH OF A CENT? *NO!*

WITH LITTLE ITCH'S CRUEL LAUGHTER RINGING IN HER EARS, THE LITTLE GIRL SEIZED HER BASKET AND RAN BACK TO THE BEEBLE-BERRY PATCH.

CARNIV GROUN

QUICKLY SHE STOOPED OVER AND PICKED ONE BEEBLEBERRY.

THEN SHE TURNED AND RAN BACK TO THE CARNIVAL.

CAR GROU

HAPPILY WAVING THE BEEBLE-BERRY, SHE RACED UP TO THE TICKET BOOTH.

HERE IT IS!

HERE'S YOUR TICKET!

ISSION 1 00

WHEN LITTLE ITCH SAW THE LITTLE GIRL STROLLING PAST, SHE COULD HARDLY BELIEVE HER EYES...

...BUT SHE PRETENDED TO BE *VERY FRIENDLY.*

COME DEARIE, I'LL TREAT YOU TO A *NICE RIDE!*

OH, GOODY!

SHE TOOK THE LITTLE GIRL OVER TO THE *AIRPLANE SPIN.*

GO ON! CLIMB RIGHT *IN!*

I LOVE TO RIDE IN SHINY AIRPLANES!

WHEN THE AIRPLANE RIDE STARTED, THE LITTLE WITCH WALKED OVER TO THE MAN WHO WORKED THE CONTROLS.

HEY, YOU!

PUTT PUTT!

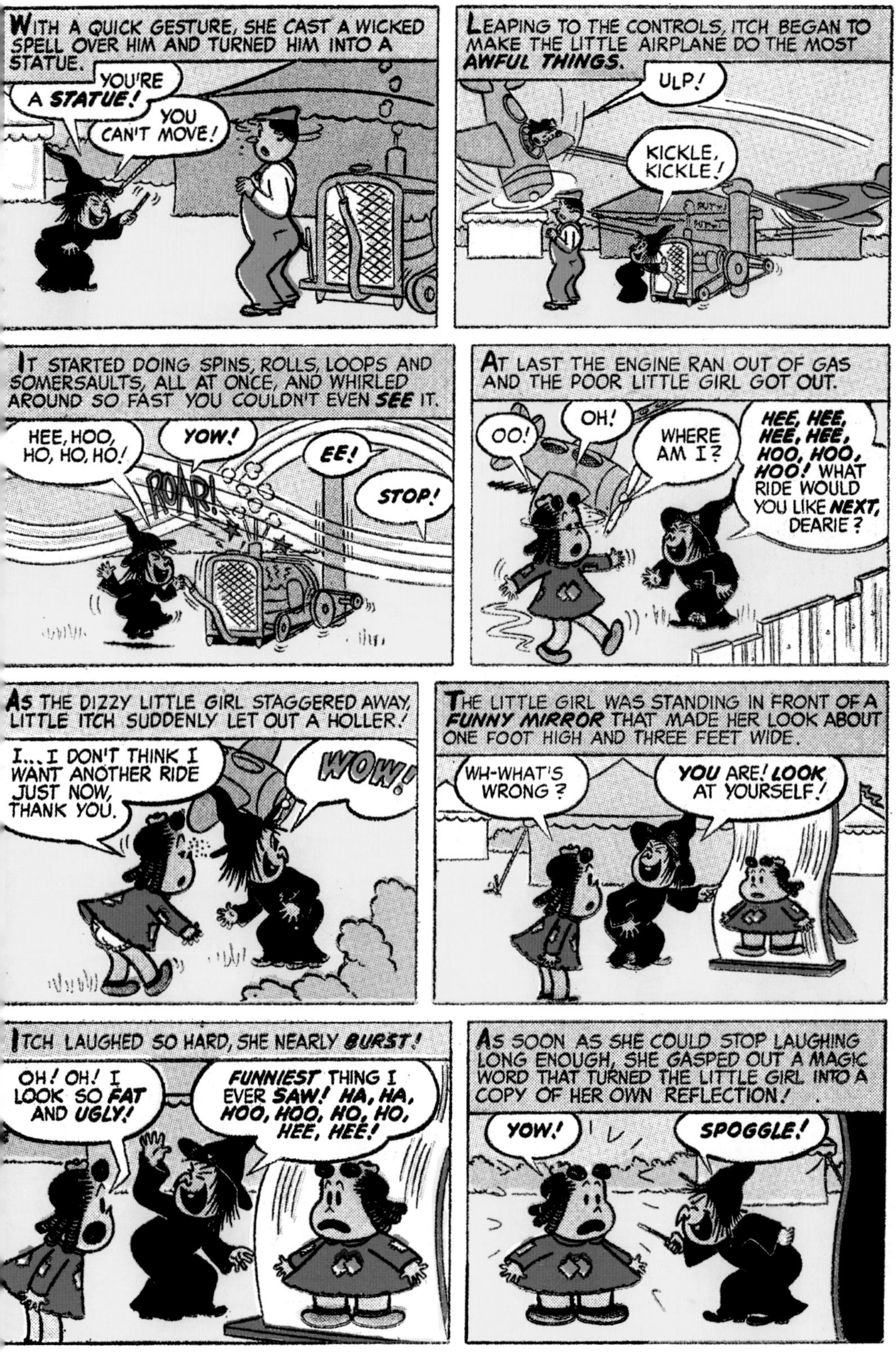
WITH A QUICK GESTURE, SHE CAST A WICKED SPELL OVER HIM AND TURNED HIM INTO A STATUE.
YOU'RE A STATUE!
YOU CAN'T MOVE!
LEAPING TO THE CONTROLS, ITCH BEGAN TO MAKE THE LITTLE AIRPLANE DO THE MOST AWFUL THINGS.
ULP!
KICKLE, KICKLE!
IT STARTED DOING SPINS, ROLLS, LOOPS AND SOMERSAULTS, ALL AT ONCE, AND WHIRLED AROUND SO FAST YOU COULDN'T EVEN SEE IT.
HEE, HOO, HO, HO, HO!
YOW!
EE!
STOP!
ROAR!
AT LAST THE ENGINE RAN OUT OF GAS AND THE POOR LITTLE GIRL GOT OUT.
OO!
OH!
WHERE AM I?
HEE, HEE, HEE, HEE, HOO, HOO, HOO! WHAT RIDE WOULD YOU LIKE NEXT, DEARIE?
AS THE DIZZY LITTLE GIRL STAGGERED AWAY, LITTLE ITCH SUDDENLY LET OUT A HOLLER!
I... I DON'T THINK I WANT ANOTHER RIDE JUST NOW, THANK YOU.
WOW!
THE LITTLE GIRL WAS STANDING IN FRONT OF A FUNNY MIRROR THAT MADE HER LOOK ABOUT ONE FOOT HIGH AND THREE FEET WIDE.
WH-WHAT'S WRONG?
YOU ARE! LOOK AT YOURSELF!
ITCH LAUGHED SO HARD, SHE NEARLY BURST!
OH! OH! I LOOK SO FAT AND UGLY!
FUNNIEST THING I EVER SAW! HA, HA, HOO, HOO, HO, HO, HEE, HEE!
AS SOON AS SHE COULD STOP LAUGHING LONG ENOUGH, SHE GASPED OUT A MAGIC WORD THAT TURNED THE LITTLE GIRL INTO A COPY OF HER OWN REFLECTION!
YOW!
SPOGGLE!

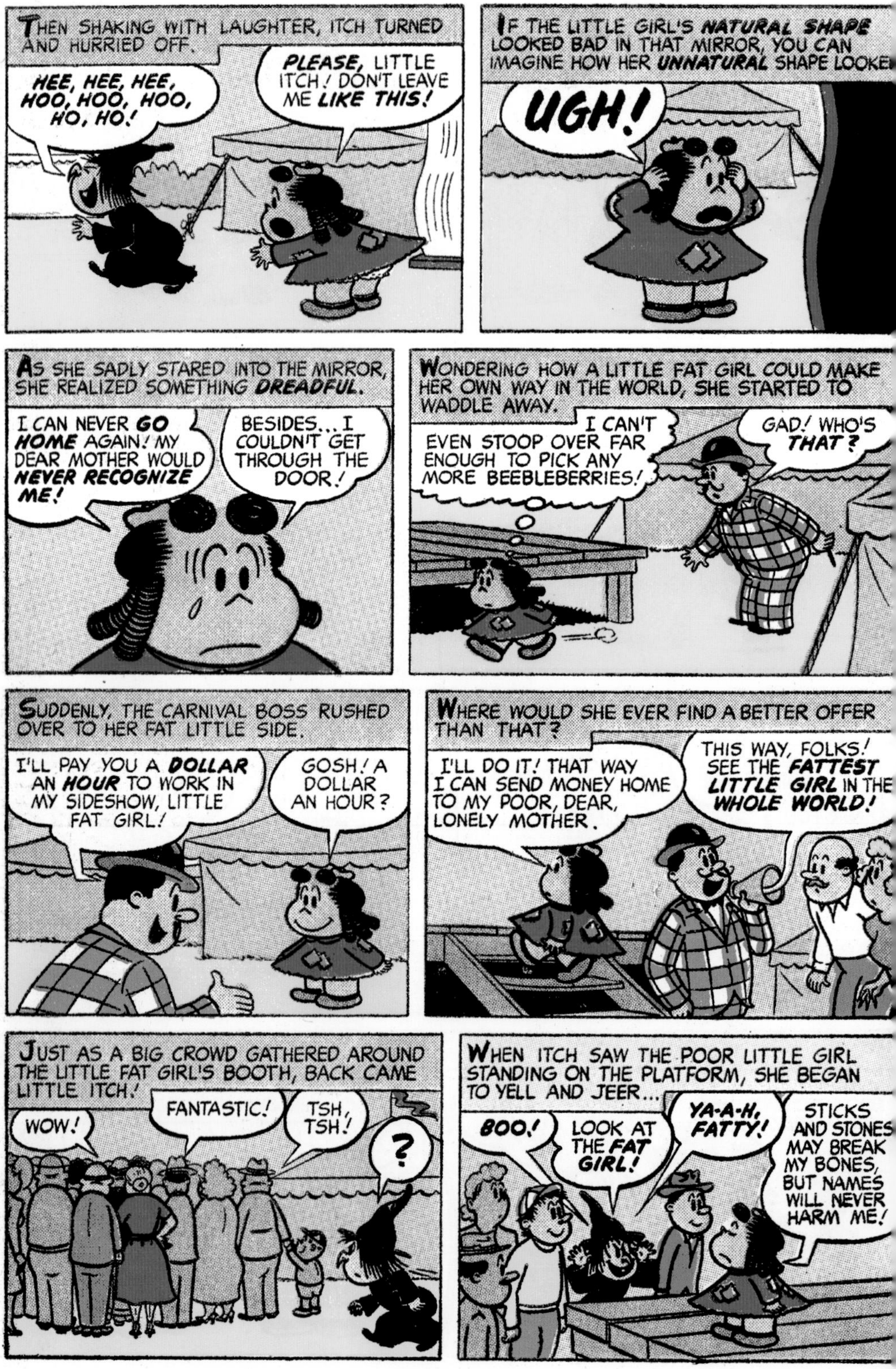
THEN SHAKING WITH LAUGHTER, ITCH TURNED AND HURRIED OFF.
HEE, HEE, HEE, HOO, HOO, HOO, HO, HO!
PLEASE, LITTLE ITCH! DON'T LEAVE ME LIKE THIS!
IF THE LITTLE GIRL'S NATURAL SHAPE LOOKED BAD IN THAT MIRROR, YOU CAN IMAGINE HOW HER UNNATURAL SHAPE LOOKED
UGH!
AS SHE SADLY STARED INTO THE MIRROR, SHE REALIZED SOMETHING DREADFUL.
I CAN NEVER GO HOME AGAIN! MY DEAR MOTHER WOULD NEVER RECOGNIZE ME!
BESIDES... I COULDN'T GET THROUGH THE DOOR!
WONDERING HOW A LITTLE FAT GIRL COULD MAKE HER OWN WAY IN THE WORLD, SHE STARTED TO WADDLE AWAY.
I CAN'T EVEN STOOP OVER FAR ENOUGH TO PICK ANY MORE BEEBLEBERRIES!
GAD! WHO'S THAT?
SUDDENLY, THE CARNIVAL BOSS RUSHED OVER TO HER FAT LITTLE SIDE.
I'LL PAY YOU A DOLLAR AN HOUR TO WORK IN MY SIDESHOW, LITTLE FAT GIRL!
GOSH! A DOLLAR AN HOUR?
WHERE WOULD SHE EVER FIND A BETTER OFFER THAN THAT?
I'LL DO IT! THAT WAY I CAN SEND MONEY HOME TO MY POOR, DEAR, LONELY MOTHER.
THIS WAY, FOLKS! SEE THE FATTEST LITTLE GIRL IN THE WHOLE WORLD!
JUST AS A BIG CROWD GATHERED AROUND THE LITTLE FAT GIRL'S BOOTH, BACK CAME LITTLE ITCH!
WOW!
FANTASTIC!
TSH, TSH!
?
WHEN ITCH SAW THE POOR LITTLE GIRL STANDING ON THE PLATFORM, SHE BEGAN TO YELL AND JEER...
BOO!
LOOK AT THE FAT GIRL!
YA-A-H, FATTY!
STICKS AND STONES MAY BREAK MY BONES, BUT NAMES WILL NEVER HARM ME!

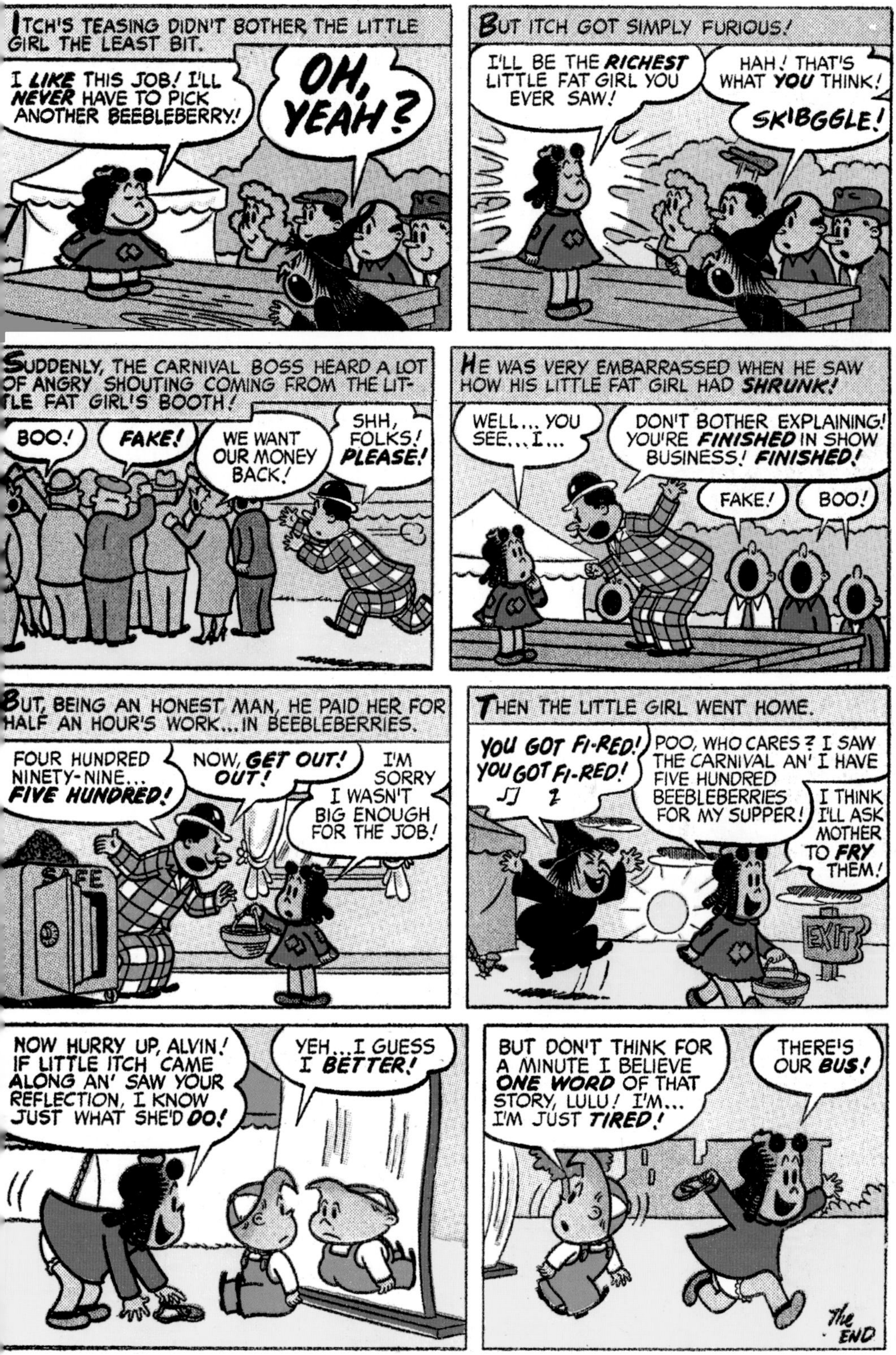
ITCH'S TEASING DIDN'T BOTHER THE LITTLE GIRL THE LEAST BIT.
I LIKE THIS JOB! I'LL NEVER HAVE TO PICK ANOTHER BEEBLEBERRY!
OH, YEAH?
BUT ITCH GOT SIMPLY FURIOUS!
I'LL BE THE RICHEST LITTLE FAT GIRL YOU EVER SAW!
HAH! THAT'S WHAT YOU THINK!
SKIBGGLE!
SUDDENLY, THE CARNIVAL BOSS HEARD A LOT OF ANGRY SHOUTING COMING FROM THE LITTLE FAT GIRL'S BOOTH!
BOO!
FAKE!
WE WANT OUR MONEY BACK!
SHH, FOLKS! PLEASE!
HE WAS VERY EMBARRASSED WHEN HE SAW HOW HIS LITTLE FAT GIRL HAD SHRUNK!
WELL... YOU SEE... I...
DON'T BOTHER EXPLAINING! YOU'RE FINISHED IN SHOW BUSINESS! FINISHED!
FAKE!
BOO!
BUT, BEING AN HONEST MAN, HE PAID HER FOR HALF AN HOUR'S WORK... IN BEEBLEBERRIES.
FOUR HUNDRED NINETY-NINE... FIVE HUNDRED!
NOW, GET OUT! OUT!
I'M SORRY I WASN'T BIG ENOUGH FOR THE JOB!
SAFE
THEN THE LITTLE GIRL WENT HOME.
YOU GOT FI-RED! YOU GOT FI-RED!
POO, WHO CARES? I SAW THE CARNIVAL AN' I HAVE FIVE HUNDRED BEEBLEBERRIES FOR MY SUPPER!
I THINK I'LL ASK MOTHER TO FRY THEM!
EXIT
NOW HURRY UP, ALVIN! IF LITTLE ITCH CAME ALONG AN' SAW YOUR REFLECTION, I KNOW JUST WHAT SHE'D DO!
YEH... I GUESS I BETTER!
BUT DON'T THINK FOR A MINUTE I BELIEVE ONE WORD OF THAT STORY, LULU! I'M... I'M JUST TIRED!
THERE'S OUR BUS!
The END

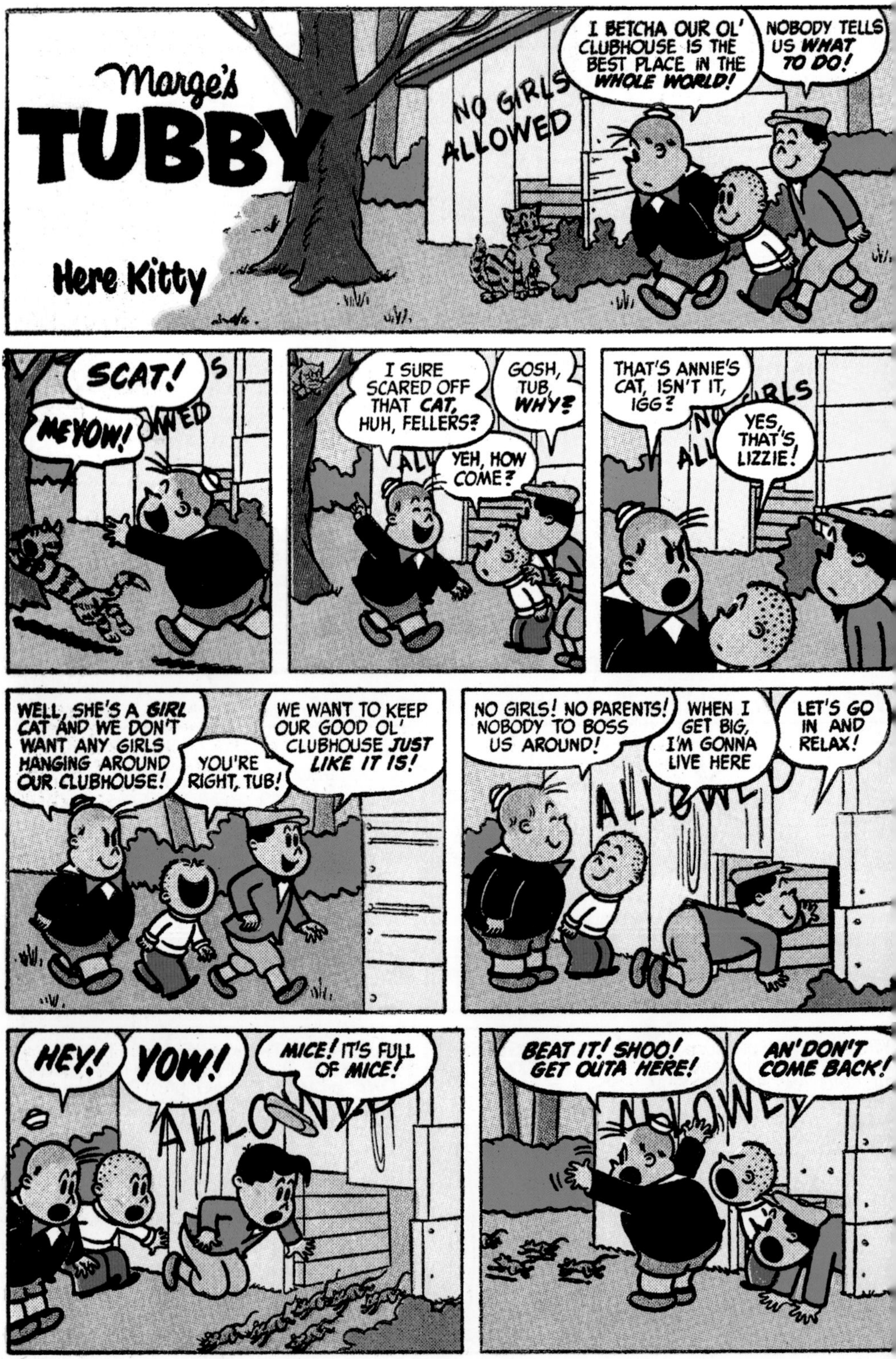
Marge's
TUBBY
Here Kitty
NO GIRLS ALLOWED
I BETCHA OUR OL' CLUBHOUSE IS THE BEST PLACE IN THE WHOLE WORLD!
NOBODY TELLS US WHAT TO DO!
SCAT!
MEYOW!
I SURE SCARED OFF THAT CAT, HUH, FELLERS?
GOSH, TUB, WHY?
YEH, HOW COME?
THAT'S ANNIE'S CAT, ISN'T IT, IGG?
YES, THAT'S LIZZIE!
WELL, SHE'S A GIRL CAT AND WE DON'T WANT ANY GIRLS HANGING AROUND OUR CLUBHOUSE!
YOU'RE RIGHT, TUB!
WE WANT TO KEEP OUR GOOD OL' CLUBHOUSE JUST LIKE IT IS!
NO GIRLS! NO PARENTS! NOBODY TO BOSS US AROUND!
WHEN I GET BIG, I'M GONNA LIVE HERE
LET'S GO IN AND RELAX!
HEY!
YOW!
MICE! IT'S FULL OF MICE!
BEAT IT! SHOO! GET OUTA HERE!
AN' DON'T COME BACK!

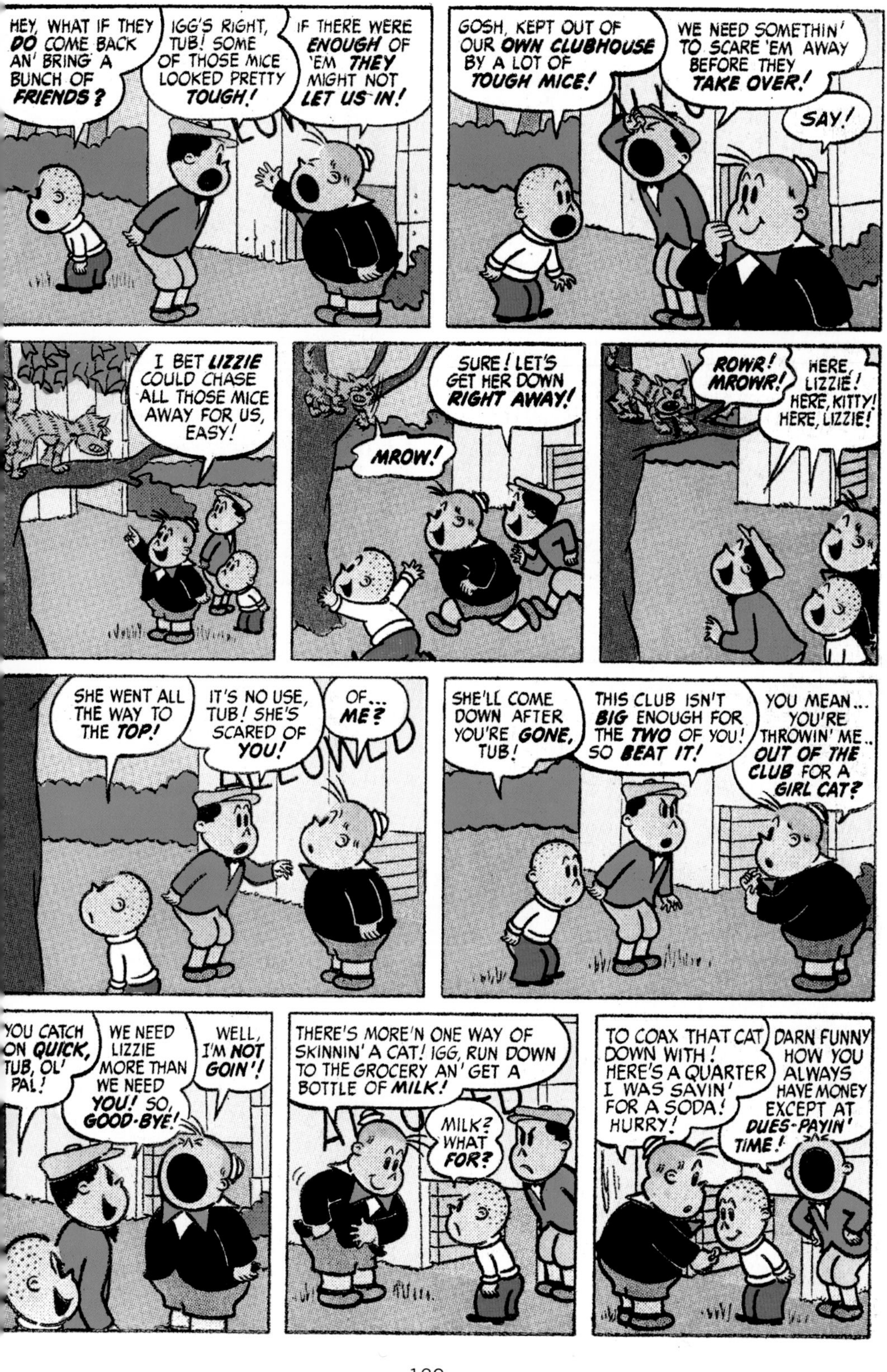
HEY, WHAT IF THEY DO COME BACK AN' BRING A BUNCH OF FRIENDS?
IGG'S RIGHT, TUB! SOME OF THOSE MICE LOOKED PRETTY TOUGH!
IF THERE WERE ENOUGH OF 'EM THEY MIGHT NOT LET US IN!
GOSH, KEPT OUT OF OUR OWN CLUBHOUSE BY A LOT OF TOUGH MICE!
WE NEED SOMETHIN' TO SCARE 'EM AWAY BEFORE THEY TAKE OVER!
SAY!
I BET LIZZIE COULD CHASE ALL THOSE MICE AWAY FOR US, EASY!
SURE! LET'S GET HER DOWN RIGHT AWAY!
MROW!
ROWR! MROWR!
HERE, LIZZIE! HERE, KITTY! HERE, LIZZIE!
SHE WENT ALL THE WAY TO THE TOP!
IT'S NO USE, TUB! SHE'S SCARED OF YOU!
OF... ME?
SHE'LL COME DOWN AFTER YOU'RE GONE, TUB!
THIS CLUB ISN'T BIG ENOUGH FOR THE TWO OF YOU! SO BEAT IT!
YOU MEAN... YOU'RE THROWIN' ME... OUT OF THE CLUB FOR A GIRL CAT?
YOU CATCH ON QUICK, TUB, OL' PAL!
WE NEED LIZZIE MORE THAN WE NEED YOU! SO, GOOD-BYE!
WELL, I'M NOT GOIN'!
THERE'S MORE'N ONE WAY OF SKINNIN' A CAT! IGG, RUN DOWN TO THE GROCERY AN' GET A BOTTLE OF MILK!
MILK? WHAT FOR?
TO COAX THAT CAT DOWN WITH! HERE'S A QUARTER I WAS SAVIN' FOR A SODA! HURRY!
DARN FUNNY HOW YOU ALWAYS HAVE MONEY EXCEPT AT DUES-PAYIN' TIME!

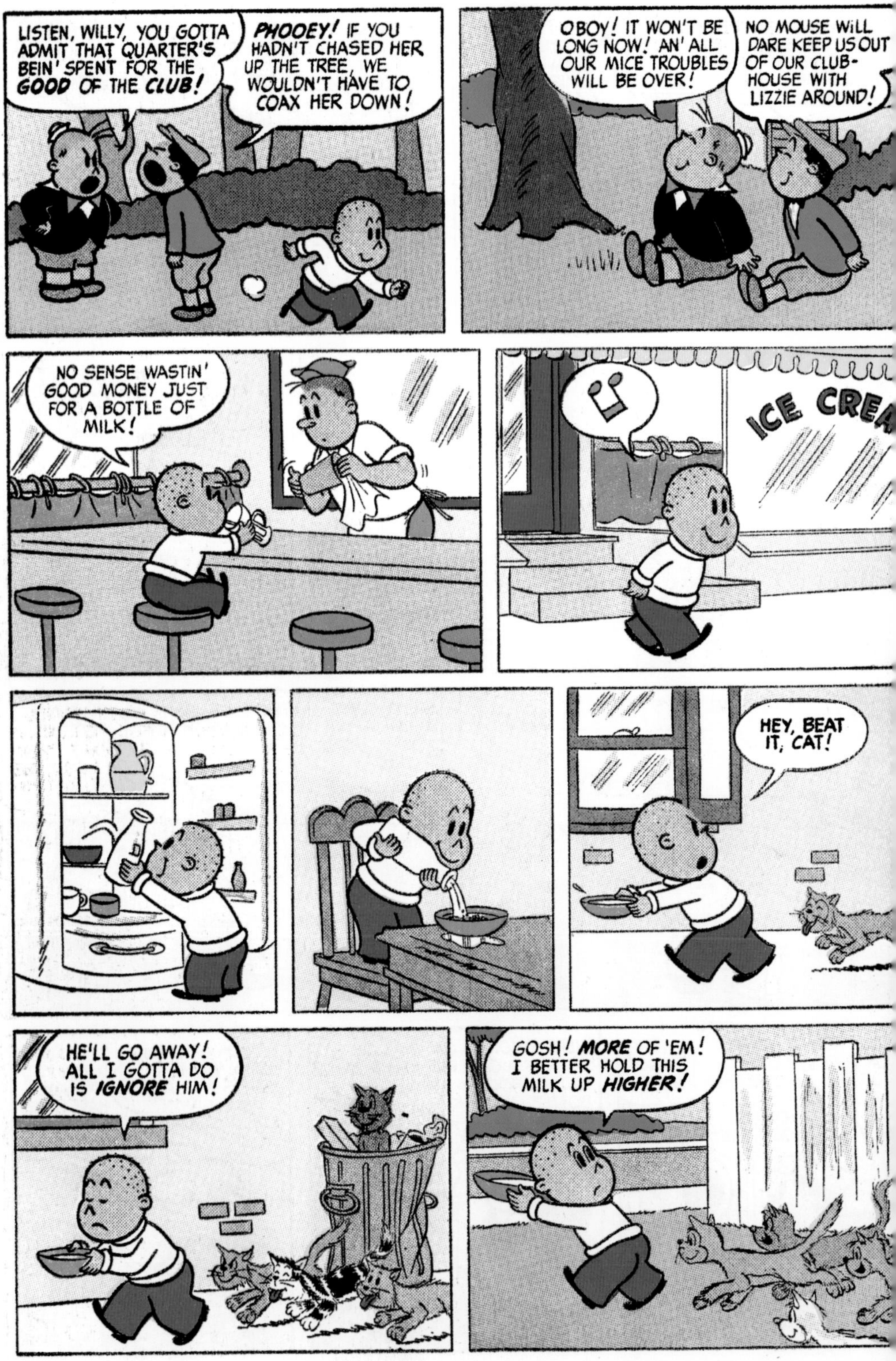
LISTEN, WILLY, YOU GOTTA ADMIT THAT QUARTER'S BEIN' SPENT FOR THE GOOD OF THE CLUB!
PHOOEY! IF YOU HADN'T CHASED HER UP THE TREE, WE WOULDN'T HAVE TO COAX HER DOWN!
OBOY! IT WON'T BE LONG NOW! AN' ALL OUR MICE TROUBLES WILL BE OVER!
NO MOUSE WILL DARE KEEP US OUT OF OUR CLUB-HOUSE WITH LIZZIE AROUND!
NO SENSE WASTIN' GOOD MONEY JUST FOR A BOTTLE OF MILK!
ICE CREA
HEY, BEAT IT, CAT!
HE'LL GO AWAY! ALL I GOTTA DO IS IGNORE HIM!
GOSH! MORE OF 'EM! I BETTER HOLD THIS MILK UP HIGHER!

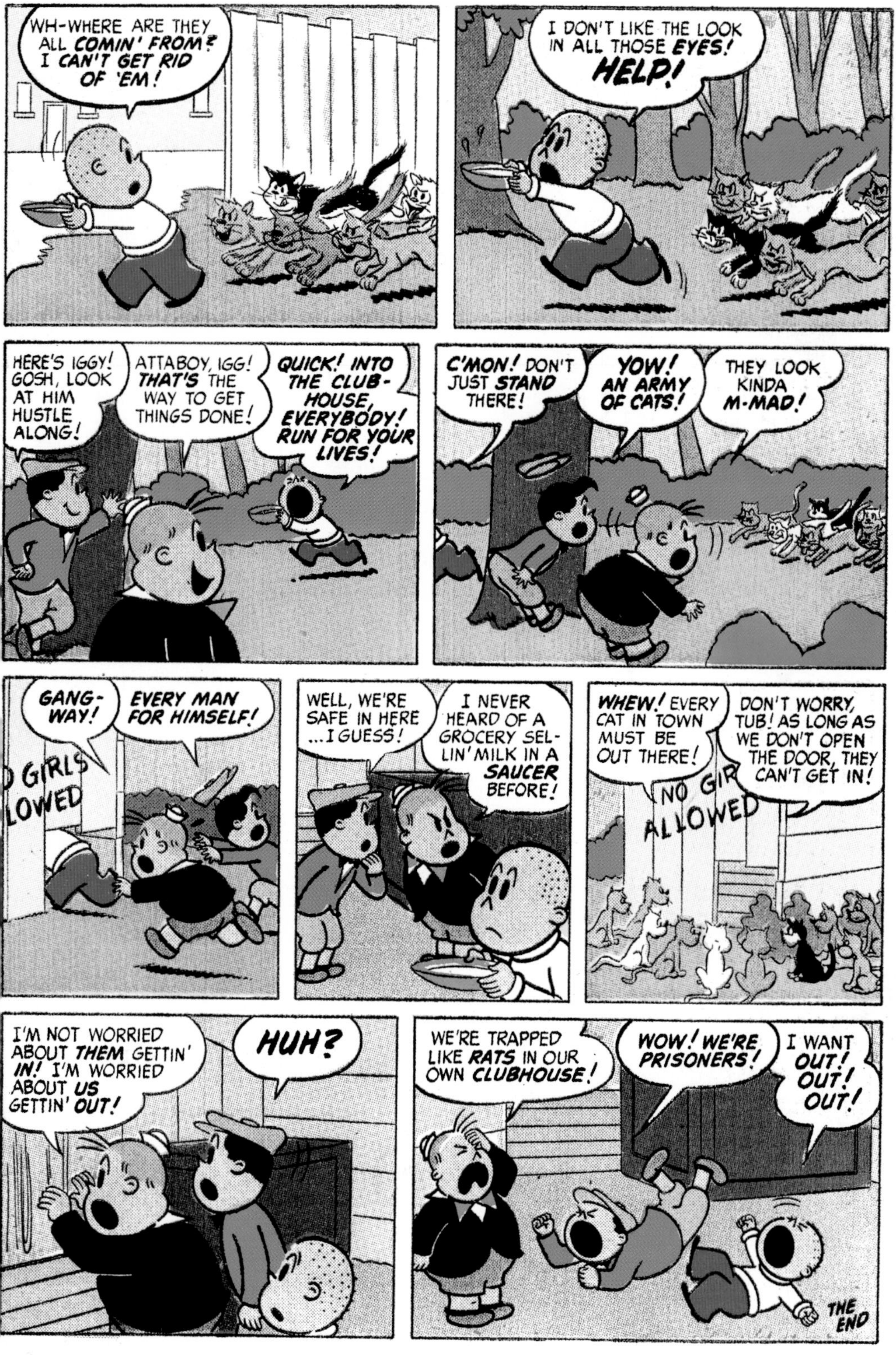
WH-WHERE ARE THEY ALL COMIN' FROM? I CAN'T GET RID OF 'EM!
I DON'T LIKE THE LOOK IN ALL THOSE EYES! HELP!
HERE'S IGGY! GOSH, LOOK AT HIM HUSTLE ALONG!
ATTABOY, IGG! THAT'S THE WAY TO GET THINGS DONE!
QUICK! INTO THE CLUB-HOUSE, EVERYBODY! RUN FOR YOUR LIVES!
C'MON! DON'T JUST STAND THERE!
YOW! AN ARMY OF CATS!
THEY LOOK KINDA M-MAD!
GANG-WAY!
EVERY MAN FOR HIMSELF!
WELL, WE'RE SAFE IN HERE ...I GUESS!
I NEVER HEARD OF A GROCERY SEL-LIN' MILK IN A SAUCER BEFORE!
WHEW! EVERY CAT IN TOWN MUST BE OUT THERE!
DON'T WORRY, TUB! AS LONG AS WE DON'T OPEN THE DOOR, THEY CAN'T GET IN!
NO GIR ALLOWED
I'M NOT WORRIED ABOUT THEM GETTIN' IN! I'M WORRIED ABOUT US GETTIN' OUT!
HUH?
WE'RE TRAPPED LIKE RATS IN OUR OWN CLUBHOUSE!
WOW! WE'RE PRISONERS!
I WANT OUT! OUT! OUT!
THE END

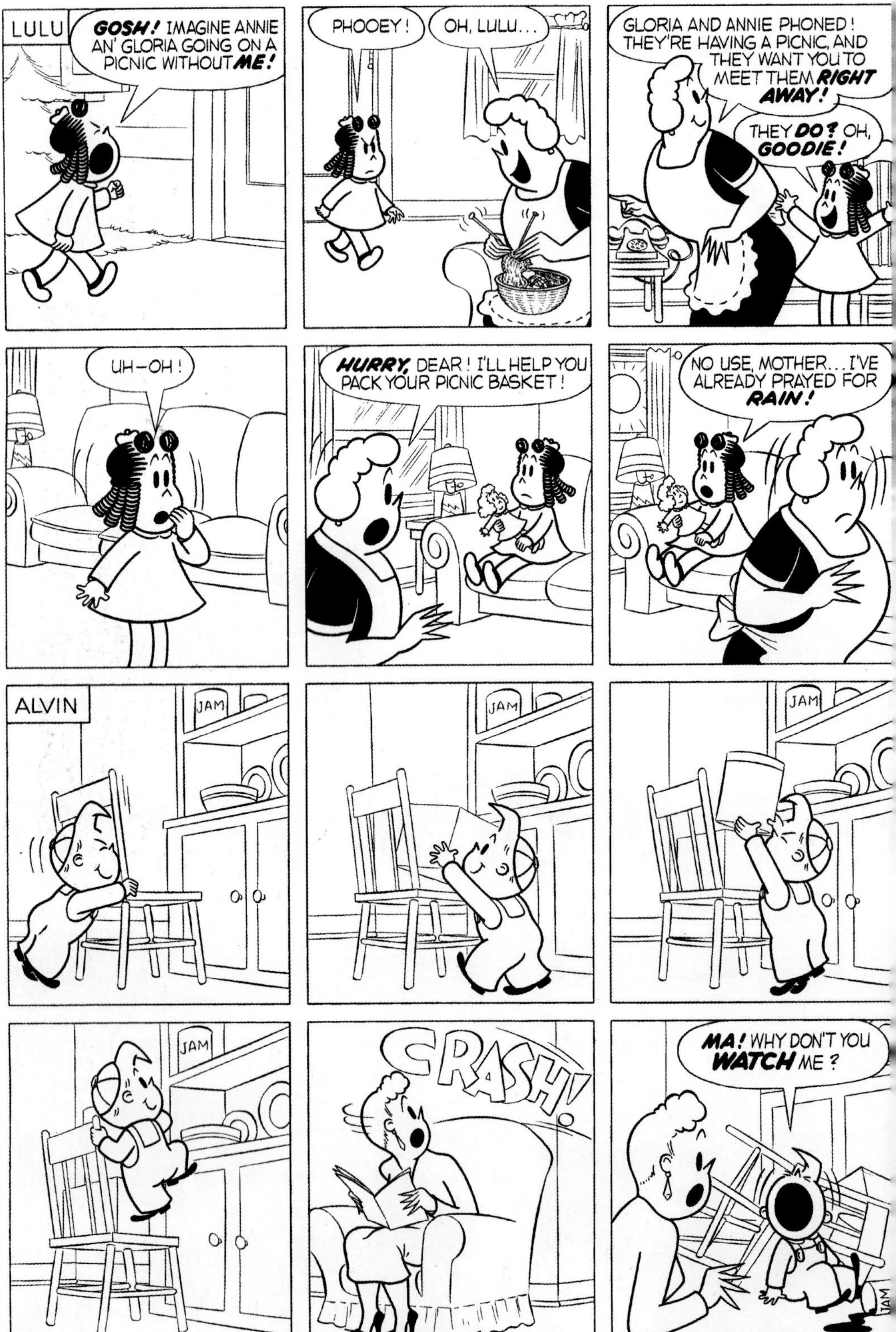

LULU
GOSH! IMAGINE ANNIE AN' GLORIA GOING ON A PICNIC WITHOUT ME!
PHOOEY!
OH, LULU...
GLORIA AND ANNIE PHONED! THEY'RE HAVING A PICNIC, AND THEY WANT YOU TO MEET THEM RIGHT AWAY!
THEY DO? OH, GOODIE!
UH-OH!
HURRY, DEAR! I'LL HELP YOU PACK YOUR PICNIC BASKET!
NO USE, MOTHER... I'VE ALREADY PRAYED FOR RAIN!
ALVIN
JAM
JAM
JAM
JAM
CRASH!
MA! WHY DON'T YOU WATCH ME?
JAM

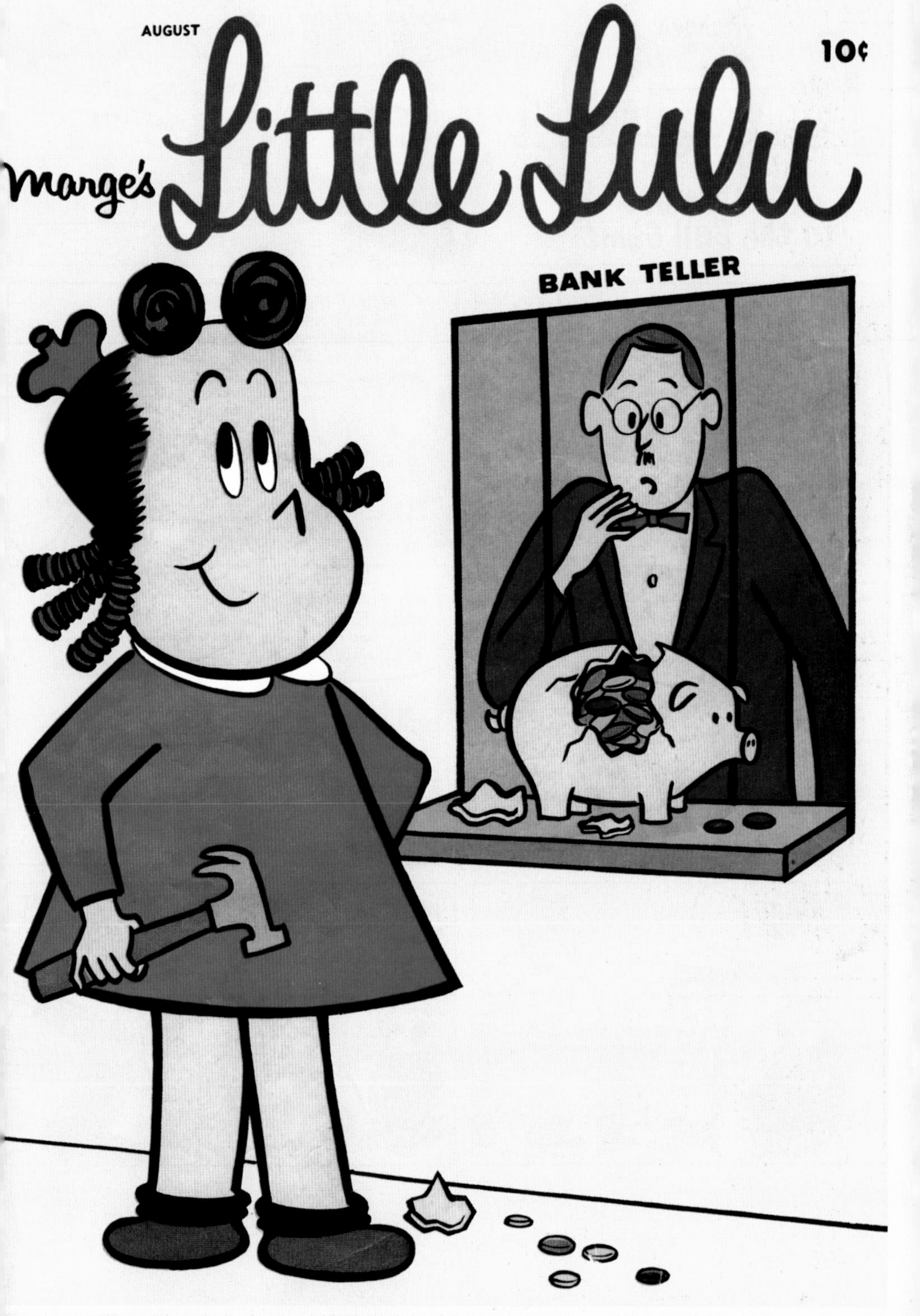
AUGUST
marge's Little Lulu
10¢
BANK TELLER

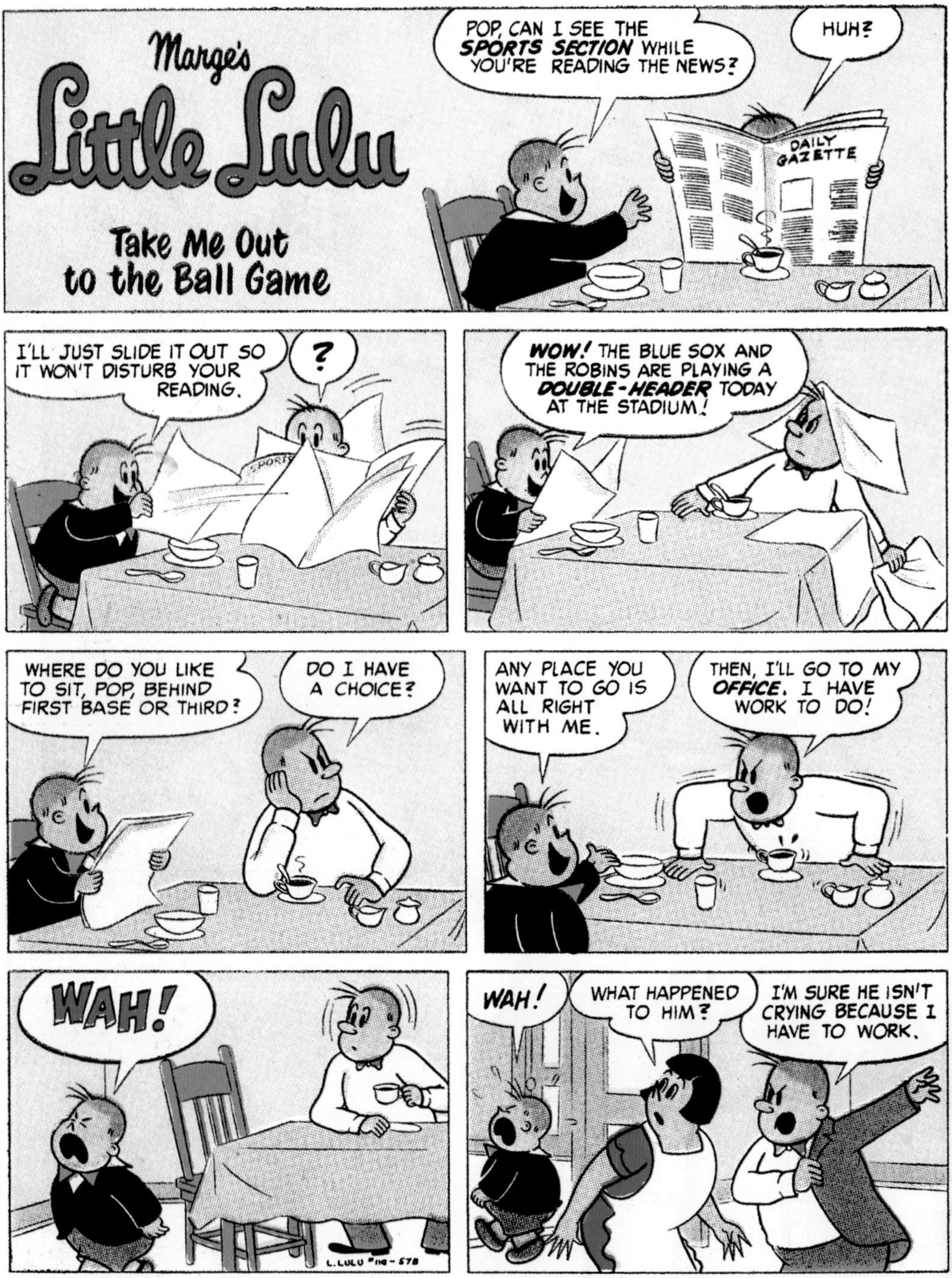
Marge's Little Lulu
Take Me Out to the Ball Game
POP, CAN I SEE THE SPORTS SECTION WHILE YOU'RE READING THE NEWS?
HUH?
DAILY GAZETTE
I'LL JUST SLIDE IT OUT SO IT WON'T DISTURB YOUR READING.
?
WOW! THE BLUE SOX AND THE ROBINS ARE PLAYING A DOUBLE-HEADER TODAY AT THE STADIUM!
WHERE DO YOU LIKE TO SIT, POP, BEHIND FIRST BASE OR THIRD?
DO I HAVE A CHOICE?
ANY PLACE YOU WANT TO GO IS ALL RIGHT WITH ME.
THEN, I'LL GO TO MY OFFICE. I HAVE WORK TO DO!
WAH!
WAH!
WHAT HAPPENED TO HIM?
I'M SURE HE ISN'T CRYING BECAUSE I HAVE TO WORK.

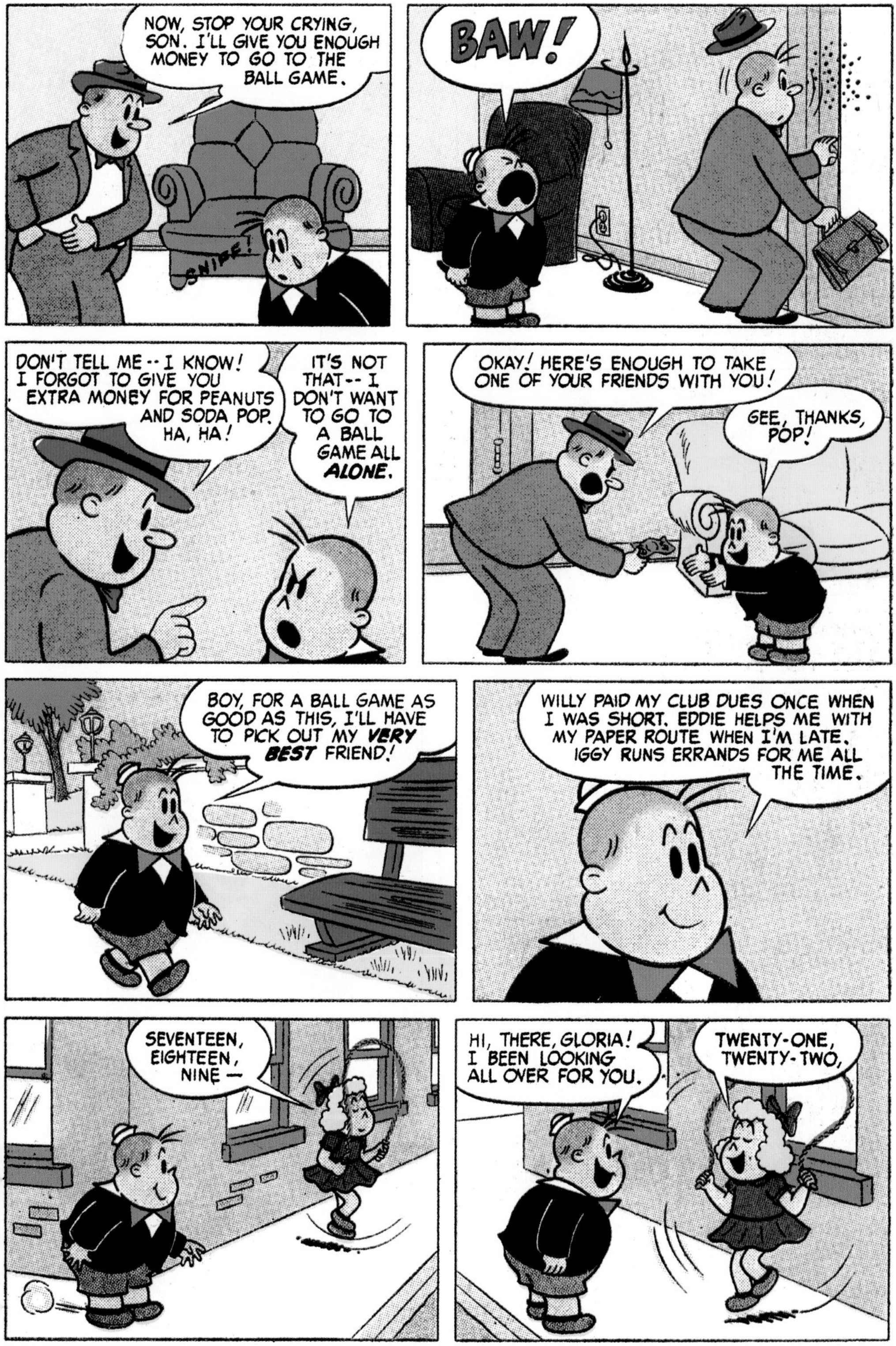
NOW, STOP YOUR CRYING, SON. I'LL GIVE YOU ENOUGH MONEY TO GO TO THE BALL GAME.
SNIFF!
BAW!
DON'T TELL ME -- I KNOW! I FORGOT TO GIVE YOU EXTRA MONEY FOR PEANUTS AND SODA POP. HA, HA!
IT'S NOT THAT -- I DON'T WANT TO GO TO A BALL GAME ALL ALONE.
OKAY! HERE'S ENOUGH TO TAKE ONE OF YOUR FRIENDS WITH YOU!
GEE, THANKS, POP!
BOY, FOR A BALL GAME AS GOOD AS THIS, I'LL HAVE TO PICK OUT MY VERY BEST FRIEND!
WILLY PAID MY CLUB DUES ONCE WHEN I WAS SHORT. EDDIE HELPS ME WITH MY PAPER ROUTE WHEN I'M LATE. IGGY RUNS ERRANDS FOR ME ALL THE TIME.
SEVENTEEN, EIGHTEEN, NINE —
HI, THERE, GLORIA! I BEEN LOOKING ALL OVER FOR YOU.
TWENTY-ONE, TWENTY-TWO,

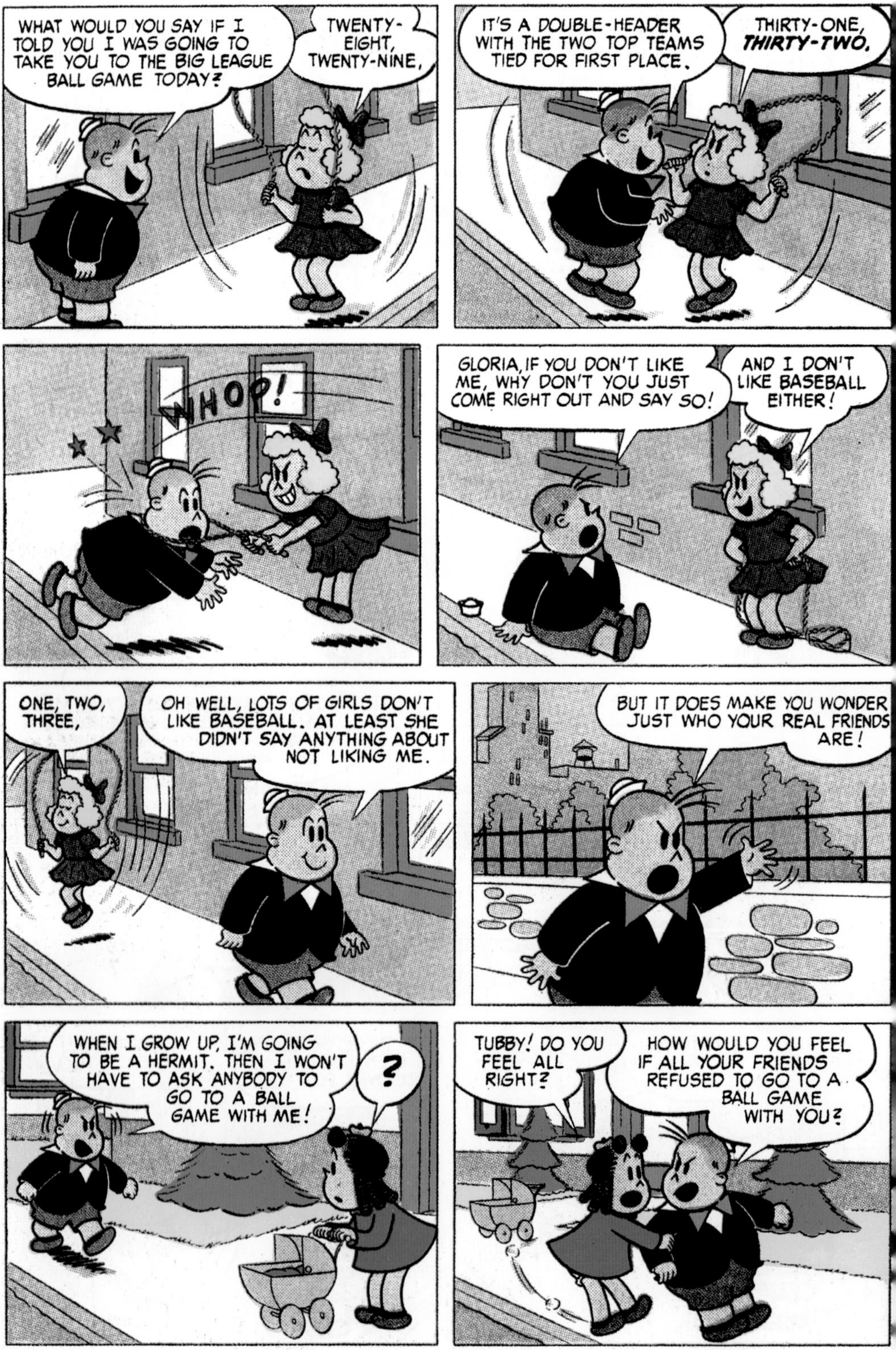
WHAT WOULD YOU SAY IF I TOLD YOU I WAS GOING TO TAKE YOU TO THE BIG LEAGUE BALL GAME TODAY?
TWENTY-EIGHT, TWENTY-NINE,
IT'S A DOUBLE-HEADER WITH THE TWO TOP TEAMS TIED FOR FIRST PLACE.
THIRTY-ONE, THIRTY-TWO.
WHOP!
GLORIA, IF YOU DON'T LIKE ME, WHY DON'T YOU JUST COME RIGHT OUT AND SAY SO!
AND I DON'T LIKE BASEBALL EITHER!
ONE, TWO, THREE,
OH WELL, LOTS OF GIRLS DON'T LIKE BASEBALL. AT LEAST SHE DIDN'T SAY ANYTHING ABOUT NOT LIKING ME.
BUT IT DOES MAKE YOU WONDER JUST WHO YOUR REAL FRIENDS ARE!
WHEN I GROW UP, I'M GOING TO BE A HERMIT. THEN I WON'T HAVE TO ASK ANYBODY TO GO TO A BALL GAME WITH ME!
?
TUBBY! DO YOU FEEL ALL RIGHT?
HOW WOULD YOU FEEL IF ALL YOUR FRIENDS REFUSED TO GO TO A BALL GAME WITH YOU?

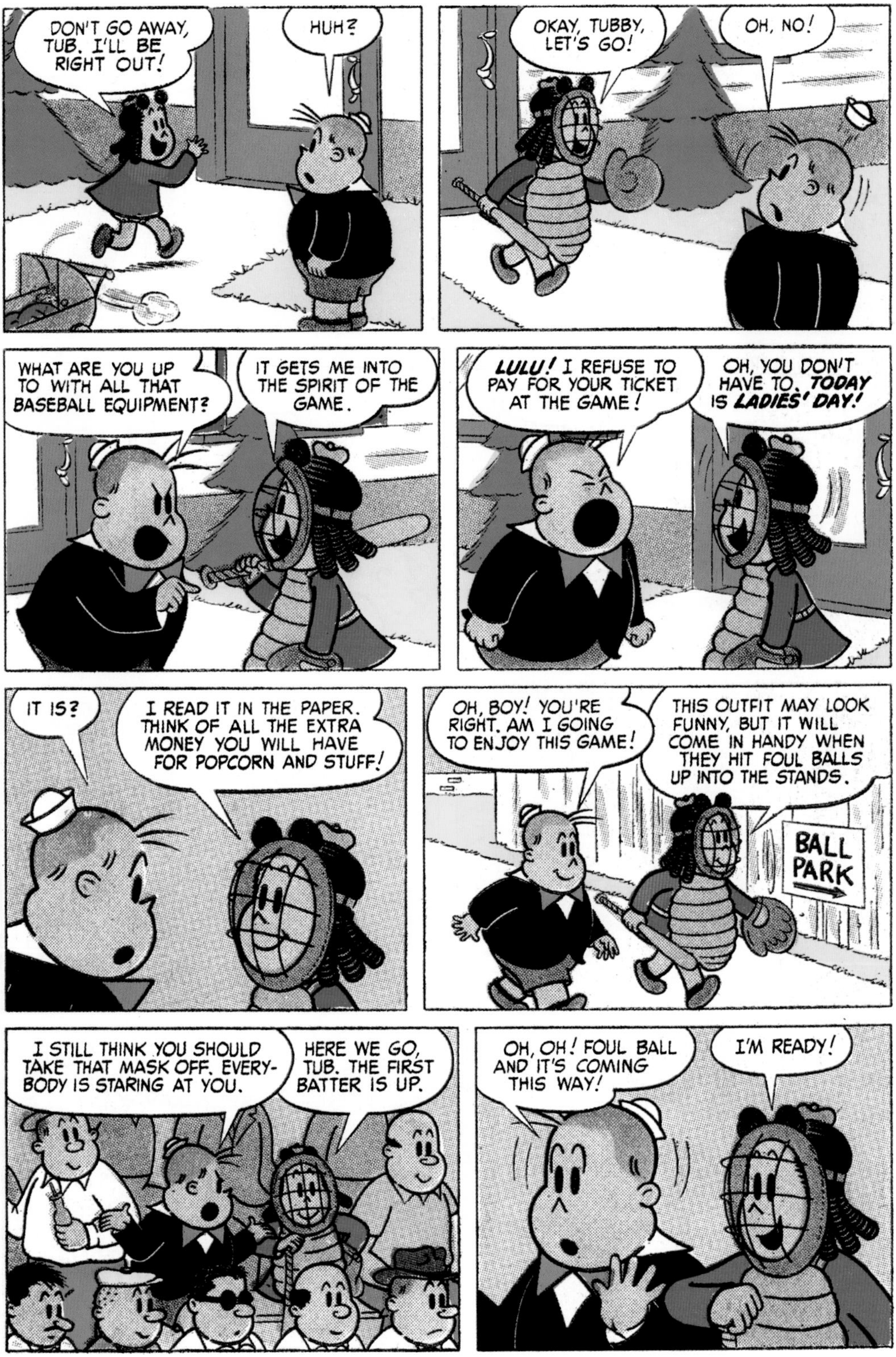
DON'T GO AWAY, TUB. I'LL BE RIGHT OUT!
HUH?
OKAY, TUBBY, LET'S GO!
OH, NO!
WHAT ARE YOU UP TO WITH ALL THAT BASEBALL EQUIPMENT?
IT GETS ME INTO THE SPIRIT OF THE GAME.
LULU! I REFUSE TO PAY FOR YOUR TICKET AT THE GAME!
OH, YOU DON'T HAVE TO. TODAY IS LADIES' DAY!
IT IS?
I READ IT IN THE PAPER. THINK OF ALL THE EXTRA MONEY YOU WILL HAVE FOR POPCORN AND STUFF!
OH, BOY! YOU'RE RIGHT. AM I GOING TO ENJOY THIS GAME!
THIS OUTFIT MAY LOOK FUNNY, BUT IT WILL COME IN HANDY WHEN THEY HIT FOUL BALLS UP INTO THE STANDS.
BALL PARK
I STILL THINK YOU SHOULD TAKE THAT MASK OFF. EVERYBODY IS STARING AT YOU.
HERE WE GO, TUB. THE FIRST BATTER IS UP.
OH, OH! FOUL BALL AND IT'S COMING THIS WAY!
I'M READY!

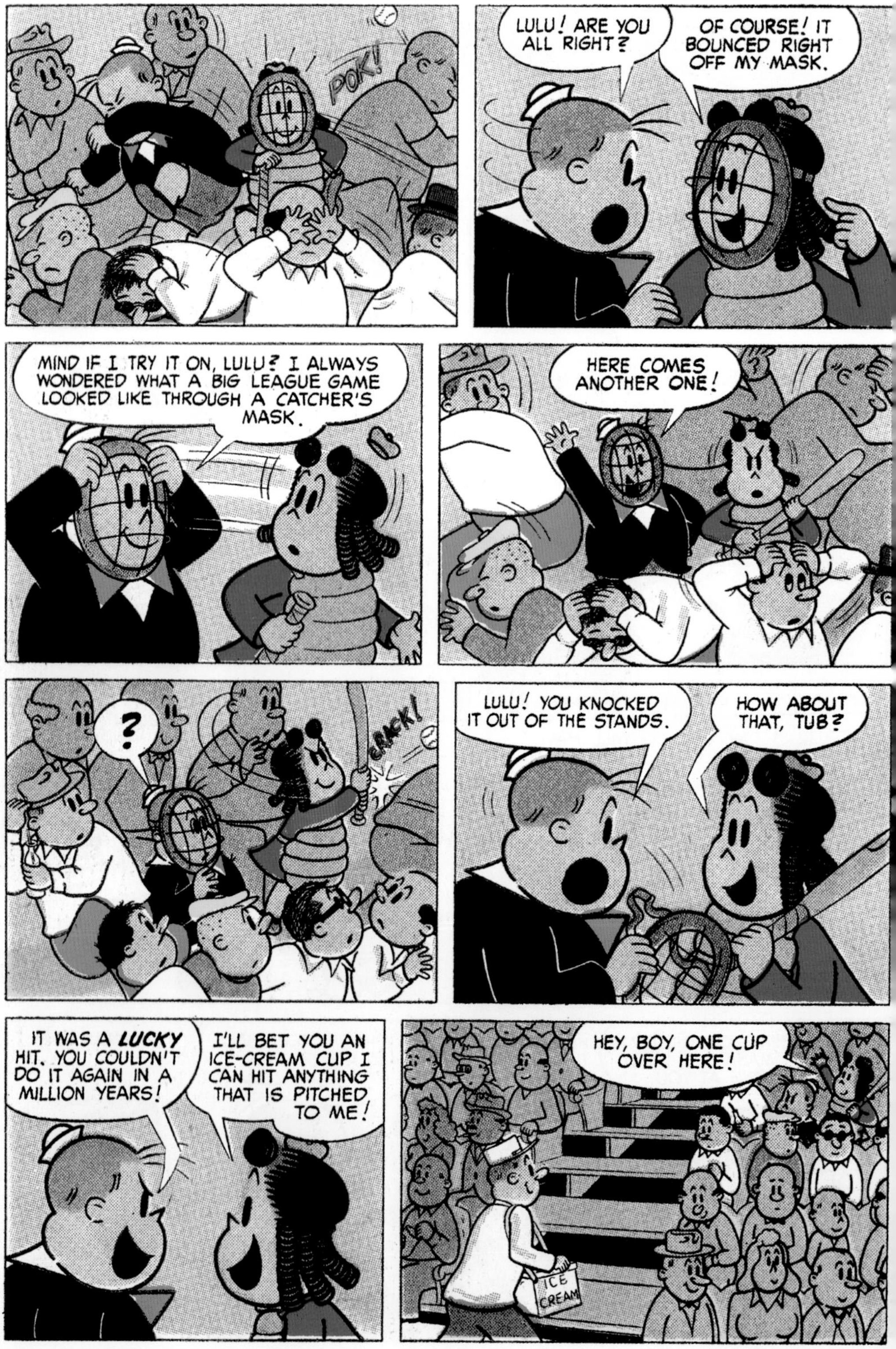

POK!
LULU! ARE YOU ALL RIGHT?
OF COURSE! IT BOUNCED RIGHT OFF MY MASK.
MIND IF I TRY IT ON, LULU? I ALWAYS WONDERED WHAT A BIG LEAGUE GAME LOOKED LIKE THROUGH A CATCHER'S MASK.
HERE COMES ANOTHER ONE!
?
CRACK!
LULU! YOU KNOCKED IT OUT OF THE STANDS.
HOW ABOUT THAT, TUB?
IT WAS A ***LUCKY*** HIT. YOU COULDN'T DO IT AGAIN IN A MILLION YEARS!
I'LL BET YOU AN ICE-CREAM CUP I CAN HIT ANYTHING THAT IS PITCHED TO ME!
HEY, BOY, ONE CUP OVER HERE!
ICE CREAM

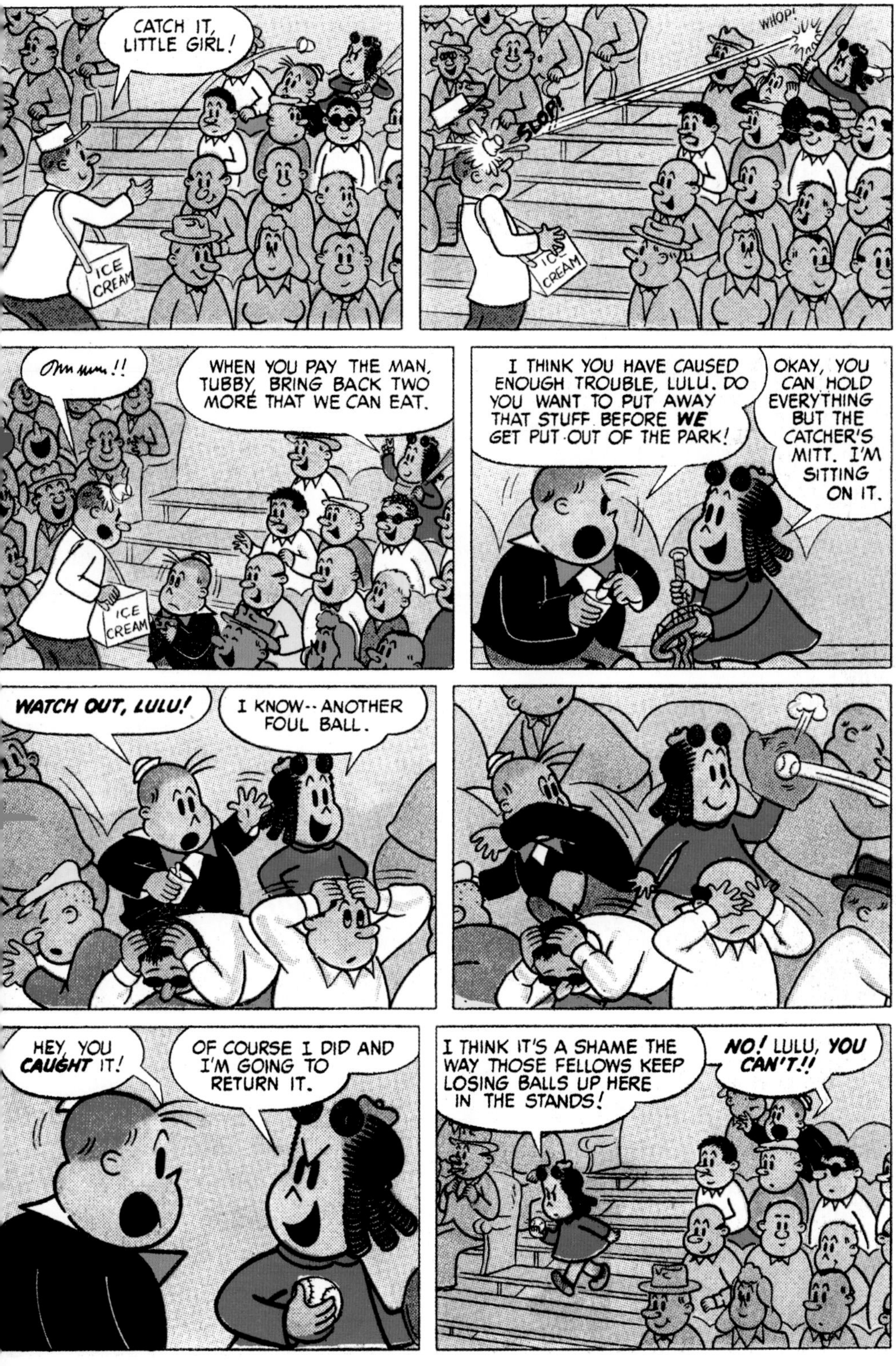

CATCH IT, LITTLE GIRL!
WHOP!
SPOP!
Omm mm!!
WHEN YOU PAY THE MAN, TUBBY, BRING BACK TWO MORE THAT WE CAN EAT.
I THINK YOU HAVE CAUSED ENOUGH TROUBLE, LULU. DO YOU WANT TO PUT AWAY THAT STUFF BEFORE WE GET PUT OUT OF THE PARK!
OKAY, YOU CAN HOLD EVERYTHING BUT THE CATCHER'S MITT. I'M SITTING ON IT.
WATCH OUT, LULU!
I KNOW-- ANOTHER FOUL BALL.
HEY, YOU CAUGHT IT!
OF COURSE I DID AND I'M GOING TO RETURN IT.
I THINK IT'S A SHAME THE WAY THOSE FELLOWS KEEP LOSING BALLS UP HERE IN THE STANDS!
NO! LULU, YOU CAN'T!!

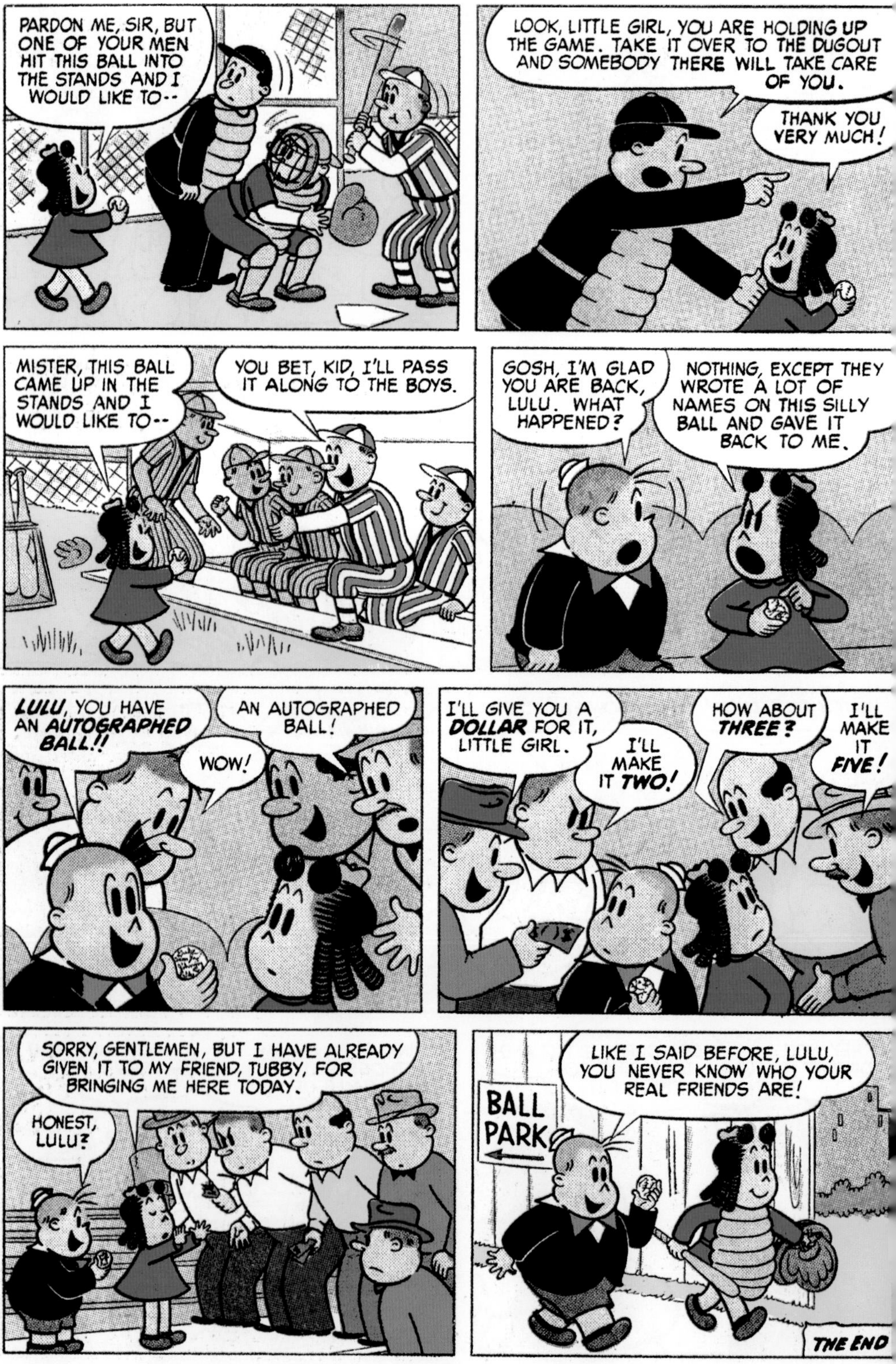
PARDON ME, SIR, BUT ONE OF YOUR MEN HIT THIS BALL INTO THE STANDS AND I WOULD LIKE TO--
LOOK, LITTLE GIRL, YOU ARE HOLDING UP THE GAME. TAKE IT OVER TO THE DUGOUT AND SOMEBODY THERE WILL TAKE CARE OF YOU.
THANK YOU VERY MUCH!
MISTER, THIS BALL CAME UP IN THE STANDS AND I WOULD LIKE TO--
YOU BET, KID, I'LL PASS IT ALONG TO THE BOYS.
GOSH, I'M GLAD YOU ARE BACK, LULU. WHAT HAPPENED?
NOTHING, EXCEPT THEY WROTE A LOT OF NAMES ON THIS SILLY BALL AND GAVE IT BACK TO ME.
LULU, YOU HAVE AN AUTOGRAPHED BALL!!
WOW!
AN AUTOGRAPHED BALL!
I'LL GIVE YOU A DOLLAR FOR IT, LITTLE GIRL.
I'LL MAKE IT TWO!
HOW ABOUT THREE?
I'LL MAKE IT FIVE!
SORRY, GENTLEMEN, BUT I HAVE ALREADY GIVEN IT TO MY FRIEND, TUBBY, FOR BRINGING ME HERE TODAY.
HONEST, LULU?
BALL PARK
LIKE I SAID BEFORE, LULU, YOU NEVER KNOW WHO YOUR REAL FRIENDS ARE!
THE END

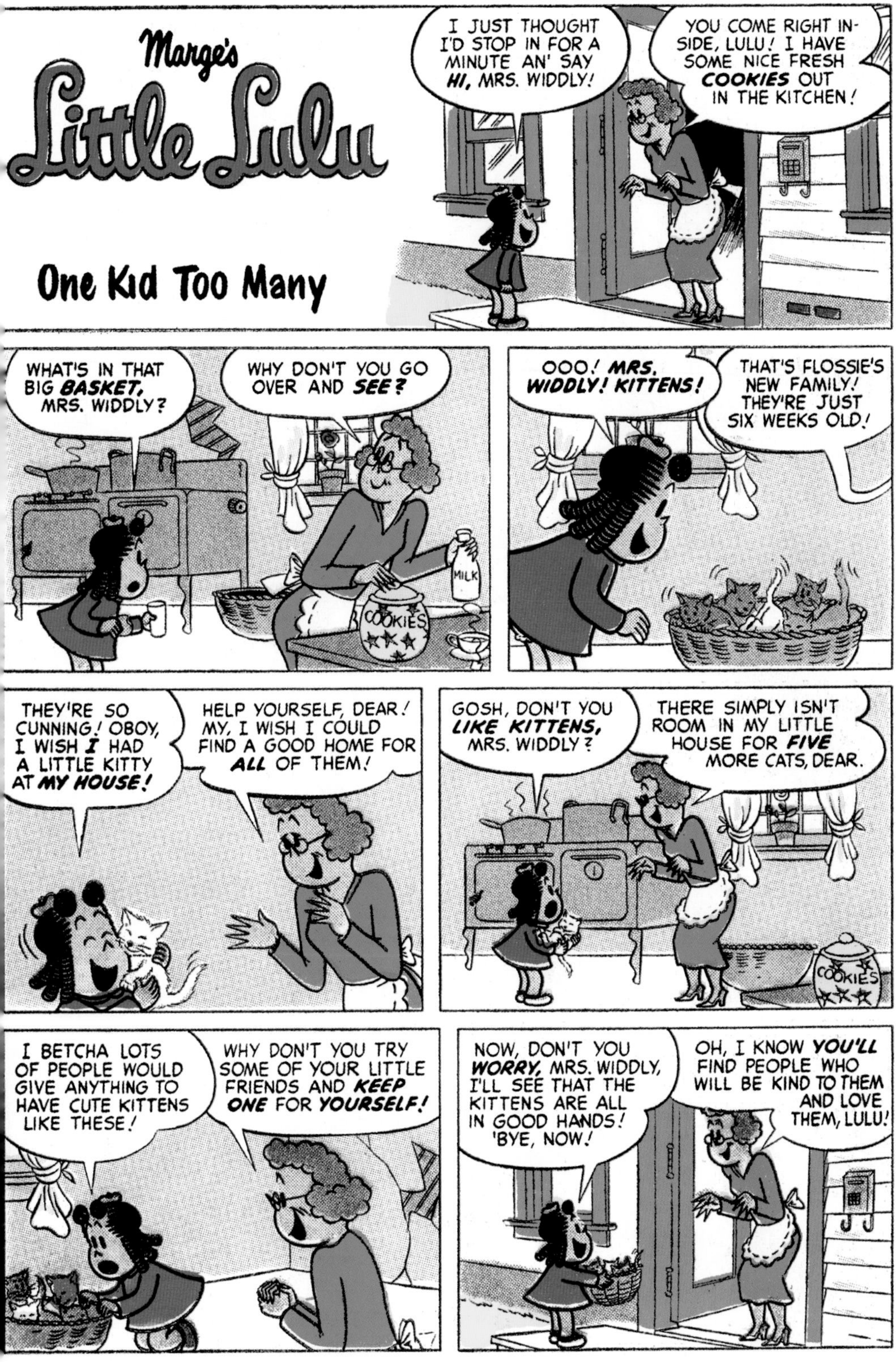
Marge's
Little Lulu
One Kid Too Many
I JUST THOUGHT I'D STOP IN FOR A MINUTE AN' SAY HI, MRS. WIDDLY!
YOU COME RIGHT INSIDE, LULU! I HAVE SOME NICE FRESH COOKIES OUT IN THE KITCHEN!
WHAT'S IN THAT BIG BASKET, MRS. WIDDLY?
WHY DON'T YOU GO OVER AND SEE?
MILK
COOKIES
OOO! MRS. WIDDLY! KITTENS!
THAT'S FLOSSIE'S NEW FAMILY! THEY'RE JUST SIX WEEKS OLD!
THEY'RE SO CUNNING! OBOY, I WISH I HAD A LITTLE KITTY AT MY HOUSE!
HELP YOURSELF, DEAR! MY, I WISH I COULD FIND A GOOD HOME FOR ALL OF THEM!
GOSH, DON'T YOU LIKE KITTENS, MRS. WIDDLY?
THERE SIMPLY ISN'T ROOM IN MY LITTLE HOUSE FOR FIVE MORE CATS, DEAR.
COOKIES
I BETCHA LOTS OF PEOPLE WOULD GIVE ANYTHING TO HAVE CUTE KITTENS LIKE THESE!
WHY DON'T YOU TRY SOME OF YOUR LITTLE FRIENDS AND KEEP ONE FOR YOURSELF!
NOW, DON'T YOU WORRY, MRS. WIDDLY, I'LL SEE THAT THE KITTENS ARE ALL IN GOOD HANDS! 'BYE, NOW!
OH, I KNOW YOU'LL FIND PEOPLE WHO WILL BE KIND TO THEM AND LOVE THEM, LULU!

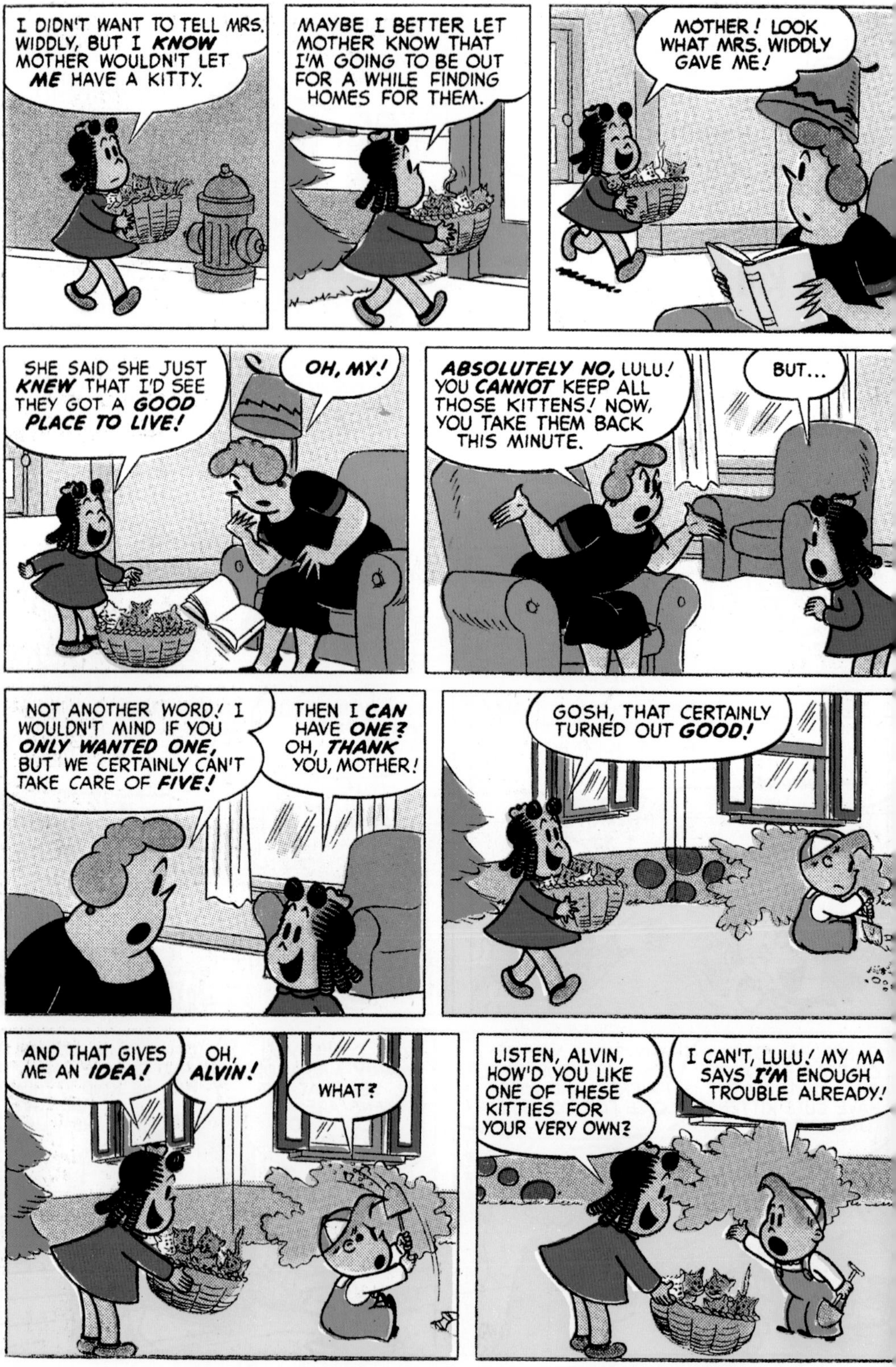
I DIDN'T WANT TO TELL MRS. WIDDLY, BUT I KNOW MOTHER WOULDN'T LET ME HAVE A KITTY.
MAYBE I BETTER LET MOTHER KNOW THAT I'M GOING TO BE OUT FOR A WHILE FINDING HOMES FOR THEM.
MOTHER! LOOK WHAT MRS. WIDDLY GAVE ME!
SHE SAID SHE JUST KNEW THAT I'D SEE THEY GOT A GOOD PLACE TO LIVE!
OH, MY!
ABSOLUTELY NO, LULU! YOU CANNOT KEEP ALL THOSE KITTENS! NOW, YOU TAKE THEM BACK THIS MINUTE.
BUT...
NOT ANOTHER WORD! I WOULDN'T MIND IF YOU ONLY WANTED ONE, BUT WE CERTAINLY CAN'T TAKE CARE OF FIVE!
THEN I CAN HAVE ONE? OH, THANK YOU, MOTHER!
GOSH, THAT CERTAINLY TURNED OUT GOOD!
AND THAT GIVES ME AN IDEA!
OH, ALVIN!
WHAT?
LISTEN, ALVIN, HOW'D YOU LIKE ONE OF THESE KITTIES FOR YOUR VERY OWN?
I CAN'T, LULU! MY MA SAYS I'M ENOUGH TROUBLE ALREADY!

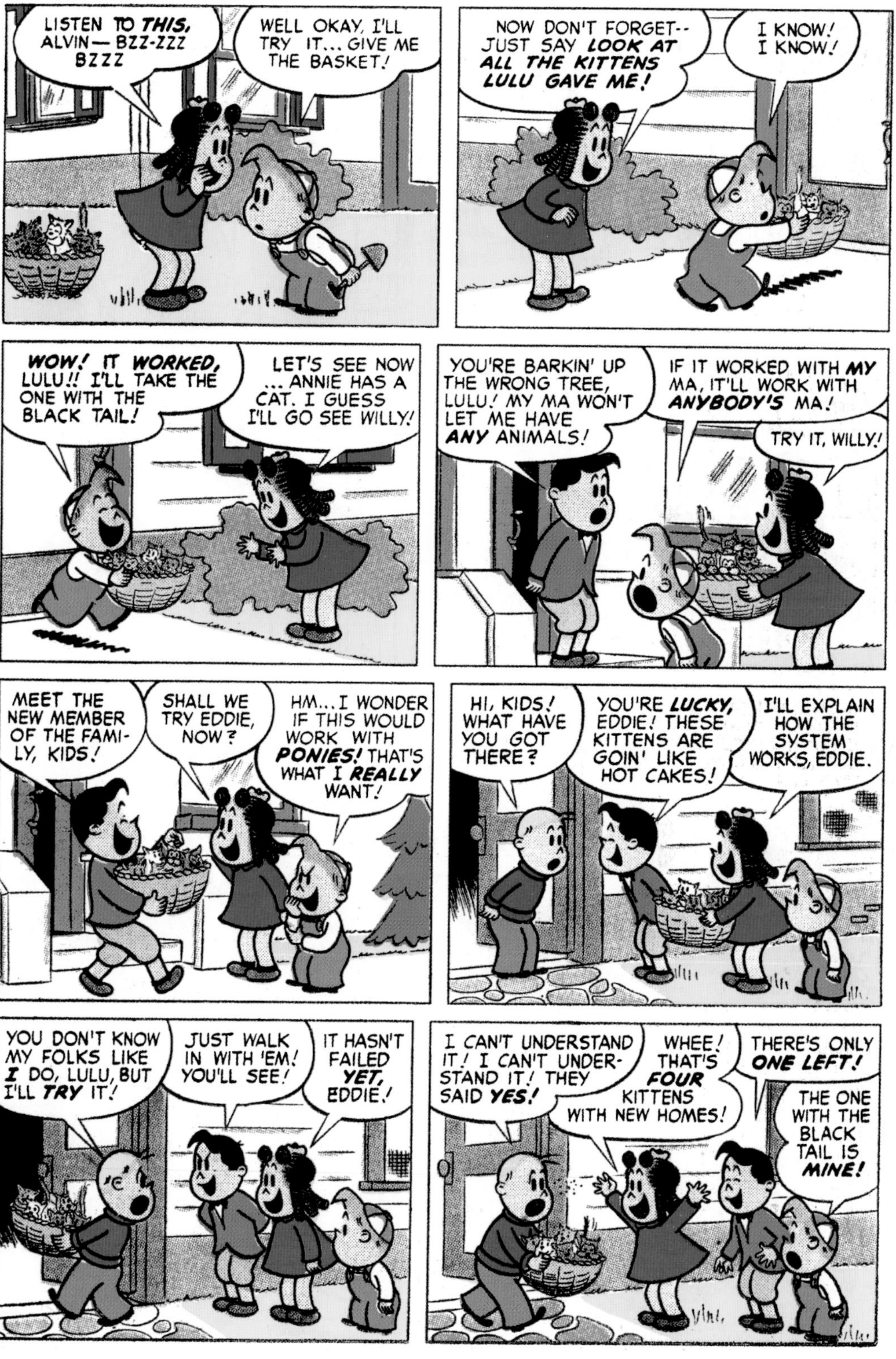
LISTEN TO THIS, ALVIN— BZZ-ZZZ BZZZ
WELL OKAY, I'LL TRY IT... GIVE ME THE BASKET!
NOW DON'T FORGET-- JUST SAY LOOK AT ALL THE KITTENS LULU GAVE ME!
I KNOW! I KNOW!
WOW! IT WORKED, LULU!! I'LL TAKE THE ONE WITH THE BLACK TAIL!
LET'S SEE NOW ... ANNIE HAS A CAT. I GUESS I'LL GO SEE WILLY!
YOU'RE BARKIN' UP THE WRONG TREE, LULU! MY MA WON'T LET ME HAVE ANY ANIMALS!
IF IT WORKED WITH MY MA, IT'LL WORK WITH ANYBODY'S MA!
TRY IT, WILLY!
MEET THE NEW MEMBER OF THE FAMILY, KIDS!
SHALL WE TRY EDDIE, NOW?
HM...I WONDER IF THIS WOULD WORK WITH PONIES! THAT'S WHAT I REALLY WANT!
HI, KIDS! WHAT HAVE YOU GOT THERE?
YOU'RE LUCKY, EDDIE! THESE KITTENS ARE GOIN' LIKE HOT CAKES!
I'LL EXPLAIN HOW THE SYSTEM WORKS, EDDIE.
YOU DON'T KNOW MY FOLKS LIKE I DO, LULU, BUT I'LL TRY IT!
JUST WALK IN WITH 'EM! YOU'LL SEE!
IT HASN'T FAILED YET, EDDIE!
I CAN'T UNDERSTAND IT! I CAN'T UNDERSTAND IT! THEY SAID YES!
WHEE! THAT'S FOUR KITTENS WITH NEW HOMES!
THERE'S ONLY ONE LEFT!
THE ONE WITH THE BLACK TAIL IS MINE!

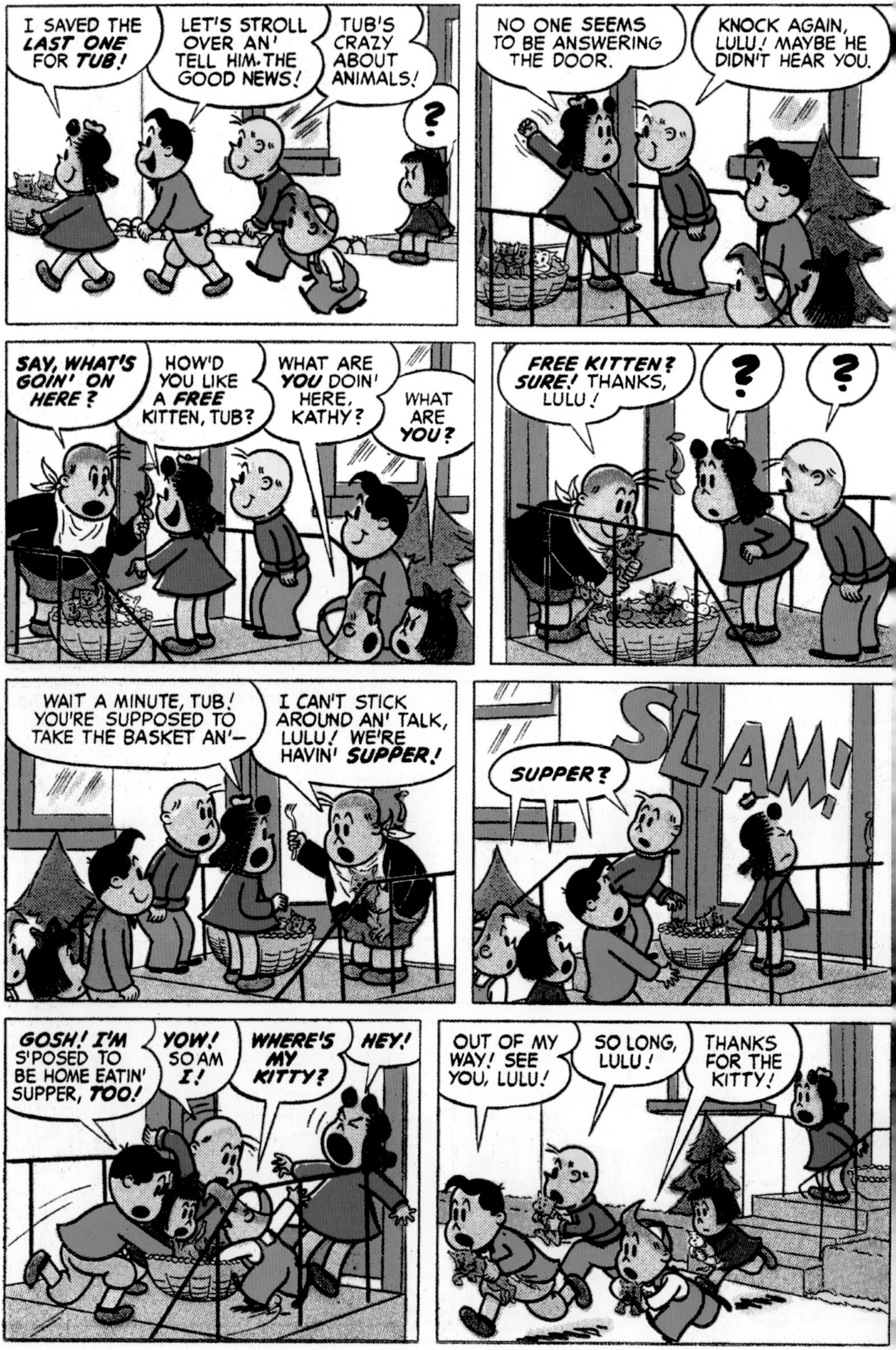
I SAVED THE LAST ONE FOR TUB!
LET'S STROLL OVER AN' TELL HIM THE GOOD NEWS!
TUB'S CRAZY ABOUT ANIMALS!
?
NO ONE SEEMS TO BE ANSWERING THE DOOR.
KNOCK AGAIN, LULU! MAYBE HE DIDN'T HEAR YOU.
SAY, WHAT'S GOIN' ON HERE?
HOW'D YOU LIKE A FREE KITTEN, TUB?
WHAT ARE YOU DOIN' HERE, KATHY?
WHAT ARE YOU?
FREE KITTEN? SURE! THANKS, LULU!
?
?
WAIT A MINUTE, TUB! YOU'RE SUPPOSED TO TAKE THE BASKET AN'—
I CAN'T STICK AROUND AN' TALK, LULU! WE'RE HAVIN' SUPPER!
SLAM!
SUPPER?
GOSH! I'M S'POSED TO BE HOME EATIN' SUPPER, TOO!
YOW! SO AM I!
WHERE'S MY KITTY?
HEY!
OUT OF MY WAY! SEE YOU, LULU!
SO LONG, LULU!
THANKS FOR THE KITTY!

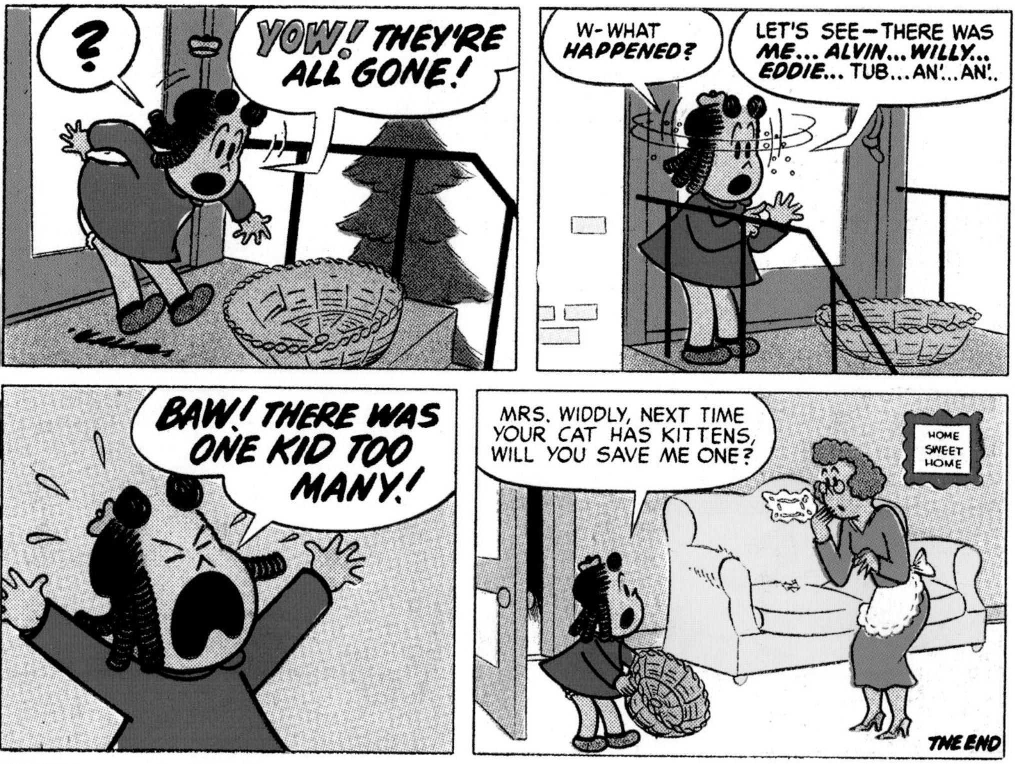
?
YOW! THEY'RE ALL GONE!
W-WHAT HAPPENED?
LET'S SEE—THERE WAS ME... ALVIN... WILLY... EDDIE... TUB... AN'... AN'..
BAW! THERE WAS ONE KID TOO MANY!
MRS. WIDDLY, NEXT TIME YOUR CAT HAS KITTENS, WILL YOU SAVE ME ONE?
HOME SWEET HOME
THE END

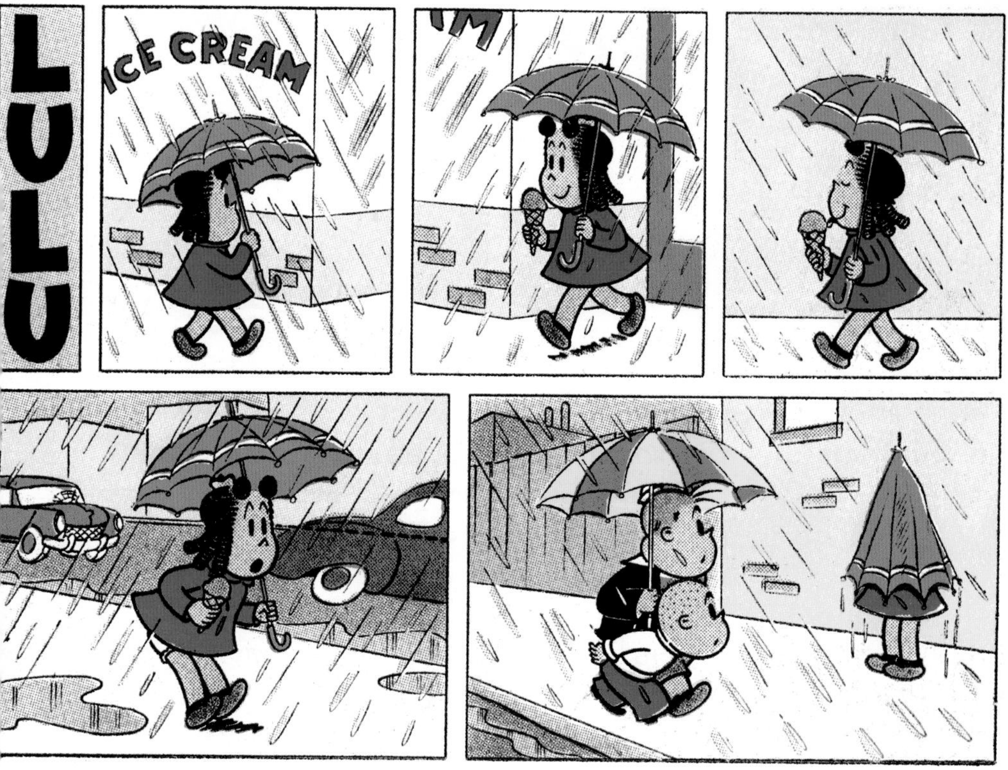
LULU
ICE CREAM

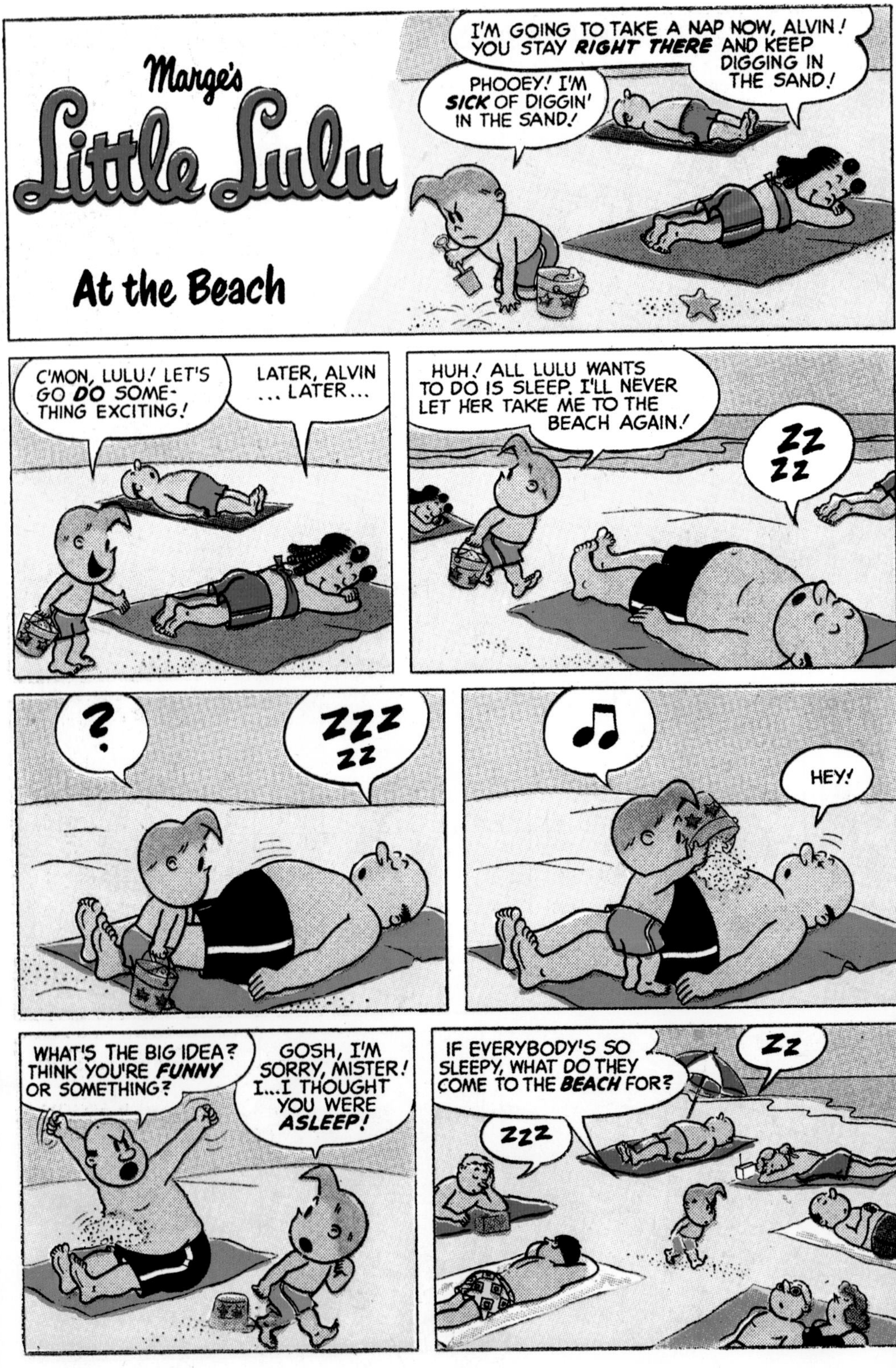
Marge's
Little Lulu
At the Beach
I'M GOING TO TAKE A NAP NOW, ALVIN! YOU STAY RIGHT THERE AND KEEP DIGGING IN THE SAND!
PHOOEY! I'M SICK OF DIGGIN' IN THE SAND!
C'MON, LULU! LET'S GO DO SOMETHING EXCITING!
LATER, ALVIN ... LATER...
HUH! ALL LULU WANTS TO DO IS SLEEP. I'LL NEVER LET HER TAKE ME TO THE BEACH AGAIN!
ZZ ZZ
?
ZZZ ZZ
HEY!
WHAT'S THE BIG IDEA? THINK YOU'RE FUNNY OR SOMETHING?
GOSH, I'M SORRY, MISTER! I...I THOUGHT YOU WERE ASLEEP!
IF EVERYBODY'S SO SLEEPY, WHAT DO THEY COME TO THE BEACH FOR?
ZZ
ZZZ

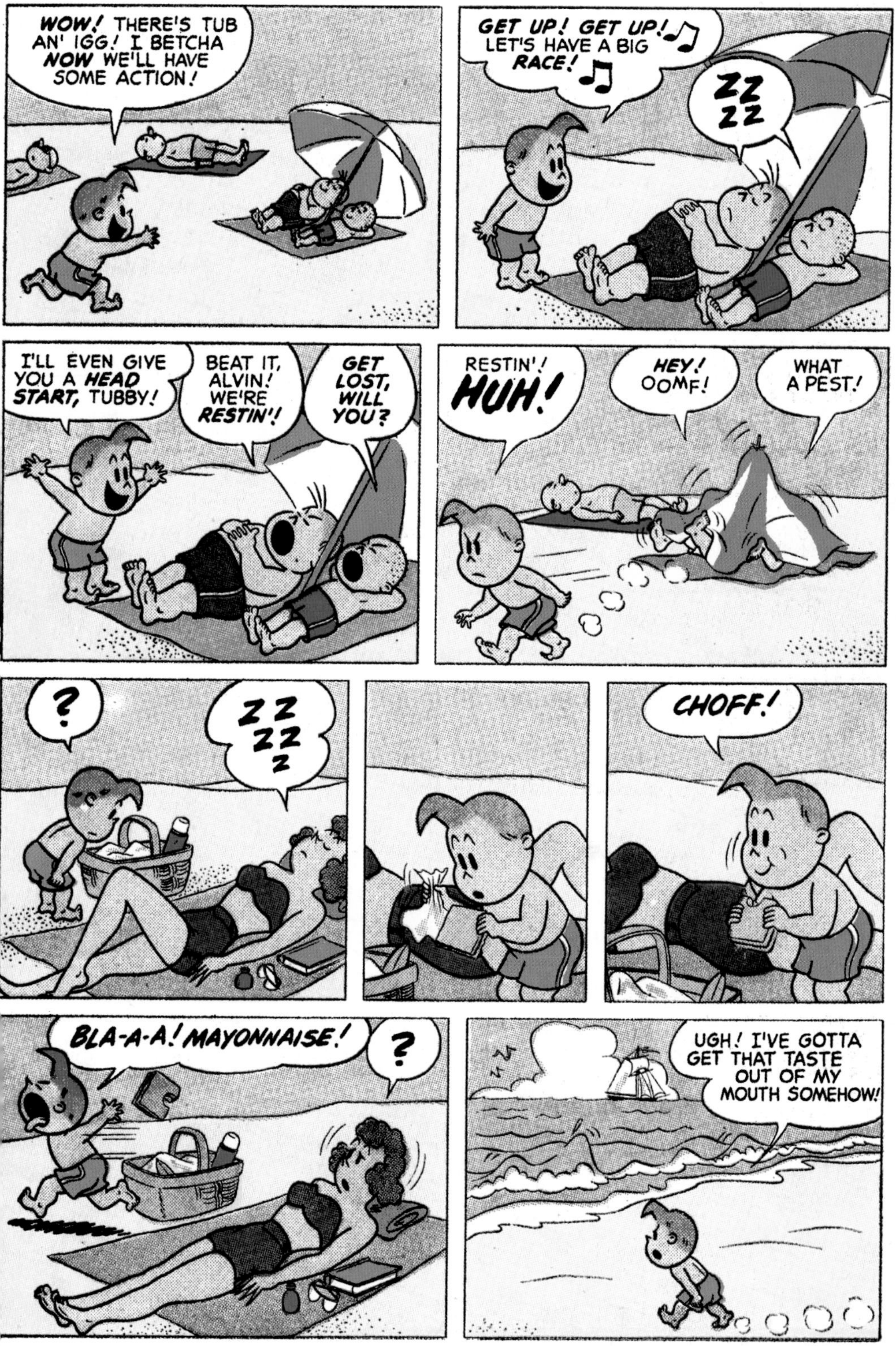

WOW! THERE'S TUB AN' IGG! I BETCHA NOW WE'LL HAVE SOME ACTION!
GET UP! GET UP! LET'S HAVE A BIG RACE!
ZZ ZZ
I'LL EVEN GIVE YOU A HEAD START, TUBBY!
BEAT IT, ALVIN! WE'RE RESTIN'!
GET LOST, WILL YOU?
RESTIN'! HUH!
HEY! OOMF!
WHAT A PEST!
?
Z Z Z Z Z
CHOFF!
BLA-A-A! MAYONNAISE!
?
UGH! I'VE GOTTA GET THAT TASTE OUT OF MY MOUTH SOMEHOW!

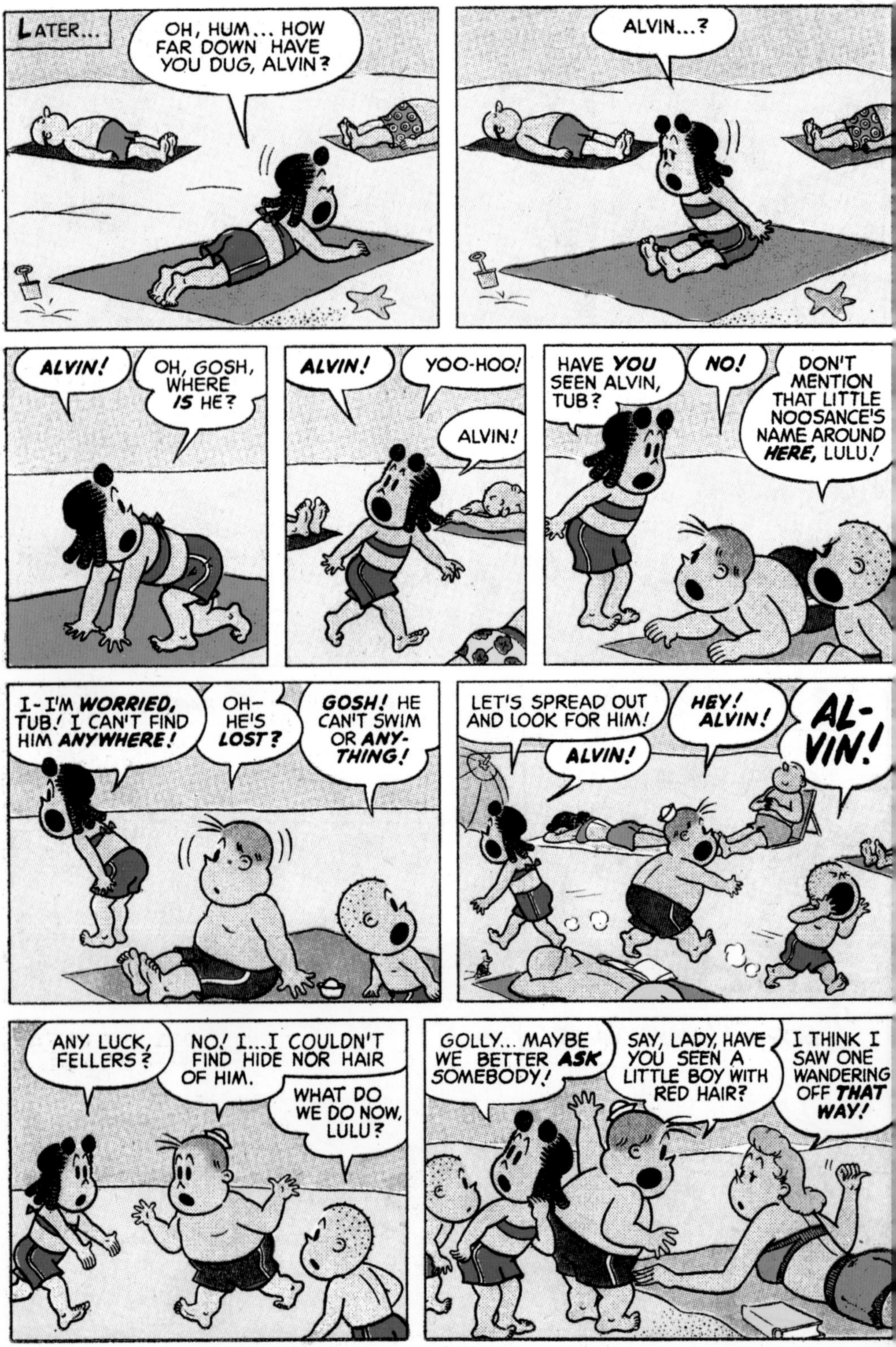
LATER...
OH, HUM... HOW FAR DOWN HAVE YOU DUG, ALVIN?
ALVIN...?
ALVIN!
OH, GOSH, WHERE IS HE?
ALVIN!
YOO-HOO!
ALVIN!
HAVE YOU SEEN ALVIN, TUB?
NO!
DON'T MENTION THAT LITTLE NOOSANCE'S NAME AROUND HERE, LULU!
I-I'M WORRIED, TUB! I CAN'T FIND HIM ANYWHERE!
OH— HE'S LOST?
GOSH! HE CAN'T SWIM OR ANY-THING!
LET'S SPREAD OUT AND LOOK FOR HIM!
ALVIN!
HEY! ALVIN!
AL-VIN!
ANY LUCK, FELLERS?
NO! I...I COULDN'T FIND HIDE NOR HAIR OF HIM.
WHAT DO WE DO NOW, LULU?
GOLLY... MAYBE WE BETTER ASK SOMEBODY!
SAY, LADY, HAVE YOU SEEN A LITTLE BOY WITH RED HAIR?
I THINK I SAW ONE WANDERING OFF THAT WAY!

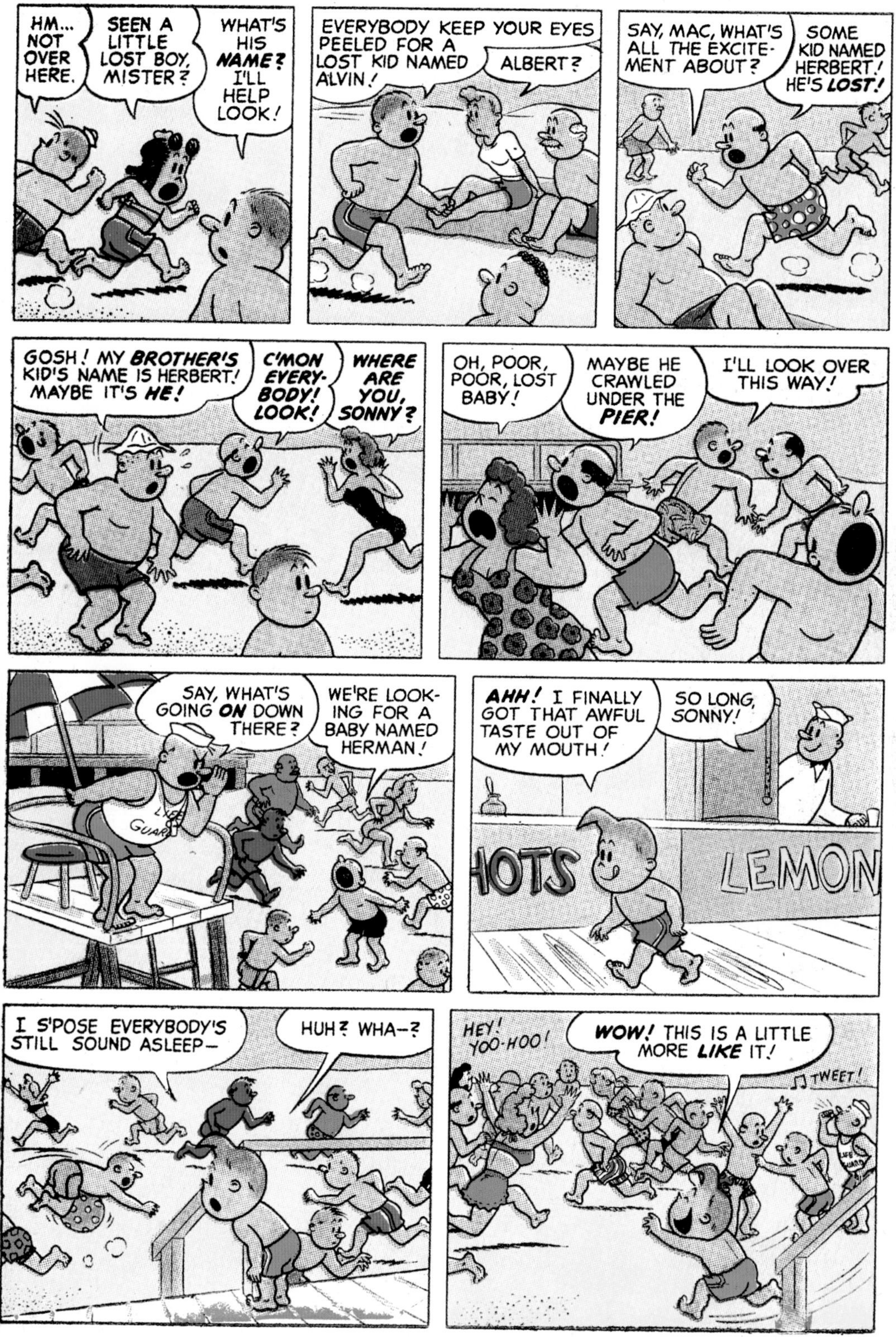
HM... NOT OVER HERE.
SEEN A LITTLE LOST BOY, MISTER?
WHAT'S HIS NAME? I'LL HELP LOOK!
EVERYBODY KEEP YOUR EYES PEELED FOR A LOST KID NAMED ALVIN!
ALBERT?
SAY, MAC, WHAT'S ALL THE EXCITEMENT ABOUT?
SOME KID NAMED HERBERT! HE'S LOST!
GOSH! MY BROTHER'S KID'S NAME IS HERBERT! MAYBE IT'S HE!
C'MON EVERYBODY! LOOK!
WHERE ARE YOU, SONNY?
OH, POOR, POOR, LOST BABY!
MAYBE HE CRAWLED UNDER THE PIER!
I'LL LOOK OVER THIS WAY!
SAY, WHAT'S GOING ON DOWN THERE?
WE'RE LOOKING FOR A BABY NAMED HERMAN!
LIFE GUARD
AHH! I FINALLY GOT THAT AWFUL TASTE OUT OF MY MOUTH!
SO LONG, SONNY!
HOTS
LEMON
I S'POSE EVERYBODY'S STILL SOUND ASLEEP—
HUH? WHA—?
HEY! YOO-HOO!
WOW! THIS IS A LITTLE MORE LIKE IT!
TWEET!

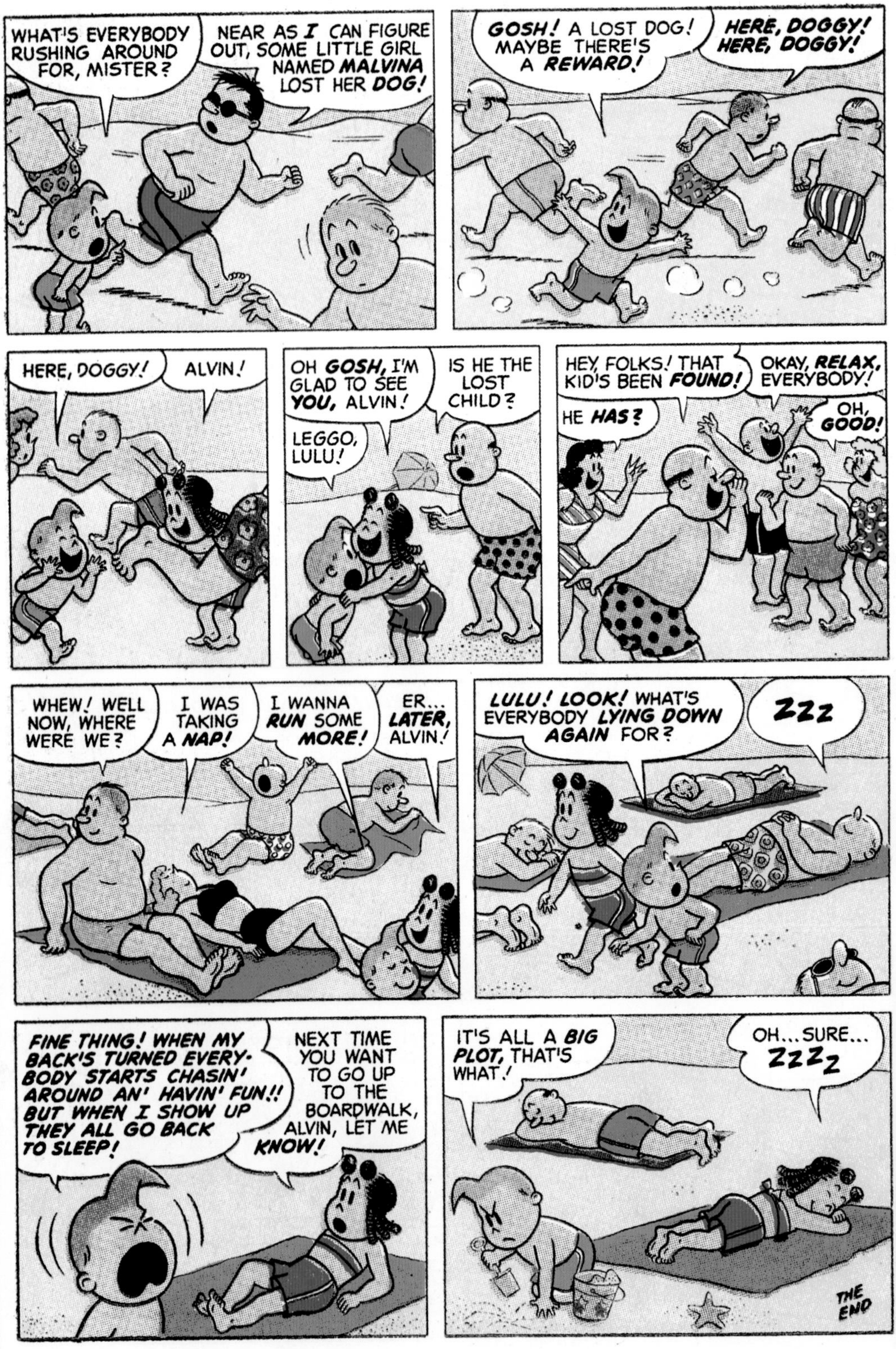
WHAT'S EVERYBODY RUSHING AROUND FOR, MISTER?
NEAR AS I CAN FIGURE OUT, SOME LITTLE GIRL NAMED MALVINA LOST HER DOG!
GOSH! A LOST DOG! MAYBE THERE'S A REWARD!
HERE, DOGGY! HERE, DOGGY!
HERE, DOGGY!
ALVIN!
OH GOSH, I'M GLAD TO SEE YOU, ALVIN!
IS HE THE LOST CHILD?
LEGGO, LULU!
HEY, FOLKS! THAT KID'S BEEN FOUND!
OKAY, RELAX, EVERYBODY!
HE HAS?
OH, GOOD!
WHEW! WELL NOW, WHERE WERE WE?
I WAS TAKING A NAP!
I WANNA RUN SOME MORE!
ER... LATER, ALVIN!
LULU! LOOK! WHAT'S EVERYBODY LYING DOWN AGAIN FOR?
ZZZ
FINE THING! WHEN MY BACK'S TURNED EVERY-BODY STARTS CHASIN' AROUND AN' HAVIN' FUN!! BUT WHEN I SHOW UP THEY ALL GO BACK TO SLEEP!
NEXT TIME YOU WANT TO GO UP TO THE BOARDWALK, ALVIN, LET ME KNOW!
IT'S ALL A BIG PLOT, THAT'S WHAT!
OH... SURE... ZZZZ
THE END

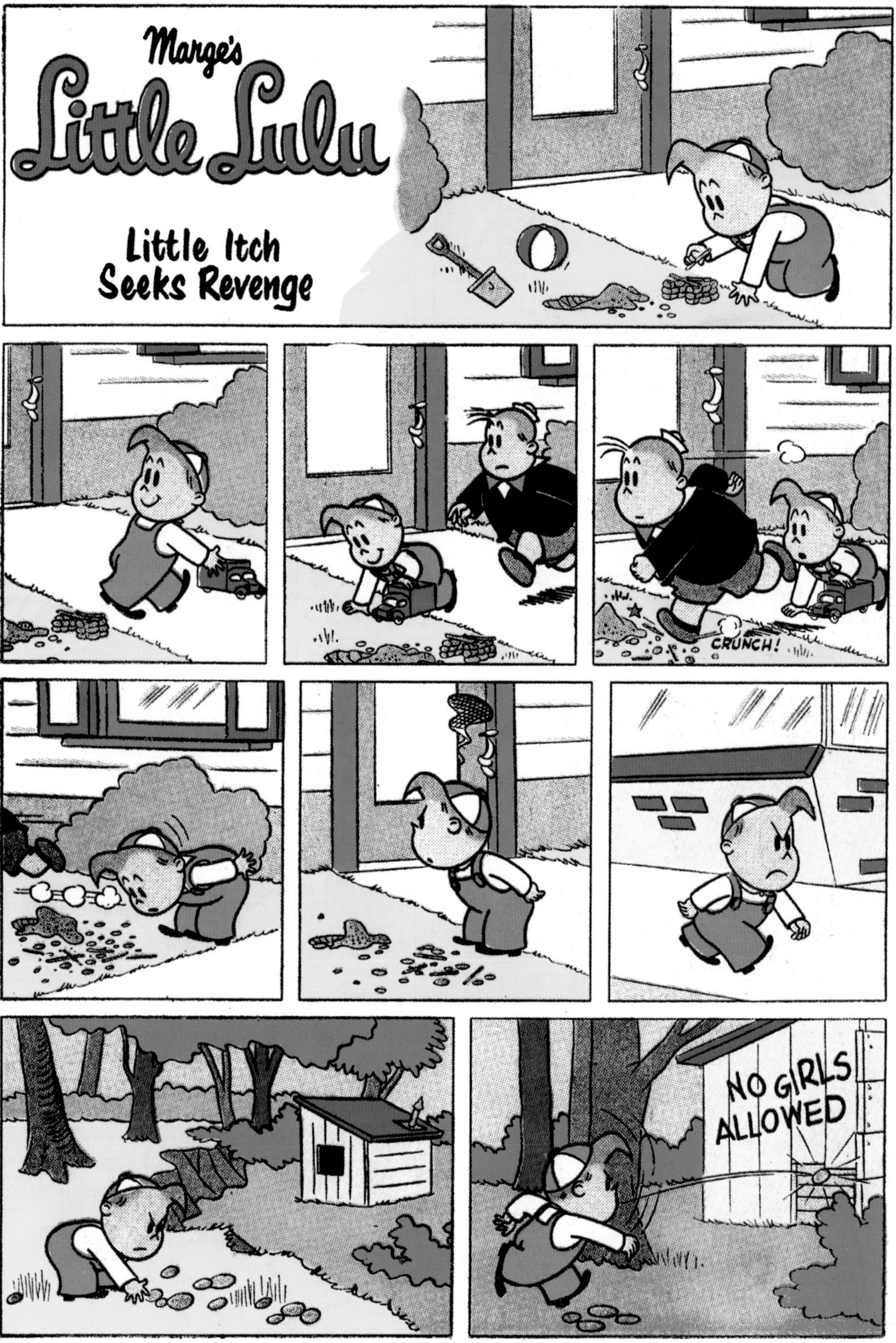
Marge's
Little Lulu
Little Itch
Seeks Revenge
CRUNCH!
NO GIRLS
ALLOWED

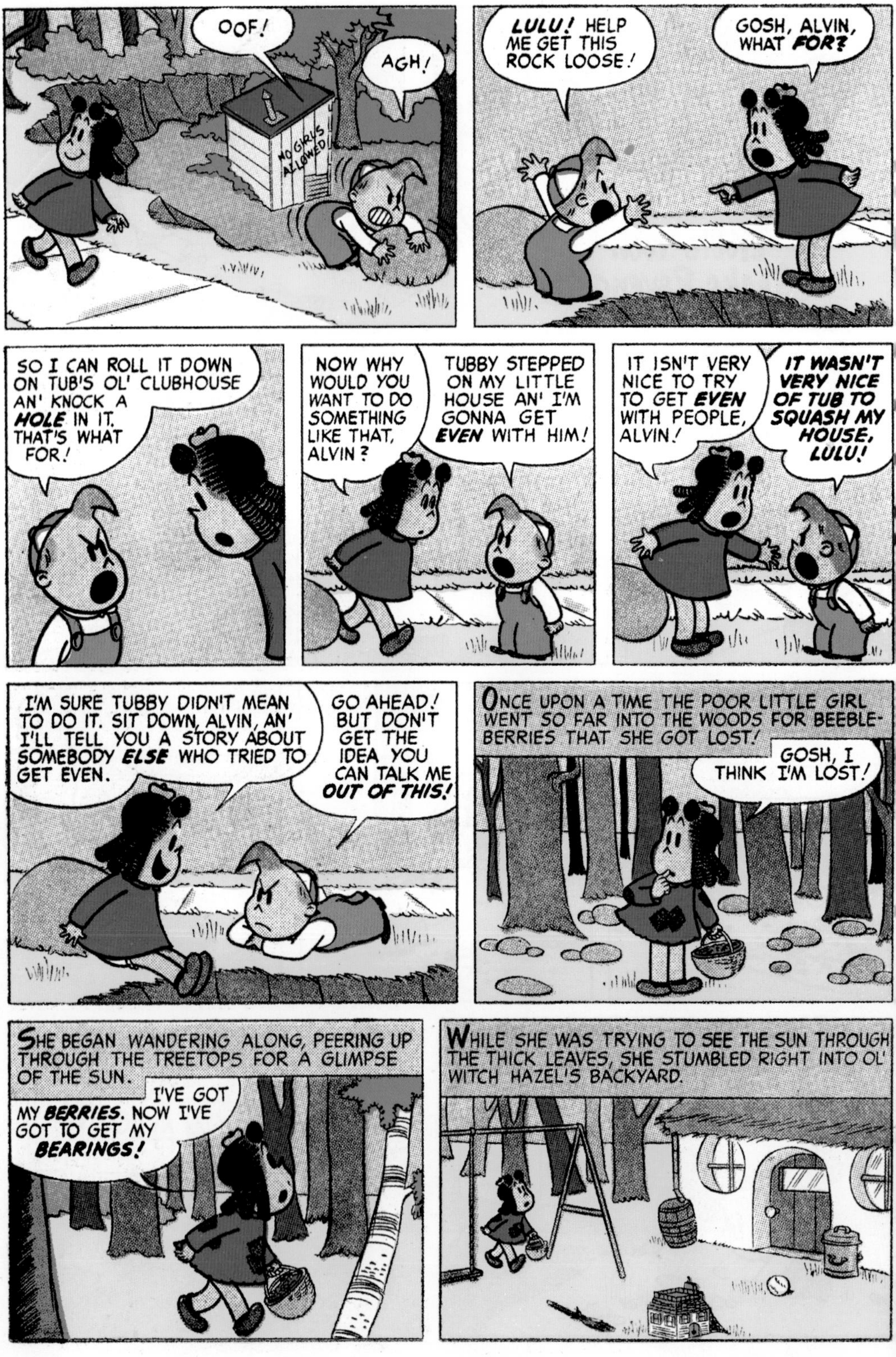
OOF!
AGH!
NO GIRLS ALLOWED!
LULU! HELP ME GET THIS ROCK LOOSE!
GOSH, ALVIN, WHAT FOR?
SO I CAN ROLL IT DOWN ON TUB'S OL' CLUBHOUSE AN' KNOCK A HOLE IN IT. THAT'S WHAT FOR!
NOW WHY WOULD YOU WANT TO DO SOMETHING LIKE THAT, ALVIN?
TUBBY STEPPED ON MY LITTLE HOUSE AN' I'M GONNA GET EVEN WITH HIM!
IT ISN'T VERY NICE TO TRY TO GET EVEN WITH PEOPLE, ALVIN!
IT WASN'T VERY NICE OF TUB TO SQUASH MY HOUSE, LULU!
I'M SURE TUBBY DIDN'T MEAN TO DO IT. SIT DOWN, ALVIN, AN' I'LL TELL YOU A STORY ABOUT SOMEBODY ELSE WHO TRIED TO GET EVEN.
GO AHEAD! BUT DON'T GET THE IDEA YOU CAN TALK ME OUT OF THIS!
ONCE UPON A TIME THE POOR LITTLE GIRL WENT SO FAR INTO THE WOODS FOR BEEBLE-BERRIES THAT SHE GOT LOST!
GOSH, I THINK I'M LOST!
SHE BEGAN WANDERING ALONG, PEERING UP THROUGH THE TREETOPS FOR A GLIMPSE OF THE SUN.
I'VE GOT MY BERRIES. NOW I'VE GOT TO GET MY BEARINGS!
WHILE SHE WAS TRYING TO SEE THE SUN THROUGH THE THICK LEAVES, SHE STUMBLED RIGHT INTO OL' WITCH HAZEL'S BACKYARD.

SMACK IN THE MIDDLE OF THE YARD WAS LITTLE ITCH'S FAVORITE DOLL HOUSE.

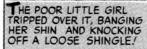

THE POOR LITTLE GIRL TRIPPED OVER IT, BANGING HER SHIN AND KNOCKING OFF A LOOSE SHINGLE!

RUBBING HER BUMPED SHIN, SHE HOPPED OFF ON ONE FOOT.

OW!

OW!

OW!

WHEN THE WITCHES CAME HOME, LITTLE ITCH SAW THE BROKEN SHINGLE RIGHT AWAY!

YOW! SOMEBODY SMASHED THE ROOF OF MY DOLL HOUSE.

OH, HOW SHE HOWLED AND HOLLERED AND SCREECHED.

BAW! IT'S RUINED! RUINED!

OW! MY EARS!

SHE NEARLY DROVE HER OL' AUNTIE OUT OF HER EVIL OLD MIND!

STOP YELLING AND FIX IT!

NO! I WANT TO FIX WHOEVER DID IT!

GRABBING HER MAGIC WAND, SHE STREAKED DOWN THE TRAIL THE LITTLE GIRL MADE WHEN SHE HOPPED AWAY.

ON THE EDGE OF TOWN, ITCH FINALLY CAUGHT UP TO THE POOR LITTLE GIRL.

OH ... SO SHE'S THE GUILTY ONE!

GOODY! I'M NOT LOST ANY MORE.

SILENTLY, ITCH STALKED HER DOWN THE STREET.

FIRST, I'LL JUMP ON HER BACK AND YANK HER HAIR!

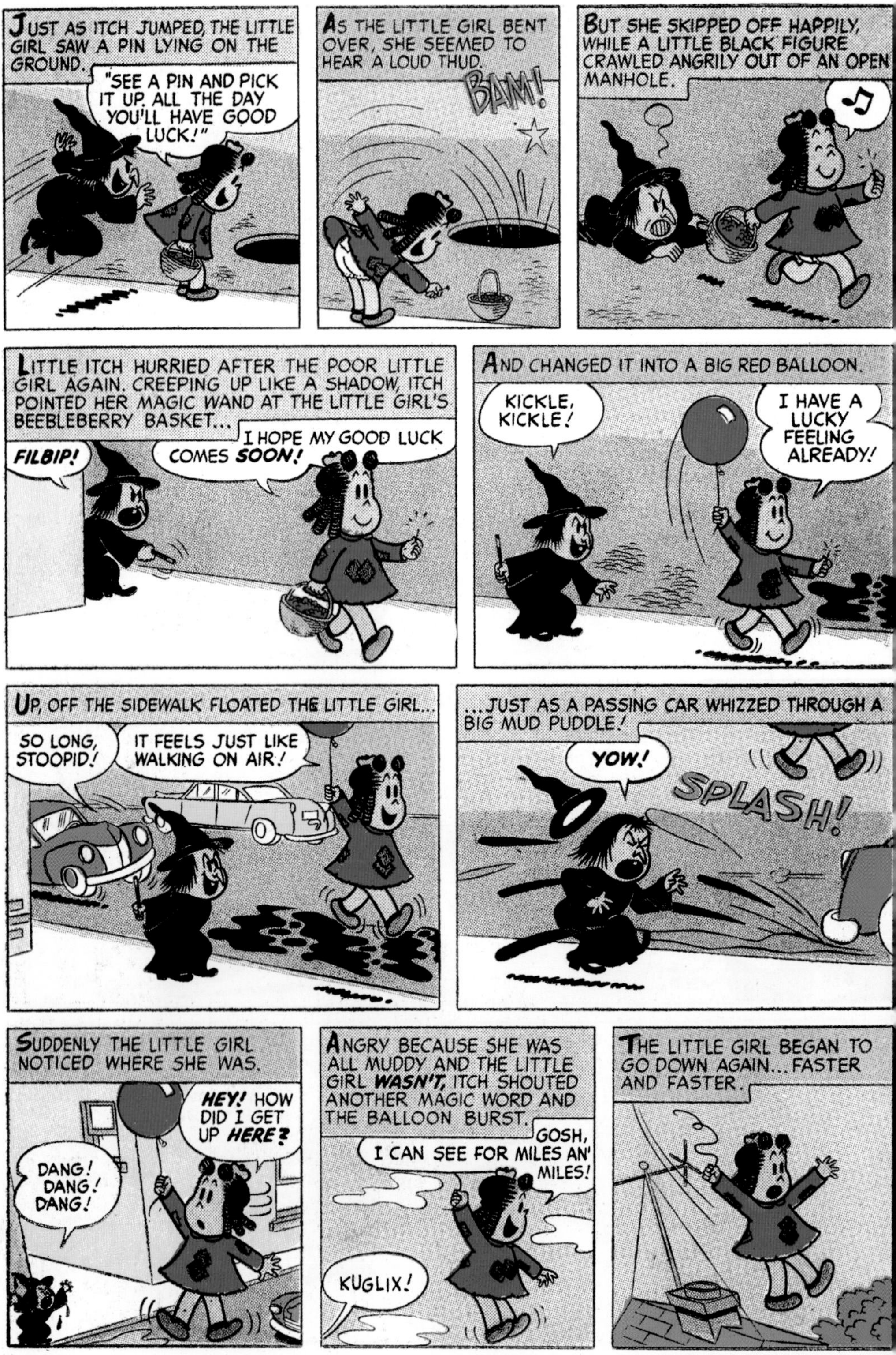
JUST AS ITCH JUMPED, THE LITTLE GIRL SAW A PIN LYING ON THE GROUND.
"SEE A PIN AND PICK IT UP, ALL THE DAY YOU'LL HAVE GOOD LUCK!"
AS THE LITTLE GIRL BENT OVER, SHE SEEMED TO HEAR A LOUD THUD.
BAM!
BUT SHE SKIPPED OFF HAPPILY, WHILE A LITTLE BLACK FIGURE CRAWLED ANGRILY OUT OF AN OPEN MANHOLE.
LITTLE ITCH HURRIED AFTER THE POOR LITTLE GIRL AGAIN. CREEPING UP LIKE A SHADOW, ITCH POINTED HER MAGIC WAND AT THE LITTLE GIRL'S BEEBLEBERRY BASKET...
FILBIP!
I HOPE MY GOOD LUCK COMES SOON!
AND CHANGED IT INTO A BIG RED BALLOON.
KICKLE, KICKLE!
I HAVE A LUCKY FEELING ALREADY!
UP, OFF THE SIDEWALK FLOATED THE LITTLE GIRL...
SO LONG, STOOPID!
IT FEELS JUST LIKE WALKING ON AIR!
...JUST AS A PASSING CAR WHIZZED THROUGH A BIG MUD PUDDLE!
YOW!
SPLASH!
SUDDENLY THE LITTLE GIRL NOTICED WHERE SHE WAS.
HEY! HOW DID I GET UP HERE?
DANG! DANG! DANG!
ANGRY BECAUSE SHE WAS ALL MUDDY AND THE LITTLE GIRL WASN'T, ITCH SHOUTED ANOTHER MAGIC WORD AND THE BALLOON BURST.
GOSH, I CAN SEE FOR MILES AN' MILES!
KUGLIX!
THE LITTLE GIRL BEGAN TO GO DOWN AGAIN... FASTER AND FASTER.

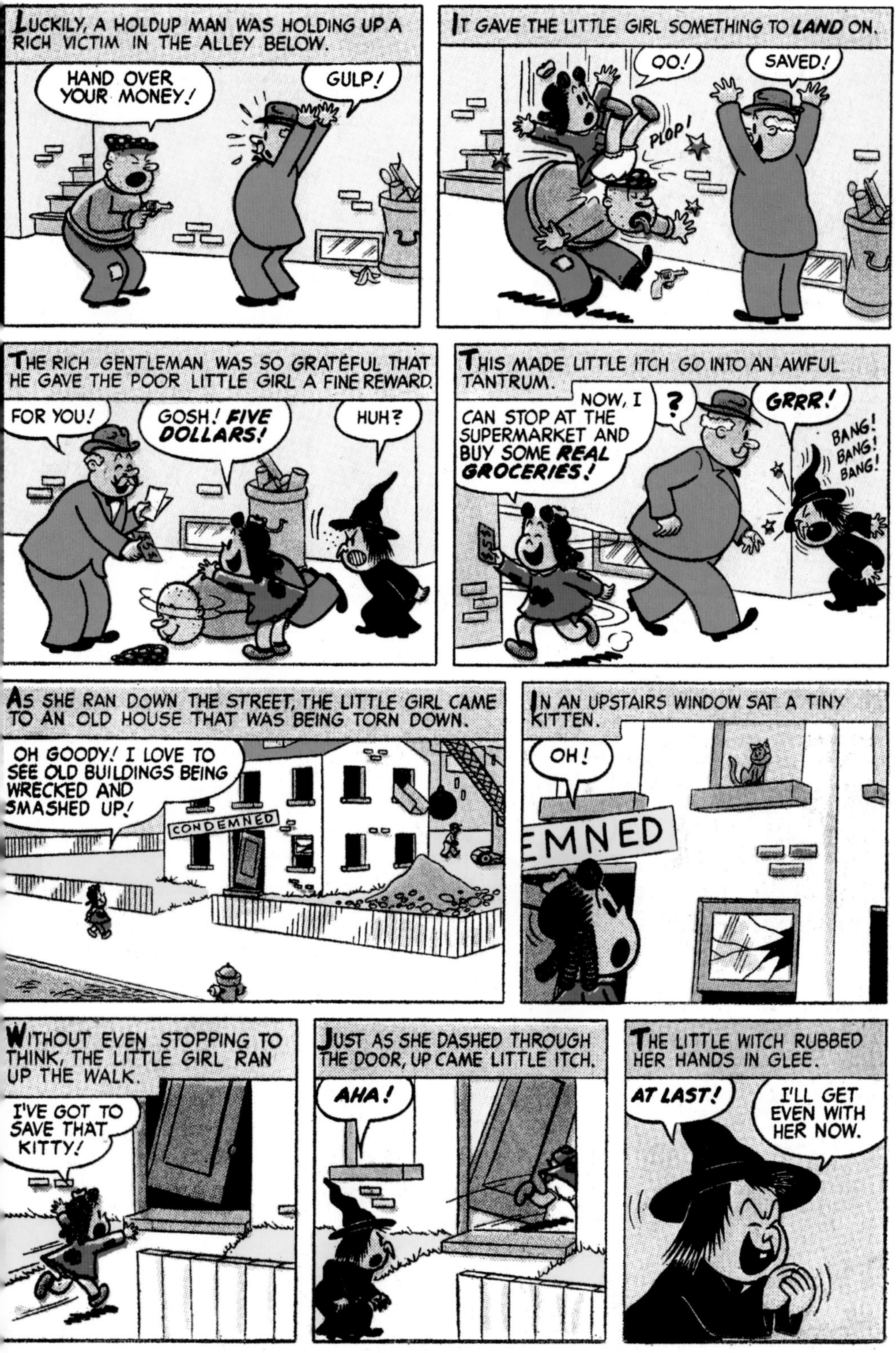
LUCKILY, A HOLDUP MAN WAS HOLDING UP A RICH VICTIM IN THE ALLEY BELOW.
HAND OVER YOUR MONEY!
GULP!
IT GAVE THE LITTLE GIRL SOMETHING TO LAND ON.
OO!
SAVED!
PLOP!
THE RICH GENTLEMAN WAS SO GRATEFUL THAT HE GAVE THE POOR LITTLE GIRL A FINE REWARD.
FOR YOU!
GOSH! FIVE DOLLARS!
HUH?
THIS MADE LITTLE ITCH GO INTO AN AWFUL TANTRUM.
NOW, I CAN STOP AT THE SUPERMARKET AND BUY SOME REAL GROCERIES!
?
GRRR!
BANG! BANG! BANG!
AS SHE RAN DOWN THE STREET, THE LITTLE GIRL CAME TO AN OLD HOUSE THAT WAS BEING TORN DOWN.
OH GOODY! I LOVE TO SEE OLD BUILDINGS BEING WRECKED AND SMASHED UP!
CONDEMNED
IN AN UPSTAIRS WINDOW SAT A TINY KITTEN.
OH!
EMNED
WITHOUT EVEN STOPPING TO THINK, THE LITTLE GIRL RAN UP THE WALK.
I'VE GOT TO SAVE THAT KITTY!
JUST AS SHE DASHED THROUGH THE DOOR, UP CAME LITTLE ITCH.
AHA!
THE LITTLE WITCH RUBBED HER HANDS IN GLEE.
AT LAST!
I'LL GET EVEN WITH HER NOW.

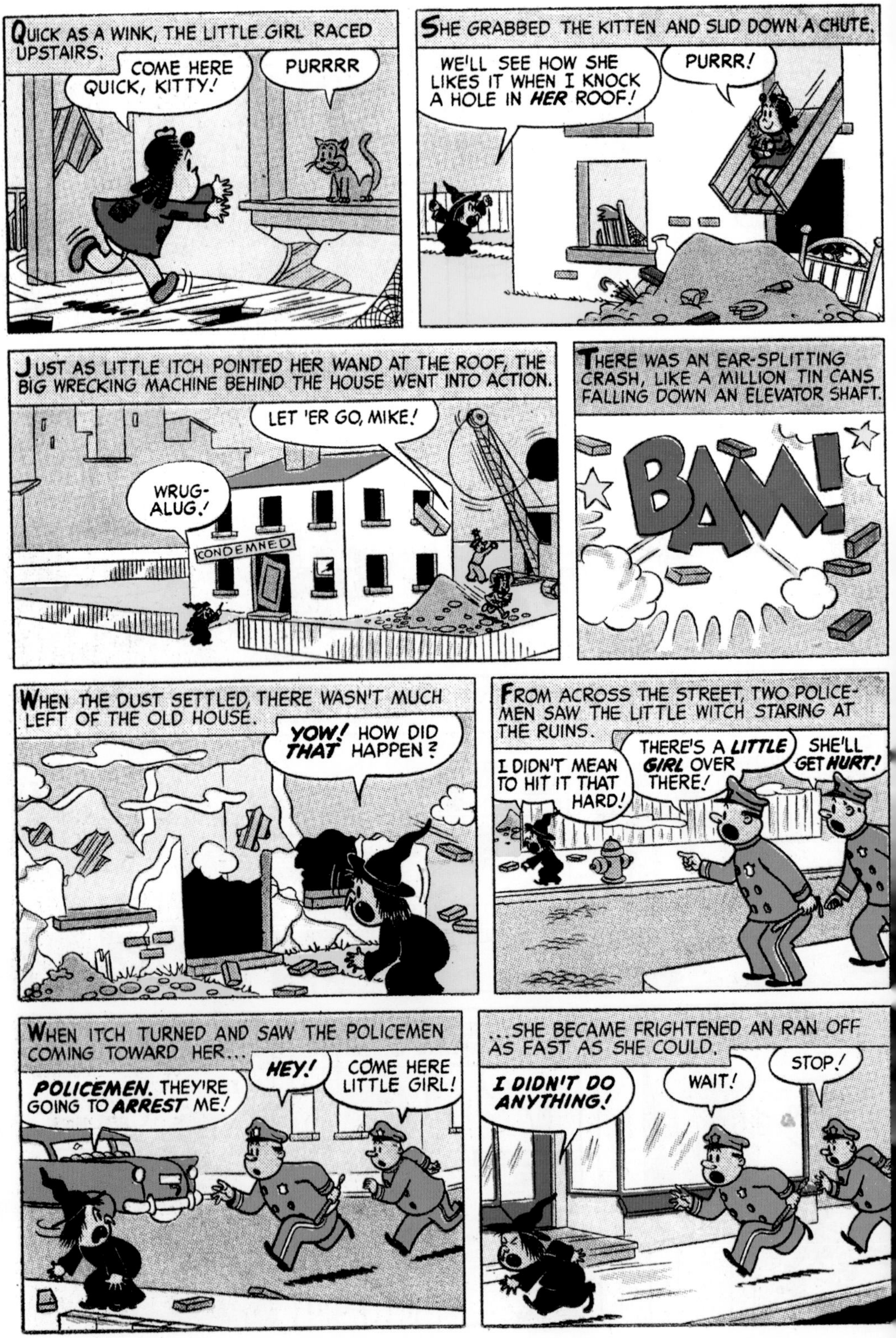
QUICK AS A WINK, THE LITTLE GIRL RACED UPSTAIRS.
COME HERE QUICK, KITTY!
PURRRR
SHE GRABBED THE KITTEN AND SLID DOWN A CHUTE.
WE'LL SEE HOW SHE LIKES IT WHEN I KNOCK A HOLE IN HER ROOF!
PURRR!
JUST AS LITTLE ITCH POINTED HER WAND AT THE ROOF, THE BIG WRECKING MACHINE BEHIND THE HOUSE WENT INTO ACTION.
LET 'ER GO, MIKE!
WRUG-ALUG!
CONDEMNED
THERE WAS AN EAR-SPLITTING CRASH, LIKE A MILLION TIN CANS FALLING DOWN AN ELEVATOR SHAFT.
BAM!
WHEN THE DUST SETTLED, THERE WASN'T MUCH LEFT OF THE OLD HOUSE.
YOW! HOW DID THAT HAPPEN?
FROM ACROSS THE STREET, TWO POLICEMEN SAW THE LITTLE WITCH STARING AT THE RUINS.
I DIDN'T MEAN TO HIT IT THAT HARD!
THERE'S A LITTLE GIRL OVER THERE!
SHE'LL GET HURT!
WHEN ITCH TURNED AND SAW THE POLICEMEN COMING TOWARD HER...
POLICEMEN. THEY'RE GOING TO ARREST ME!
HEY!
COME HERE LITTLE GIRL!
...SHE BECAME FRIGHTENED AN RAN OFF AS FAST AS SHE COULD.
I DIDN'T DO ANYTHING!
WAIT!
STOP!

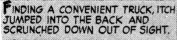
FINDING A CONVENIENT TRUCK, ITCH JUMPED INTO THE BACK AND SCRUNCHED DOWN OUT OF SIGHT.

AS THE TRUCK ROLLED AWAY SHE SNICKERED AT HOW **CLEVERLY** SHE HAD ESCAPED.

KICKLE, KICKLE!

SHE SNICKERED AND GIGGLED ALL THE WAY TO THE RIVER.

KICKLE, KICKLE, KICKLE, KICKLE, KICKLE!

CITY GARBAGE
TRUCK NO. 3

BUT SHE STOPPED SNICKERING WHEN SHE SLID OFF THE END OF A PIER ONTO A GARBAGE SCOW.

CITY GARBAGE
TRUCK NO. 3

SITTING ON TOP OF **THIS SCOW**, WITH COFFEE GROUNDS DOWN HER DRESS AND AN ORANGE RIND ON HER HEAD, LITTLE ITCH WAS TOWED OUT TO SEA.

BAW! HELP!

IT WAS A LONG SWIM, BUT SHE FINALLY GOT HOME LATE THAT NIGHT.

I GUESS SHE DRANK PLENTY OF **MILK** BEFORE SHE STARTED SWIMMIN', HUH LULU?

MILK?

SURE...FROM THE **COW** SHE WAS RIDIN' ON!

A GARBAGE SCOW ISN'T A COW, ALVIN.

OH...WELL, I GUESS I WON'T BUST UP TUB'S CLUBHOUSE, LULU!

NO GIRLS ALLOWED

OH, I'M SO GLAD I CHANGED YOUR MIND FOR YOU, ALVIN!

YOU DIDN'T CHANGE MY MIND, LULU! I JUST REMEMBERED --TUBBY'S GONNA SHOW ME HIS COLLECTION OF OLD COINS TODAY!

THE END

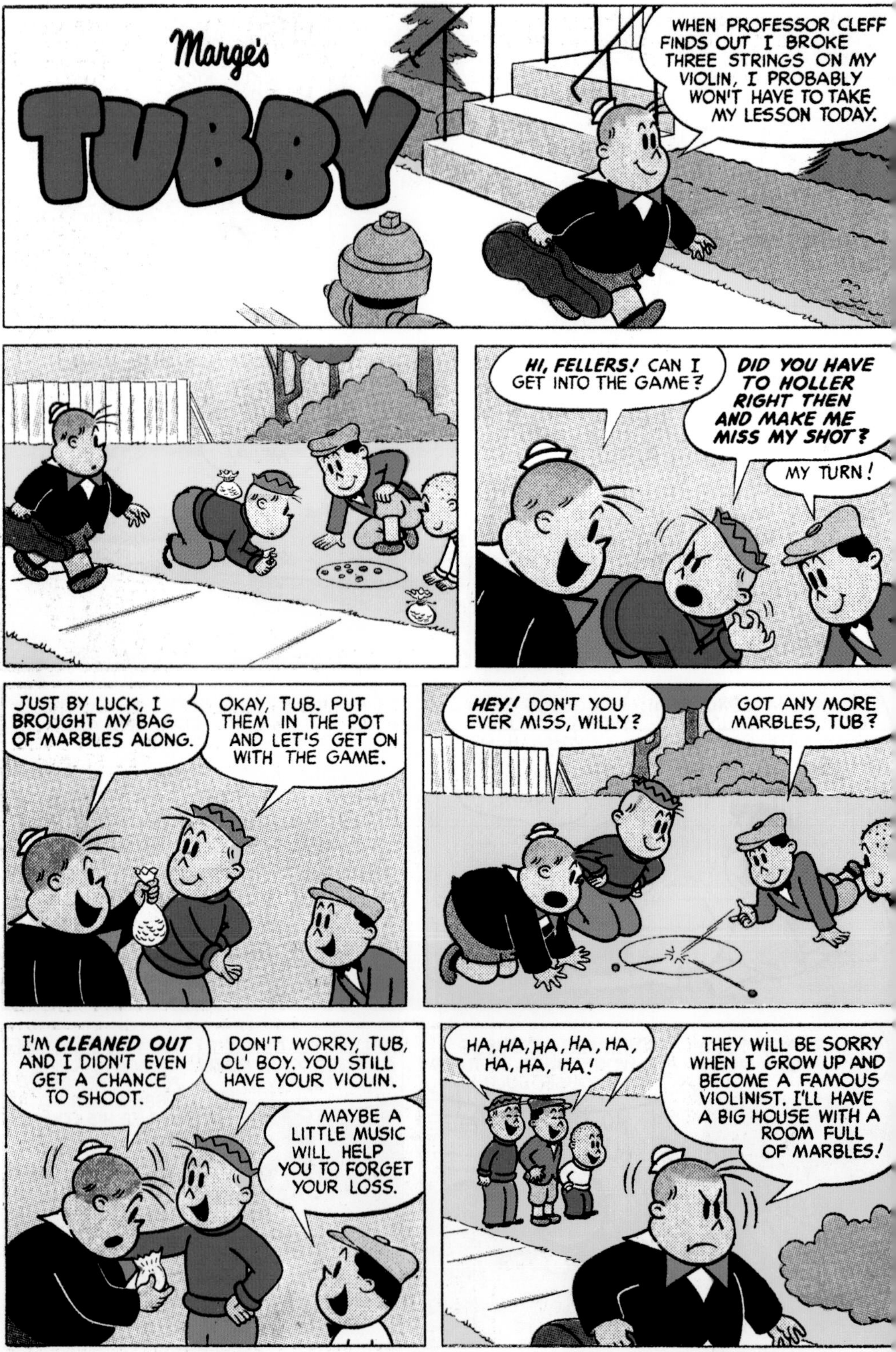
Marge's
TUBBY
WHEN PROFESSOR CLEFF FINDS OUT I BROKE THREE STRINGS ON MY VIOLIN, I PROBABLY WON'T HAVE TO TAKE MY LESSON TODAY.
HI, FELLERS! CAN I GET INTO THE GAME?
DID YOU HAVE TO HOLLER RIGHT THEN AND MAKE ME MISS MY SHOT?
MY TURN!
JUST BY LUCK, I BROUGHT MY BAG OF MARBLES ALONG.
OKAY, TUB. PUT THEM IN THE POT AND LET'S GET ON WITH THE GAME.
HEY! DON'T YOU EVER MISS, WILLY?
GOT ANY MORE MARBLES, TUB?
I'M CLEANED OUT AND I DIDN'T EVEN GET A CHANCE TO SHOOT.
DON'T WORRY, TUB, OL' BOY. YOU STILL HAVE YOUR VIOLIN.
MAYBE A LITTLE MUSIC WILL HELP YOU TO FORGET YOUR LOSS.
HA, HA, HA, HA, HA, HA, HA, HA!
THEY WILL BE SORRY WHEN I GROW UP AND BECOME A FAMOUS VIOLINIST. I'LL HAVE A BIG HOUSE WITH A ROOM FULL OF MARBLES!

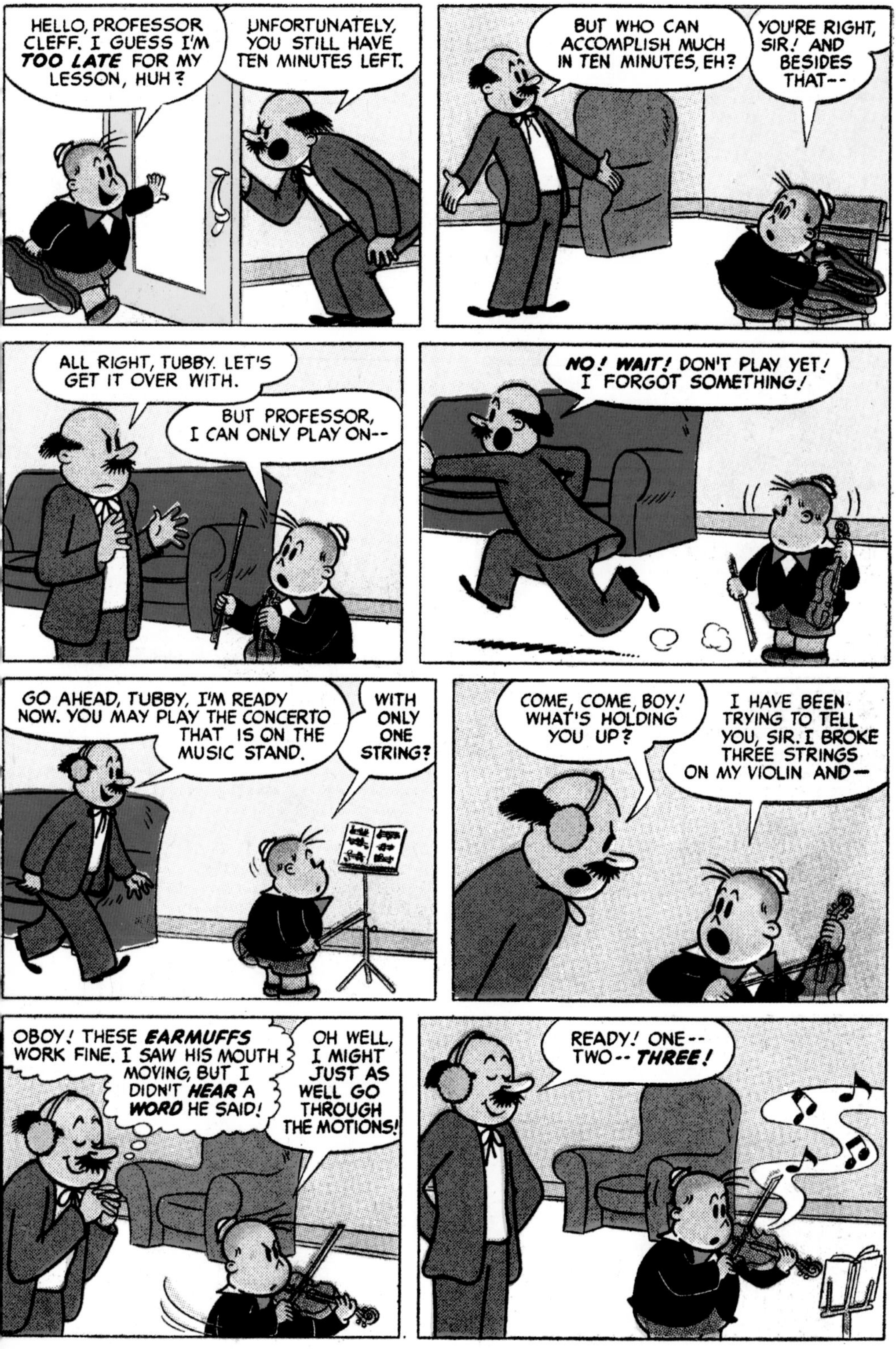
HELLO, PROFESSOR CLEFF. I GUESS I'M TOO LATE FOR MY LESSON, HUH?
UNFORTUNATELY, YOU STILL HAVE TEN MINUTES LEFT.
BUT WHO CAN ACCOMPLISH MUCH IN TEN MINUTES, EH?
YOU'RE RIGHT, SIR! AND BESIDES THAT--
ALL RIGHT, TUBBY. LET'S GET IT OVER WITH.
BUT PROFESSOR, I CAN ONLY PLAY ON--
NO! WAIT! DON'T PLAY YET! I FORGOT SOMETHING!
GO AHEAD, TUBBY, I'M READY NOW. YOU MAY PLAY THE CONCERTO THAT IS ON THE MUSIC STAND.
WITH ONLY ONE STRING?
COME, COME, BOY! WHAT'S HOLDING YOU UP?
I HAVE BEEN TRYING TO TELL YOU, SIR. I BROKE THREE STRINGS ON MY VIOLIN AND—
OBOY! THESE EARMUFFS WORK FINE. I SAW HIS MOUTH MOVING, BUT I DIDN'T HEAR A WORD HE SAID!
OH WELL, I MIGHT JUST AS WELL GO THROUGH THE MOTIONS!
READY! ONE-- TWO-- THREE!

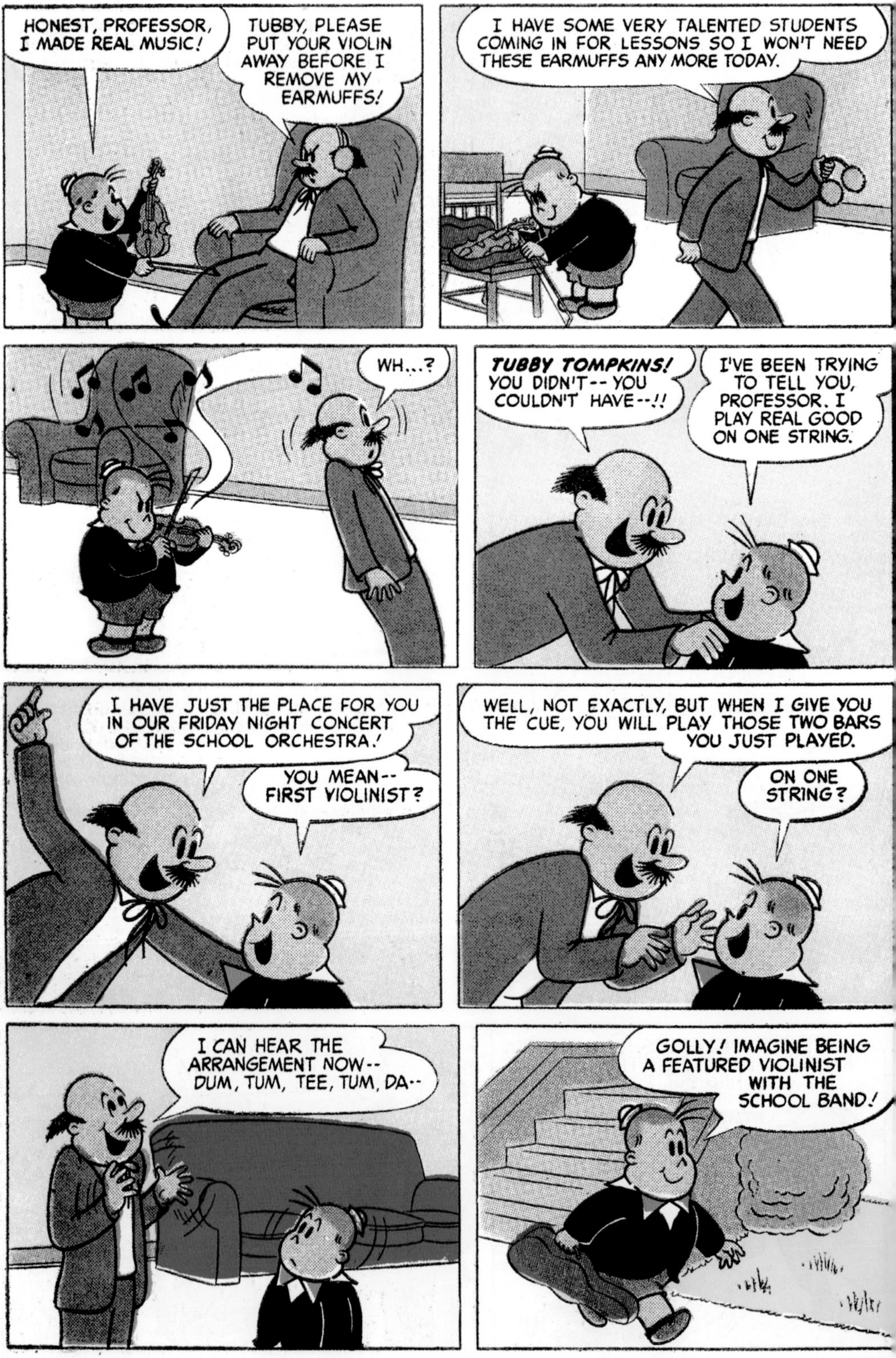
HONEST, PROFESSOR, I MADE REAL MUSIC!
TUBBY, PLEASE PUT YOUR VIOLIN AWAY BEFORE I REMOVE MY EARMUFFS!
I HAVE SOME VERY TALENTED STUDENTS COMING IN FOR LESSONS SO I WON'T NEED THESE EARMUFFS ANY MORE TODAY.
WH...?
TUBBY TOMPKINS! YOU DIDN'T-- YOU COULDN'T HAVE--!!
I'VE BEEN TRYING TO TELL YOU, PROFESSOR. I PLAY REAL GOOD ON ONE STRING.
I HAVE JUST THE PLACE FOR YOU IN OUR FRIDAY NIGHT CONCERT OF THE SCHOOL ORCHESTRA!
YOU MEAN-- FIRST VIOLINIST?
WELL, NOT EXACTLY, BUT WHEN I GIVE YOU THE CUE, YOU WILL PLAY THOSE TWO BARS YOU JUST PLAYED.
ON ONE STRING?
I CAN HEAR THE ARRANGEMENT NOW-- DUM, TUM, TEE, TUM, DA--
GOLLY! IMAGINE BEING A FEATURED VIOLINIST WITH THE SCHOOL BAND!

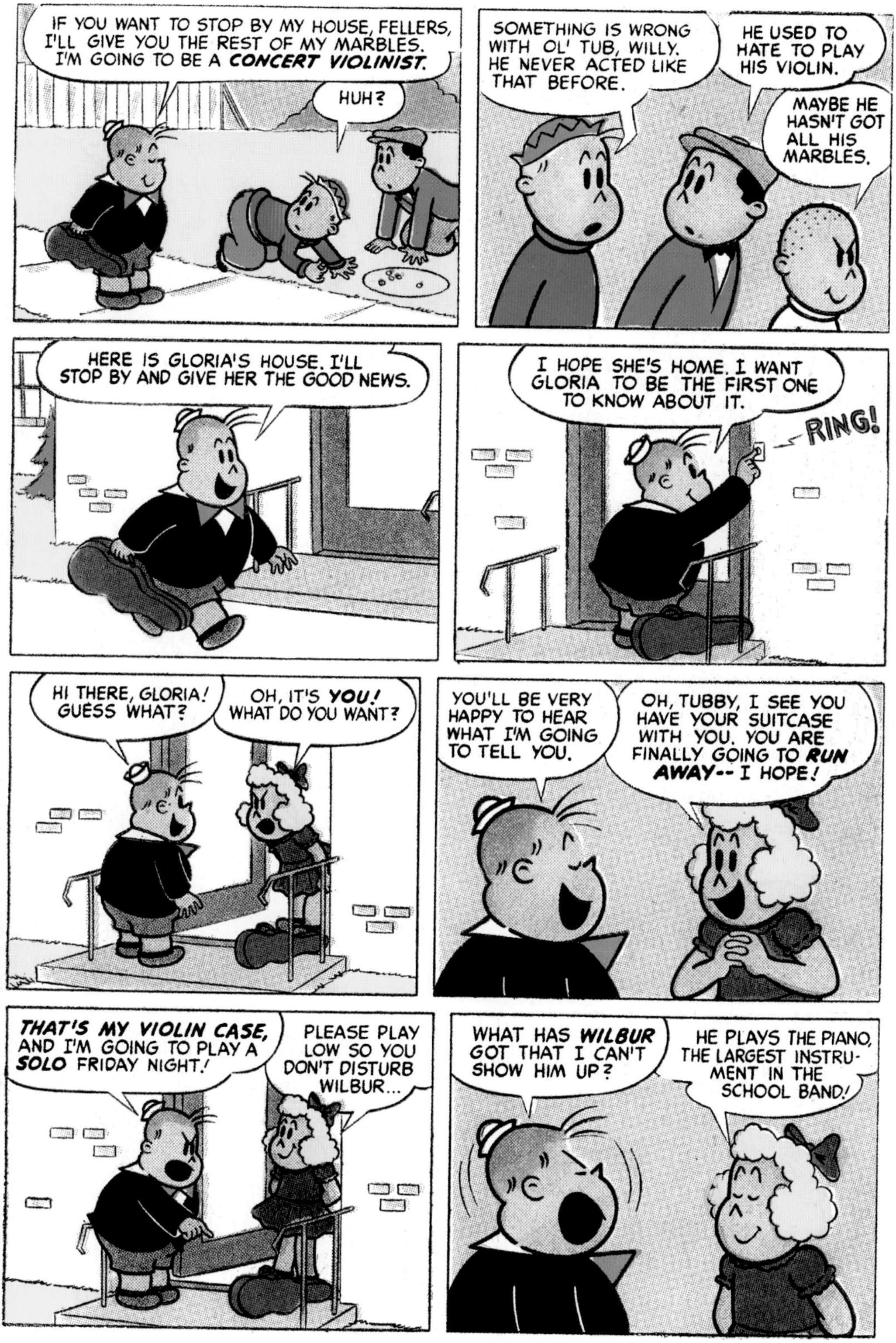
IF YOU WANT TO STOP BY MY HOUSE, FELLERS, I'LL GIVE YOU THE REST OF MY MARBLES. I'M GOING TO BE A CONCERT VIOLINIST.
HUH?
SOMETHING IS WRONG WITH OL' TUB, WILLY. HE NEVER ACTED LIKE THAT BEFORE.
HE USED TO HATE TO PLAY HIS VIOLIN.
MAYBE HE HASN'T GOT ALL HIS MARBLES.
HERE IS GLORIA'S HOUSE. I'LL STOP BY AND GIVE HER THE GOOD NEWS.
I HOPE SHE'S HOME. I WANT GLORIA TO BE THE FIRST ONE TO KNOW ABOUT IT.
RING!
HI THERE, GLORIA! GUESS WHAT?
OH, IT'S YOU! WHAT DO YOU WANT?
YOU'LL BE VERY HAPPY TO HEAR WHAT I'M GOING TO TELL YOU.
OH, TUBBY, I SEE YOU HAVE YOUR SUITCASE WITH YOU. YOU ARE FINALLY GOING TO RUN AWAY-- I HOPE!
THAT'S MY VIOLIN CASE, AND I'M GOING TO PLAY A SOLO FRIDAY NIGHT!
PLEASE PLAY LOW SO YOU DON'T DISTURB WILBUR...
WHAT HAS WILBUR GOT THAT I CAN'T SHOW HIM UP?
HE PLAYS THE PIANO, THE LARGEST INSTRU-MENT IN THE SCHOOL BAND!

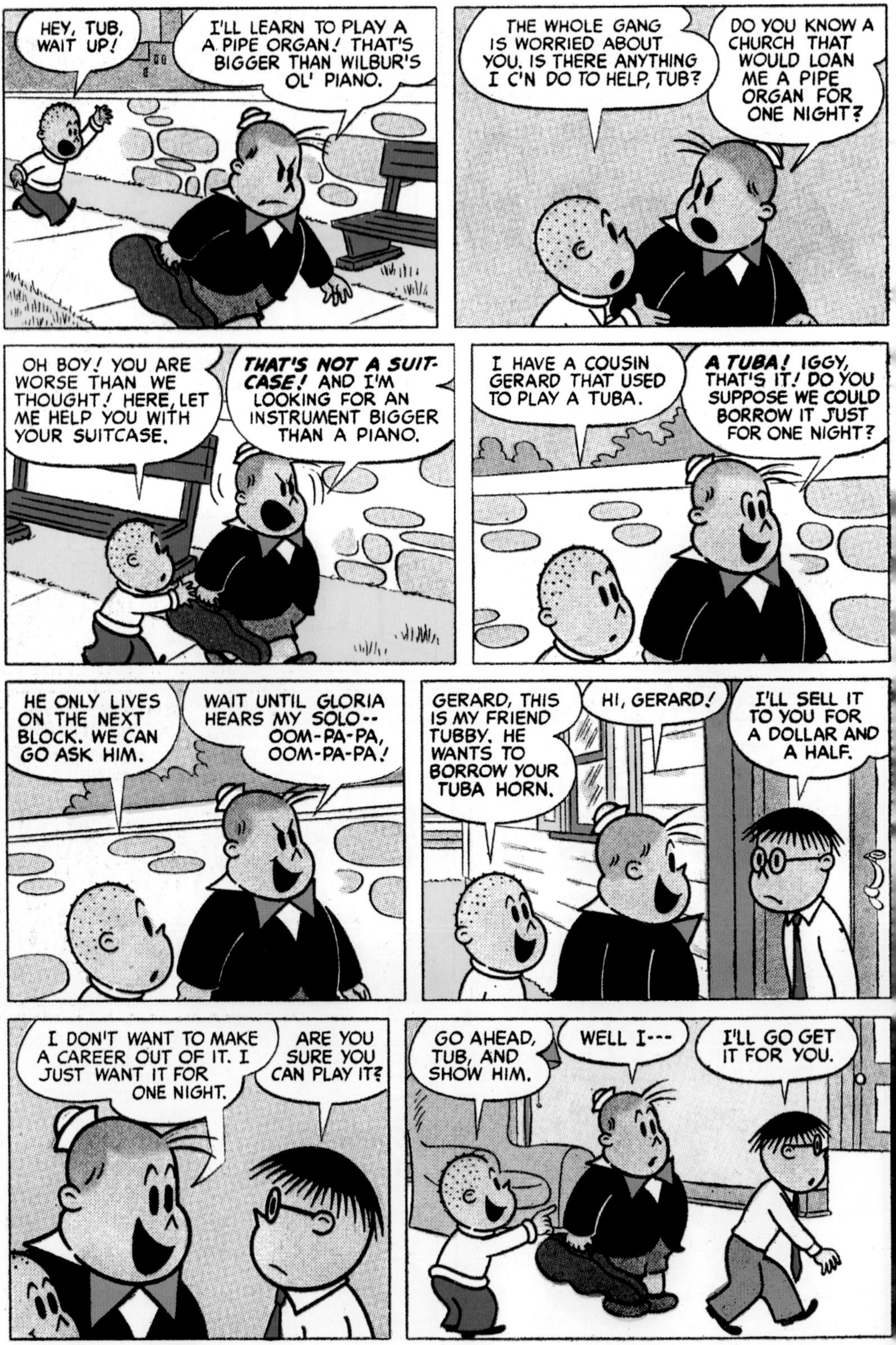
HEY, TUB, WAIT UP!
I'LL LEARN TO PLAY A A PIPE ORGAN! THAT'S BIGGER THAN WILBUR'S OL' PIANO.
THE WHOLE GANG IS WORRIED ABOUT YOU. IS THERE ANYTHING I C'N DO TO HELP, TUB?
DO YOU KNOW A CHURCH THAT WOULD LOAN ME A PIPE ORGAN FOR ONE NIGHT?
OH BOY! YOU ARE WORSE THAN WE THOUGHT! HERE, LET ME HELP YOU WITH YOUR SUITCASE.
THAT'S NOT A SUITCASE! AND I'M LOOKING FOR AN INSTRUMENT BIGGER THAN A PIANO.
I HAVE A COUSIN GERARD THAT USED TO PLAY A TUBA.
A TUBA! IGGY, THAT'S IT! DO YOU SUPPOSE WE COULD BORROW IT JUST FOR ONE NIGHT?
HE ONLY LIVES ON THE NEXT BLOCK. WE CAN GO ASK HIM.
WAIT UNTIL GLORIA HEARS MY SOLO-- OOM-PA-PA, OOM-PA-PA!
GERARD, THIS IS MY FRIEND TUBBY. HE WANTS TO BORROW YOUR TUBA HORN.
HI, GERARD!
I'LL SELL IT TO YOU FOR A DOLLAR AND A HALF.
I DON'T WANT TO MAKE A CAREER OUT OF IT. I JUST WANT IT FOR ONE NIGHT.
ARE YOU SURE YOU CAN PLAY IT?
GO AHEAD, TUB, AND SHOW HIM.
WELL I---
I'LL GO GET IT FOR YOU.

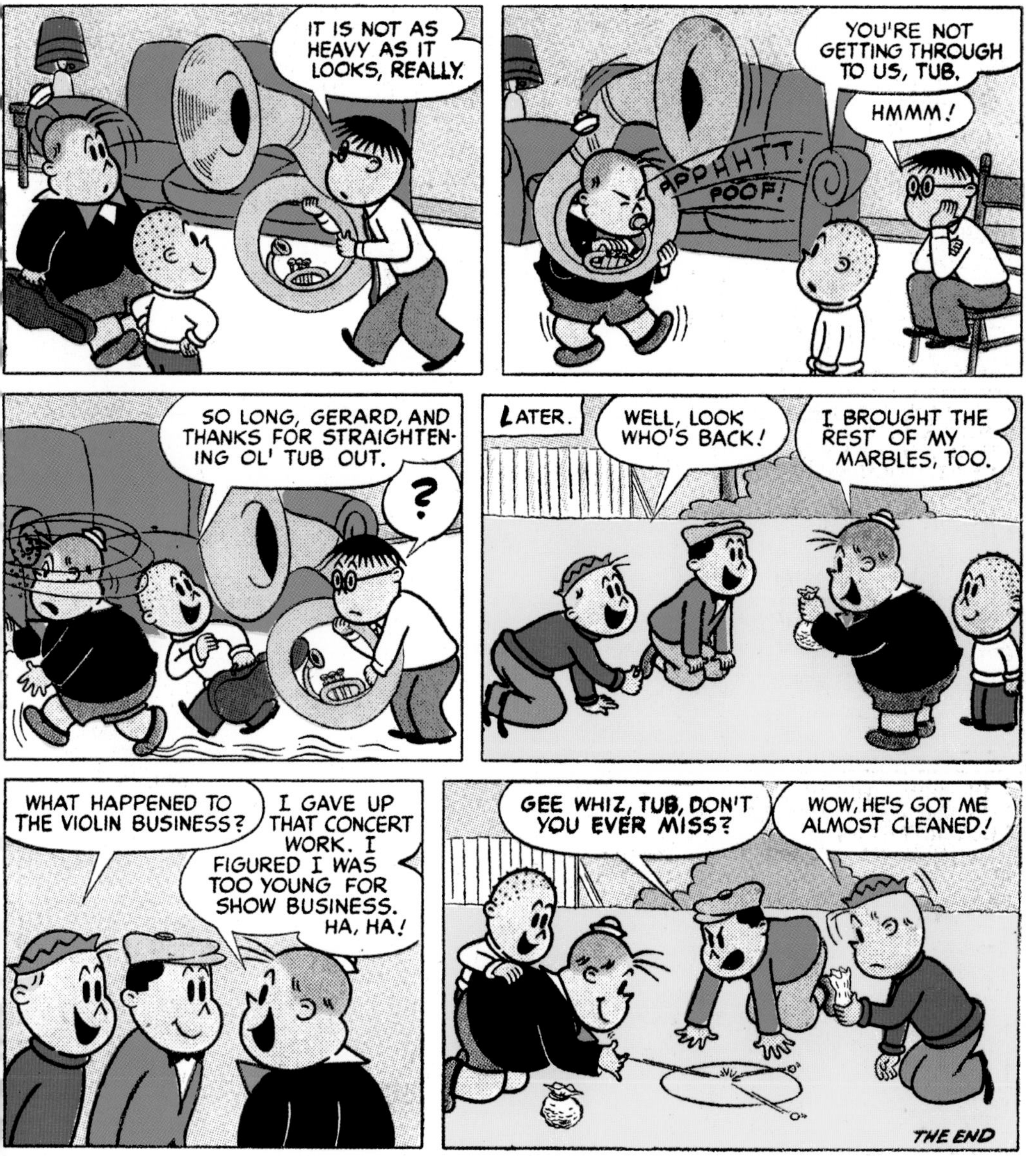
IT IS NOT AS HEAVY AS IT LOOKS, REALLY.
YOU'RE NOT GETTING THROUGH TO US, TUB.
HMMM!
PPPHHTT!
POOF!
SO LONG, GERARD, AND THANKS FOR STRAIGHTENING OL' TUB OUT.
?
LATER.
WELL, LOOK WHO'S BACK!
I BROUGHT THE REST OF MY MARBLES, TOO.
WHAT HAPPENED TO THE VIOLIN BUSINESS?
I GAVE UP THAT CONCERT WORK. I FIGURED I WAS TOO YOUNG FOR SHOW BUSINESS. HA, HA!
GEE WHIZ, TUB, DON'T YOU EVER MISS?
WOW, HE'S GOT ME ALMOST CLEANED!
THE END

Little Lulu

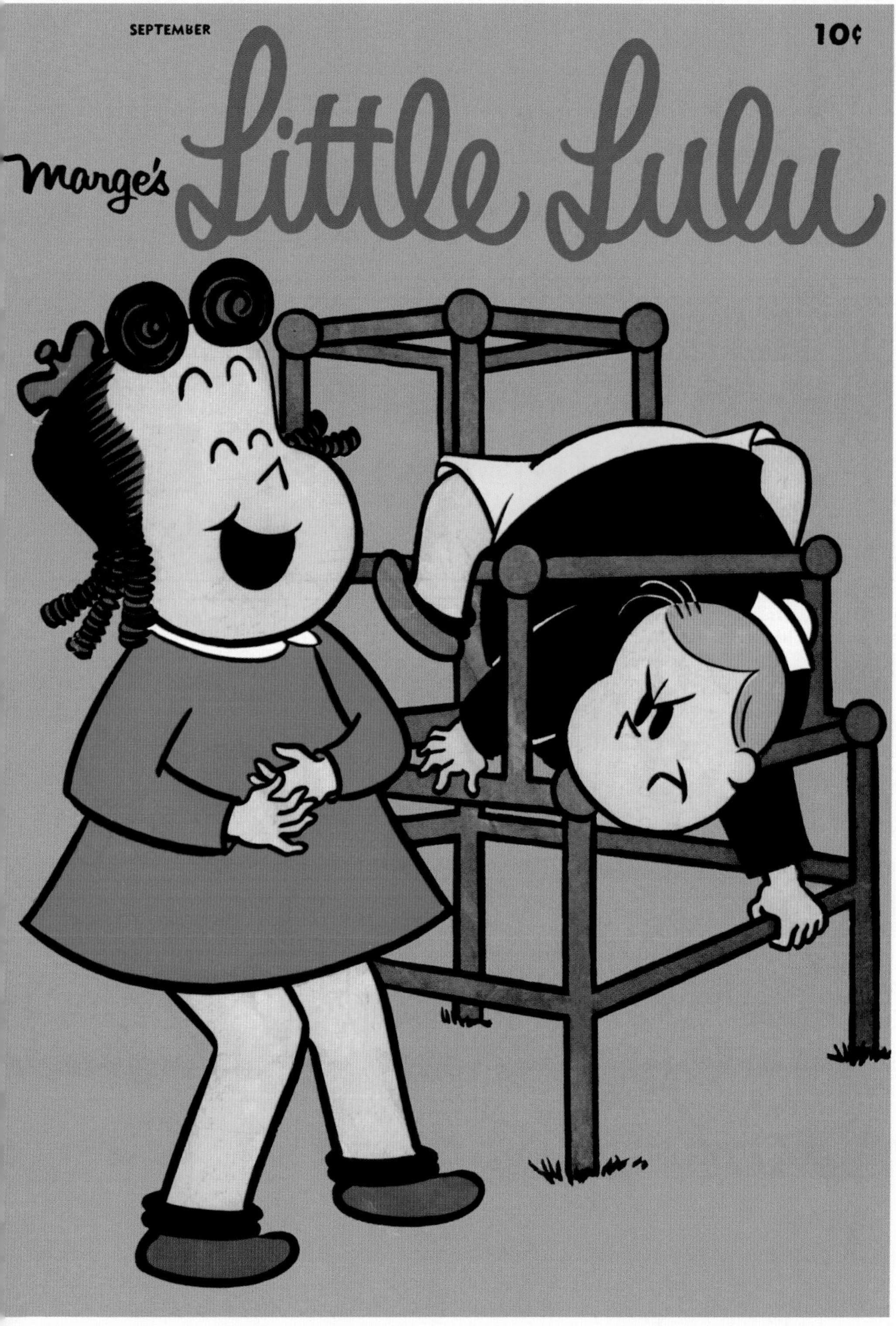
SEPTEMBER
10¢
Marge's Little Lulu

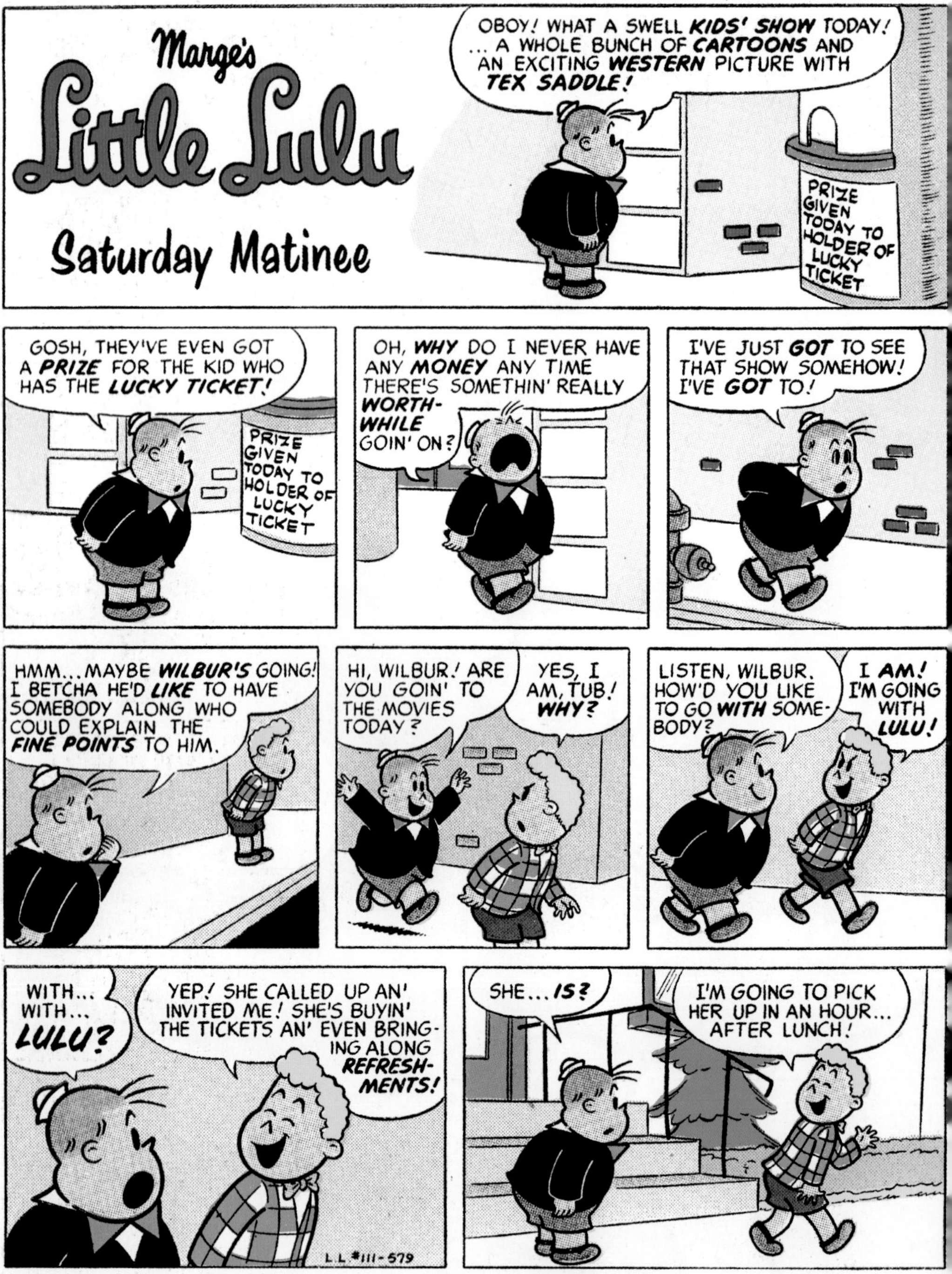
Marge's Little Lulu
Saturday Matinee
OBOY! WHAT A SWELL KIDS' SHOW TODAY! ... A WHOLE BUNCH OF CARTOONS AND AN EXCITING WESTERN PICTURE WITH TEX SADDLE!
PRIZE GIVEN TODAY TO HOLDER OF LUCKY TICKET
GOSH, THEY'VE EVEN GOT A PRIZE FOR THE KID WHO HAS THE LUCKY TICKET!
PRIZE GIVEN TODAY TO HOLDER OF LUCKY TICKET
OH, WHY DO I NEVER HAVE ANY MONEY ANY TIME THERE'S SOMETHIN' REALLY WORTH-WHILE GOIN' ON?
I'VE JUST GOT TO SEE THAT SHOW SOMEHOW! I'VE GOT TO!
HMM... MAYBE WILBUR'S GOING! I BETCHA HE'D LIKE TO HAVE SOMEBODY ALONG WHO COULD EXPLAIN THE FINE POINTS TO HIM.
HI, WILBUR! ARE YOU GOIN' TO THE MOVIES TODAY?
YES, I AM, TUB! WHY?
LISTEN, WILBUR. HOW'D YOU LIKE TO GO WITH SOME-BODY?
I AM! I'M GOING WITH LULU!
WITH... WITH... LULU?
YEP! SHE CALLED UP AN' INVITED ME! SHE'S BUYIN' THE TICKETS AN' EVEN BRING-ING ALONG REFRESH-MENTS!
L.L. #111-579
SHE... IS?
I'M GOING TO PICK HER UP IN AN HOUR... AFTER LUNCH!

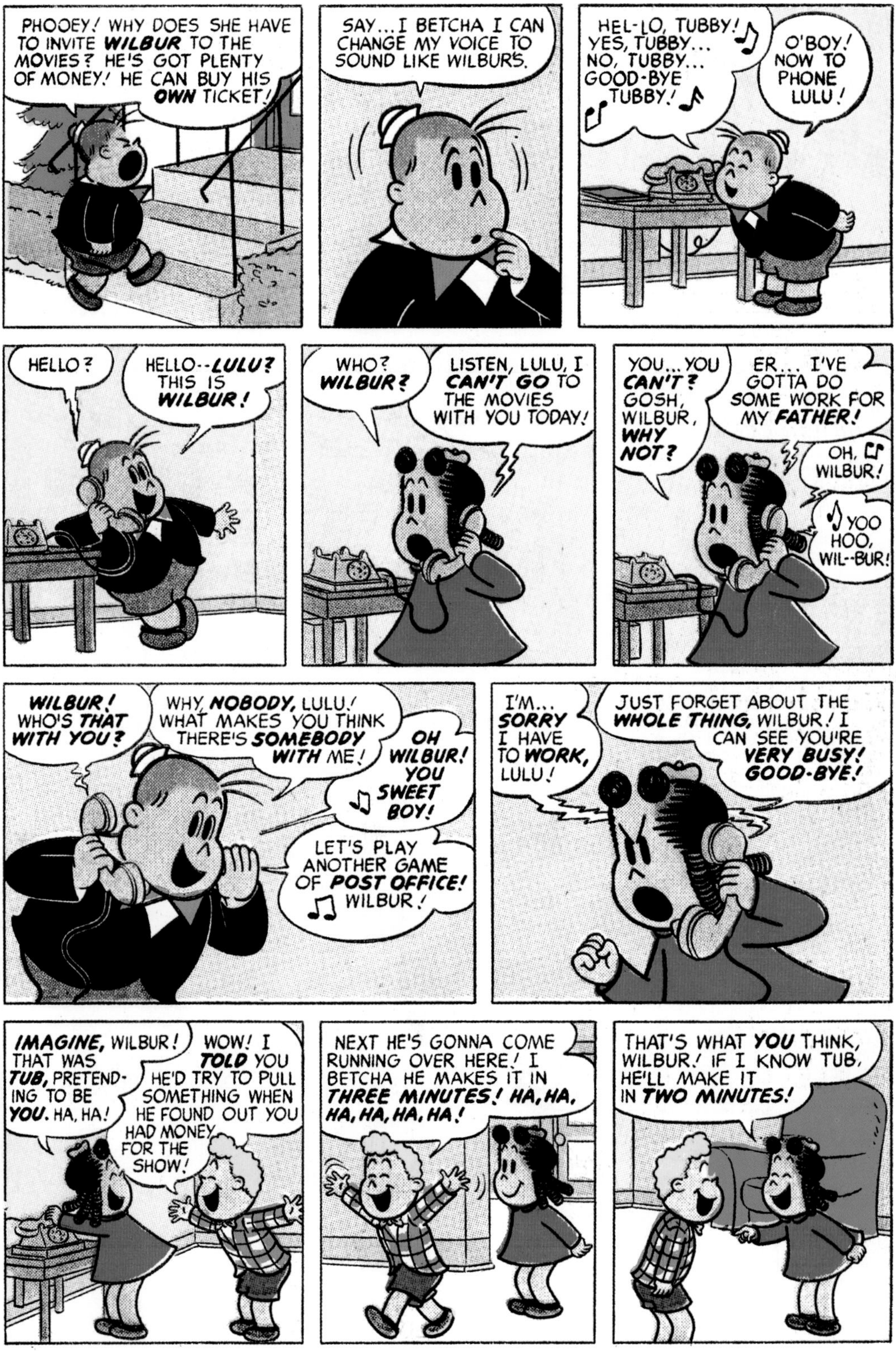
PHOOEY! WHY DOES SHE HAVE TO INVITE WILBUR TO THE MOVIES? HE'S GOT PLENTY OF MONEY! HE CAN BUY HIS OWN TICKET!
SAY...I BETCHA I CAN CHANGE MY VOICE TO SOUND LIKE WILBUR'S.
HEL-LO, TUBBY! YES, TUBBY... NO, TUBBY... GOOD-BYE TUBBY!
O'BOY! NOW TO PHONE LULU!
HELLO?
HELLO--LULU? THIS IS WILBUR!
WHO? WILBUR?
LISTEN, LULU, I CAN'T GO TO THE MOVIES WITH YOU TODAY!
YOU...YOU CAN'T? GOSH, WILBUR, WHY NOT?
ER... I'VE GOTTA DO SOME WORK FOR MY FATHER!
OH, WILBUR!
YOO HOO, WIL-BUR!
WILBUR! WHO'S THAT WITH YOU?
WHY, NOBODY, LULU! WHAT MAKES YOU THINK THERE'S SOMEBODY WITH ME!
OH WILBUR! YOU SWEET BOY!
LET'S PLAY ANOTHER GAME OF POST OFFICE! WILBUR!
I'M... SORRY I HAVE TO WORK, LULU!
JUST FORGET ABOUT THE WHOLE THING, WILBUR! I CAN SEE YOU'RE VERY BUSY! GOOD-BYE!
IMAGINE, WILBUR! THAT WAS TUB, PRETENDING TO BE YOU. HA, HA!
WOW! I TOLD YOU HE'D TRY TO PULL SOMETHING WHEN HE FOUND OUT YOU HAD MONEY FOR THE SHOW!
NEXT HE'S GONNA COME RUNNING OVER HERE! I BETCHA HE MAKES IT IN THREE MINUTES! HA, HA, HA, HA, HA, HA!
THAT'S WHAT YOU THINK, WILBUR! IF I KNOW TUB, HE'LL MAKE IT IN TWO MINUTES!

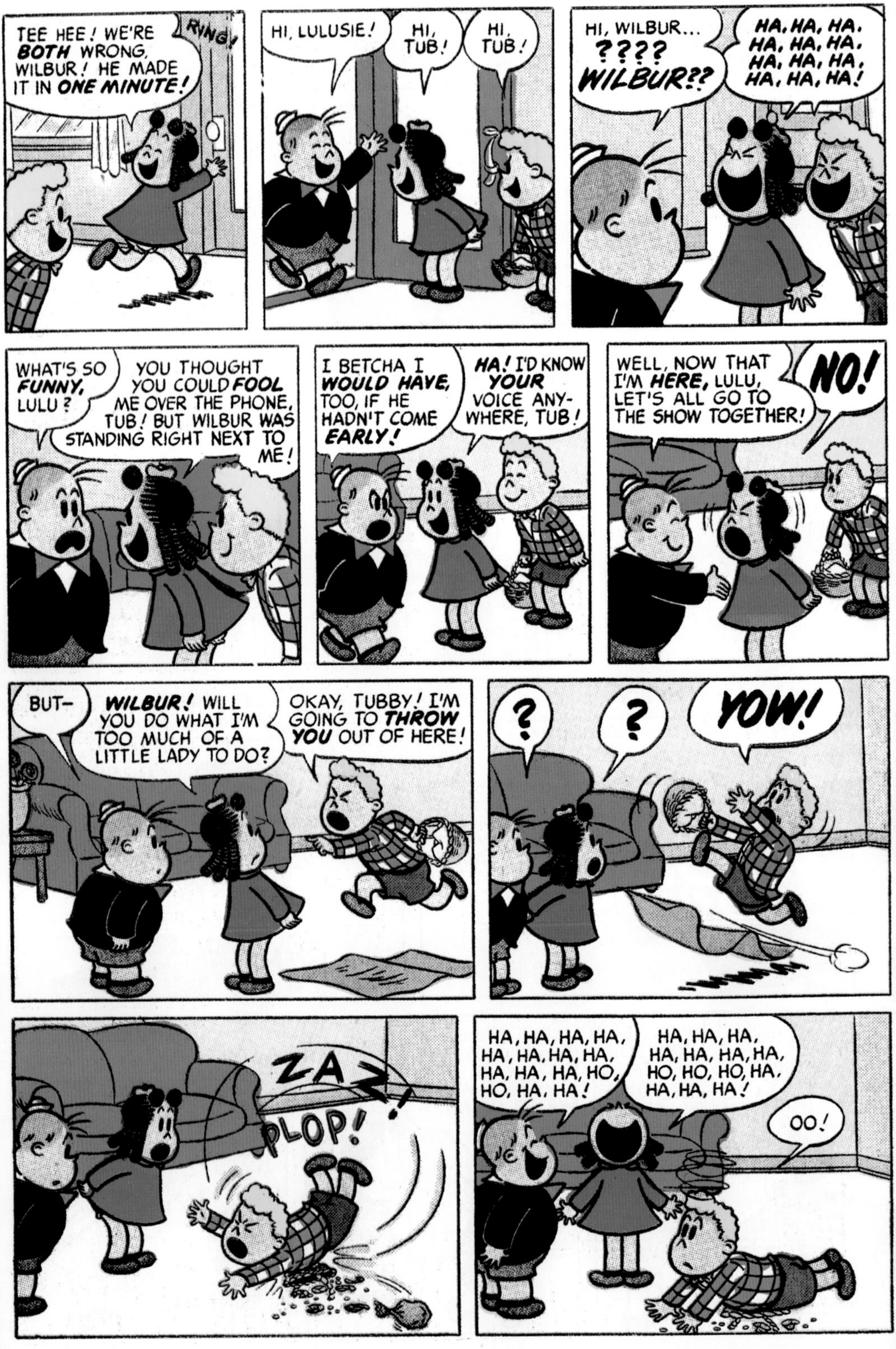
TEE HEE! WE'RE BOTH WRONG, WILBUR! HE MADE IT IN ONE MINUTE!
RING!
HI, LULUSIE!
HI, TUB!
HI, TUB!
HI, WILBUR... ???? WILBUR??
HA, HA, HA, HA, HA, HA, HA, HA, HA, HA, HA, HA!
WHAT'S SO FUNNY, LULU?
YOU THOUGHT YOU COULD FOOL ME OVER THE PHONE, TUB! BUT WILBUR WAS STANDING RIGHT NEXT TO ME!
I BETCHA I WOULD HAVE, TOO, IF HE HADN'T COME EARLY!
HA! I'D KNOW YOUR VOICE ANYWHERE, TUB!
WELL, NOW THAT I'M HERE, LULU, LET'S ALL GO TO THE SHOW TOGETHER!
NO!
BUT–
WILBUR! WILL YOU DO WHAT I'M TOO MUCH OF A LITTLE LADY TO DO?
OKAY, TUBBY! I'M GOING TO THROW YOU OUT OF HERE!
?
?
YOW!
ZAZ!
PLOP!
HA, HA, HA, HA, HA, HA, HA, HA, HA, HA, HA, HO, HO, HA, HA!
HA, HA, HA, HA, HA, HA, HA, HO, HO, HO, HA, HA, HA, HA!
OO!

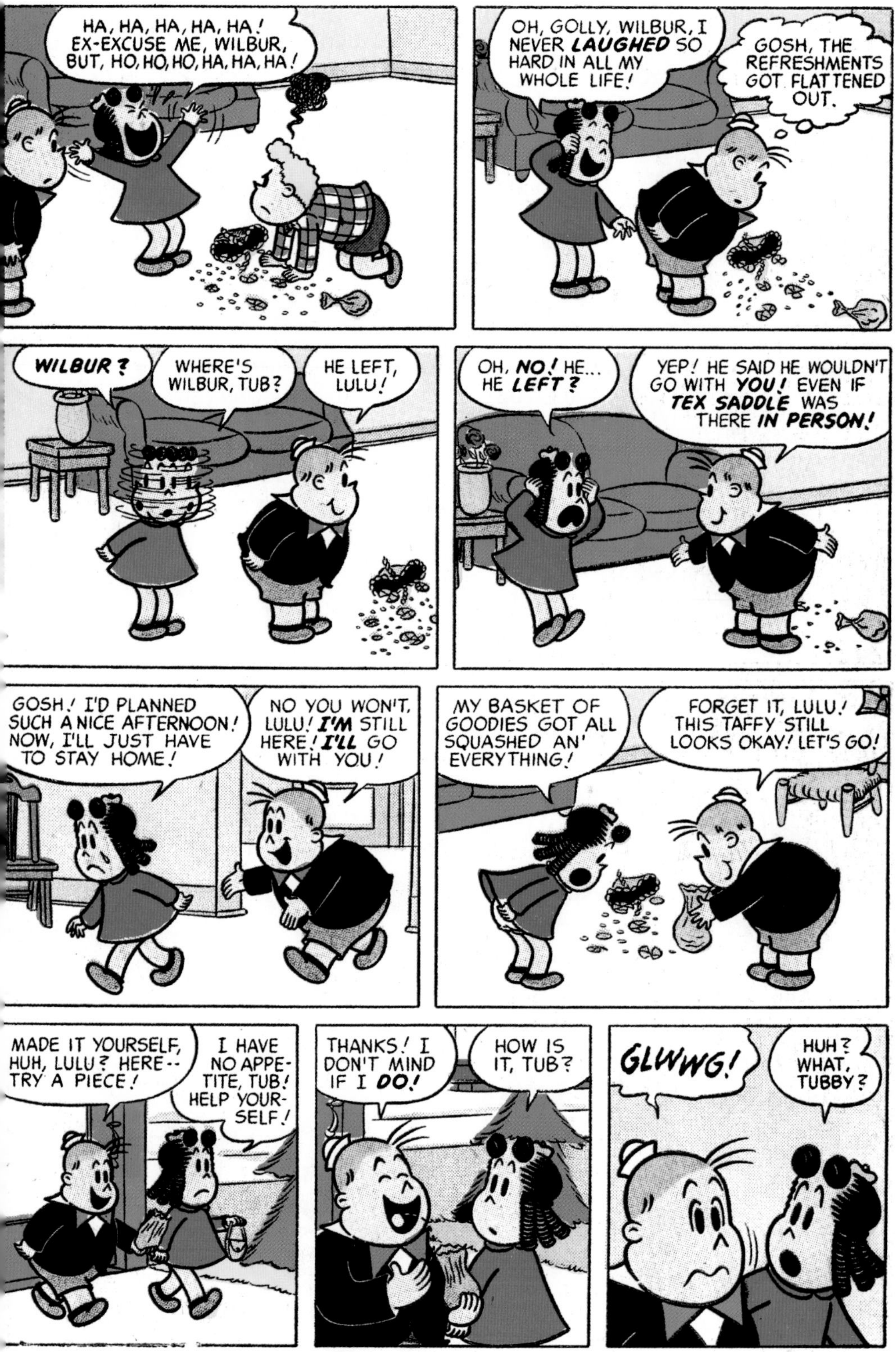
HA, HA, HA, HA, HA! EX-EXCUSE ME, WILBUR, BUT, HO, HO, HO, HA, HA, HA!
OH, GOLLY, WILBUR, I NEVER LAUGHED SO HARD IN ALL MY WHOLE LIFE!
GOSH, THE REFRESHMENTS GOT FLATTENED OUT.
WILBUR?
WHERE'S WILBUR, TUB?
HE LEFT, LULU!
OH, NO! HE... HE LEFT?
YEP! HE SAID HE WOULDN'T GO WITH YOU! EVEN IF TEX SADDLE WAS THERE IN PERSON!
GOSH! I'D PLANNED SUCH A NICE AFTERNOON! NOW, I'LL JUST HAVE TO STAY HOME!
NO YOU WON'T, LULU! I'M STILL HERE! I'LL GO WITH YOU!
MY BASKET OF GOODIES GOT ALL SQUASHED AN' EVERYTHING!
FORGET IT, LULU! THIS TAFFY STILL LOOKS OKAY! LET'S GO!
MADE IT YOURSELF, HUH, LULU? HERE-- TRY A PIECE!
I HAVE NO APPETITE, TUB! HELP YOURSELF!
THANKS! I DON'T MIND IF I DO!
HOW IS IT, TUB?
GLWWG!
HUH? WHAT, TUBBY?

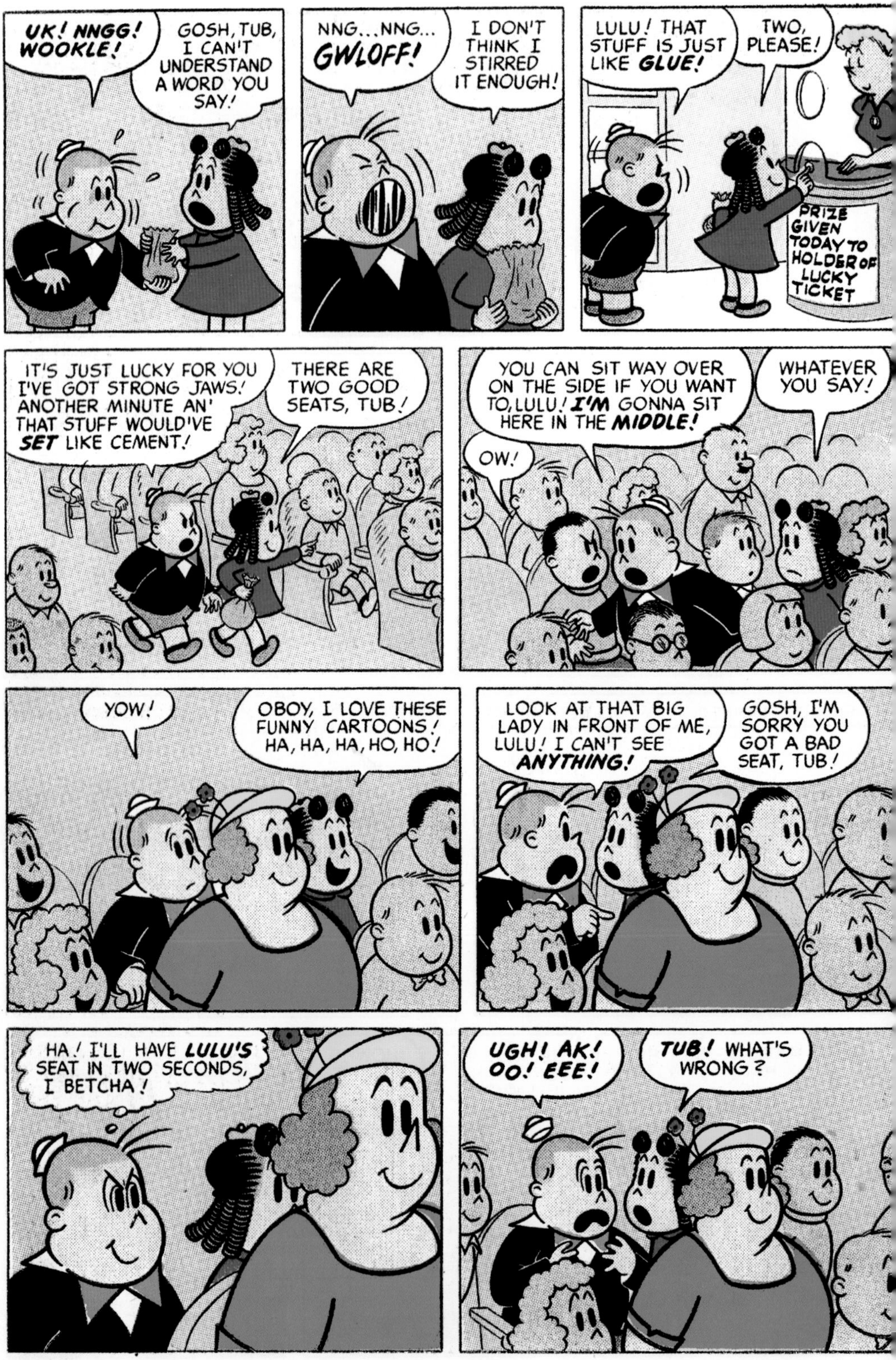
UK! NNGG! WOOKLE!
GOSH, TUB, I CAN'T UNDERSTAND A WORD YOU SAY!
NNG...NNG... GWLOFF!
I DON'T THINK I STIRRED IT ENOUGH!
LULU! THAT STUFF IS JUST LIKE GLUE!
TWO, PLEASE!
PRIZE GIVEN TODAY TO HOLDER OF LUCKY TICKET
IT'S JUST LUCKY FOR YOU I'VE GOT STRONG JAWS! ANOTHER MINUTE AN' THAT STUFF WOULD'VE SET LIKE CEMENT!
THERE ARE TWO GOOD SEATS, TUB!
YOU CAN SIT WAY OVER ON THE SIDE IF YOU WANT TO, LULU! I'M GONNA SIT HERE IN THE MIDDLE!
WHATEVER YOU SAY!
OW!
YOW!
OBOY, I LOVE THESE FUNNY CARTOONS! HA, HA, HA, HO, HO!
LOOK AT THAT BIG LADY IN FRONT OF ME, LULU! I CAN'T SEE ANYTHING!
GOSH, I'M SORRY YOU GOT A BAD SEAT, TUB!
HA! I'LL HAVE LULU'S SEAT IN TWO SECONDS, I BETCHA!
UGH! AK! OO! EEE!
TUB! WHAT'S WRONG?

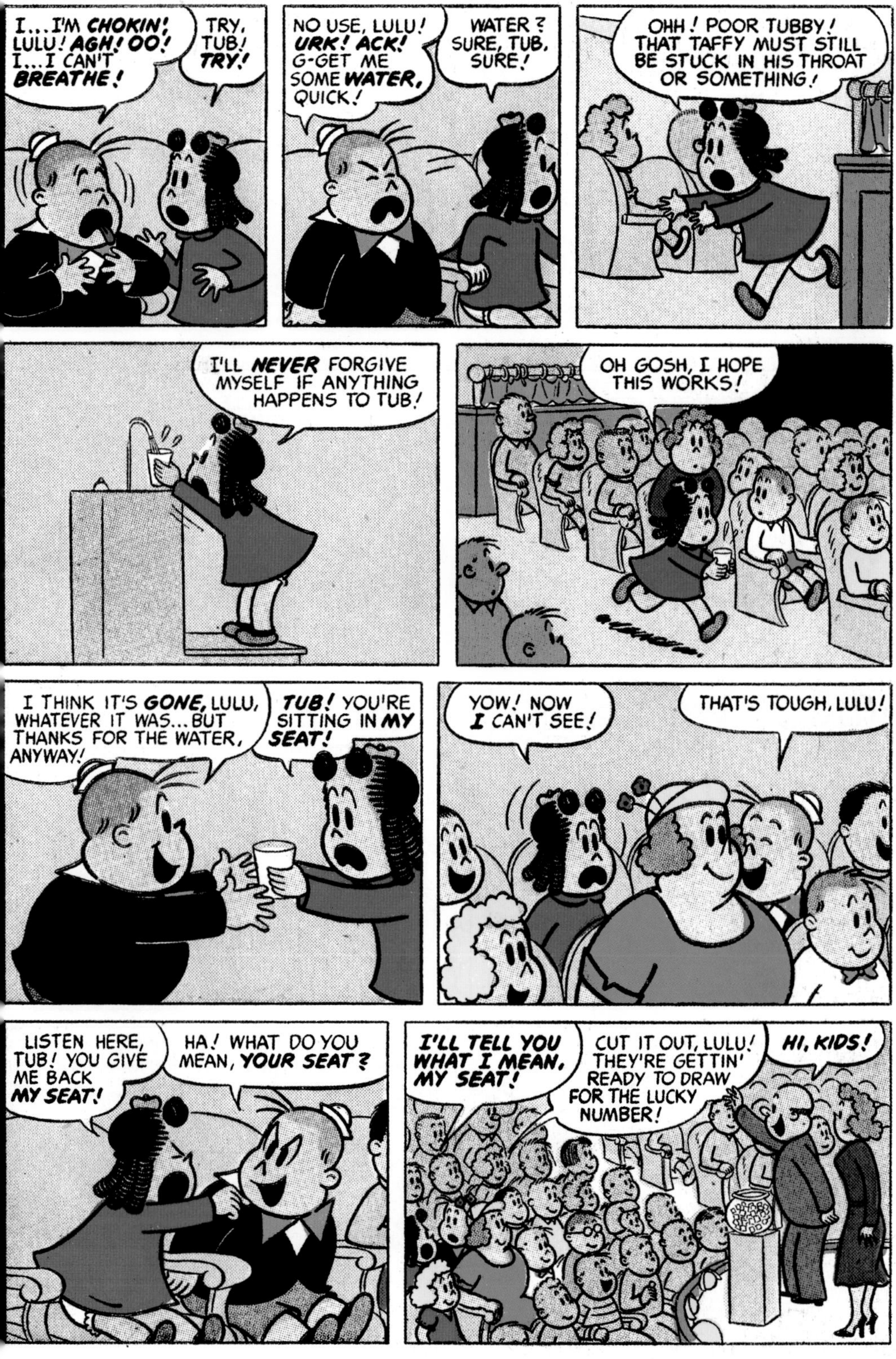

I...I'M CHOKIN'! LULU! AGH! OO! I...I CAN'T BREATHE!
TRY, TUB! TRY!
NO USE, LULU! URK! ACK! G-GET ME SOME WATER, QUICK!
WATER? SURE, TUB, SURE!
OHH! POOR TUBBY! THAT TAFFY MUST STILL BE STUCK IN HIS THROAT OR SOMETHING!
I'LL NEVER FORGIVE MYSELF IF ANYTHING HAPPENS TO TUB!
OH GOSH, I HOPE THIS WORKS!
I THINK IT'S GONE, LULU, WHATEVER IT WAS...BUT THANKS FOR THE WATER, ANYWAY!
TUB! YOU'RE SITTING IN MY SEAT!
YOW! NOW I CAN'T SEE!
THAT'S TOUGH, LULU!
LISTEN HERE, TUB! YOU GIVE ME BACK MY SEAT!
HA! WHAT DO YOU MEAN, YOUR SEAT?
I'LL TELL YOU WHAT I MEAN, MY SEAT!
CUT IT OUT, LULU! THEY'RE GETTIN' READY TO DRAW FOR THE LUCKY NUMBER!
HI, KIDS!

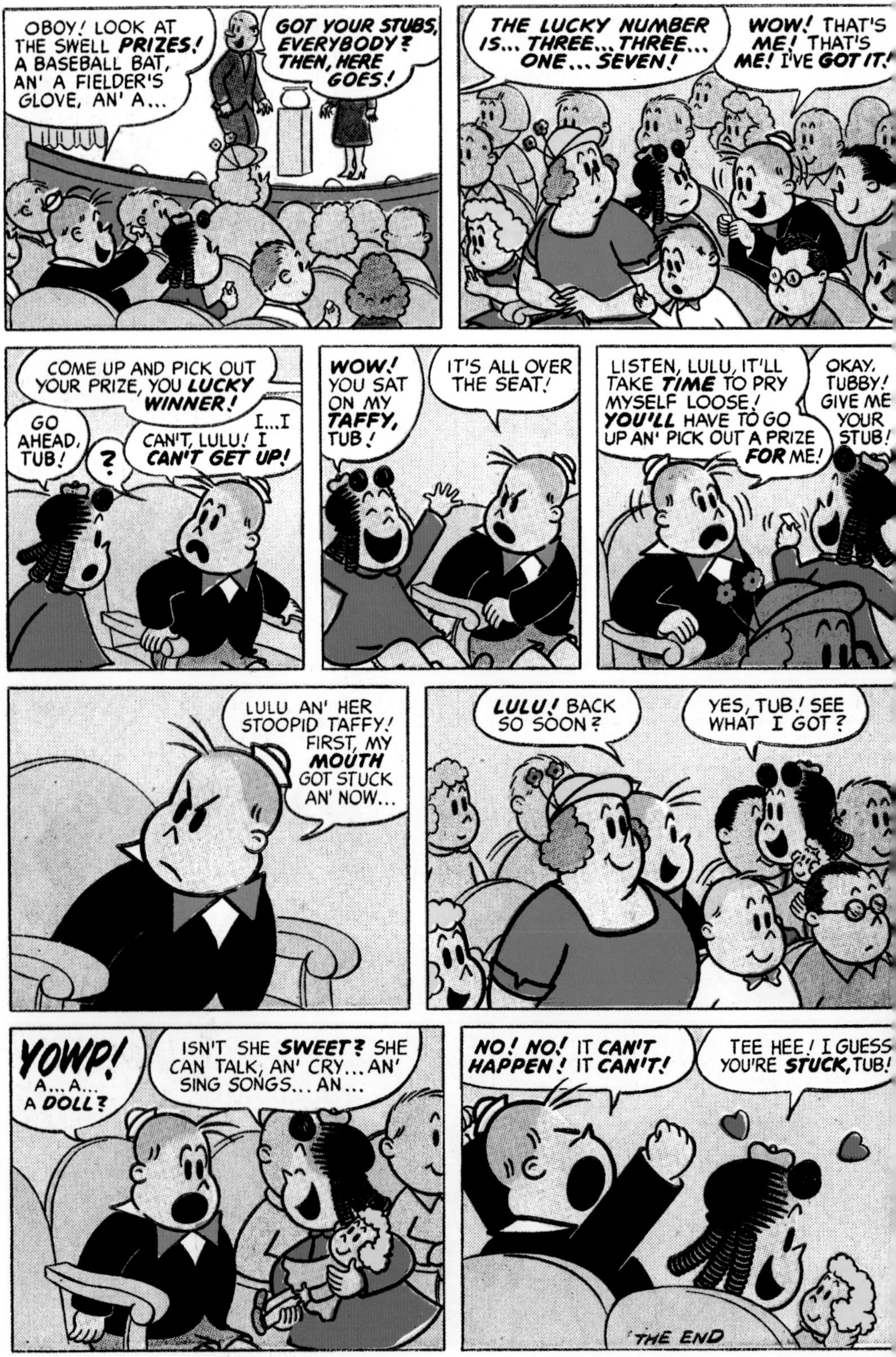
OBOY! LOOK AT THE SWELL PRIZES! A BASEBALL BAT, AN' A FIELDER'S GLOVE, AN' A...
GOT YOUR STUBS, EVERYBODY? THEN, HERE GOES!
THE LUCKY NUMBER IS... THREE... THREE... ONE... SEVEN!
WOW! THAT'S ME! THAT'S ME! I'VE GOT IT!
COME UP AND PICK OUT YOUR PRIZE, YOU LUCKY WINNER!
GO AHEAD, TUB!
?
I...I CAN'T, LULU! I CAN'T GET UP!
WOW! YOU SAT ON MY TAFFY, TUB!
IT'S ALL OVER THE SEAT!
LISTEN, LULU, IT'LL TAKE TIME TO PRY MYSELF LOOSE! YOU'LL HAVE TO GO UP AN' PICK OUT A PRIZE FOR ME!
OKAY, TUBBY! GIVE ME YOUR STUB!
LULU AN' HER STOOPID TAFFY! FIRST, MY MOUTH GOT STUCK AN' NOW...
LULU! BACK SO SOON?
YES, TUB! SEE WHAT I GOT?
YOWP! A... A... A DOLL?
ISN'T SHE SWEET? SHE CAN TALK, AN' CRY... AN' SING SONGS... AN...
NO! NO! IT CAN'T HAPPEN! IT CAN'T!
TEE HEE! I GUESS YOU'RE STUCK, TUB!
THE END

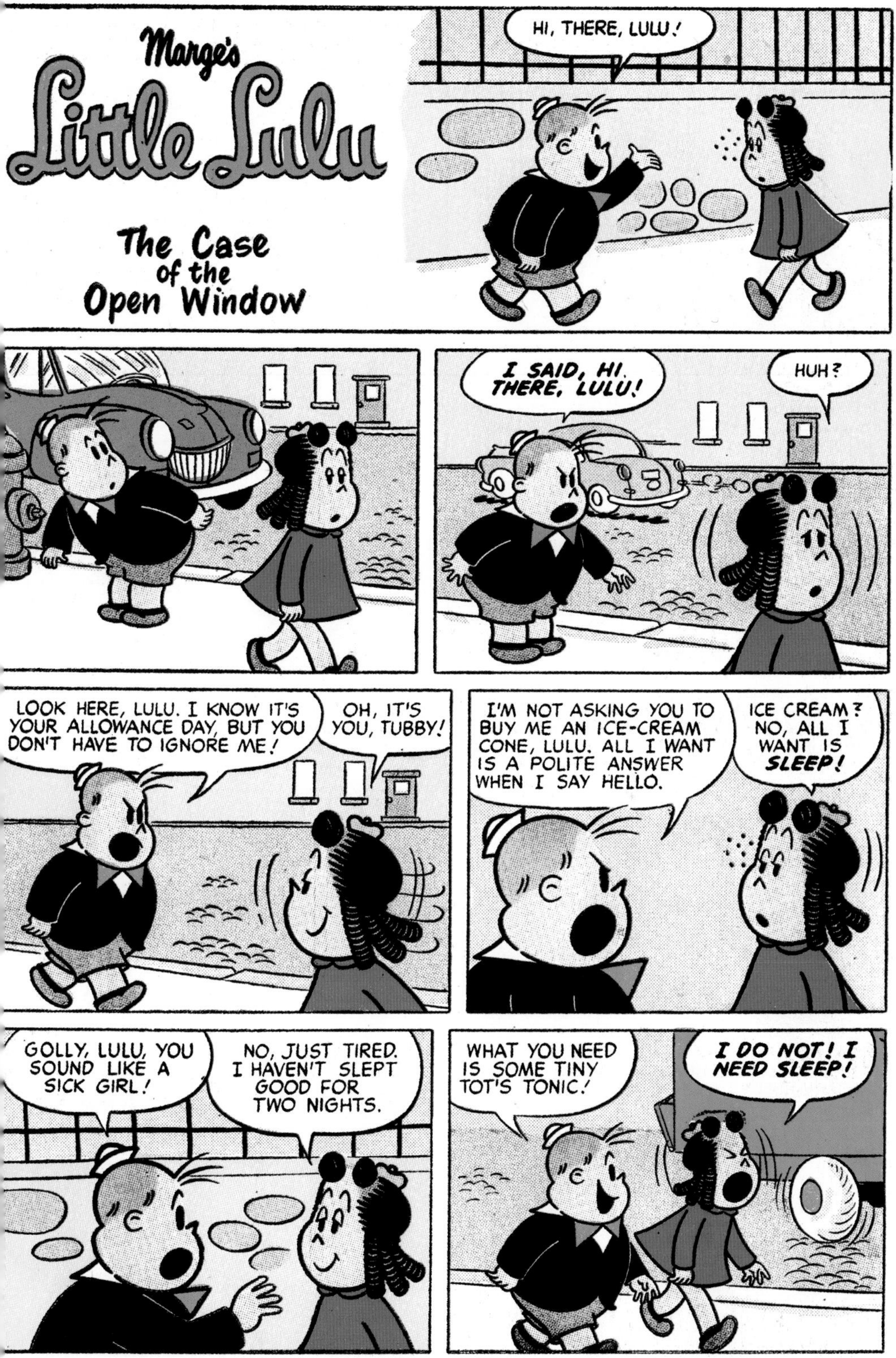
Marge's
Little Lulu
The Case of the Open Window
HI, THERE, LULU!
I SAID, HI THERE, LULU!
HUH?
LOOK HERE, LULU. I KNOW IT'S YOUR ALLOWANCE DAY, BUT YOU DON'T HAVE TO IGNORE ME!
OH, IT'S YOU, TUBBY!
I'M NOT ASKING YOU TO BUY ME AN ICE-CREAM CONE, LULU. ALL I WANT IS A POLITE ANSWER WHEN I SAY HELLO.
ICE CREAM? NO, ALL I WANT IS SLEEP!
GOLLY, LULU, YOU SOUND LIKE A SICK GIRL!
NO, JUST TIRED. I HAVEN'T SLEPT GOOD FOR TWO NIGHTS.
WHAT YOU NEED IS SOME TINY TOT'S TONIC!
I DO NOT! I NEED SLEEP!

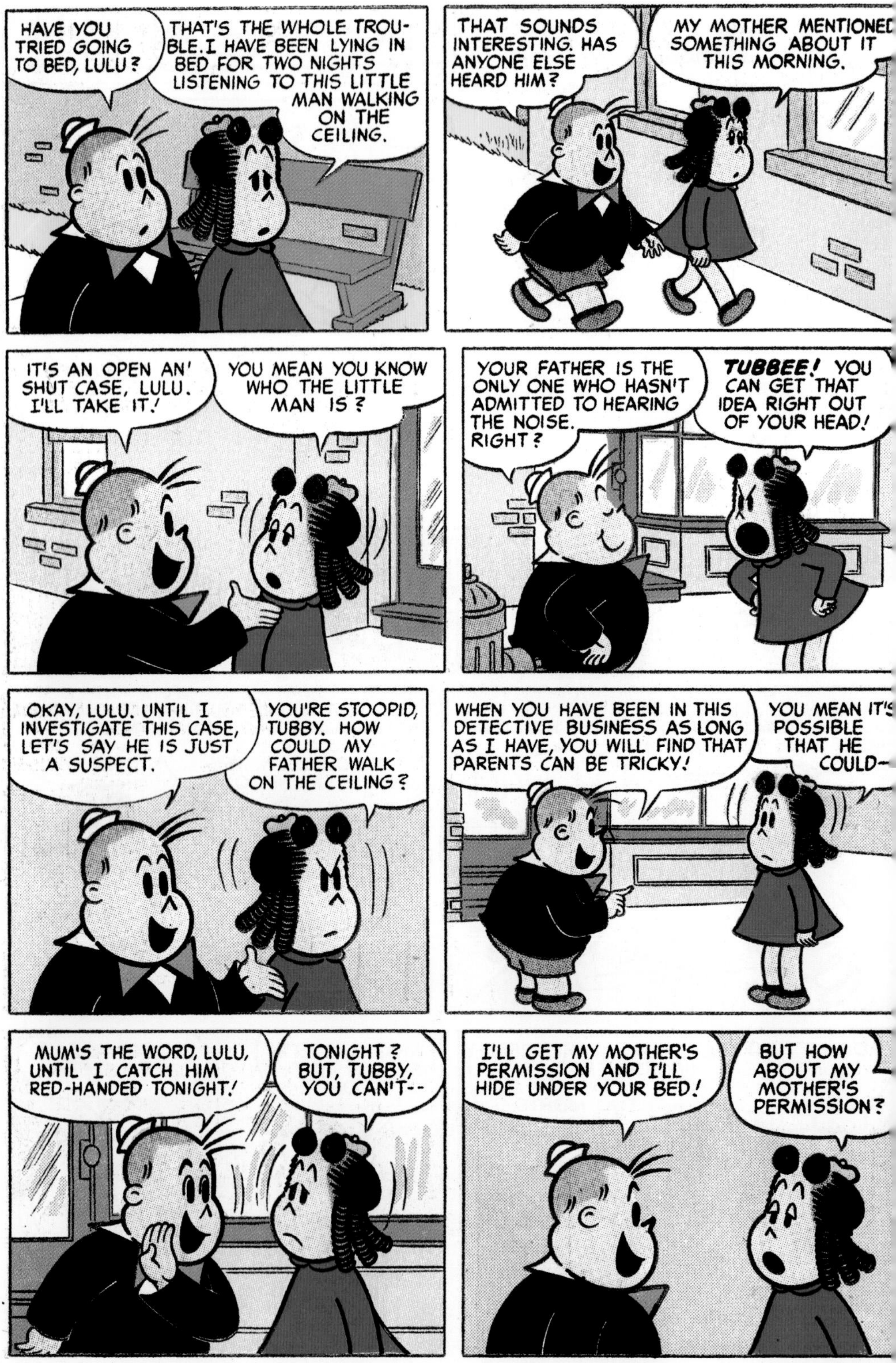
HAVE YOU TRIED GOING TO BED, LULU?
THAT'S THE WHOLE TROUBLE. I HAVE BEEN LYING IN BED FOR TWO NIGHTS LISTENING TO THIS LITTLE MAN WALKING ON THE CEILING.
THAT SOUNDS INTERESTING. HAS ANYONE ELSE HEARD HIM?
MY MOTHER MENTIONED SOMETHING ABOUT IT THIS MORNING.
IT'S AN OPEN AN' SHUT CASE, LULU. I'LL TAKE IT!
YOU MEAN YOU KNOW WHO THE LITTLE MAN IS?
YOUR FATHER IS THE ONLY ONE WHO HASN'T ADMITTED TO HEARING THE NOISE. RIGHT?
TUBBEE! YOU CAN GET THAT IDEA RIGHT OUT OF YOUR HEAD!
OKAY, LULU. UNTIL I INVESTIGATE THIS CASE, LET'S SAY HE IS JUST A SUSPECT.
YOU'RE STOOPID, TUBBY. HOW COULD MY FATHER WALK ON THE CEILING?
WHEN YOU HAVE BEEN IN THIS DETECTIVE BUSINESS AS LONG AS I HAVE, YOU WILL FIND THAT PARENTS CAN BE TRICKY!
YOU MEAN IT'S POSSIBLE THAT HE COULD--
MUM'S THE WORD, LULU, UNTIL I CATCH HIM RED-HANDED TONIGHT!
TONIGHT? BUT, TUBBY, YOU CAN'T--
I'LL GET MY MOTHER'S PERMISSION AND I'LL HIDE UNDER YOUR BED!
BUT HOW ABOUT MY MOTHER'S PERMISSION?

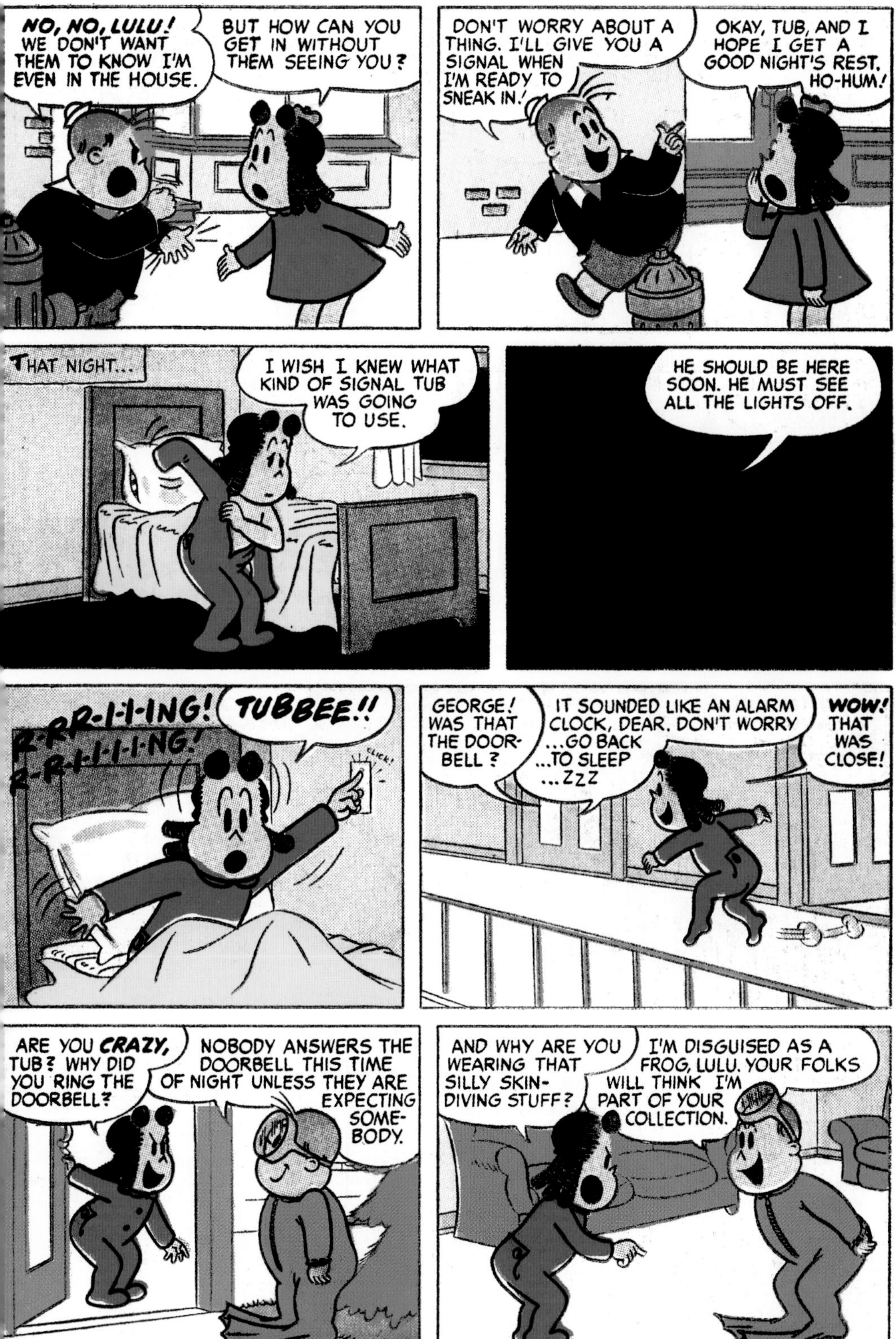
NO, NO, LULU! WE DON'T WANT THEM TO KNOW I'M EVEN IN THE HOUSE.
BUT HOW CAN YOU GET IN WITHOUT THEM SEEING YOU?
DON'T WORRY ABOUT A THING. I'LL GIVE YOU A SIGNAL WHEN I'M READY TO SNEAK IN!
OKAY, TUB, AND I HOPE I GET A GOOD NIGHT'S REST. HO-HUM!
THAT NIGHT...
I WISH I KNEW WHAT KIND OF SIGNAL TUB WAS GOING TO USE.
HE SHOULD BE HERE SOON. HE MUST SEE ALL THE LIGHTS OFF.
R-RR-I-I-ING! R-RR-I-I-ING! R-R-I-I-I-I-NG!
TUBBEE!!
CLICK!
GEORGE! WAS THAT THE DOOR-BELL?
IT SOUNDED LIKE AN ALARM CLOCK, DEAR. DON'T WORRY ...GO BACK ...TO SLEEP ...ZZZ
WOW! THAT WAS CLOSE!
ARE YOU CRAZY, TUB? WHY DID YOU RING THE DOORBELL?
NOBODY ANSWERS THE DOORBELL THIS TIME OF NIGHT UNLESS THEY ARE EXPECTING SOME-BODY.
AND WHY ARE YOU WEARING THAT SILLY SKIN-DIVING STUFF?
I'M DISGUISED AS A FROG, LULU. YOUR FOLKS WILL THINK I'M PART OF YOUR COLLECTION.

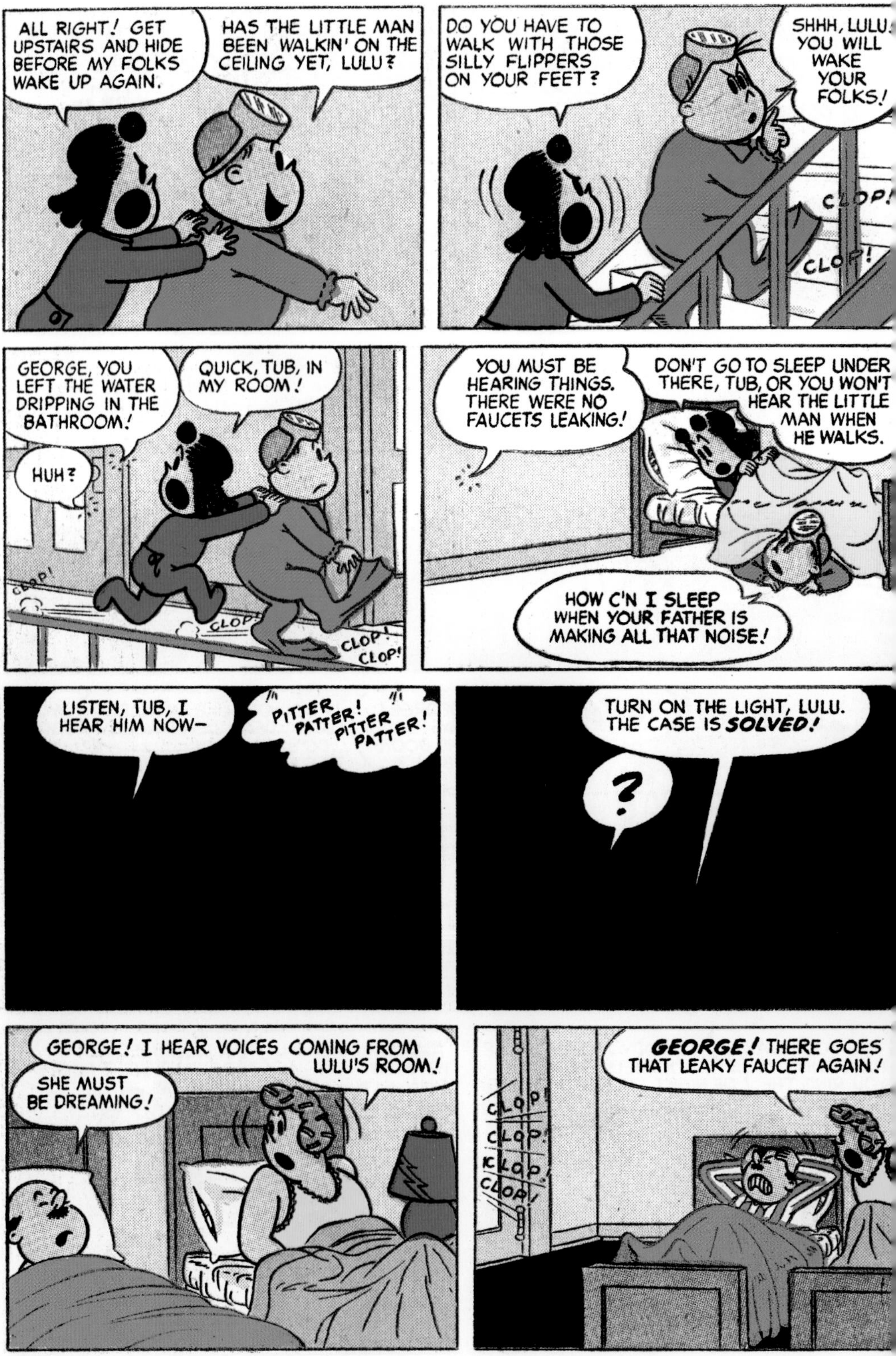
ALL RIGHT! GET UPSTAIRS AND HIDE BEFORE MY FOLKS WAKE UP AGAIN.
HAS THE LITTLE MAN BEEN WALKIN' ON THE CEILING YET, LULU?
DO YOU HAVE TO WALK WITH THOSE SILLY FLIPPERS ON YOUR FEET?
SHHH, LULU! YOU WILL WAKE YOUR FOLKS!
CLOP!
CLOP!
GEORGE, YOU LEFT THE WATER DRIPPING IN THE BATHROOM!
QUICK, TUB, IN MY ROOM!
HUH?
CLOP!
CLOP!
CLOP!
CLOP!
YOU MUST BE HEARING THINGS. THERE WERE NO FAUCETS LEAKING!
DON'T GO TO SLEEP UNDER THERE, TUB, OR YOU WON'T HEAR THE LITTLE MAN WHEN HE WALKS.
HOW C'N I SLEEP WHEN YOUR FATHER IS MAKING ALL THAT NOISE!
LISTEN, TUB, I HEAR HIM NOW—
PITTER PATTER! PITTER PATTER!
TURN ON THE LIGHT, LULU. THE CASE IS SOLVED!
?
GEORGE! I HEAR VOICES COMING FROM LULU'S ROOM!
SHE MUST BE DREAMING!
GEORGE! THERE GOES THAT LEAKY FAUCET AGAIN!
CLOP!
CLOP!
KLOP!
CLOP!

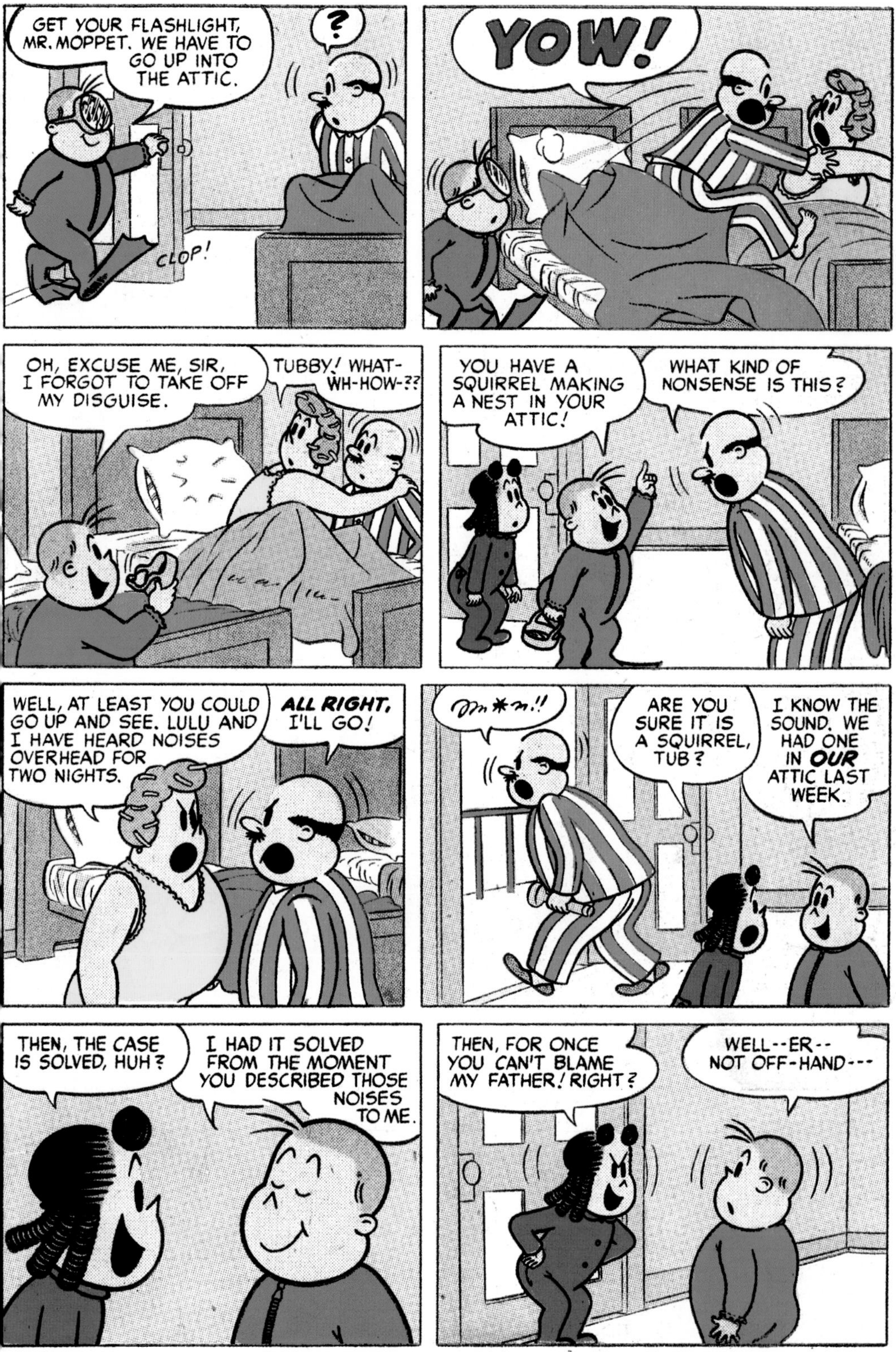
GET YOUR FLASHLIGHT, MR. MOPPET. WE HAVE TO GO UP INTO THE ATTIC.
?
CLOP!
YOW!
OH, EXCUSE ME, SIR, I FORGOT TO TAKE OFF MY DISGUISE.
TUBBY! WHAT- WH-HOW-??
YOU HAVE A SQUIRREL MAKING A NEST IN YOUR ATTIC!
WHAT KIND OF NONSENSE IS THIS?
WELL, AT LEAST YOU COULD GO UP AND SEE. LULU AND I HAVE HEARD NOISES OVERHEAD FOR TWO NIGHTS.
ALL RIGHT, I'LL GO!
ARE YOU SURE IT IS A SQUIRREL, TUB?
I KNOW THE SOUND. WE HAD ONE IN OUR ATTIC LAST WEEK.
THEN, THE CASE IS SOLVED, HUH?
I HAD IT SOLVED FROM THE MOMENT YOU DESCRIBED THOSE NOISES TO ME.
THEN, FOR ONCE YOU CAN'T BLAME MY FATHER! RIGHT?
WELL--ER-- NOT OFF-HAND---

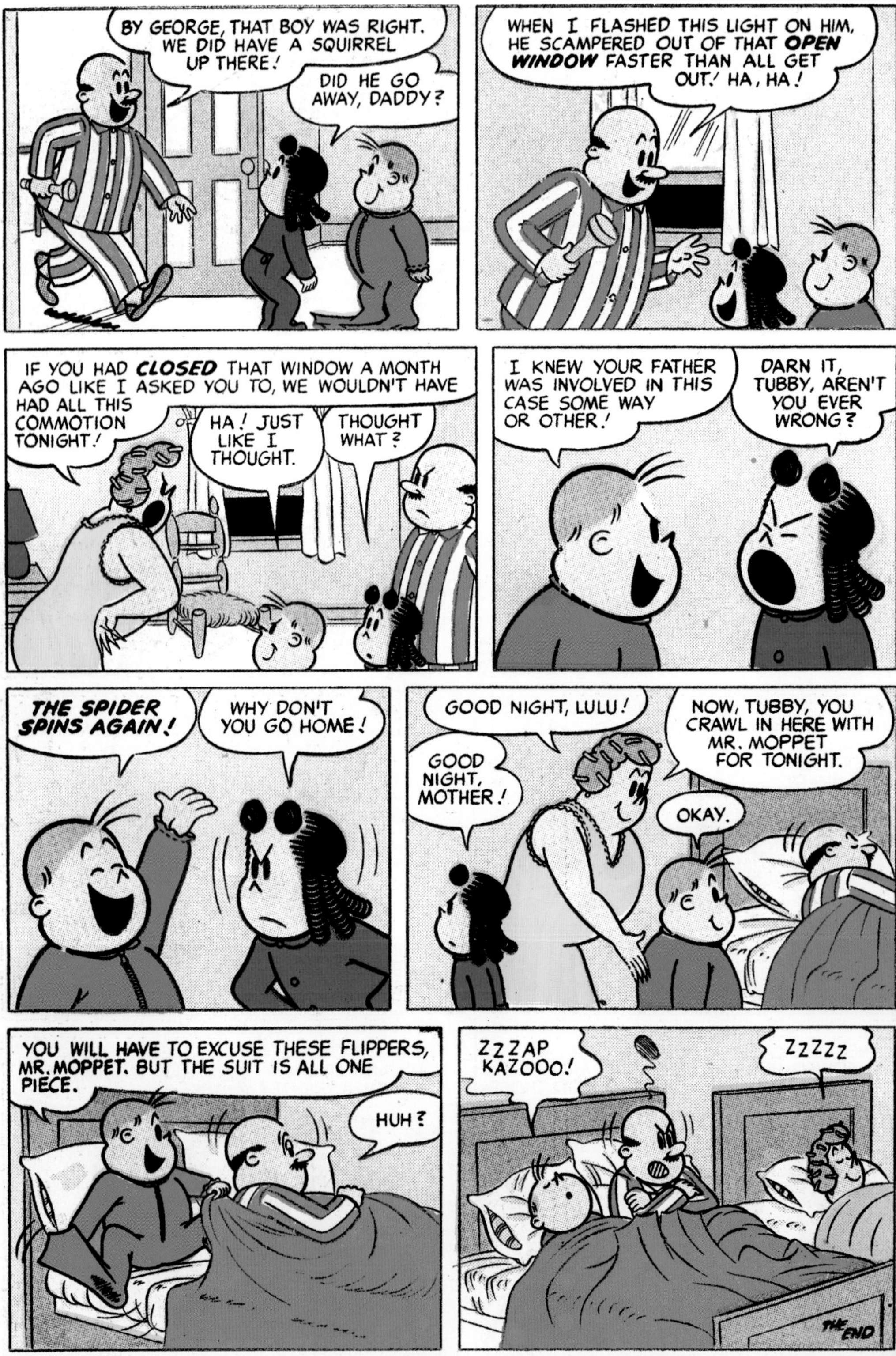

BY GEORGE, THAT BOY WAS RIGHT. WE DID HAVE A SQUIRREL UP THERE!
DID HE GO AWAY, DADDY?
WHEN I FLASHED THIS LIGHT ON HIM, HE SCAMPERED OUT OF THAT **OPEN WINDOW** FASTER THAN ALL GET OUT! HA, HA!
IF YOU HAD **CLOSED** THAT WINDOW A MONTH AGO LIKE I ASKED YOU TO, WE WOULDN'T HAVE HAD ALL THIS COMMOTION TONIGHT!
HA! JUST LIKE I THOUGHT.
THOUGHT WHAT?
I KNEW YOUR FATHER WAS INVOLVED IN THIS CASE SOME WAY OR OTHER!
DARN IT, TUBBY, AREN'T YOU EVER WRONG?
THE SPIDER SPINS AGAIN!
WHY DON'T YOU GO HOME!
GOOD NIGHT, LULU!
GOOD NIGHT, MOTHER!
NOW, TUBBY, YOU CRAWL IN HERE WITH MR. MOPPET FOR TONIGHT.
OKAY.
YOU WILL HAVE TO EXCUSE THESE FLIPPERS, MR. MOPPET. BUT THE SUIT IS ALL ONE PIECE.
HUH?
ZZZAP KAZOOO!
ZZZZZ
THE END

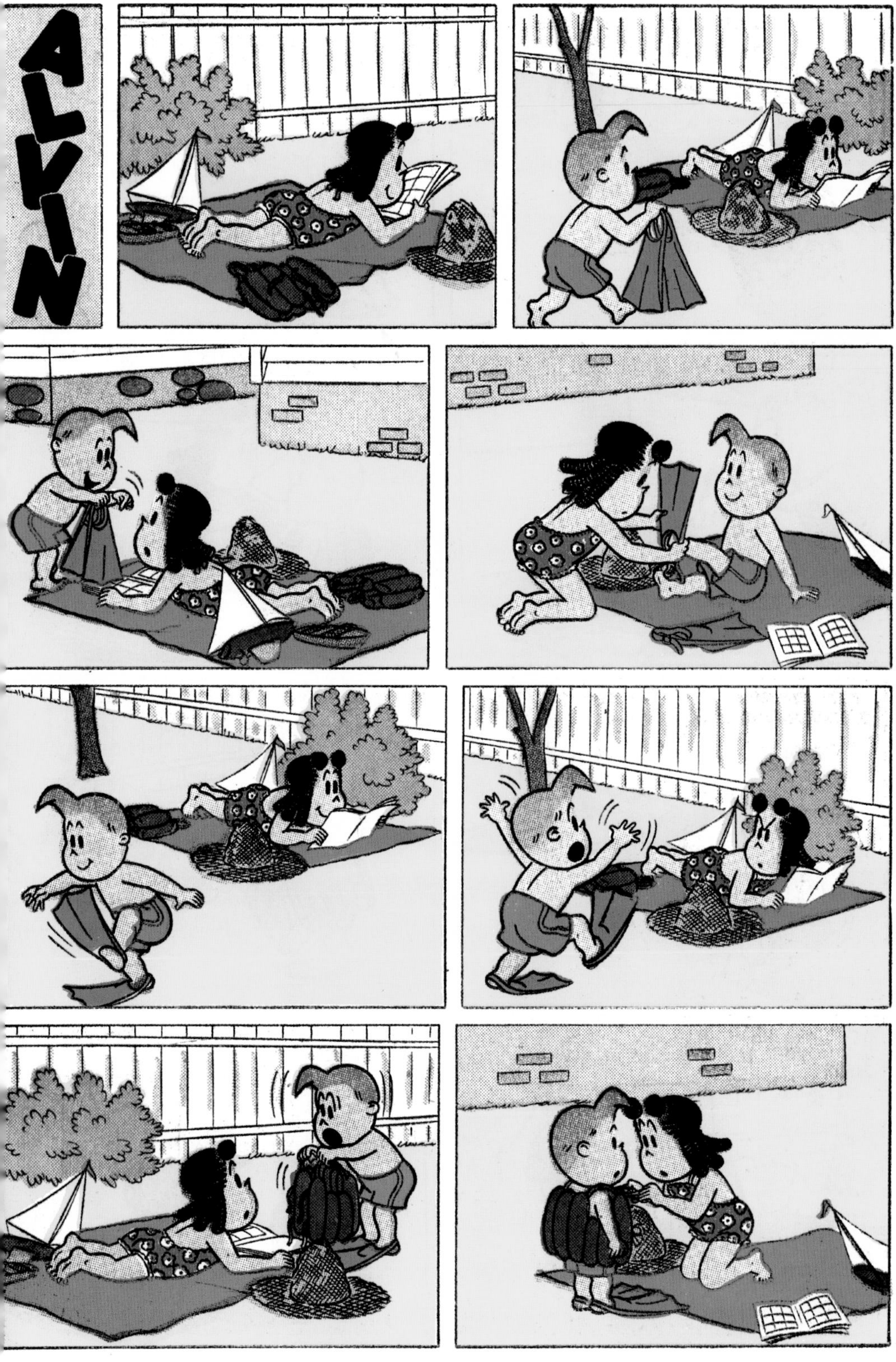
ALVIN

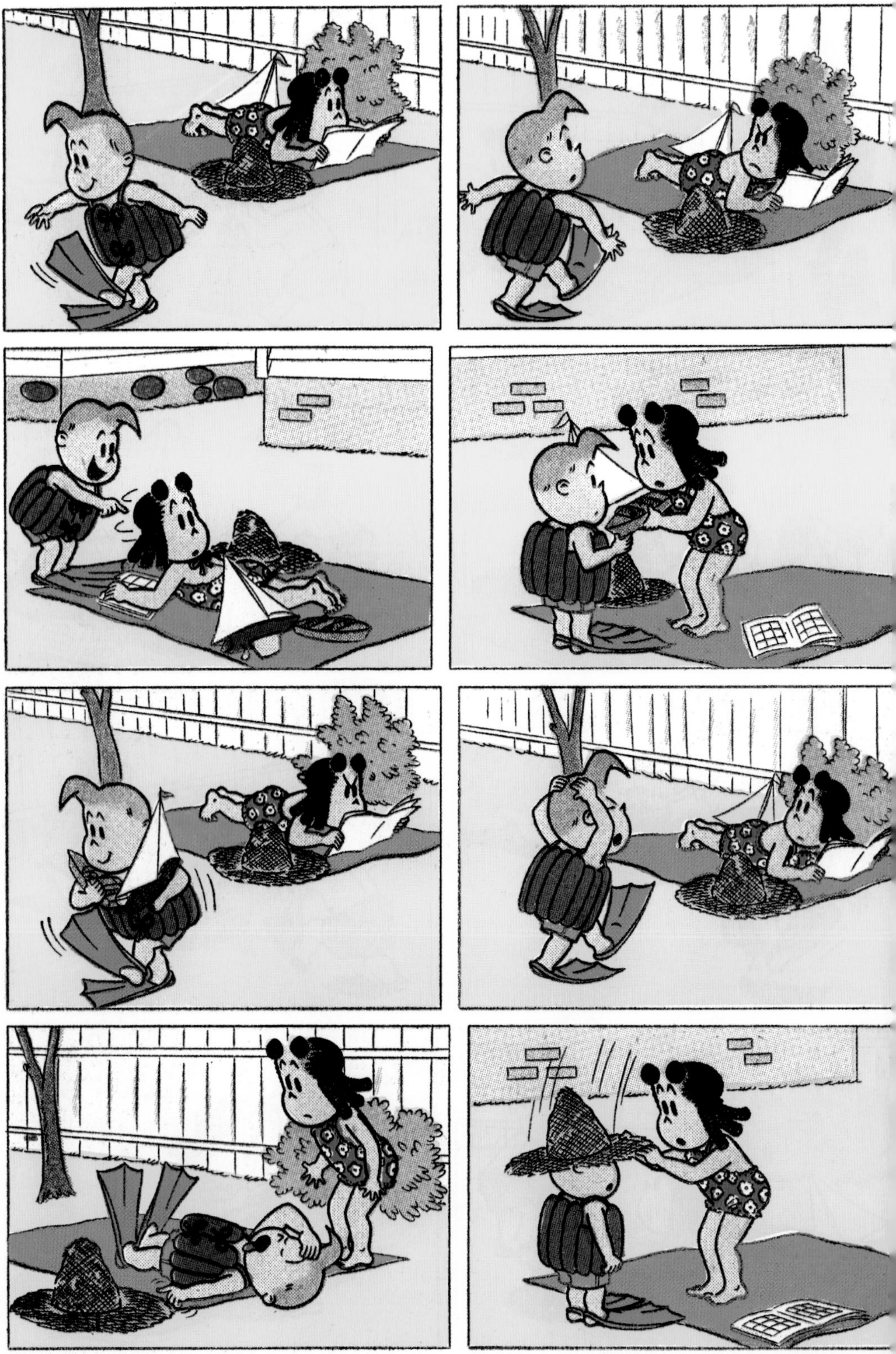

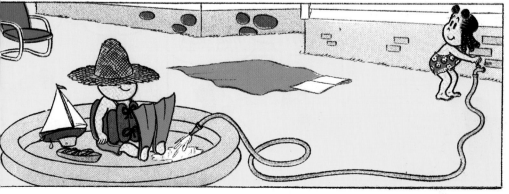

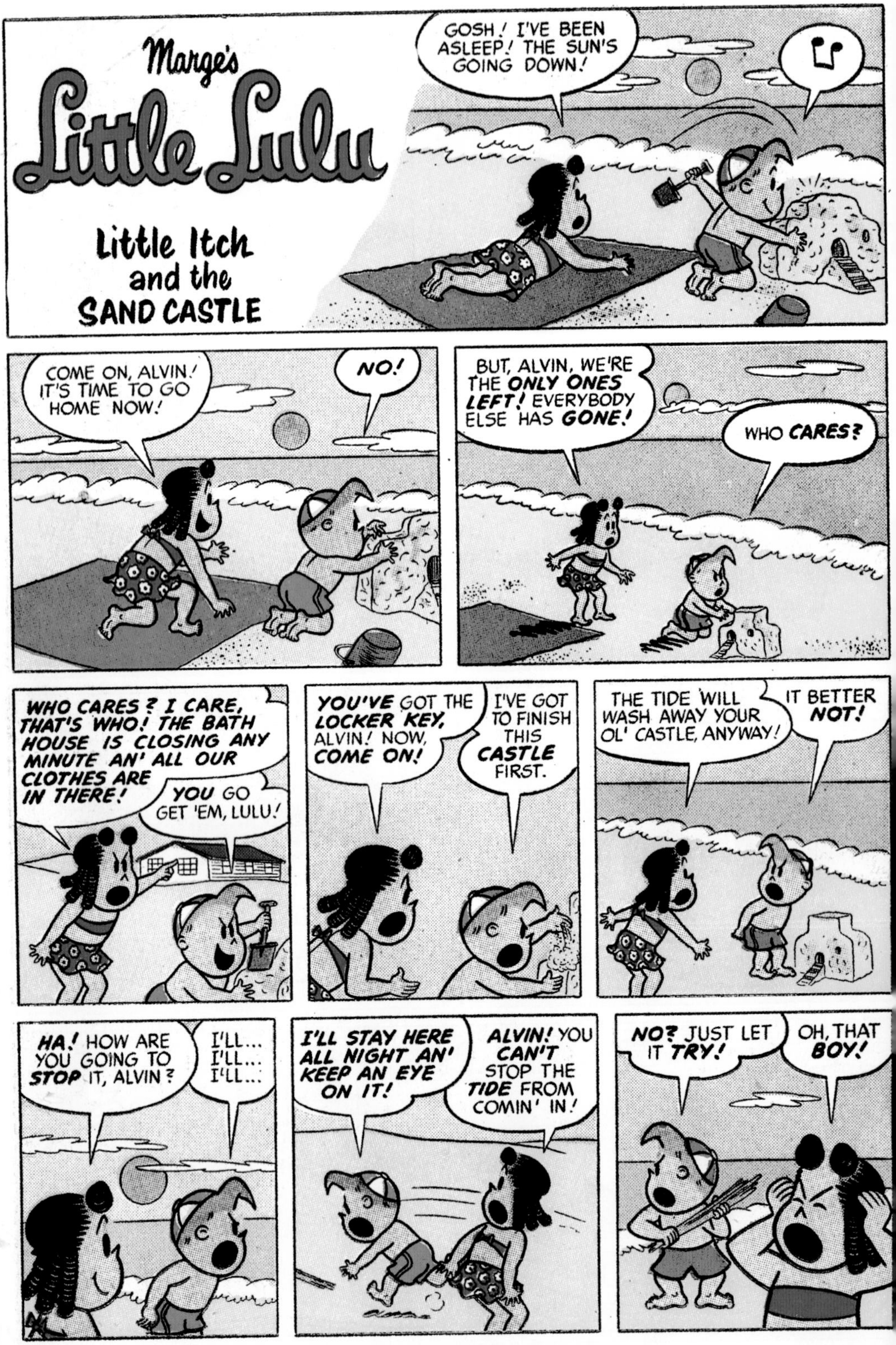
Marge's
Little Lulu
Little Itch and the SAND CASTLE
GOSH! I'VE BEEN ASLEEP! THE SUN'S GOING DOWN!
COME ON, ALVIN! IT'S TIME TO GO HOME NOW!
NO!
BUT, ALVIN, WE'RE THE ONLY ONES LEFT! EVERYBODY ELSE HAS GONE!
WHO CARES?
WHO CARES? I CARE, THAT'S WHO! THE BATH HOUSE IS CLOSING ANY MINUTE AN' ALL OUR CLOTHES ARE IN THERE!
YOU GO GET 'EM, LULU!
YOU'VE GOT THE LOCKER KEY, ALVIN! NOW, COME ON!
I'VE GOT TO FINISH THIS CASTLE FIRST.
THE TIDE WILL WASH AWAY YOUR OL' CASTLE, ANYWAY!
IT BETTER NOT!
HA! HOW ARE YOU GOING TO STOP IT, ALVIN?
I'LL... I'LL... I'LL...
I'LL STAY HERE ALL NIGHT AN' KEEP AN EYE ON IT!
ALVIN! YOU CAN'T STOP THE TIDE FROM COMIN' IN!
NO? JUST LET IT TRY!
OH, THAT BOY!

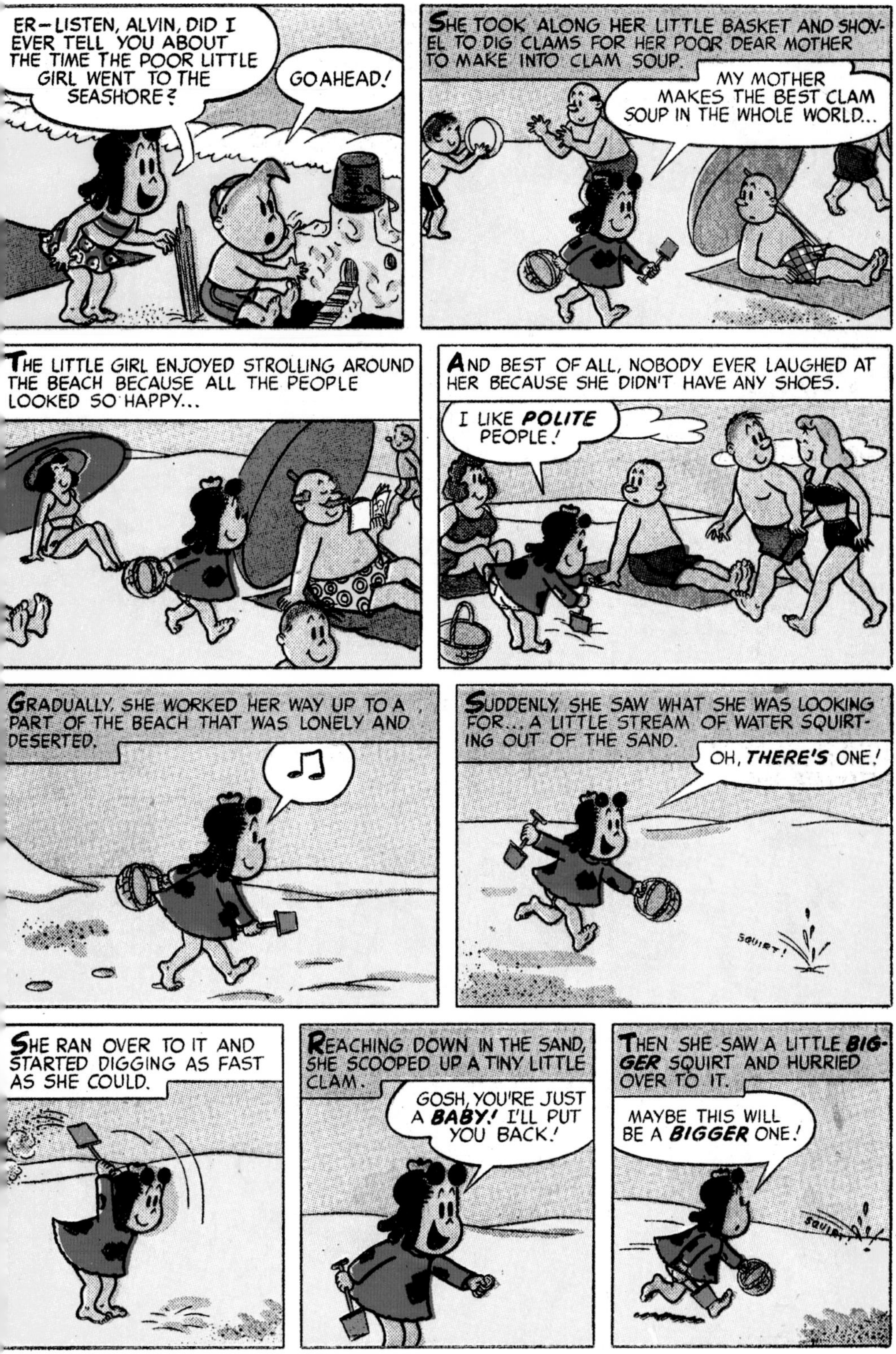
ER—LISTEN, ALVIN, DID I EVER TELL YOU ABOUT THE TIME THE POOR LITTLE GIRL WENT TO THE SEASHORE?
GO AHEAD!
SHE TOOK ALONG HER LITTLE BASKET AND SHOVEL TO DIG CLAMS FOR HER POOR DEAR MOTHER TO MAKE INTO CLAM SOUP.
MY MOTHER MAKES THE BEST CLAM SOUP IN THE WHOLE WORLD...
THE LITTLE GIRL ENJOYED STROLLING AROUND THE BEACH BECAUSE ALL THE PEOPLE LOOKED SO HAPPY...
AND BEST OF ALL, NOBODY EVER LAUGHED AT HER BECAUSE SHE DIDN'T HAVE ANY SHOES.
I LIKE POLITE PEOPLE!
GRADUALLY, SHE WORKED HER WAY UP TO A PART OF THE BEACH THAT WAS LONELY AND DESERTED.
SUDDENLY, SHE SAW WHAT SHE WAS LOOKING FOR... A LITTLE STREAM OF WATER SQUIRTING OUT OF THE SAND.
OH, THERE'S ONE!
SQUIRT!
SHE RAN OVER TO IT AND STARTED DIGGING AS FAST AS SHE COULD.
REACHING DOWN IN THE SAND, SHE SCOOPED UP A TINY LITTLE CLAM.
GOSH, YOU'RE JUST A BABY! I'LL PUT YOU BACK!
THEN SHE SAW A LITTLE BIGGER SQUIRT AND HURRIED OVER TO IT.
MAYBE THIS WILL BE A BIGGER ONE!

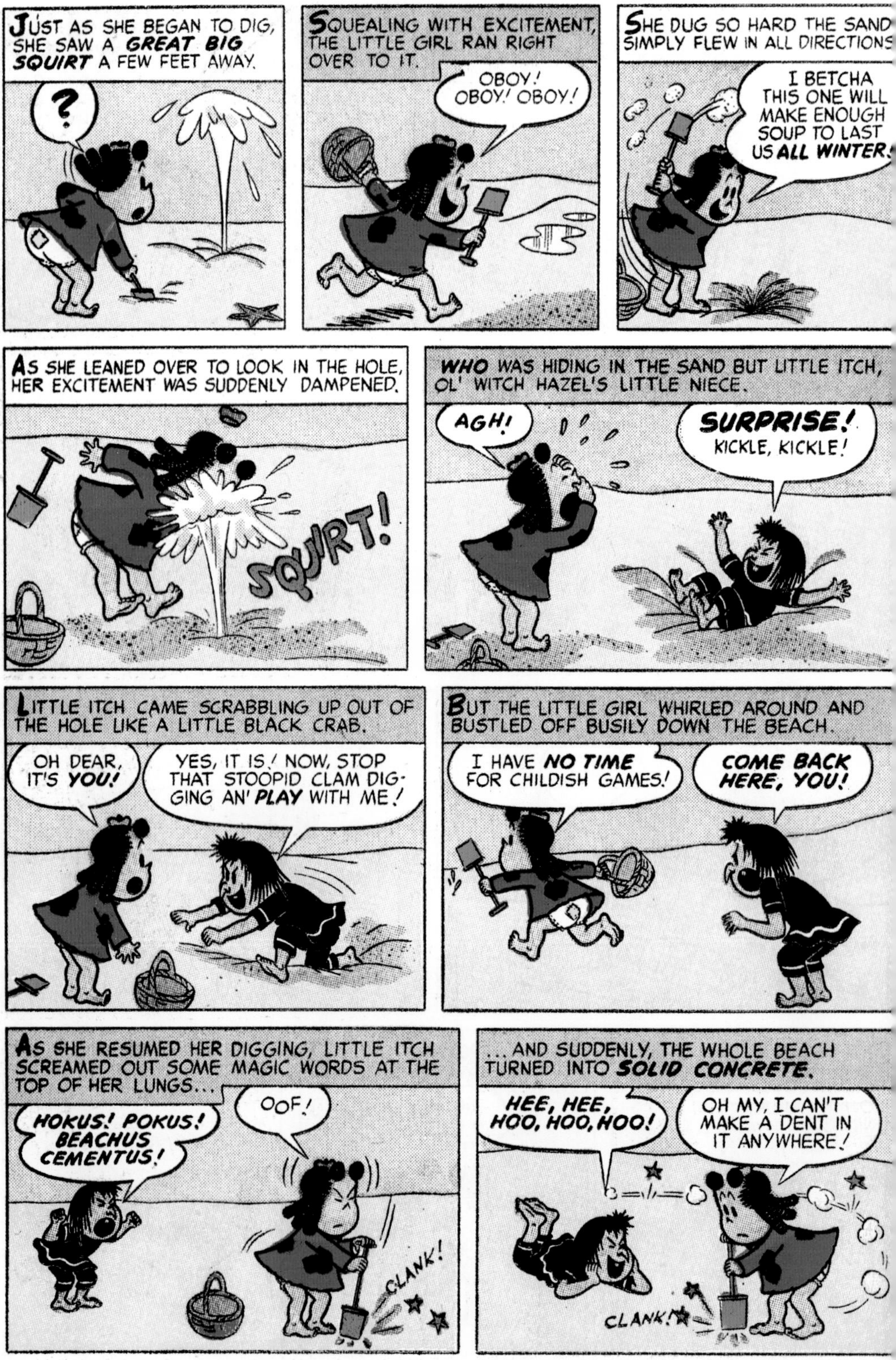

JUST AS SHE BEGAN TO DIG, SHE SAW A GREAT BIG SQUIRT A FEW FEET AWAY.
?
SQUEALING WITH EXCITEMENT, THE LITTLE GIRL RAN RIGHT OVER TO IT.
OBOY! OBOY! OBOY!
SHE DUG SO HARD THE SAND SIMPLY FLEW IN ALL DIRECTIONS
I BETCHA THIS ONE WILL MAKE ENOUGH SOUP TO LAST US ALL WINTER!
AS SHE LEANED OVER TO LOOK IN THE HOLE, HER EXCITEMENT WAS SUDDENLY DAMPENED.
SQUIRT!
WHO WAS HIDING IN THE SAND BUT LITTLE ITCH, OL' WITCH HAZEL'S LITTLE NIECE.
AGH!
SURPRISE! KICKLE, KICKLE!
LITTLE ITCH CAME SCRABBLING UP OUT OF THE HOLE LIKE A LITTLE BLACK CRAB.
OH DEAR, IT'S YOU!
YES, IT IS! NOW, STOP THAT STOOPID CLAM DIG-GING AN' PLAY WITH ME!
BUT THE LITTLE GIRL WHIRLED AROUND AND BUSTLED OFF BUSILY DOWN THE BEACH.
I HAVE NO TIME FOR CHILDISH GAMES!
COME BACK HERE, YOU!
AS SHE RESUMED HER DIGGING, LITTLE ITCH SCREAMED OUT SOME MAGIC WORDS AT THE TOP OF HER LUNGS...
HOKUS! POKUS! BEACHUS CEMENTUS!
OOF!
CLANK!
...AND SUDDENLY, THE WHOLE BEACH TURNED INTO SOLID CONCRETE.
HEE, HEE, HOO, HOO, HOO!
OH MY, I CAN'T MAKE A DENT IN IT ANYWHERE!
CLANK!

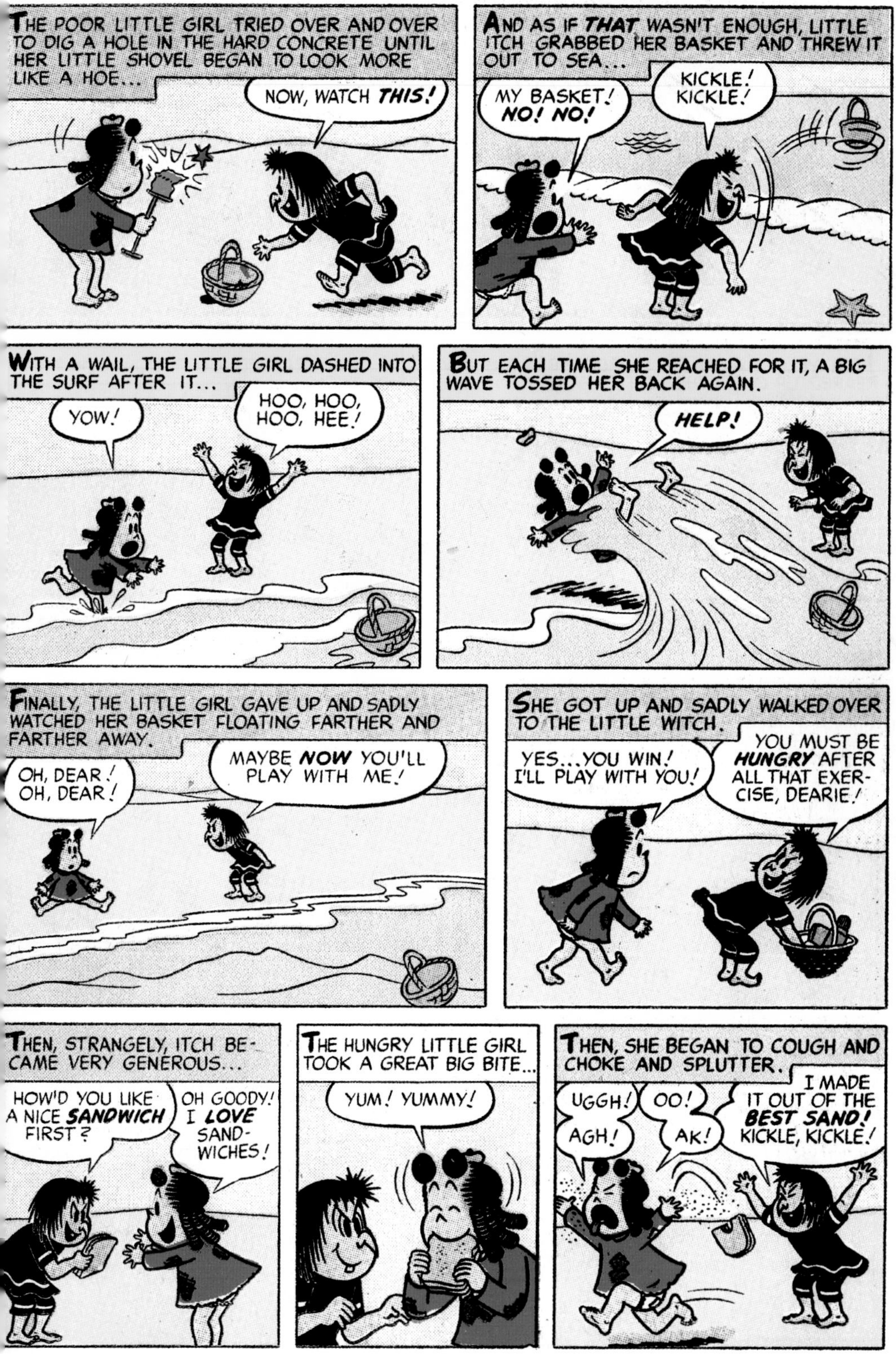
THE POOR LITTLE GIRL TRIED OVER AND OVER TO DIG A HOLE IN THE HARD CONCRETE UNTIL HER LITTLE SHOVEL BEGAN TO LOOK MORE LIKE A HOE...
NOW, WATCH THIS!
AND AS IF THAT WASN'T ENOUGH, LITTLE ITCH GRABBED HER BASKET AND THREW IT OUT TO SEA...
MY BASKET! NO! NO!
KICKLE! KICKLE!
WITH A WAIL, THE LITTLE GIRL DASHED INTO THE SURF AFTER IT...
YOW!
HOO, HOO, HOO, HEE!
BUT EACH TIME SHE REACHED FOR IT, A BIG WAVE TOSSED HER BACK AGAIN.
HELP!
FINALLY, THE LITTLE GIRL GAVE UP AND SADLY WATCHED HER BASKET FLOATING FARTHER AND FARTHER AWAY.
OH, DEAR! OH, DEAR!
MAYBE NOW YOU'LL PLAY WITH ME!
SHE GOT UP AND SADLY WALKED OVER TO THE LITTLE WITCH.
YES...YOU WIN! I'LL PLAY WITH YOU!
YOU MUST BE HUNGRY AFTER ALL THAT EXERCISE, DEARIE!
THEN, STRANGELY, ITCH BECAME VERY GENEROUS...
HOW'D YOU LIKE A NICE SANDWICH FIRST?
OH GOODY! I LOVE SANDWICHES!
THE HUNGRY LITTLE GIRL TOOK A GREAT BIG BITE...
YUM! YUMMY!
THEN, SHE BEGAN TO COUGH AND CHOKE AND SPLUTTER.
UGGH! AGH!
OO! AK!
I MADE IT OUT OF THE BEST SAND! KICKLE, KICKLE!

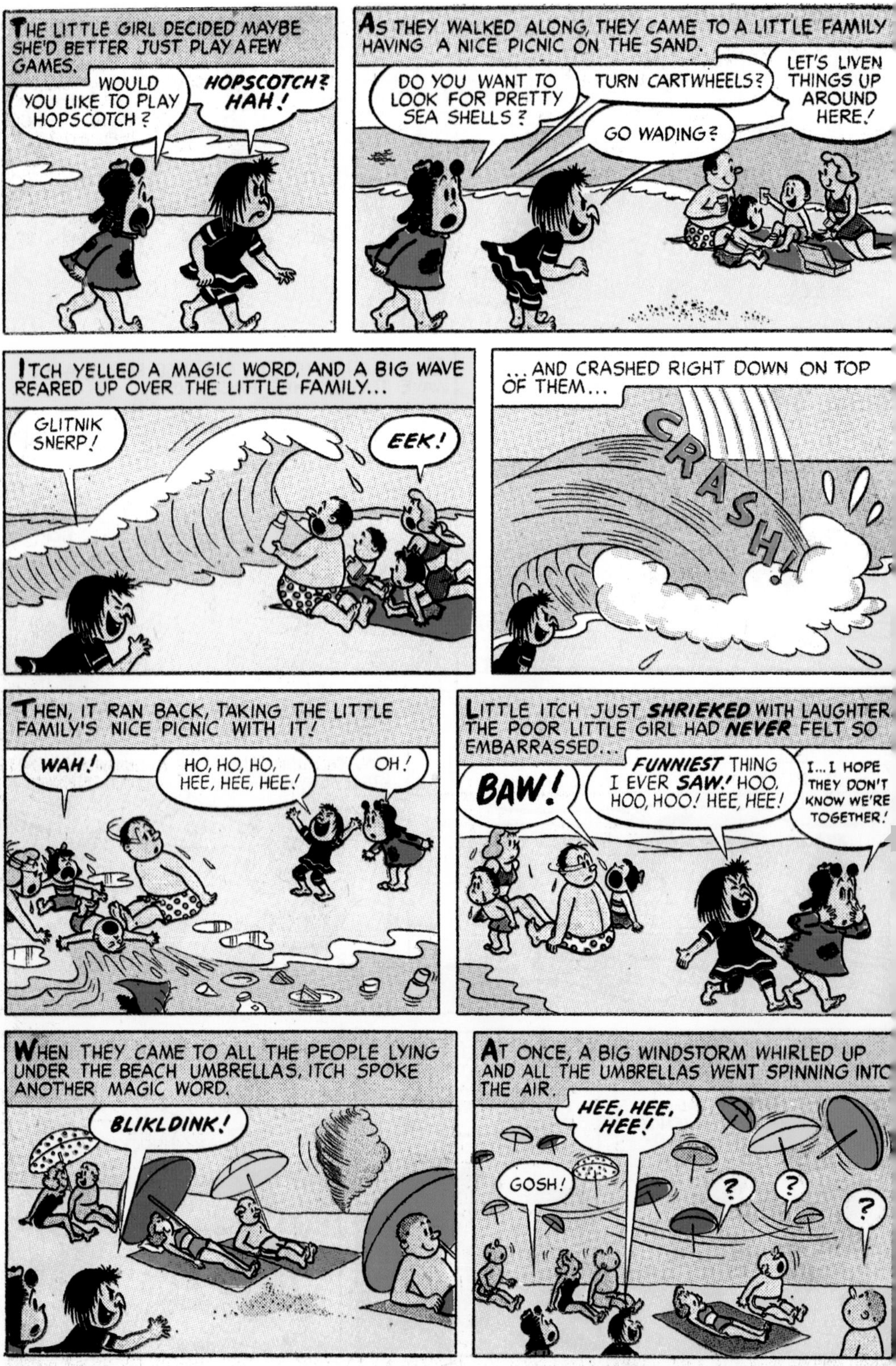

THE LITTLE GIRL DECIDED MAYBE SHE'D BETTER JUST PLAY A FEW GAMES.
WOULD YOU LIKE TO PLAY HOPSCOTCH ?
HOPSCOTCH? HAH!
AS THEY WALKED ALONG, THEY CAME TO A LITTLE FAMILY HAVING A NICE PICNIC ON THE SAND.
DO YOU WANT TO LOOK FOR PRETTY SEA SHELLS ?
TURN CARTWHEELS?
GO WADING?
LET'S LIVEN THINGS UP AROUND HERE!
ITCH YELLED A MAGIC WORD, AND A BIG WAVE REARED UP OVER THE LITTLE FAMILY...
GLITNIK SNERP!
EEK!
...AND CRASHED RIGHT DOWN ON TOP OF THEM...
CRASH!
THEN, IT RAN BACK, TAKING THE LITTLE FAMILY'S NICE PICNIC WITH IT!
WAH!
HO, HO, HO, HEE, HEE, HEE!
OH!
LITTLE ITCH JUST SHRIEKED WITH LAUGHTER. THE POOR LITTLE GIRL HAD NEVER FELT SO EMBARRASSED...
BAW!
FUNNIEST THING I EVER SAW! HOO, HOO, HOO! HEE, HEE!
I...I HOPE THEY DON'T KNOW WE'RE TOGETHER!
WHEN THEY CAME TO ALL THE PEOPLE LYING UNDER THE BEACH UMBRELLAS, ITCH SPOKE ANOTHER MAGIC WORD.
BLIKLDINK!
AT ONCE, A BIG WINDSTORM WHIRLED UP AND ALL THE UMBRELLAS WENT SPINNING INTO THE AIR.
HEE, HEE, HEE!
GOSH!
?
?
?

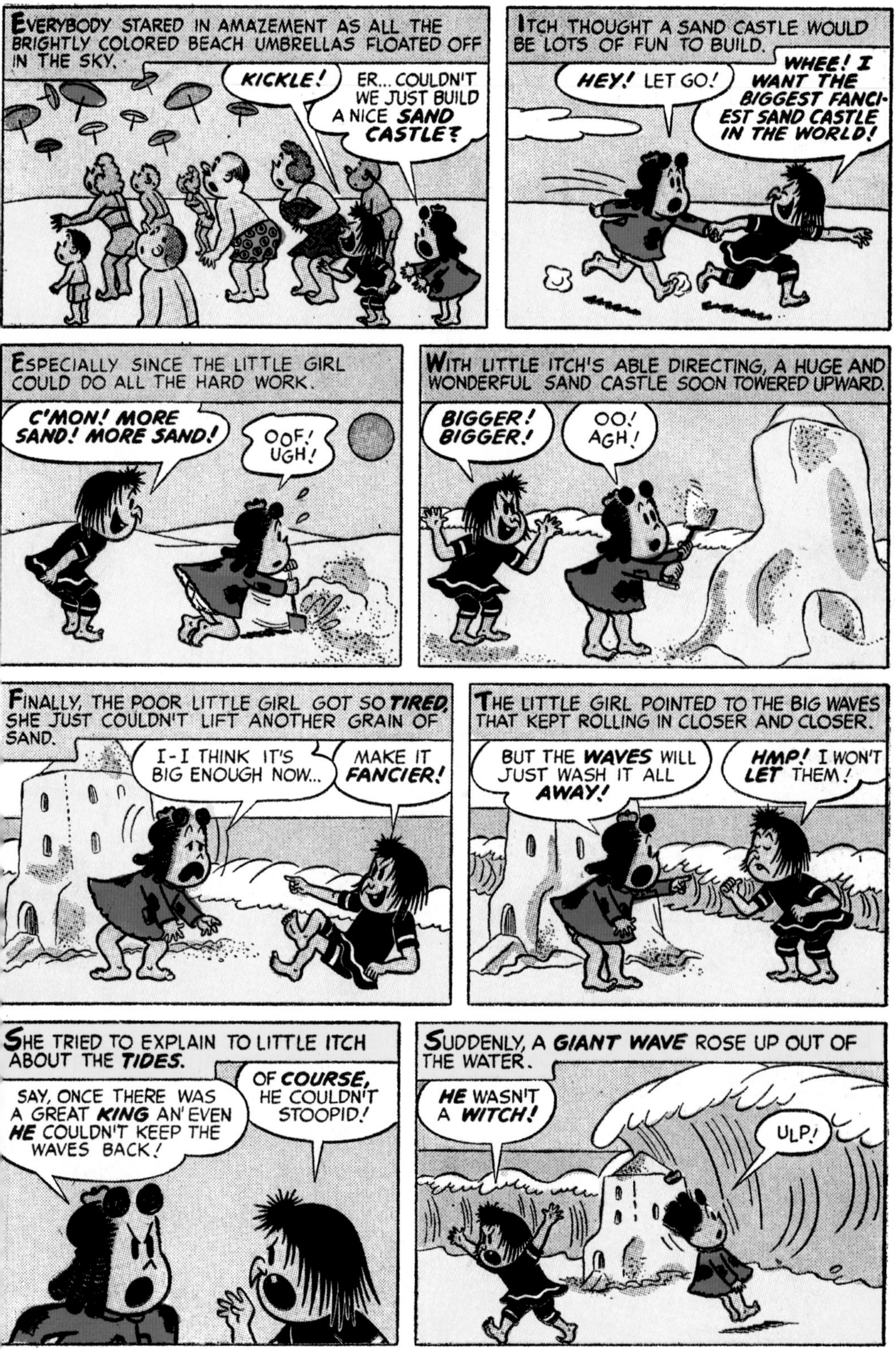
EVERYBODY STARED IN AMAZEMENT AS ALL THE BRIGHTLY COLORED BEACH UMBRELLAS FLOATED OFF IN THE SKY.
KICKLE!
ER... COULDN'T WE JUST BUILD A NICE SAND CASTLE?
ITCH THOUGHT A SAND CASTLE WOULD BE LOTS OF FUN TO BUILD.
HEY! LET GO!
WHEE! I WANT THE BIGGEST FANCI-EST SAND CASTLE IN THE WORLD!
ESPECIALLY SINCE THE LITTLE GIRL COULD DO ALL THE HARD WORK.
C'MON! MORE SAND! MORE SAND!
OOF! UGH!
WITH LITTLE ITCH'S ABLE DIRECTING, A HUGE AND WONDERFUL SAND CASTLE SOON TOWERED UPWARD.
BIGGER! BIGGER!
OO! AGH!
FINALLY, THE POOR LITTLE GIRL GOT SO TIRED, SHE JUST COULDN'T LIFT ANOTHER GRAIN OF SAND.
I-I THINK IT'S BIG ENOUGH NOW...
MAKE IT FANCIER!
THE LITTLE GIRL POINTED TO THE BIG WAVES THAT KEPT ROLLING IN CLOSER AND CLOSER.
BUT THE WAVES WILL JUST WASH IT ALL AWAY!
HMP! I WON'T LET THEM!
SHE TRIED TO EXPLAIN TO LITTLE ITCH ABOUT THE TIDES.
SAY, ONCE THERE WAS A GREAT KING AN' EVEN HE COULDN'T KEEP THE WAVES BACK!
OF COURSE, HE COULDN'T STOOPID!
SUDDENLY, A GIANT WAVE ROSE UP OUT OF THE WATER.
HE WASN'T A WITCH!
ULP!

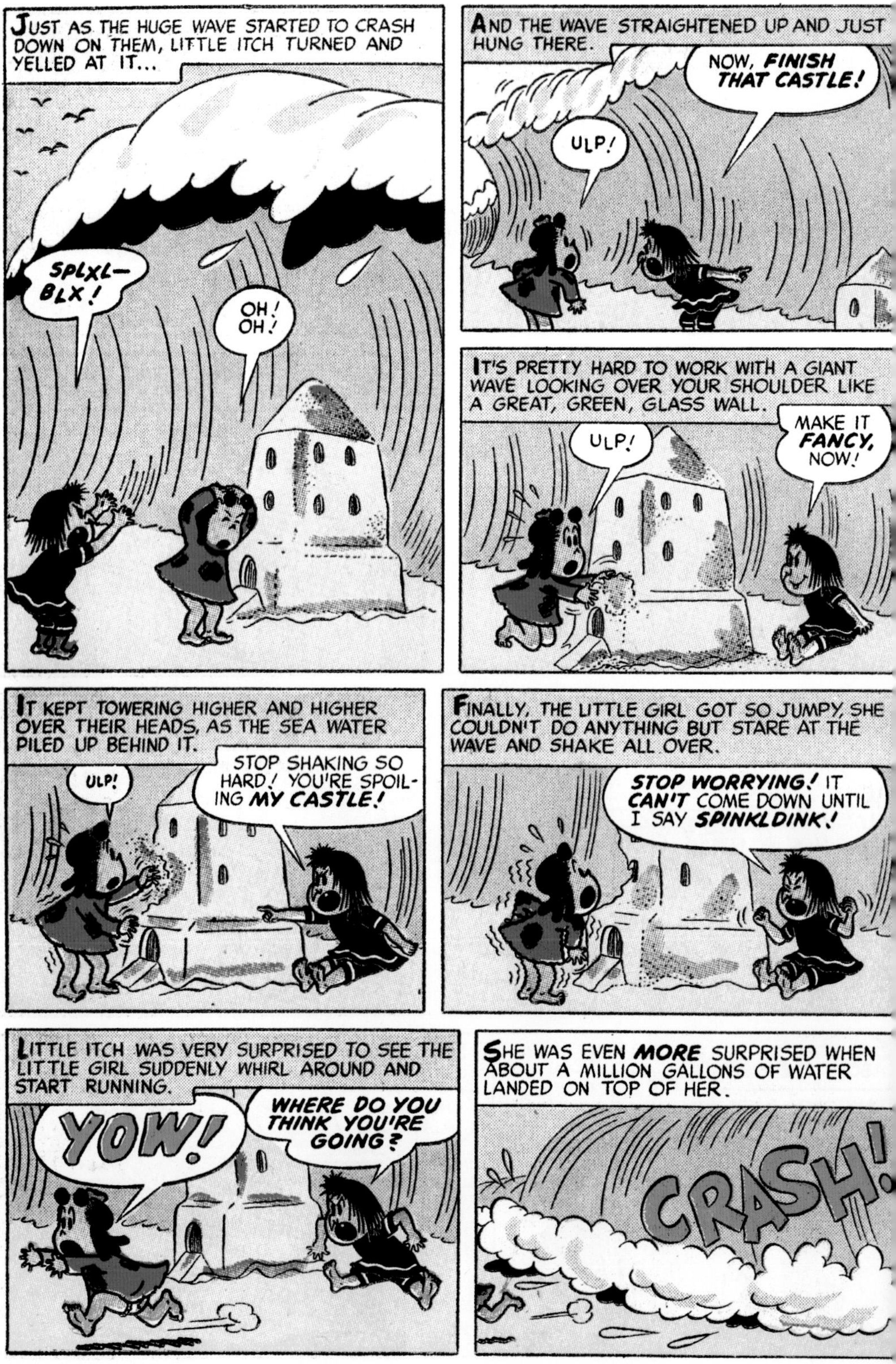
JUST AS THE HUGE WAVE STARTED TO CRASH DOWN ON THEM, LITTLE ITCH TURNED AND YELLED AT IT...
SPLXL-BLX!
OH! OH!
AND THE WAVE STRAIGHTENED UP AND JUST HUNG THERE.
NOW, FINISH THAT CASTLE!
ULP!
IT'S PRETTY HARD TO WORK WITH A GIANT WAVE LOOKING OVER YOUR SHOULDER LIKE A GREAT, GREEN, GLASS WALL.
ULP!
MAKE IT FANCY, NOW!
IT KEPT TOWERING HIGHER AND HIGHER OVER THEIR HEADS, AS THE SEA WATER PILED UP BEHIND IT.
ULP!
STOP SHAKING SO HARD! YOU'RE SPOIL-ING MY CASTLE!
FINALLY, THE LITTLE GIRL GOT SO JUMPY, SHE COULDN'T DO ANYTHING BUT STARE AT THE WAVE AND SHAKE ALL OVER.
STOP WORRYING! IT CAN'T COME DOWN UNTIL I SAY SPINKLDINK!
LITTLE ITCH WAS VERY SURPRISED TO SEE THE LITTLE GIRL SUDDENLY WHIRL AROUND AND START RUNNING.
YOW!
WHERE DO YOU THINK YOU'RE GOING?
SHE WAS EVEN MORE SURPRISED WHEN ABOUT A MILLION GALLONS OF WATER LANDED ON TOP OF HER.
CRASH!

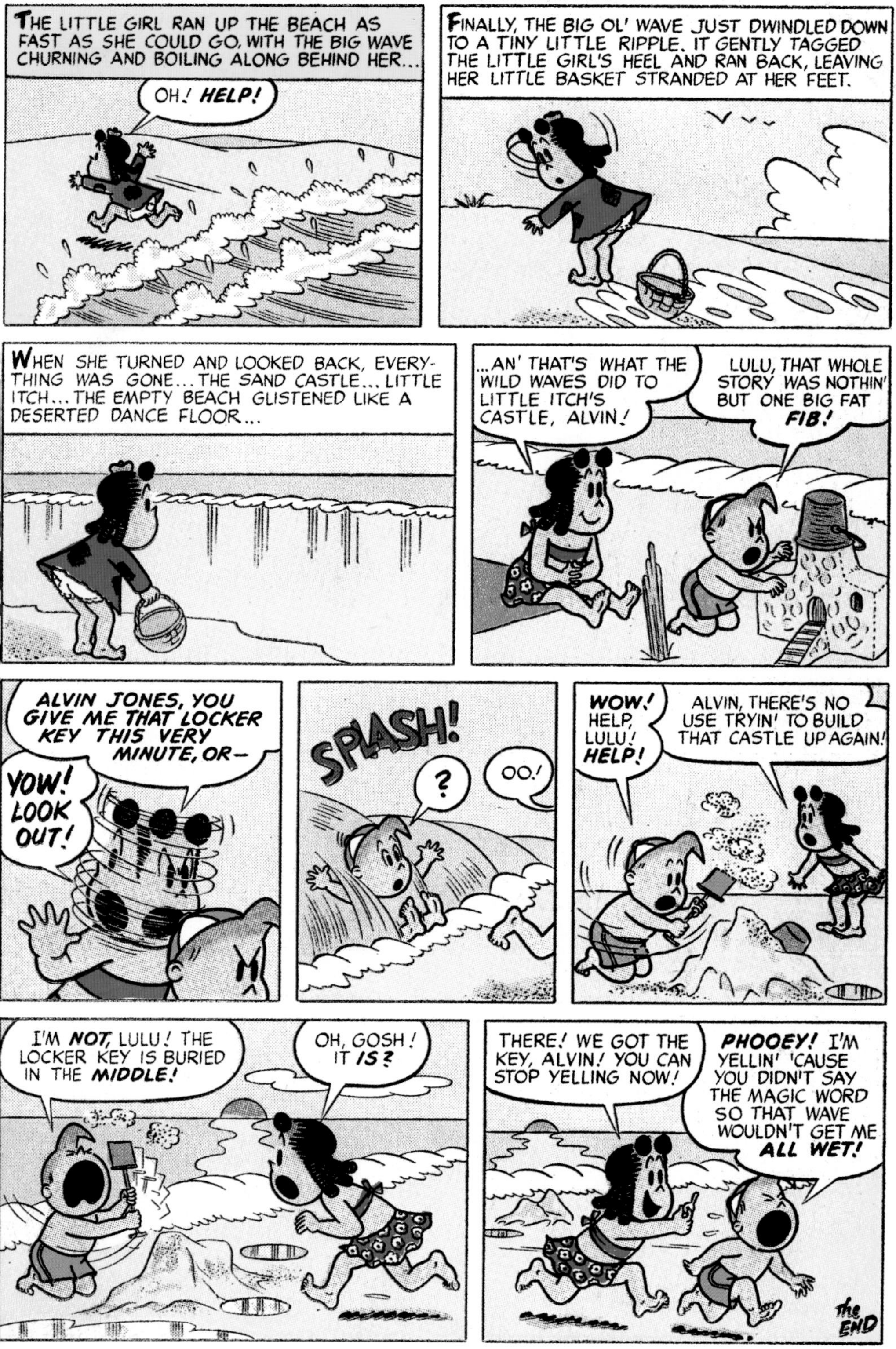
THE LITTLE GIRL RAN UP THE BEACH AS FAST AS SHE COULD GO, WITH THE BIG WAVE CHURNING AND BOILING ALONG BEHIND HER...
OH! HELP!
FINALLY, THE BIG OL' WAVE JUST DWINDLED DOWN TO A TINY LITTLE RIPPLE. IT GENTLY TAGGED THE LITTLE GIRL'S HEEL AND RAN BACK, LEAVING HER LITTLE BASKET STRANDED AT HER FEET.
WHEN SHE TURNED AND LOOKED BACK, EVERYTHING WAS GONE... THE SAND CASTLE... LITTLE ITCH... THE EMPTY BEACH GLISTENED LIKE A DESERTED DANCE FLOOR...
...AN' THAT'S WHAT THE WILD WAVES DID TO LITTLE ITCH'S CASTLE, ALVIN!
LULU, THAT WHOLE STORY WAS NOTHIN' BUT ONE BIG FAT FIB!
ALVIN JONES, YOU GIVE ME THAT LOCKER KEY THIS VERY MINUTE, OR—
YOW! LOOK OUT!
SPLASH!
?
OO!
WOW! HELP, LULU! HELP!
ALVIN, THERE'S NO USE TRYIN' TO BUILD THAT CASTLE UP AGAIN!
I'M NOT, LULU! THE LOCKER KEY IS BURIED IN THE MIDDLE!
OH, GOSH! IT IS?
THERE! WE GOT THE KEY, ALVIN! YOU CAN STOP YELLING NOW!
PHOOEY! I'M YELLIN' 'CAUSE YOU DIDN'T SAY THE MAGIC WORD SO THAT WAVE WOULDN'T GET ME ALL WET!
THE END

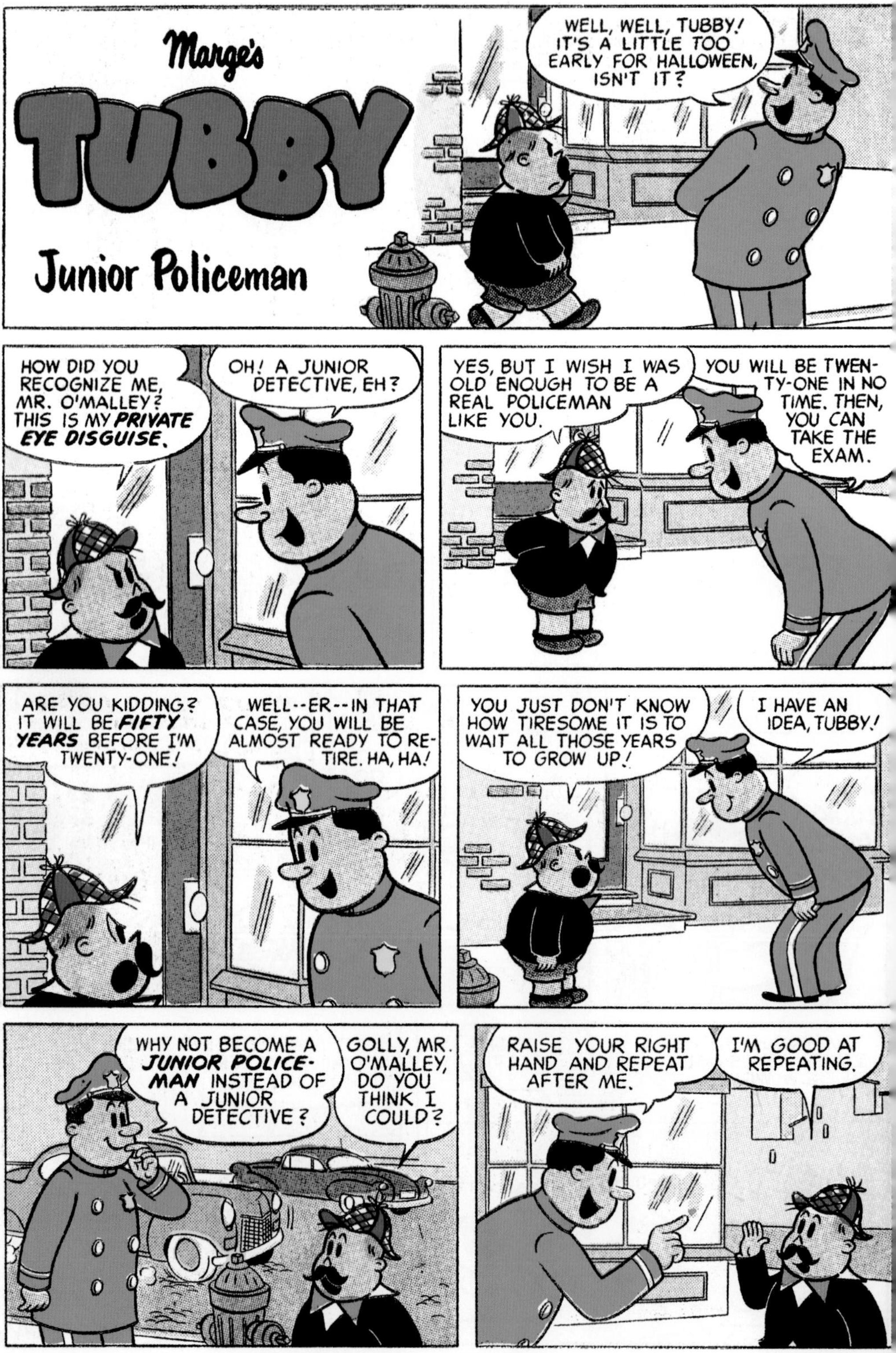
Marge's
TUBBY
Junior Policeman
WELL, WELL, TUBBY! IT'S A LITTLE TOO EARLY FOR HALLOWEEN, ISN'T IT?
HOW DID YOU RECOGNIZE ME, MR. O'MALLEY? THIS IS MY PRIVATE EYE DISGUISE.
OH! A JUNIOR DETECTIVE, EH?
YES, BUT I WISH I WAS OLD ENOUGH TO BE A REAL POLICEMAN LIKE YOU.
YOU WILL BE TWENTY-ONE IN NO TIME. THEN, YOU CAN TAKE THE EXAM.
ARE YOU KIDDING? IT WILL BE FIFTY YEARS BEFORE I'M TWENTY-ONE!
WELL--ER--IN THAT CASE, YOU WILL BE ALMOST READY TO RETIRE. HA, HA!
YOU JUST DON'T KNOW HOW TIRESOME IT IS TO WAIT ALL THOSE YEARS TO GROW UP!
I HAVE AN IDEA, TUBBY!
WHY NOT BECOME A JUNIOR POLICEMAN INSTEAD OF A JUNIOR DETECTIVE?
GOLLY, MR. O'MALLEY, DO YOU THINK I COULD?
RAISE YOUR RIGHT HAND AND REPEAT AFTER ME.
I'M GOOD AT REPEATING.

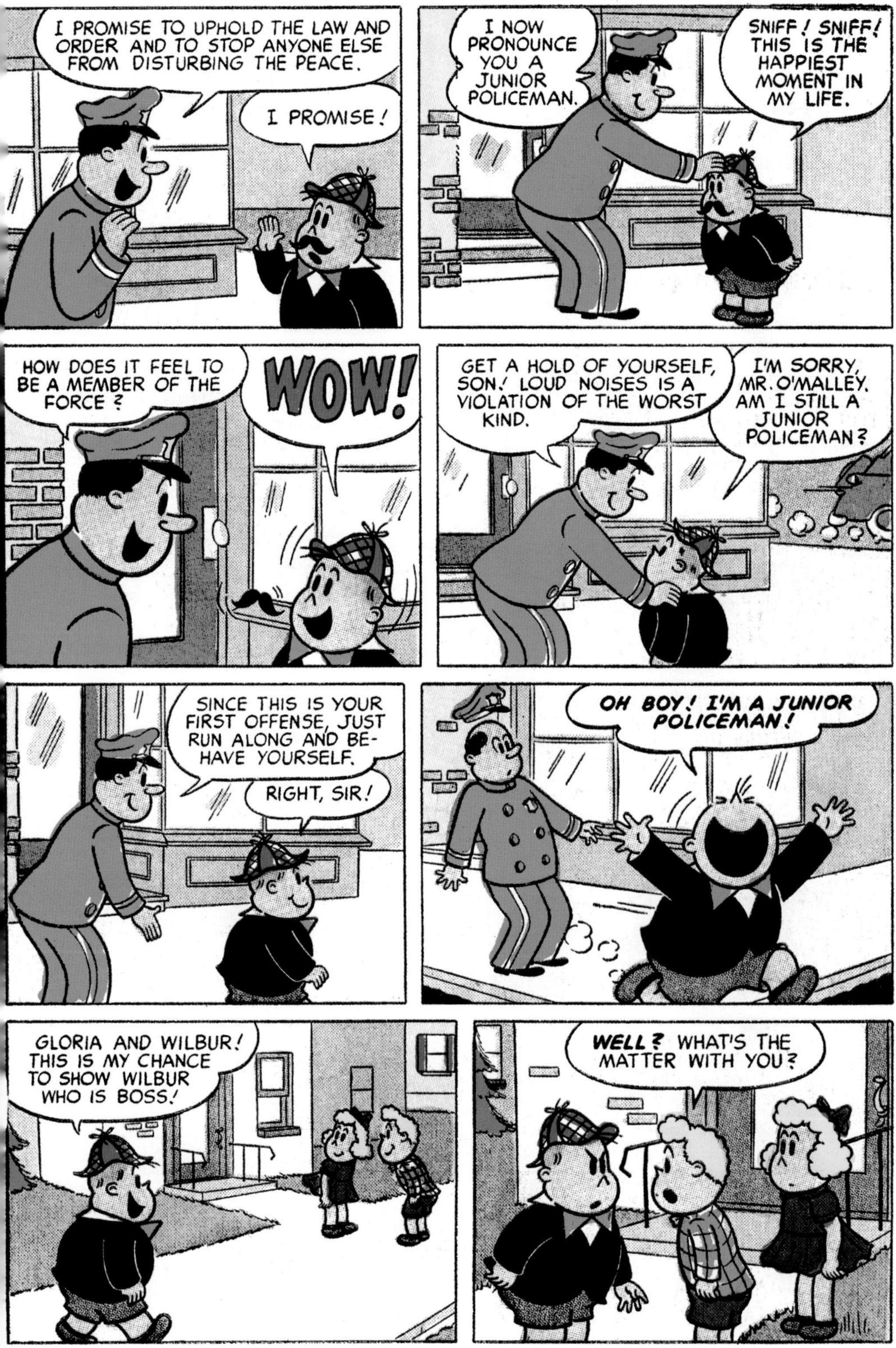
I PROMISE TO UPHOLD THE LAW AND ORDER AND TO STOP ANYONE ELSE FROM DISTURBING THE PEACE.
I PROMISE!
I NOW PRONOUNCE YOU A JUNIOR POLICEMAN.
SNIFF! SNIFF! THIS IS THE HAPPIEST MOMENT IN MY LIFE.
HOW DOES IT FEEL TO BE A MEMBER OF THE FORCE?
WOW!
GET A HOLD OF YOURSELF, SON! LOUD NOISES IS A VIOLATION OF THE WORST KIND.
I'M SORRY, MR. O'MALLEY. AM I STILL A JUNIOR POLICEMAN?
SINCE THIS IS YOUR FIRST OFFENSE, JUST RUN ALONG AND BE-HAVE YOURSELF.
RIGHT, SIR!
OH BOY! I'M A JUNIOR POLICEMAN!
GLORIA AND WILBUR! THIS IS MY CHANCE TO SHOW WILBUR WHO IS BOSS!
WELL? WHAT'S THE MATTER WITH YOU?

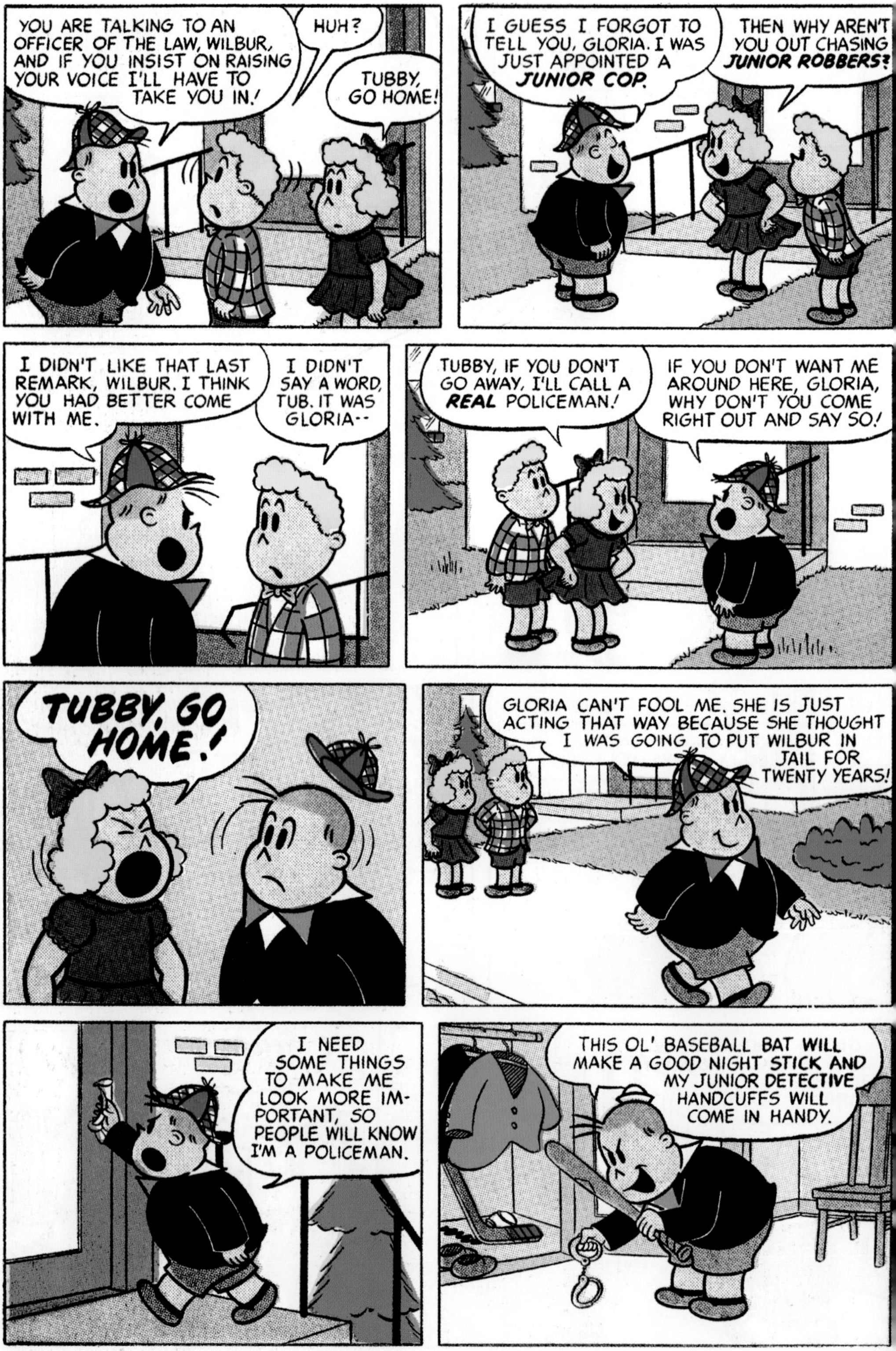
YOU ARE TALKING TO AN OFFICER OF THE LAW, WILBUR, AND IF YOU INSIST ON RAISING YOUR VOICE I'LL HAVE TO TAKE YOU IN!
HUH?
TUBBY, GO HOME!
I GUESS I FORGOT TO TELL YOU, GLORIA. I WAS JUST APPOINTED A JUNIOR COP.
THEN WHY AREN'T YOU OUT CHASING JUNIOR ROBBERS?
I DIDN'T LIKE THAT LAST REMARK, WILBUR. I THINK YOU HAD BETTER COME WITH ME.
I DIDN'T SAY A WORD, TUB. IT WAS GLORIA--
TUBBY, IF YOU DON'T GO AWAY, I'LL CALL A REAL POLICEMAN!
IF YOU DON'T WANT ME AROUND HERE, GLORIA, WHY DON'T YOU COME RIGHT OUT AND SAY SO!
TUBBY, GO HOME!
GLORIA CAN'T FOOL ME. SHE IS JUST ACTING THAT WAY BECAUSE SHE THOUGHT I WAS GOING TO PUT WILBUR IN JAIL FOR TWENTY YEARS!
I NEED SOME THINGS TO MAKE ME LOOK MORE IMPORTANT, SO PEOPLE WILL KNOW I'M A POLICEMAN.
THIS OL' BASEBALL BAT WILL MAKE A GOOD NIGHT STICK AND MY JUNIOR DETECTIVE HANDCUFFS WILL COME IN HANDY.

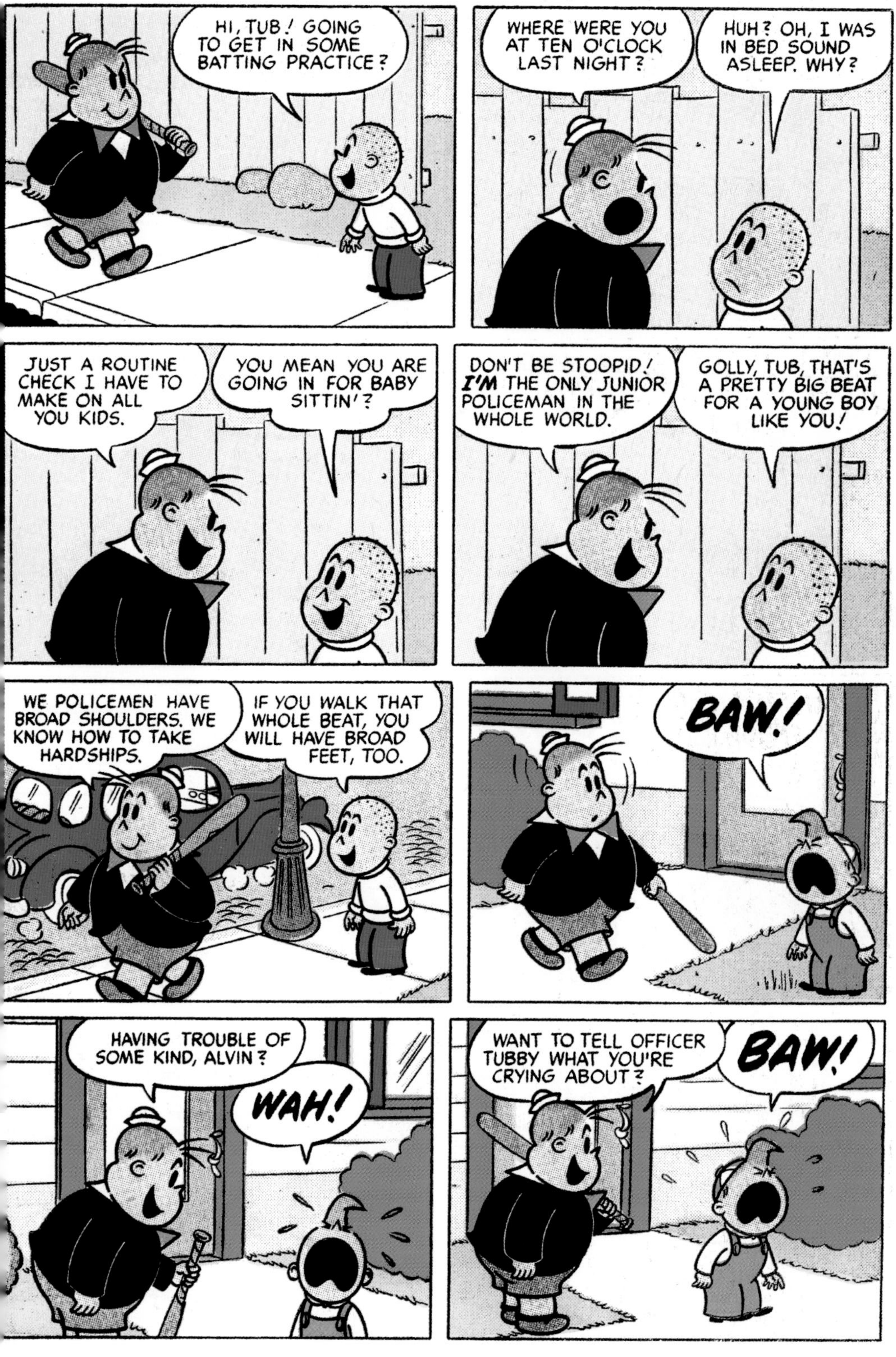
HI, TUB! GOING TO GET IN SOME BATTING PRACTICE?
WHERE WERE YOU AT TEN O'CLOCK LAST NIGHT?
HUH? OH, I WAS IN BED SOUND ASLEEP. WHY?
JUST A ROUTINE CHECK I HAVE TO MAKE ON ALL YOU KIDS.
YOU MEAN YOU ARE GOING IN FOR BABY SITTIN'?
DON'T BE STOOPID! I'M THE ONLY JUNIOR POLICEMAN IN THE WHOLE WORLD.
GOLLY, TUB, THAT'S A PRETTY BIG BEAT FOR A YOUNG BOY LIKE YOU!
WE POLICEMEN HAVE BROAD SHOULDERS. WE KNOW HOW TO TAKE HARDSHIPS.
IF YOU WALK THAT WHOLE BEAT, YOU WILL HAVE BROAD FEET, TOO.
BAW!
HAVING TROUBLE OF SOME KIND, ALVIN?
WAH!
WANT TO TELL OFFICER TUBBY WHAT YOU'RE CRYING ABOUT?
BAW!

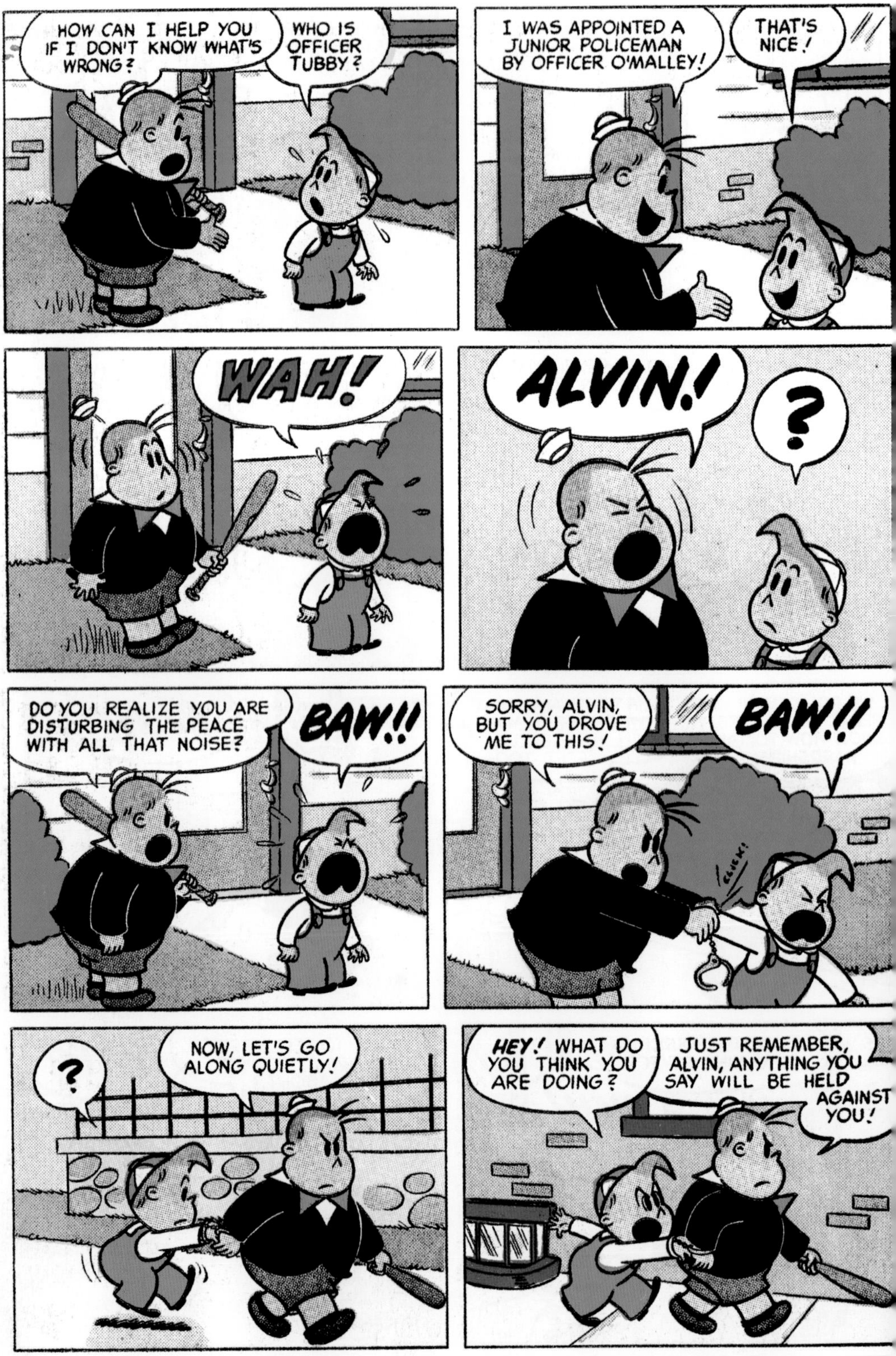
HOW CAN I HELP YOU IF I DON'T KNOW WHAT'S WRONG?
WHO IS OFFICER TUBBY?
I WAS APPOINTED A JUNIOR POLICEMAN BY OFFICER O'MALLEY!
THAT'S NICE!
WAH!
ALVIN!
?
DO YOU REALIZE YOU ARE DISTURBING THE PEACE WITH ALL THAT NOISE?
BAW!!
SORRY, ALVIN, BUT YOU DROVE ME TO THIS!
BAW!!
?
NOW, LET'S GO ALONG QUIETLY!
HEY! WHAT DO YOU THINK YOU ARE DOING?
JUST REMEMBER, ALVIN, ANYTHING YOU SAY WILL BE HELD AGAINST YOU!

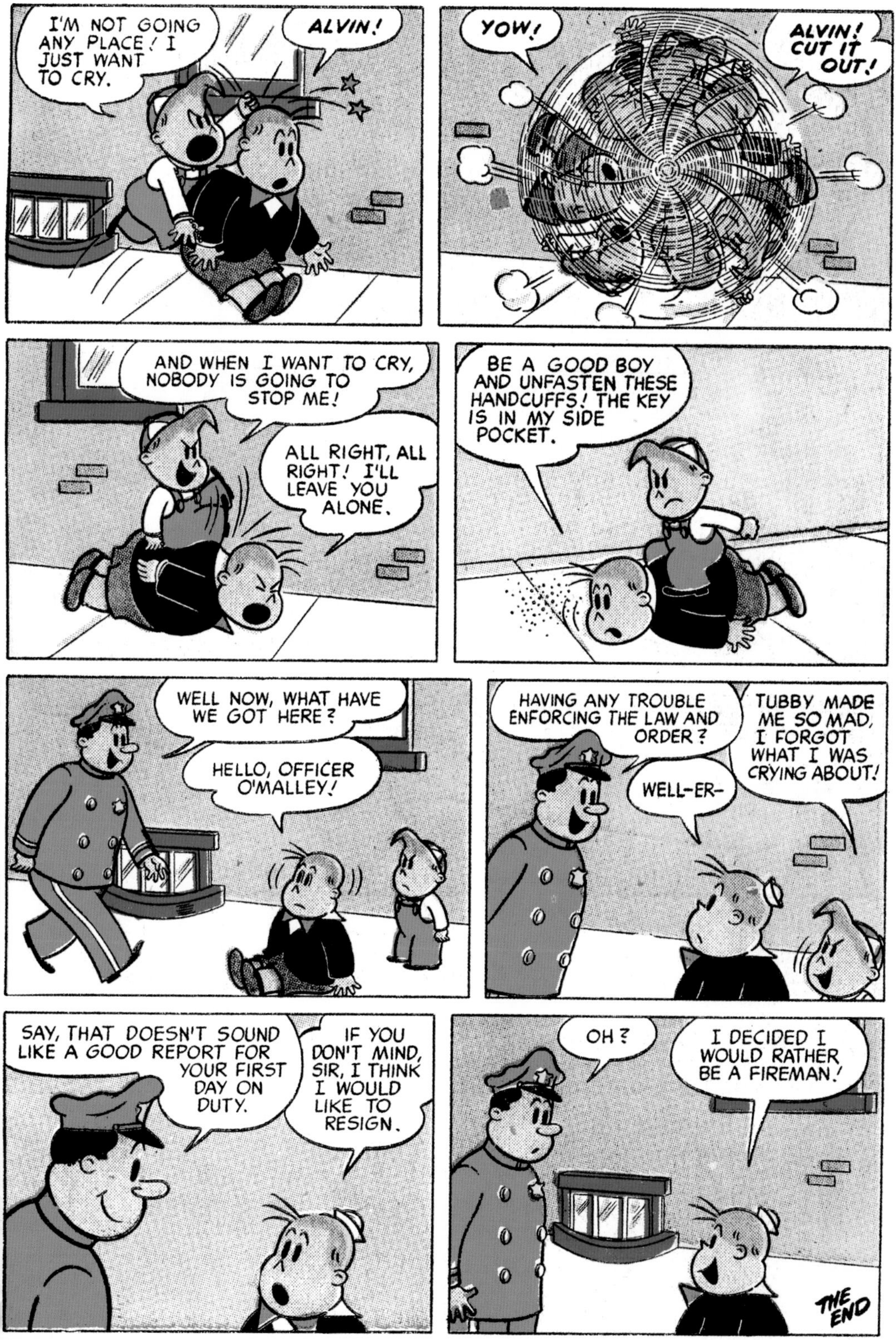
I'M NOT GOING ANY PLACE! I JUST WANT TO CRY.
ALVIN!
YOW!
ALVIN! CUT IT OUT!
AND WHEN I WANT TO CRY, NOBODY IS GOING TO STOP ME!
ALL RIGHT, ALL RIGHT! I'LL LEAVE YOU ALONE.
BE A GOOD BOY AND UNFASTEN THESE HANDCUFFS! THE KEY IS IN MY SIDE POCKET.
WELL NOW, WHAT HAVE WE GOT HERE?
HELLO, OFFICER O'MALLEY!
HAVING ANY TROUBLE ENFORCING THE LAW AND ORDER?
WELL-ER-
TUBBY MADE ME SO MAD, I FORGOT WHAT I WAS CRYING ABOUT!
SAY, THAT DOESN'T SOUND LIKE A GOOD REPORT FOR YOUR FIRST DAY ON DUTY.
IF YOU DON'T MIND, SIR, I THINK I WOULD LIKE TO RESIGN.
OH?
I DECIDED I WOULD RATHER BE A FIREMAN!
THE END

Little Lulu®

Volume 1: My Dinner with Lulu
ISBN 978-1-59307-318-3 $9.99

Volume 2: Sunday Afternoon
ISBN 978-1-59307-345-9 $9.99

Volume 3: Lulu in the Doghouse
ISBN 978-1-59307-346-6 $9.99

Volume 4: Lulu Goes Shopping
ISBN 978-1-59307-270-4 $9.99

Volume 5: Lulu Takes a Trip
ISBN 978-1-59307-317-6 $9.99

Volume 6: Letters to Santa
ISBN 978-1-59307-386-2 $9.99

Volume 7: Lulu's Umbrella Service
ISBN 978-1-59307-399-2 $9.99

Volume 8: Late for School
ISBN 978-1-59307-453-1 $9.99

Volume 9: Lucky Lulu
ISBN 978-1-59307-471-5 $9.99

Volume 10: All Dressed Up
ISBN 978-1-59307-534-7 $9.99

Volume 11: April Fools
ISBN 978-1-59307-557-6 $9.99

Volume 12: Leave It to Lulu
ISBN 978-1-59307-620-7 $9.99

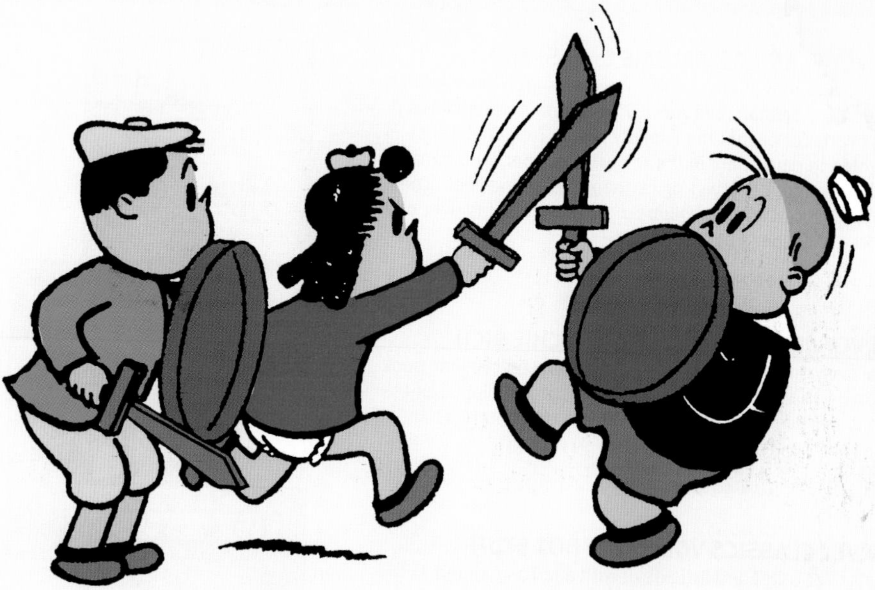

Volume 13: Too Much Fun
ISBN 978-1-59307-621-4 $9.99

Volume 14: Queen Lulu
ISBN 978-1-59307-683-2 $9.99

Volume 15: The Explorers
ISBN 978-1-59307-684-9 $9.99

Volume 16: A Handy Kid
ISBN 978-1-59307-685-6 $10.99

Volume 17: The Valentine
ISBN 978-1-59307-686-3 $10.99

Volume 18: The Expert
ISBN 978-1-59307-687-0 $10.99

FULL COLOR VOLUMES!

Volume 19: The Alamo and Other Stories
ISBN 978-1-59582-293-2 $14.99

Volume 20: The Bawlplayers and Other Stories
ISBN 978-1-59582-364-9 $14.99

Volume 21: Miss Feeny's Folly and Other Stories
ISBN 978-1-59582-365-6 $14.99

Little Lulu Color Special
ISBN 978-1-59307-613-9 $13.99

Looking for something new to read?

CHECK OUT THESE HARVEY CLASSICS TITLES FROM DARK HORSE BOOKS!

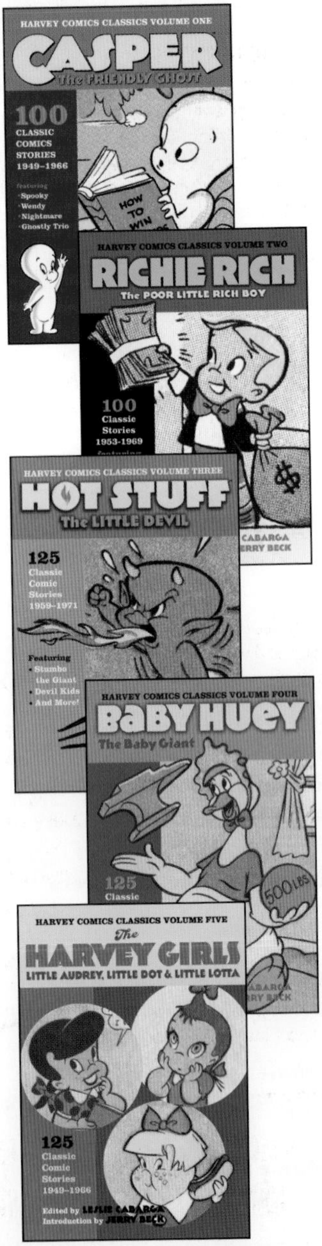
HARVEY COMICS CLASSICS VOLUME ONE
CASPER
The Friendly Ghost
100 CLASSIC COMICS STORIES 1949–1966
featuring
·Spooky
·Wendy
·Nightmare
·Ghostly Trio
HARVEY COMICS CLASSICS VOLUME TWO
RICHIE RICH
The POOR LITTLE RICH BOY
100 Classic Stories 1953-1969
HARVEY COMICS CLASSICS VOLUME THREE
HOT STUFF
The LITTLE DEVIL
125 Classic Comic Stories 1959–1971
Featuring
· Stumbo the Giant
· Devil Kids
· And More!
HARVEY COMICS CLASSICS VOLUME FOUR
BABY HUEY
The Baby Giant
500 LBS
HARVEY COMICS CLASSICS VOLUME FIVE
The HARVEY GIRLS
LITTLE AUDREY, LITTLE DOT & LITTLE LOTTA
125 Classic Comic Stories 1949–1966
Edited by LESLIE CABARGA
Introduction by JERRY BECK

HARVEY CLASSICS VOLUME 1: CASPER

It's amazing how many comics fans who grew up admiring Spider-Man, Batman, and Nick Fury still retain warm places in their hearts for Casper the Friendly Ghost. Now Dark Horse is delighted to participate in the revival of Casper, who remains among the most beloved of cartoon and comic-book icons. *Harvey Comics Classics Volume 1: Casper* contains over one hundred of Casper's best stories.

ISBN 978-1-59307-781-5

HARVEY CLASSICS VOLUME 2: RICHIE RICH

Move over, Uncle Scrooge! The richest character in comic-book history is about to get his due. This megacompilation of the essential Richie Rich collects his earliest and most substantial stories for the first time ever.

ISBN 978-1-59307-848-5

HARVEY CLASSICS VOLUME 3: HOT STUFF

Who's the hotheaded little devil with a tail as pointed as his personality? It's Hot Stuff! This adorably mischievous imp has delighted comics fans since the 1950s. This volume collects over one hundred of the funniest (and hottest!) classic cartoons featuring Hot Stuff and his pals.

ISBN 978-1-59307-914-7

HARVEY CLASSICS VOLUME 4: BABY HUEY

Oversized, oblivious, and oh-so-good-natured duckling Baby Huey first delighted audiences in 1949, but quickly lumbered his way into the bigger world of cartoons and his own comic-book series! Join Baby Huey, his baffled parents, and his duckling pals in this jumbo collection of classic stories.

ISBN 978-1-59307-977-2

HARVEY CLASSICS VOLUME 5: THE HARVEY GIRLS

They're cute, they're clever, and they're obsessive! Some of Harvey Comics' biggest stars were three "little" girls with large dreams, enormous hearts, and king-size laughs: Little Audrey, Little Dot, and Little Lotta. This book includes 125 classic tales of three amazing girls!

ISBN 978-1-59582-171-3

$19.99 each!

Find out more about these and other great Dark Horse all-ages titles at darkhorse.com!

DARK HORSE BOOKS